A
HERTFORDSHIRE VALLEY

Written and edited by Scott Hastie

Photography David Spain

Published in 1996
by Alpine Press Ltd
Station Road
Kings Langley
Hertfordshire
England
Tel: 01923 269777

ISBN: 0952863103

Acknowledgements

The production of "A Hertfordshire Valley" would not have been possible without key contributions from the following people:

Lynne Fletcher undertook all data preparation and research management for "A Hertfordshire Valley".

Debbie Elborn worked on the project as photographic assistant to David Spain.

Joyce and Tom Burke carried out important proof reading work.

The authors would like to express their gratitude to the following organisations who have all, in their various ways, offered significant support to this publication:

Kodak Ltd, Dacorum Heritage Trust, Dacorum Borough Council, Hertfordshire County Council, Sandoz Nutrition, formerly Wander (Ovaltine) Ltd, Hunton Park Management Centre,

The authors would also like to thank the following individuals and organisations whose advice, expertise and generosity have added to the quality of "A Hertfordshire Valley":

Michael Stanyon, Assistant Heritage Officer of Dacorum Borough Council, Dr. Kate Thomson and staff of the County Record Office, F. Cory-Wright of the Herts Archaeological Trust, Christine Shearman and staff of the Local Studies Library, Hertford, the staff of Watford, Hemel Hempstead, Bovingdon, Berkhamsted, Abbots Langley, Kings Langley and Tring libraries, Hemel Hempstead Local History and Museum Society, Berkhamsted Local History Society, Kings Langley Local History and Museum Society, Abbots Langley Parish Council, Bovingdon Parish Council, Watford Museum, Bovingdon History Group, Bushey Museum, Kay Sanecki of Ashridge College, Watford Industrial Society, Three Rivers Museum, S. Bradley of Berkhamsted School for Girls, Abbots Hill School Photographic Club, B. Southorn of Great Gaddesden School, Beechwood Park School, Oliver Phillips at the Watford Observer, Hemel Hempstead Gazette, Villager Newspaper, National Trust, Waterways Museum at Stoke Bruerne, M. Allaby, R. Barden, S. Belgarde, N. Birnie, J. Boxall, V. Brooks, M. Brown, P. Brown, P. Bryant, A. Burrows, R. Casserley, B. Cassell, E. M. Chapman, R. Chapman, C. Clark, P. Coneron, D. Cook, M. Corby, L. Cox, N. Cox, A. Daniels, L. Dean, R. Desborough, M. Dillon, F. W. Dobson, H. Dulley, Dr. M. Dyer, E.E. Evans, J. Fancourt, A. Faulkner, J. Fisher, M. Forsythe, J. Fowler, G. Gosling, R. Grace, J. Graham, F. Halsey, N. Halsey, J. Hands, R. Hands, D. Harrison, L. Hastie, E. Holland, B. Hosier, S. Jerrett, J. Johnson, J. Kingsley, A. C. Lindley, M. McCaul, S.McLelland, D.Miles, L. Mitchell, B. Nelson, J.B. Nunn, E. Parrot, C. Peacock, B. Pizzey, R. Prue, M. Reveley, K. Seabrook, F. Seely, A. Selby, B. Seymour-Taylor, R. Simons, J. Simpson, A. Spain, F. Steel, J. Swain, A. Taylor, L. Venables, D. Wadham, J. Wall, A. J. Ward, K. Warden, K. Watts, R. Williams, J. Wood, C. Woodstock of the New Mill Social Centre, Tring.

We are also grateful to many people who have kindly allowed us to reproduce some of their photographs to help illustrate this book: S. Bailey, M. Baldwin, M. Bass, E.D. Bruton, A. G. Burrows, Camera Craft, Hemel Hempstead, H. C. Casserley, D. Chandler, I. J. Clark, C.R.L. Coles, H. C. Doyle, J. Eastone, D. Edwards, D. S. Edwards, R. Grace, Grevilles Photographers, J. Habart, M. Hemmings, R. Hodgson, E. Holland, B. Hosier, A. How, D. Hubbard, R. Lacey, Lens of Sutton, N. Macleod, B. Morrison, V. Nunn, I. Paget-Tomlinson, I. Quelch, V. Rickard, A. Rickett, P. Smith, S. Stevens, J. Tapster, B. Wood.

The authors wish to thank Kodak Ltd. for their generous support in donating all David Spain's photographic materials required for the publication of "A Hertfordshire Valley".

Foreword

The idea for this book arose directly from our previous publications which focus upon detailed histories of specific local communities. In the course of this work, it was impossible not to become aware of a unique series of important historic developments in the surrounding area, themselves reinforced by the evolutionary influence of both the Gade and Bulbourne valleys.

It became clear that throughout the centuries, these two river valleys have been the principal influence in the development of the most economically active part of Hertfordshire. This textbook example of successful settlement, set in an area of outstanding natural beauty, is itself a fascinating story. Beginning with the Ice Age and reaching into the Twentieth Century, this book is an attempt to pull together a clear understanding of this historical process for the general reader. In addition we have aimed to capture the essence of each of the principal communities that lie within, and adjacent to, these two valleys. Although not intended to be definitive, we hope that this book does provide a well-illustrated historic guide to most of the towns and villages in the local area, and also offers a broader context for the development of each community featured. Many of the images used to illustrate this story are stunning archive photographs, many of which are being published for the first time.

We hope you enjoy this glimpse into the past.

Scott Hastie and David Spain, September 1996.

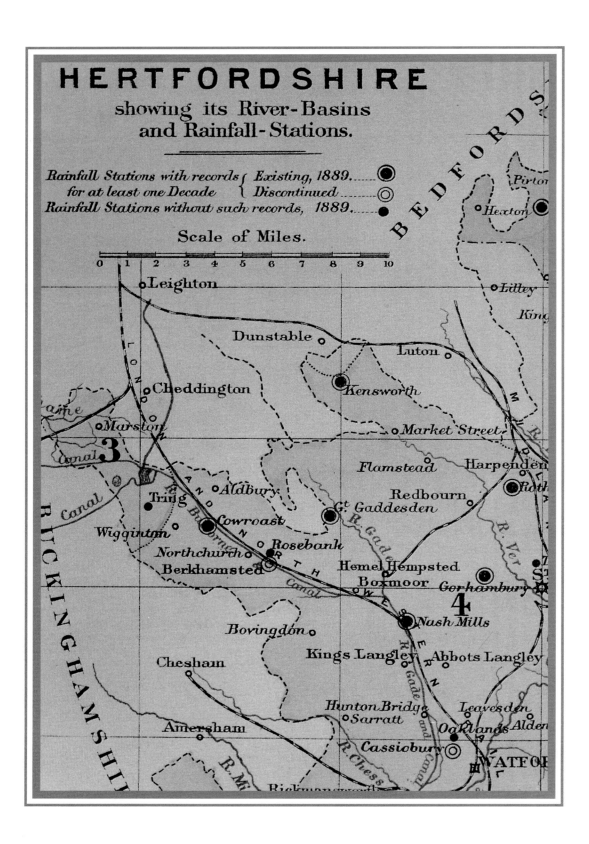

Table of Contents

Local Geography

The Ice Age

The period of maximum glaciation during the last Ice Age in Britain occured about 300,000 years ago, when great glaciers extended down the country stopping just short of Watford. By 14,000 BC these ice sheets were in retreat and by 8,500 BC the last main glacier was leaving the country, retreating north towards Scotland. At this time the British Isles did not exist as a separate entity. Britain was simply a low range of hills on the edge of the Great Northern Plain which could be visited by both early man and wild animals at will. However by 6000 BC the huge quantity of water from melted ice, which had flowed down across the terrain, meant that the English Channel and North Sea were submerged. Britain was now cut off from Continental influence until the development of boats and ships which could safely cross these new oceans.

During the Ice Age, rivers were unable to follow their normal course because of the glaciation, and their waters pooled back to form huge lakes. As the temperature thawed the glaciers, ice sheets and snowfields began to retreat northwards and vast quantities of melt water were released across the country. These waters naturally flowed towards lower ground, across what was still largely frozen terrain. Where an earlier river valley already existed, the waters tended to follow its course but where it did not, new channels were formed. The sheer power of this process was spectacular; existing river valleys like the Gade, were widened and deepened. Huge quantities of geological material were swept along by the melt waters and deposited often far away from their original source. The surface gravels that can still be found in the local valleys were deposited in the area by the flood waters of the last Ice Age. As the thawing process continued, the volume of these floods began to decline and the water was gradually able to drain into the sub-soil. The climate was warming quite rapidly to the extent that by 5,800 BC average summer temperature reached two degrees above our current average today. Vegetation now began to cover the old and scarred landscape that had been so weathered by the Ice Age. As conditions improved, tundra vegetation was gradually replaced by broad leafed woodland which was able to establish itself on this softer, warmer terrain. Birch and pine began to cover the landscape, followed later by oak, hazel, elm and lime trees. Archaeological records tell us that because of this gradual environmental change, earlier herds of large wild horses, bison and reindeer began to disappear from Britain. These were replaced by more successful woodland species such as deer, elk, wild oxen and boars.

The London Basin

In geological terms, the local valley area comprises a small part of the larger syncline or down-folding of rocks which is called the London Basin, running for about 100 miles around the Capital, stretching to Newbury in the west. It is bounded by the chalk uplands of both the Berkshire Downs and our own Chiltern Hills to the north, and fringed by the North Downs to the south. The sub-structure of the London Basin is part of a much wider deposit of chalk, which covers much of Europe and was laid down under the sea during the Upper Cretaceous period, which ended some 70 million years ago. The London Basin itself is a great layer of chalk some 600ft. deep, which is sandwiched between two layers of clay. Whilst chalk is a heavily porous substance, clay is impervious to water. Consequently the rain water which falls in the Chiltern Hills sinks down into the terrain until it reaches the London Basin, where it then collects between the two layers of clay and saturates the chalk. In parts of the local area (see watercress cultivation on page 26) it is therefore possible to sink artesian wells through this first layer of clay and recover huge quantities of water from the underlying chalk bed. The hilltops of the Gade and Bulbourne valleys have some deposits of clay on their higher reaches, whilst the soils of the lower slopes are often masked by the glacial sands and gravels that were carried to the area during the last Ice Age. Nearly all deposits in the area contain a preponderance of flints and the local earth is dominated by these mixed constituents. The most common local soil types are dominated by parent material known either as 'boulder clay', 'clay with flint' or 'glacial gravel'.

Hertfordshire Puddingstone

It may be difficult for us in Hertfordshire to believe, but puddingstone is one of the world's rarest rocks. It occurs in pieces which vary from a few inches to several feet across. Puddingstone is a conglomerate of small pebbles bonded together by silicon to form solid rock. When broken, it shows a cross section of pebbles which give it the plum-pudding appearance which accounts for its name. All puddingstone is several million years old and its formation began when small, mainly flint, pebbles were deposited in river beds and then later covered by London clay. This puddingstone mixture was subsequently compressed and bonded together during the Ice Age, becoming strong enough to resist crushing. When the ice melted, large pieces of this rock were tumbled by the flood water to produce the rounded blocks that are still underneath the local fields today. Created by the precise conditions prevailing locally during the last Ice Age, nearly all the puddingstone in the world is found in Hertfordshire and most of it lies in the Gade and Bulbourne valleys. Puddingstone has an exceptionally hard surface and its earliest known application was as a Stone Age quern, which was a primitive mill stone used for grinding corn. Stone Age culture also used circles of puddingstone in its ritual worship and, because of the deliberate incorporation of some pagan beliefs into the Christian faith by Pope Gregory's missionaries (circa AD 601), it is still possible to find some puddingstone built into the walls and foundations of many local churches. Although in some ways an ideal material due to its strength, puddingstone has never been widely used as a building material, simply because of its scarce supply. However there are one or two rare buildings in Hertfordshire built entirely of puddingstone. A small structure in Radlett was unfortunately demolished in the 1970's, but one house survives on the Westbrook Hay estate (see page 146); the old Ice House at Ashridge (see page 197) is also built entirely of puddingstone. This local rock was sometimes used for grave markers and coffin stones and Great Gaddesden churchyard is a good example of this, with some large puddingstone boulders still marking graves. Local superstitions surrounding puddingstone are many and various; in some cases the rock was put on top of the coffin to protect the deceased as many local people believed puddingstone warded off evil spirits and could bring good luck. For this reason, it is not unusual to see pieces of the rock laid by local cottage doors or gate posts. These local practices have give rise to puddingstone's alternative names of Angel stone, Hagstone or Witchstone. Although its exterior surface is similar to concrete and dull, when sliced through puddingstone can be very attractive. Consequently it was used for jewellery, ornaments and some small table tops during Victorian times, when it was discovered that puddingstone could take a very high polish, which showed off the spectacular variety of colours in its constituent pebbles.

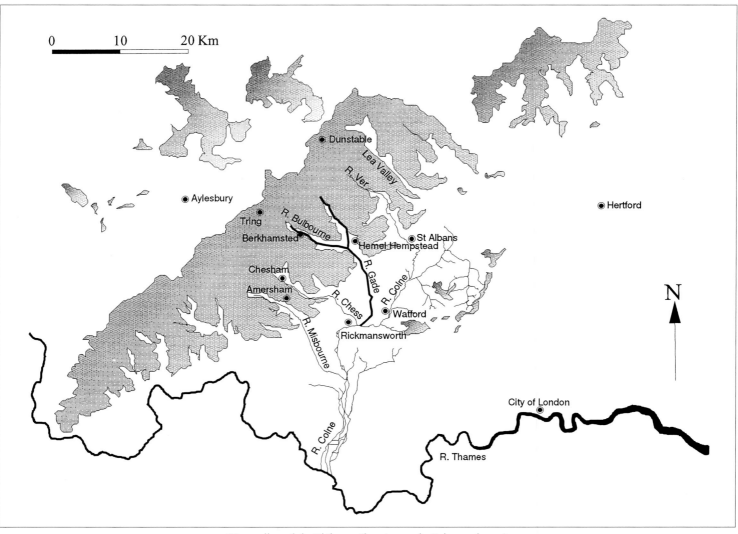

River valleys of the Chilterns (focusing on the Colne catchment).

The River Valleys

The rivers in Hertfordshire vary in both their size and their vigour as they flow through the county. Some of these rivers have dry grass beds with no headsprings to feed them and, because of this, their upper water supply relies totally on surface drainage from the surrounding hills. Another type of river has an intermittent flow and is known as a Bourne. These streams usually have a source higher up the river valley, although sometimes this source can be at a lower level, dependent on the water level in the chalk sub-soil. Two layers of chalk are concerned with this supply of water to our local rivers. One is an upper permeable layer which soaks up the rain like a sponge and the other layer is a much denser material, known as middle chalk, which offers considerable resistance to water penetration. This latter layer allows the water to run along the valley in relatively shallow underground channels until it has the opportunity to percolate to the surface in the form of a spring or a well. A typical example of this process is the Bourne Gutter, (see page 9), which is an irregular stream flowing into the River Bulbourne at Bourne End.

The River Bulbourne

Towards its northern end at Berkhamsted, the River Bulbourne has created the most spectacular valley in Hertfordshire. At its narrowest point, it displays slopes that rise up to 300ft. on either side. However today this great old river is little more than an insignificant stream and for over half its length the Bulbourne is dying in its bed. The demands of an increasing population have of course lowered the level of the local water table, but the key factor behind the demise of the River Bulbourne was the arrival of the Grand Junction Canal, which promptly usurped the majority of its water supply from

1797. The Bulbourne currently rises near the Cow Roast, half way between Berkhamsted and Tring. This is approximately 3 miles from its original source near the hamlet of Bulbourne, which lies close to the border with Buckinghamshire. In its heyday the River Bulbourne was a full and fast flowing river, powering many local water mills and also helping to provide water defences for the great earthworks of Berkhamsted Castle. In these early days the river yielded a healthy crop of eels and excellent fresh fish for the local Royal establishments. As recently as the early Twentieth Century, it was still possible to fish for excellent wild specimens of trout and golden carp in the River Bulbourne.

From its source to its junction with the River Gade at Two Waters near Apsley, the River Bulbourne falls about 100ft. The river has two unreliable tributaries: an ancient 60 yard trickle down St. John's Well Lane at Berkhamsted (see page 205) which is unlikely to flow again and the Bourne Gutter which gave Bourne End its name. From Dudswell, the Bulbourne flows past St. Mary's, Northchurch, and into Berkhamsted. Here, prior to the cutting of the canal, the river had turned much of the town's central area into little more than an unhealthy swamp. Leaving Berkhamsted, the river then runs beneath Castle Street and into Lower Mill, flowing under Bank Mill Lane. From this point the Bulbourne can be seen at its fullest extent as it travels through the meadows past Broadway Church and on to Bourne End. Here we can find the first of the old watercress beds and trout farms for which the pure chalk streams and small lagoons of the River Bulbourne are ideal. From this point the river then winds on to Winkwell and across Boxmoor, where it joins the River Gade at Two Waters.

The River Gade

The River Gade covers little more than 20 miles in the course of its meandering from its source below Hudnall Common, near Little Gaddesden, until its three-way meeting with two local rivers, the Chess and the Colne, near Rickmansworth. In common with the Bulbourne, the Gade also suffers from a much reduced flow. This is not really surprising when one considers that in 1947 the growing post-war town of Hemel Hempstead successfully obtained an order for the daily extraction of up to four and a half million gallons of water from the River Gade at Piccotts End. The River Gade also has a chalk bed and was formerly home to many fine watercress beds, especially in its upper reaches. Here it is still possible to admire the fullest and most picturesque part of the river's course on the stretch of clear water between Great Gaddesden and Water End. From this point the Gade flows through Piccotts End and down across Gadebridge Park. It then passes along the length of the Marlowes, where it has been widened to become the focal point of Hemel Hempstead's Water Gardens, which were built as part of the New Town development. Below the town centre at Two Waters, the River Gade is joined by the River Bulbourne flowing into it from across Boxmoor. The enlarged River Gade, together with the canal, takes a course through Two Waters and Apsley and on to Kings Langley, where it flows under the M25 towards the Grove. It then passes through the Cassiobury estate and deeper into the Three Rivers District above Cassio Bridge, near the Metropolitan railway line. Here the Gade again flows alongside the canal, past the site of John Dickinson's Paper Mill at Croxley Green and travels across Common Moor to Rickmansworth. It then joins the canal below Lot Mead Lock and travels down to Batchworth. By this time it has flowed into the waters of the River Colne which will eventually carry it out, via the Thames, into the open sea at Southend. Extensive watercress cultivation in the pure chalk waters was also popular at this end of the valley in the Croxley Green, Rickmansworth and Cassiobury areas (see page 26).

Bourne Gutter

We know from surviving records that the irregular stream called the Bourne Gutter, which provided the hamlet of Bourne End with its name, only flows when levels of local rainfall exceed 30 inches in the preceding twelve months. At the beginning of March 1926, it was a continuous stream for about 400 yards, above the junction of the lanes from Bottom and Lower Farms. We also know that the Spring of 1951 was one of the Bourne Gutter's fuller periods. A well established local tradition believes that the flow of this stream is 'woe water' and its appearance a sure signal of impending disaster, pestilence or war.

Tring Brook

At the beginning of the Nineteenth Century, underground channels were built at Tring to direct the natural springs at Dunsdale and Miswell into the local brook, swelling it to the sizeable flow known as the Tring Brook. This flow of water was then used from 1825 to power the large silk mill which was built in Brook Street by William Kay. Further upstream, before it was diverted by the Canal Company, this Brook used to flow through New Mill, close to the Baptist Church in Sutton Close. Here the Baptist community used its waters at the old mill head to carry out their baptisms. Its course from the Pond outside the old mill house is not certain, but it is thought to run under both the old Fire Station in Brook Street and the Cattle Market near the Robin Hood pub. The likely source of the Brook is somewhere in Tring Park.

Tring Reservoirs

Shortly after the construction of the Grand Junction Canal, it became obvious that there were insufficient water supplies at the Tring Summit, where vast quantities of water were required to enable the boats to progress through the various locks. Consequently a large reservoir was built at Wilstone, some three quarters of a mile from the canal. A steam-engine was used to pump water from the Reservoir into the Wendover branch and then into the main canal. However, with the success of the canal system, the demand for water became insatiable and by 1817 two more reservoirs were built at Tringford and Startop End. Both these new reservoirs supplied the main canal and also the Aylesbury branch which joins at Marsworth. The original Wilstone Reservoir needed to be enlarged in 1811 and again in 1827, with a second and third reservoir built beside it in 1839. When these reservoirs were all connected, the total capacity of water at all four had been raised to 500 million gallons.

All these reservoirs had been sited at the highest point possible, close to the summit level in order to save unnecessary pumping. They were built largely by hand and, like the canal itself, were a major engineering undertaking of their day. Today the habitat offered by the Tring reservoirs has meant they have become important ornithological sites and Tring is currently the home of the British Trust for Ornithology. In 1918 the black-necked grebe nested for the first time in England on Marsworth Reservoir and in 1938 the very first pairs of little ringed plovers in England were recorded on Startop End. Tring reservoirs are also a key location for keen fishermen and several prize specimens caught there are on display at Tring Museum. The best of these include a 26 pound pike and a 13 pound bream, which were both caught at the Wilstone Reservoir.

Woodland

The dominant historical theme of the surrounding countryside is one of progressive and often sudden forest clearance. By 6000 BC the deciduous forest and woodland was well established across the local landscape and it was this type of densely wooded terrain that faced the first settlers. The early peoples in the Mesolithic period led a hunter-gatherer life style and the impact they made on the landscape was therefore modest. They used fire, both for heat and driving animals and they also cleared some relatively small areas for grazing, with their flint axes. It wasn't until the Neolithic period (from 3,500 BC) that the destruction of the wildwood began to intensify and early man began to settle in small temporary farmsteads and clear land to grow his crops. Periods of regeneration still took place because these early Neolithic communities simply moved on when their immediate soil became exhausted and too poor for continuing cultivation. The areas which were settled later, towards the end of the Neolithic period, tended to remain occupied during the early Bronze Age (2300-1400 BC). The tools that were available during both the Bronze Age and later Iron Age, now made the efficient clearing of forest and the on-going cultivation of soil much easier. The archaeological evidence of extensive iron smelting hearths in the area of the Cow Roast and the Ashridge Estate (see Early Settlement page 12) suggests that the charcoal used in the furnaces would have involved considerable woodland clearance. The sophisticated and highly organised style of farming estates introduced to this valley by the Romans (54 BC-450 AD) was systematically destroyed by the invading Nordic raiders, whose impact on the countryside became very significant. These peoples of the Anglo-Saxon period (AD 450-1066) settled and farmed here in their own style, creating the nucleus of the communities which today are the modern towns and villages of the Gade and Bulbourne valleys. The Saxons systematically cleared areas of woodland and drained valleys, introducing their own system of open field agriculture (see page 22). However the first wholesale clearance of forest in West Hertfordshire took place in the mid Tenth Century, and was ordered by Abbot Wuslin. This was followed by more far reaching clearances conducted from St. Albans Abbey, one century later. These clearances created new and large tracts of land that were now available as arable land or as pasture. Throughout the Norman period the valleys were farmed principally for the benefit of the Abbey at St. Albans and the Royal community established at Berkhamsted Castle. Sufficient woodland was still left around each village settlement to allow for the supply of its daily needs in terms of fuel, wild food and pannage for pigs etc. Throughout the Thirteenth and Fourteenth Centuries clearance continued unabated in the valleys, helping to finance the Royal establishments at Berkhamsted, Kings Langley and also the important Monastery at Ashridge.

Mature standard trees, were not now being replaced nearly as fast as they were being used. From 1500 the indigenous oak and ash trees were being used for the great beams and planks employed in the extensive house and shipbuilding programmes of the Tudor period. However by this time some thought had been given to woodland management, and the traditional techniques of coppicing and pollarding became established to help protect stocks of trees such as Hazel, Beech and Lime. Coppicing was a technique which cut the tree near to the ground, and left the remaining stump to reliably re-sprout, producing multi-stemmed shoots and poles. It took between 10 and 30 years to rotate the wood supply in a formal coppice. Pollarding uses the same techniques, but instead cuts the trees at head height, producing thinner poles of wood. This was done partly to protect the otherwise lower stumps with their sweet young shoots, from pigs left to forage for nuts and other wild food. Most of the villages in the valley still have some surrounding areas of both coppice and wood pasture. Because of its pliability, hazel was used for fences and hurdles, whilst beech, which was relatively easy to turn, was used for early furniture and tool handles. Despite the early management of the natural woodland characteristic of this area, timber had still become a scarce resource nationally by the middle of the Seventeenth Century. In 1664 it was necessary for Charles II to introduce laws which rationed its supply and tried to ensure the recycling of wood where possible. East of Berkhamsted there is a particularly fine stretch of woodland at Frithsden, with an extensive area of old beech pollards situated on the edge of Berkhamsted Common.

Local Wildlife

If we include the various specimens of trees and bushes, there are over one thousand different wild plants to be found growing in Hertfordshire. The county is fortunate in that it enjoys a wide variety of natural habitats, including areas of natural woodland which still offer wild flowers some chance of survival. It is reassuring to know that most of the varieties recorded in Hertfordshire by the pioneer botanists of the mid-Nineteenth Century can still be found somewhere, if you know where to look. The predominant chalk downland of the valley area is of course less natural than the woodland it replaced. However these chalk grasslands are still host to many wild vetches that act as food plants for some butterflies and therefore help to make the countryside attractive to insect life. Historically the air of Hertfordshire has always been

"The Stile" by Joe Graham.

considered to be sweet and healthy, when compared with the early industrial smogs of the major cities. It is true to say that the local air stayed relatively unpolluted until the beginning of the Twentieth Century and this has contributed to its healthy insect population. The biggest threat to local wildlife, is the rapidly expanding human population which has more than quadrupled since the beginning of this Century. Insects and wild plants suffer when natural habitat is lost to houses and domestic gardens. Whilst adult butterflies gain in access to sweet flower nectars, many of the primary food plants for their larvae, such as nettles, are uprooted as weeds. Increasingly wild mammals of the local countryside have been chased from the peace of their natural habitats by the spread of construction work and noisy road traffic. The survivors have tended to become increasingly domesticated. In addition to rats and field mice, it is now not uncommon to see squirrels, badgers, foxes and even muntjac deer prowling the fringes of modern housing areas looking for titbits of sustenance. With its reservoirs, canal-side habitats and gravel pits, the Gade valley is particularly rich in dragonflies, hosting approximately half of the 42 known British species. Despite its proximity to London, the valley remains an excellent area for bird watching. However the increasing spread of urbanisation and modern agricultural practices have not made it easy for some species. Much of the local deciduous woodland has long since been felled and replaced with conifers which are far less attractive to most species of birds. The old oaks and other mature secluded trees that once provided excellent nesting sites for jackdaws, stock doves and owls are gradually disappearing. However tracts of beech woods, oak, birch and hornbeam still survive in the Bulbourne valley, notably at Ashridge and also in the Tring and Aldbury district. Despite the fact that Hertfordshire is an inland county it still manages to host up to 290 species of birds. In addition to reservoirs, the local gravel pits of the two valleys have also been responsible for the successful spread of breeding species such as the great crested grebe, little ringed plover and common tern. The reservoirs at Tring are however probably best known for their migrants and winter visitors. One of only two heronries in Hertfordshire is located at these reservoirs, where up to a dozen pairs nest in the adjacent reed beds and trees.

The Present Landscape

Surrounding the various built-up areas that make up the towns and villages of the locality, much of the valley is part of the Metropolitan Green Belt. The northern portion of this Green Belt is made up of the Chiltern Hills which are part of the Chiltern Area of Outstanding Natural Beauty. Within the Gade and Bulbourne valleys there are also many conservation areas, for example, in parts of Aldbury, Tring and old Hemel Hempstead. The National Trust have been managing over 3,500 acres of the Ashridge Estate since 1928 and the Boxmoor Trust is responsible for the maintenance and conservation work of another 400 acres further down the valley. Since 1964 the Herts and Middlesex Wildlife Trust have been active in the area, helping to maintain and protect natural habitats by creating over 40 Nature Reserves in the two counties. Local examples of their work in the valleys can be found at Long Deans in Nash Mills, Alpine Meadow which is close to Berkhamsted Common and at Duchie's Piece in the Aldbury Woodland. The chalk hills of the Chilterns which are mainly more than 400ft. above sea level, slope down to the east and are interspersed with narrow valleys. To the south and east of the Chiltern Hills , the land is lower and the scenery changes. The valleys of the Bulbourne and the Gade, which rise in the Chilterns, run across more open rolling countryside which is largely given over to agricultural production. At Berkhamsted, the narrowness of the Bulbourne valley is at its most accentuated and the road, canal and railway that provide the principal route north, are all squeezed very close together at several points.

The local environment remains pleasant with large areas of land still given over to pasture, semi-natural woodland or commons. Agriculture is still the predominant feature of the valleys' landscape. Associated with this is the area's equitable climate which generally comprises mild winters and pleasantly warm summers. It is worth noting that even in the late Twentieth Century, approximately two thirds of the total land surface of Hertfordshire is given over to agriculture which remains an important industry. Cereal growing has a strong hold in the valley area and is supplemented by extensive grassland pastures which support livestock. Some of the heavier London clay-based soils on the upper slopes are ideal for cattle grazing and dairy production. To date, given the survival of the Green Belt, the greatest threat to the environment has been more natural. The tree population suffered devastating losses from the outbreak of Dutch Elm disease in the late 60's and early 70's, and the surrounding countryside continues to lose many of its beech trees due to stress and disease. Perhaps the biggest continuing hazard, other than traffic pollution, comes from the rapidly expanding numbers of the harmless looking grey squirrel. These small rodents breed fast and run wild throughout the area, disabling trees by stripping the bark. If the squirrel population is not controlled, it could have a disastrous effect on what little remains of our natural woodland.

Whippendell Woods.

Early Settlement

The fertile river valleys of the Gade and the Bulbourne provided early man with a route through the dense woodland that covered the hillsides, and they were also a good source of food. Unfortunately any evidence left to indicate the presence of early Stone Age man, from the Palaeolithic period, will most likely have been carried away by the sheer volume of flood waters which swept down the valleys following the retreat of the last Ice Age, circa 8000 BC. However, such a presence was clearly possible and there have been the occasional finds, in areas like the Colne valley, of flint hand-held hunting axes from the Acheulian period which dates from some 200,000 years ago. A 'flint factory floor' dating from this period was found near Kensworth. We do know that in the Upper Palaeolithic period (circa 25,000 BC), the Lea Valley in Hertfordshire had been reached by groups of hunters with flint spears. At this point in history there would have been no tree cover on what was largely tundra-like vegetation and it has been suggested that these later Palaeolithic peoples were mainly meat eaters who hunted larger animals like wild horses, oxen and reindeer that were then roaming around the local landscape.

The harsh landscape of the Palaeolithic Period.

The first people that we know for sure made an impact locally are the hunters and gatherers from the Mesolithic period (circa 6000 BC), who gradually moved northwards up the valleys of south east England following the last Ice Age. Large quantities of their small flint tools, called microliths, have been found especially in the Lea, Stort and Colne valleys. More locally these Mesolithic tribesmen gradually moved up the Gade valley leaving evidence in the form of single axes, and some undated microliths have been found in the Kings Langley, Bedmond and Hemel Hempstead areas. By 6000 BC the local landscape was no longer tundra, but was made up of rather dense and mixed deciduous woodland. Mesolithic man attempted some small scale clearance of trees in his areas of temporary settlement. The Mesolithic period in Britain is characterised by the first appearance of some cereal production, together with the keeping of some domesticated animals. When Fishery Lake in Boxmoor was excavated, many ancient pot boilers were found. These were large round flint stones, some six inches in diameter, which were heated in open fires and used to warm water. These finds confirmed that the wider area was part of a Mesolithic site and a tranchet axe head from 6000 BC was also found in the waters of the lake. Although they liked to live close to rivers and lakes, the Mesolithic peoples favoured upland sites for settlement. Here the soils were better drained and the woodland was less dense. These early clearings on upland slopes were also the sites favoured by the last Stone Age tribes from the Neolithic period which dates from 3000 BC.

Neolithic Man

As recently as five years ago, it was thought there could have been no successful Neolithic settlement in the valleys of the Gade and the Bulbourne. No evidence had been found to contradict this theory and historians confidently considered that the clay topped chalk-lands to the north of London would have been too heavy for Neolithic man to work without the benefit of the improved tools which were introduced by the later Bronze and Iron Age civilisations. However these theories had to be rapidly revised when startling finds of eight new sites were made, on the south-eastern slopes of both the Gade and the Bulbourne valleys, in 1991. These discoveries were made during the construction of over 11 miles of dual carriageway for the A41 by-pass. With the benefit of the latest archaeological techniques, this major road scheme was a superb opportunity to examine an entire section cut through the chalk valley and, with the benefit of hindsight, was always likely to revise the evidence for long term settlement in the area. We now know that during the early Neolithic period, domestic sites were established on the slopes of both valleys. Some woodland clearance, together with grazing by domesticated cattle and pigs, would have lead to a gradual reduction in tree cover with the animals stripping bark from the trees.

An important site was to become known as the Neolithic Village at Rucklers Lane. The size of this settlement, which surprised all the experts, featured two long parallel lines of elongated Neolithic housing pits and post holes set some 70 metres apart. Another site was found 300 metres to the north at Apsley and the excavated areas of both sites together covered 28,212 square metres. Later in the Neolithic period, both round and flat based pottery bowls were made and these featured extensive surface decoration in what has become known as the Peterborough ware tradition. These two sites yielded over 800 such pottery sherds, together with stone tools such as fashioned arrow heads, hollow flakes, scrapers and blades. Although the local flint used was of a poor quality, the cutting edges of these tools were beautifully and carefully worked. Another major Neolithic site, discovered during the A41 roadworks, was further north in the Bulbourne valley between Berkhamsted and Tring. This was at Bottom House Lane and featured 40 parallel ditches running east to west across the road corridor. These ditches were found to be associated with Neolithic pottery and it was obvious that flint was also knapped here. Over 2,500 features were excavated on this particular site which also contained the post holes of later Bronze and Iron Age dwellings.

Bronze Age

It was not unusual for the areas settled during the later Neolithic period to have been inherited by the early Bronze Age peoples who continued to develop the agricultural practices and animal husbandry of these previous communities. These early settlers were now aided by the first metal tools which were chiefly axes and daggers made of fashioned bronze. They also introduced new styles of pottery with both beakers and collared urns coming into regular use. A tell-tale indication of the presence of early Bronze Age civilisation is the round barrows they built nearby for burials. Two such burial mounds can be found on Chipperfield Common and date from the early Bronze Age (2700-1400 BC). These barrows were originally surrounded by ditches which, over time, have gradually been filled in by soil erosion from the mounds themselves. Typically they contain the ashes of a single cremation, in a pottery vessel, and sometimes are accompanied by various ceremonial items intended for use in the next world. However a feature of the later Bronze Age (from 1200 BC) is the disappearance of this practice of using burial mounds. This later period is characterised by the dramatic increase in finds of bronze metal work with large hoards of this material being discovered in local rivers and lakes. We also see the first defensive hill forts, similar to that discovered at Ivinghoe Beacon. It appears that these early forts were also used to store supplies of grain and other agricultural produce gathered in from the smaller farming settlements in the surrounding valleys. Many late Bronze Age peoples now lived in circular fenced settlements known as ringworks. These consisted of a number of small circular huts, built close to a rectangular four post structure which was the likely local grain store. At this time there appears to have been a concerted effort to clear and colonise new areas of land for farming. The introduction of spelt wheat as a crop, which better tolerates more poorly drained clay soils, contributed to the success of this process.

Iron Age

From around 600 BC the knowledge of iron making spread into our valley area and the introduction of new iron tools made it much easier to both clear the forest and cultivate the soil. Given the beginnings of a more effective style of agriculture, the nomadic style of life preferred by the Stone Age peoples now came to an end. A feature of the early Iron Age in the Chilterns is the remarkably fine quality of the pottery ware which is found within the old farmstead and hill fort sites. Part of a Celtic sword, still in its scabbard, and dating from the First Century BC was found in the watercress beds at Bourne End, whilst an iron lynch pin from a Celtic chariot was found at Kings Langley. This lynch pin featured an enamel decorated head and both these important pieces are now in the custody of the British Museum. With Iron Age Chieftains established in the early hill forts, the tribal territories established in the Bronze Age had now become important centres of strength and wealth which were worth defending. This meant that for the first time wider conflict and power struggles began to enter the life of what, until then, had been a relatively peaceful area.

Typical Iron Age settlement.

Grims Dyke

The need for boundary markers and early defensive positions could well be part of the explanation for Grims Dyke. Grims Dyke (or ditch) is a related group of contour dykes which flank the Bulbourne valley and are known collectively as Grims Dyke. They form part of an extensive series of linear defences, traces of which can still be found extending over the chalk areas of Wiltshire, Hampshire, Oxfordshire, Berkshire and

Buckinghamshire and into London near Harrow. These dykes were initially constructed as territorial or farming estate boundaries, although it is likely that they also had some related social and religious functions. Local portions of Grims Dyke can still be seen at Wigginton and on Berkhamsted Common, running towards Potten End. In its hey-day, Grims Ditch would have been a deeply dug trench, surmounted by bracken covered ramparts, at least 15ft. high. Said by many historians to date from the Saxon period, it is perfectly possible that Grims Ditch could date from the much earlier Iron Age, and indeed some pottery sherds, attributed to this earlier period, have been found in the basal fill of Grims Dyke.

The first recorded invasion of Britain occurred around 150 BC, when powerful and wealthy tribes from the area of the Marne valley, near Paris, crossed the English Channel and invaded the south-east of Britain. This Belgic tribe, known to the Romans as the Catuvellauni, gradually took control of this area extending their influence from early centres of settlement in St. Albans. With their sea-faring heritage, the Catuvellauni were the first peoples to exploit the local rivers, controlling the fords and using the river system as a part of their highway communications. The majority of the numerous gold, silver and bronze Iron Age coins found in the valleys, date from the rule of the Catuvellaunian King Tasciovanus. For example a gold stater of Tasciovanus has been found at Kings Langley and a similar silver coin found at Gaddesden. Both these coins date from 25-20 BC. A group of pottery cinerary urns have also been uncovered from an Iron Age Belgic cremation cemetery, which was found by a group of school children in Aldbury in 1943. Numerous coins dating from the reign of Tasciovanus's son Cunobelin (AD 10-43) have also been found in both the Gade and the Bulbourne valleys. There was a significant increase in settlement in the river valleys during the late Iron Age and this development was accelerated by the growing contacts and influence of the Roman Empire, which was now beginning to spread its tentacles northwards from Italy and into Gaul. The Roman military expeditions, launched by Caesar from Gaul, first reached Britain in 55 BC. However before the Roman Empire could begin to influence the rather primitive Celtic civilisation it encountered, it first had to defeat the resistance of the Belgic tribes, in particular the Catuvellauni, who already ruled most of south-east England. There was a series of pitched battles before Caesar's troops attacked the base belonging to King Cassivellanus and successfully routed their enemy. Historians have speculated that the most likely site of this decisive battle was at either Wheathampsted or the early hill fort of Ravensburgh Castle on the Herts./Beds. border. A more recent suggestion is that it could have occurred around the Iron Age Fort at the Aubreys, near Redbourn. Once subjugated, trading contacts between the Romans and the Iron Age Chiefs continued until the full scale Roman invasion of Britain in AD 43. During the First Century BC, wheel thrown pottery was introduced to the area and the first industrial and trading areas begin to appear. At Berkhamsted and St. Albans, and especially at the Cow Roast site which we discuss a little later, there is evidence of organised iron production, large scale potteries and coin minting. Some surviving Romano-British shaft furnaces, together with some funeral urns dating from 30 BC, were also found in Berkhamsted during the construction of Bridgewater Middle School in 1969.

The Romans

With the arrival of the Romans, our favoured valley was soon transformed from a quiet backwater into one of the most highly developed areas in Britain. The Romans had their eyes firmly on the fertile lands of the Gade and Bulbourne valleys which were adjacent to the major city of Verulamium they soon established at St. Albans. Verulamium offered the various estate owners a well organised market for their produce, access to craftsmen and builders, supplies of metalwork, pottery and building materials, wine, cloth and importantly a regular supply of slaves. The Bulbourne valley was also a part of the route they established for one of the major highways, Akeman Street, which the Romans built to link Verulamium to Cirencester. Their impressive road system, together with the benefits of improved town planning derived from Roman civilisation, made a considerable and immediate impact on the local area. Under Roman organisation, most of the local countryside was split up into a series of estates, each with a large villa as its operational centre. These villas served as homes to the wealthy families, but were also working farms which included barns, granaries and workers' accommodation. In both the Gade and the Bulbourne valleys, the available archaeological evidence appears to indicate that these villas were regularly spaced about two miles apart along the valley floor. The Roman occupation continued from AD 43-500 and the villas from the early part of this period were often half timbered structures with painted plaster walls, flanked by corridors. In the Second Century, these first buildings were replaced by more substantial masonry structures which often included decorative mosaic floors and under-floor (hypocaust) heating systems. Such estates were often designed as self-sufficient units and produced their own metalwork, pottery and lime for plaster.

The first Roman finds in the Gade valley were made in the burial ground of Box Lane Chapel in August 1837 and these were the remains of two cremation burials, one contained in a green glass jar and the other in a blue-green glass bottle. Later in 1850 the remains of a Roman building and well were found in ground which is now part of the car park of Hemel Hempstead's Railway Station. At Kings Langley, during construction of the Roman Gardens estate, the foundations of a substantial Second Century masonry built villa was uncovered in 1981. This villa consisted of an impressive suite of rooms to the east and west which were controlled by corridors to the north and south; evidence of a hypocaust and bathhouse was also found on the site. In 1851 Sir John Evans excavated a Roman site on the east side of Boxmoor House (now Boxmoor

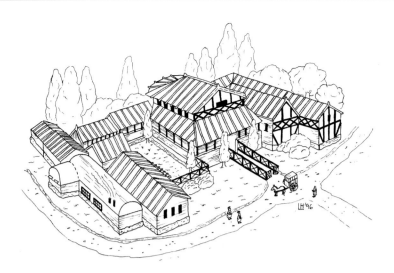

Roman Villa, circa 350AD.

House School). Here he unearthed a relatively simple four room structure with related tessellated paving. A later excavation in 1966, revealed a larger eleven room villa with mortared flint walls, which had been reduced to seven rooms by the Fourth Century AD. This building, considered to be of some wealth, also featured a hypocaust and at least three different mosaics. Although no villa has yet been found at Bourne End, the pattern of their distribution down the valley, indicates the presence of one is likely, particularly as historians believe that Akeman Street probably crossed the River Bulbourne at this point. Consequently it was no surprise when a hoard of 40 Roman coins was found at Bourne End in 1976.

The important discovery of a large Roman villa at Gadebridge Park was made in 1963 during the construction of the Leighton Buzzard Road. Surviving archaeological evidence indicates that, from its earliest timber-built phase, this villa had clearly undergone four different stages of construction before its extensive modernisation in the Fourth Century AD. By this time, the large winged corridor house now had its own separate gate house with a further range of farm buildings which together formed an outer courtyard. Five of the villa's nine rooms had under-floor heating systems and, from AD 325, a feature of the Gadebridge estate was its large bathing pool with five steps down from the terrace. Roman pools of this kind are very rare and this is the only example known to exist in Britain. In terms of its size, the only comparable Roman pool to survive in this country, is the famous one in the City of Bath. Another exciting find at Gadebridge was a well preserved basement room with painted plaster work decorated in purple and orange. This important villa, which was excavated by the archaeologist David Neal between 1963-68, made a key contribution to our knowledge of the development of Roman villas in Britain.

There has been no significant Roman structure properly unearthed at Berkhamsted, although there are some indications of a Roman villa on the golf course at Ashridge and evidence of a smaller Roman building has been located to the north of the Castle. However another major villa site was uncovered at Northchurch, during housing development for the construction of the Springwood estate in the 1970's. Roman occupation on this site dates from AD 60 and culminated circa AD 100 with an eight room villa which featured two 'wing' rooms at the end of the corridor. About AD 70 this building seems to have been abandoned for some 40-50 years. Substantial re-building then seems to have taken place on the site after AD 339 when a small bath house was added, together with some mosaics and painted plaster work. There is evidence of mixed farming on this Roman site at Northchurch, including cattle, sheep, pigs, goats, horses and ducks. There are also indications that this riverside

Sepulchral remains found at Box Lane, 1837.

villa may have been involved in farming of trout, oysters and freshwater mussels.

A very important site, further north at the Cow Roast, differs from all the others in that it is much larger and offers indications of a substantial Romano-British settlement which grew up alongside Akeman Street. Excavations have been conducted on this site since 1972, centering first on an orchard near the Cow Roast Inn, then at the marina and latterly on the hillside to the north. The whole area is now protected as an Ancient Monument and it has officially been designated as an early Roman town. Huge quantities of pottery have been recovered from both the marina and orchard sites and these include examples of glossy red Samian ware from Gaul. There are also clear signs of the industrial production of iron with fourteen separate well shafts for water and over two tons of iron slag and cinder already discovered at the Cow Roast. Finds of Roman coinage dating from Claudius (AD 41-54) to Honorius (AD 395-423) indicate an unbroken sequence of Roman occupation of around 400 years at the Cow Roast. When the Grand Junction Canal was being dug (1793-97), a legionary's helmet of the First Century AD was found in the mud at Norcott Hill. This became known as the Tring Helmet and is now held by the British Museum. The Roman Akeman Street travelled through Tring itself and its name is preserved in the town, albeit on a different road to this ancient main thoroughfare, whose route instead skirted the town.

When the Roman military occupation of Britain ended in the first decade of the Fifth Century, Saxon peoples from the harsher climates of Northern Europe gradually began to settle in Britain, intermingling their stock with the declining native British population. Sometimes these two peoples fought for supremacy, otherwise they co-existed peacefully. The progressive influence of the departed Roman civilisation began to decline as the country gradually came under Saxon control. During the Fifth Century AD the nation underwent a considerable influx of foreign tribesmen who were Anglo-Saxons, Danes, Jutes, or Norsemen. The more aggressive of these Nordic raiders made it their business to drive out any remaining Celtic tribes from Hertfordshire. They also systematically destroyed all the Roman buildings, in order to introduce their own style of life. By AD 527 the whole of Hertfordshire was included in the kingdom of East Saxony which was ruled by King Erkewin. The valleys of the Gade and the Bulbourne naturally formed part of the entry routes of these Saxon colonists who began to settle and farm land here, clearing woodland and systematically draining water-logged ground. They lived in family based clans and introduced their open field system of agriculture to Britain. They were very industrious pioneers, energetically burning scrub and clearing hundreds of acres before the Norman Conquest. They grew oats, barley and wheat on land that was ploughed by oxen. Pigs were also an important part of the village economy and were grazed, semi-wild, in the woodland. These Saxon settlers lived in huts built of mud and sticks, often sunk into the ground for warmth. Their communities also had larger halls built with logs for storage and the whole community was fenced to protect it from sudden attack. Unlike the earlier primitive settlements on higher ground, the chosen sites of the Anglo-Saxons tended to be on the gravel terraces, just above the lowest parts of the valley floors. It was these early settlements, established between AD 450 and 1066, which formed the pattern of the towns and villages that are dotted along the river valleys of the Gade and Bulbourne today.

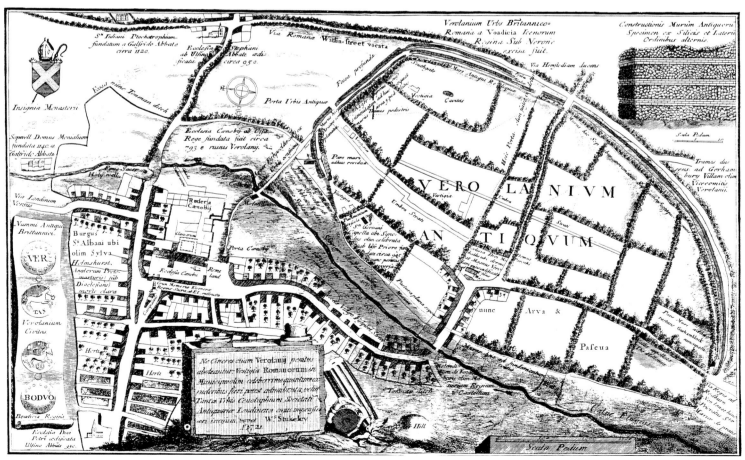

Plan of the Roman city of Verulamium.

Royal Patronage

It is doubtful whether there are any other largely rural areas of England that can lay claim to such a richly consistent historical pattern. In particular the continuing Royal presence, in both the Gade and Bulbourne valleys, offers us an illuminating example which runs through the centuries. By following its thread, we can see how many of the great events in England's history became closely interwoven with the evolution and development of our own particular local area.

Saxons

Initially the Saxon culture imported to Britain was quite harsh, although by the Seventh Century the spreading influence of Christianity made everyday life more humane. Apart from a mid Ninth Century Christian seal, found at Witchcraft Bottom in Little Gaddesden, and a circular bronze brooch from the same period, the only definite Saxon remains, as yet discovered, are some portions of the south and west walls of St. Mary's Parish Church at Northchurch. However it is quite likely that there were also earlier Saxon churches at Bovingdon, Abbots Langley and Great Gaddesden. As an explanation for this apparently limited amount of religious provision, surviving place names indicate that the pattern of Saxon settlement in the valley was relatively sparse, when compared with elsewhere in Hertfordshire. There are few local names ending in 'leah' meaning clearing, which indicates that Saxon clearance here was late. One such leah, 'Langelei', (which at this time included both Kings and Abbots Langley) was given by the Saxons, Ethelwine the Black and his wife Alfleda, to the Abbot Leofstan, the 12th Abbot of St. Albans. Hemel Hempstead first appears in records of lands in the district when 'Hamele' was granted to the Bishop of London in AD 705. In AD 793 King Offa founded the St. Albans Abbey on the site of the martyred Roman soldier, Alban.

By the time of the Norman Conquest, Edmar a Thane serving under Earl Harold, lived at Berkhamsted and ruled the local area. Two brothers, who were Earl Leofwin's men, supervised Hemel Hempstead, while Alwin, a Thane of King Edward, held Aldbury. Following the successful Norman invasion, despite the fact that William the Conqueror had given assurances that local landowners would retain rights and ownership of their local estates, he promptly confiscated them all when he had consolidated his power. All the local manors were awarded to his half-brother Robert, the Count of Mortain who was now resident at Berkhamsted Castle. This soon became an impressive Norman castle and it was now an important centre of power, used to subjugate the local area throughout the Norman period.

Detail from the Bayeaux Tapestry, showing William the Conqueror (centre) with Robert Count of Mortain (right).

Following the Norman invasion of Britain in 1066, William the Conqueror accepted the surrender of the Saxon nobles at Berkhamsted. Following an unsuccessful rebellion against Henry I, Berkhamsted Castle was then substantially rebuilt by the King's Chancellor, Randolph. Later, from 1155-65, it became home to the much venerated and betrayed priest, Thomas à Beckett. The castle then became a favoured residence of Henry II who in 1156 granted the merchants and traders of Berkhamsted exemption from all taxes and tolls throughout his kingdom. By 1189 Berkhamsted Castle was in the ownership of Prince John, later King John, and infamous brother of the crusading King Richard I. Because King John reneged on various pledges made in the Magna Carta, Berkhamsted Castle was successfully besieged in December 1216 by aggrieved English Barons, aided by Prince Louis of France. Consequent damage to the castle was repaired during the reign of Henry III (1216-72).

Berkhamstead Castle

In 1272 Edmund, Earl of Cornwall inherited the castle, where he had been born. Four years later he founded the important monastery at Ashridge which was finally dedicated in 1286. The community of monks at Ashridge was established primarily to safeguard a Holy relic. This was a casket said to contain some of the blood of Christ which had been brought back to England by Edmund's father, King Richard I. In 1276 a second local Royal residence was established by Eleanor of Castille, the wife of Edward I (1272-1307). In the Gade valley at Kings Langley, she created a Royal hunting park of 126 acres and provided it with a splendid Plantagenet Palace. Nearby the lands of Shendish had been held by the Chenduit family until 1276. The Chenduits are likely descendants of Ralf, a Sergeant at Berkhamsted Castle who had been "given land of the capital manor of Langley" by his Lord, Robert Count of Mortain.

In 1290 Edward I held a Parliament at Ashridge Monastery and by 1296 he was embroiled in a long and bloody conflict with the rebellious Scots, led by William Wallace. In 1300, accompanied by his son Edward of Caenarfon, the first Prince of Wales, he departed from the Royal Palace at Kings Langley to campaign in Scotland. However, brave Wallace was not defeated until 1305 and the struggle was promptly renewed by a new King of the Scots, Robert the Bruce in 1306. In 1308 Edward II, who had succeeded his father in 1307, built a Dominican Friary on a site adjacent to the Royal Palace at Kings Langley. This developed to become "the richest house of Dominican preachers, in all England". Prior to this Royal patronage, a smaller community of friars lived on a small moated site to the south of Kings Langley. This was known as "Little London", a more modest friary which occupied ground close to where the M25 Gade Valley Viaduct crosses the valley.

The King also granted Berkhamsted Castle to his favourite, Piers Gaveston, but by 1315 the betrayed lover of Edward II had been murdered and buried at the Church of the Dominican Friary in Kings Langley. In 1349 the Palace at Kings Langley was used by Edward III as his seat of Government during the Black Death. Around this time the King also carried out extensive repairs to the decaying fabric of Berkhamsted Castle, before granting it to his son, Edward, the Black Prince.

The Black Prince

Based at Berkhamsted Castle, the Black Prince enjoyed spectacular military success in the Hundred Years War against the French and King John of France was imprisoned at the castle, following the Battle of Poitiers in 1356.

Richard II, the eldest surviving son of the Black Prince, grew up as a boy at the Royal Palace at Kings Langley, and became very fond of the area. Two scenes in Shakespeare's play Richard II are set at Kings Langley, one in the Palace itself and another in the garden. However his reign was not a happy one and during the period of the Peasants Revolt in 1381, there was much unrest around the Castle of Berkhamsted. This discontent was mainly concerned with the levying of additional taxes to help pay for the continuing Hundred Years War against the French. Following the King's betrayal and incarceration at Pontefract Castle, Richard was first buried at the Friary Church in Kings Langley. Subsequently his body was removed to Westminster Abbey on the instructions of Henry V. Richard's fondness for the area adds plausibility to the story that his portable altar was hidden away and then re-found in a barn on Harthall Farm, near Kings Langley, during the late Sixteenth Century. This ancient Royal artefact is now known as the Wilton Diptych and consists of two panels of oak, painted on both sides. The exquisite paintings on this devotional object are considered to represent the most outstanding surviving example of English medieval painting. In 1929 the Wilton Diptych was acquired by the National Gallery. In 1341 Edmund de Langley was born at Kings Langley, later becoming the first Duke of York. On his death in 1402, Edmund was also first buried at the Friary Church. However in 1574, on the orders of Queen Elizabeth I, his body was moved to the local Parish Church in Kings Langley.

We know that Henry V spent time at Kings Langley in 1414, but the last significant Royal presence at the palace was when it became the official residence of his wife, Queen Joan of Navarre. Its decline was hastened by a disastrously destructive fire which occurred in 1431. The castle at Berkhamsted however remained in Royal favour a little longer, and the Town was accorded further privileges derived from a Charter issued by Edward IV (1442-83) This stipulated that no other market could be established within an 11 mile radius of Berkhamsted. The last member of the Royal Family to live at Berkhamsted Castle was Cecily, Duchess of York, who remained at the castle as a widow from 1460 until her death in 1496. The Duchess was an important historical figure who had been mother to two kings, Edward IV and Richard III. She was also grandmother to Edward and Richard, the two Princes who were so treacherously murdered in the Tower of London in 1483.

In 1452 Robert Whittingham inherited the Estate of Pendley, near Tring. He served as Keeper of the Wardrobe to Margaret of Anjou and was a leading soldier and loyal servant of the Crown. He was subsequently Knighted following the Battle of St. Albans in 1461. His tomb can still be found in the Memorial Chapel at the Parish Church of St. John the Baptist in Aldbury. Whittingham's daughter Mary, married the son of Yorkist Sir Ralph Verney and this union established the branch of the Verney family who were to live on the Pendley estate for the next four generations. Mary's husband, the 2nd Sir Ralph Verney died in 1528, and was laid to rest in a fine tomb at the Parish Church of all Saints at Kings Langley.

A panel of the Wilton Diptych, showing Richard II kneeling.

The will of Cecily Duchess of York provided for a substantial bequest to her gentleman friend, Edward de La Hay. He was another leading landowner of the day who lived at Westbrook Hay, near Bovingdon. The reign of Henry VIII, and the Dissolution of the Monasteries, spelt the end for the community of monks who had thrived under 250 years of Royal patronage at Ashridge. The house and estate were promptly claimed for the Crown and the King's three children, Edward, Mary and Elizabeth then divided their time between Hatfield House and Ashridge. From this time the Royal status of both Berkhamsted and Kings Langley waned considerably. King Henry VIII, who by now spent most of his time at Hampton Court, had courted Anne Boleyn at Lockers Park, Hemel Hempstead.

Henry VIII.

Perhaps as a result of this, he conferred his local favours upon this town, awarding it the important status of Bailiwick in 1539. Following the Dissolution of the Monasteries, in that same year, the King had become, in effect, the Lord of the Manor for Hemel Hempstead. It was therefore in his direct financial interest to help the local community to build on its already prosperous agricultural trade. Also in 1539, King Henry VIII granted the manorial estate of Abbots Langley, which he had confiscated from the Abbot of St. Albans, to his distinguished and loyal military commander Sir Richard Lee. This parcel of land included Hunton Bridge and Langleybury. Locally the King also granted the Rectory and Advowson of Great Gaddesden to William Halsey and in 1546 he gave the Manor of Cassio to Sir Richard Morison. Sir Richard began to build the Manor House at Cassiobury which was then inherited in 1580 by his son Charles Morison. Charles Morison built an additional house on Langley Hill at Kings Langley.

In 1553 Mary Tudor came to the throne and in 1557 she sent men to Ashridge in order to arrest her sister, Princess Elizabeth, who was suspected of being involved in a plot to prevent Queen Mary's projected marriage to Philip, the King of Spain. There is a surviving Tudor portrait of the moment of Elizabeth's arrest which still hangs in the Manor House at Little Gaddesden. Following her own accession to the throne in 1558, Queen Elizabeth never returned to Ashridge. Prior to 1581 the land at Boxmoor had been given to the Earl of Leicester by the Queen, who also granted the parsonages of both Tring and Wigginton to the Dean and Chapter of Christchurch College, Oxford. At Berkhamsted in 1580, the fine mansion house of Berkhamsted Place was built by Sir Edward Carey, who was Keeper of the Jewels to Elizabeth I. He was allowed to use some of the stone-work from the derelict Royal castle in the construction of this substantial house. By 1604 Thomas Egerton (1540-1617), Lord Keeper to Queen Elizabeth I and Lord Chancellor to James I, was the owner of the Ashridge estate. Thomas Egerton's son, who became the first Earl of Bridgewater, was also a leading Royalist and Ashridge was later ransacked by Cromwell's troops during the Civil War.

Although we can already see a pattern whereby lands would be granted by the reigning Sovereign to favoured ministers, courtiers and servants, this was a process which intensified considerably following the Royalist versus Parliamentary struggles of the Civil Wars (1642-51). Many of the great houses and estates, which survived locally into the Twentieth Century, were established by leading families who had taken the not inconsiderable risk of supporting the Royalist cause. Most were handsomely rewarded by a grateful sovereign, following the Restoration of the Monarchy in 1660.

In 1616 the Estate of Langleybury was conveyed to Prince Charles (later King Charles I), under the supervision of several trustees, who included Francis Bacon, then living nearby on the Gorehambury Estate at St. Albans. During this time the Royal Prince used the building which is now the Kings Lodge, a licensed restaurant in Hunton Bridge, as his hunting lodge. In 1612 Berkhamsted Place had been owned by Henry, Prince of Wales. This was prior to the tenure of the new King, Charles I, who awarded this estate to his tutor and nurse, Thomas and Mary Murray. Some local Royalists did perish in the struggles of the Civil Wars. In March 1649 Arthur Capel, owner of the Cassiobury estate and a leading supporter of Charles I, was beheaded and Sir Edmund Verney of Pendley, loyal Standard Bearer to King Charles, died at the Battle of Edgehill. The Grove estate, near Watford, was home to another leading Royalist, Edward Hyde the 1st Earl of Clarendon, who was made Lord Chancellor following the Restoration of the King. Arthur Capel of the Cassiobury estate, eldest son of the beheaded Arthur, was awarded the titles of Viscount Malden and Earl of Essex by the newly crowned Charles II. Between 1674-1680, the King's architect, Hugh May, helped the Earl of Essex to rebuild Cassiobury House. Sir Thomas Halsey, who lived at The Golden Parsonage in Great Gaddesden, was another important figure of the day who achieved distinction as a Judge during the reign of Charles II.

By 1662 Berkhamsted Place was home to the King's Chief Cook, John Sayer and Ashlyns Hall was home to Francis Wethered, his Comptroller of Works. Despite a Charter awarded by James I in 1618, the town of Berkhamsted had fallen further from favour because it had shown distinct Parliamentary sympathies during the Civil Wars. In 1684 Charles II had kept some faith with the other old Royal community of Kings Langley by granting its inhabitants immunity from tolls charged at any other market in England. The Tring Park estate was given to Henry Guy, who was Lord of the Bedchamber to Charles II and already wealthy enough to engage Sir Christopher Wren as architect for the building of his fine mansion.

By 1705 Sir William Gore had possession of the lands at Tring Park; Sir William was a former Lord Mayor of London who had also served as Under Steward to Queen Katherine. In 1711 the classically Georgian structure of Langleybury House was built by Sir Robert Raymond, who was later to become Lord Chief Justice of England (1724-32). William Capel (1697-1743) resident at Cassiobury, served as Gentleman of the Bedchamber to George II, when he was Prince of Wales. He later became Keeper of both St. James and Hyde Parks for the King. At the Grove the title of Clarendon had remained in the Hyde family until the death of the 4th Earl in 1753. Thomas Villiers, who purchased the Grove, was subsequently awarded the title of Earl of Clarendon in 1776 in recognition of his diplomatic work.

In 1811 Sir Astley Paston Cooper (1768-1841) purchased the estate of Gadebridge, near Hemel Hempstead. He was a distinguished surgeon who successfully operated to remove a tumour from the head of George IV in 1821. He was subsequently made Surgeon General to King George IV and also served King William IV and Queen Victoria in that capacity. Between 1846-1848, Cassiobury House was used by Queen Adelaide as her Royal residence and in 1847 Baron Rokeby, who had served with distinction as a Major General at the Battle of Sebastopol in the Crimean War, built himself a fine house and estate at Hazelwood, near Abbots Langley. Resident at the Grove, George Frederick William Villiers (1800-75) was unusually awarded both the Order of the Garter and the Insignia of the Bath by a grateful Queen Victoria.

These honours were given principally in recognition of his service as Lord Lieutenant of Ireland. In 1872 the Tring Park estate was purchased by leading banker Nathaniel Rothschild who became the first Jew to be elevated to the peerage as Lord Rothschild of Tring in 1872. Visitors to Tring Park included King Edward VII and King George V. Although declining, a pattern of some Royal connections with the local area continued into the Twentieth Century. Both Queen Victoria and King Edward VII paid regular visits to the homes of the Earls of Essex and Clarendon at Cassiobury and the Grove respectively. In 1902 Edward VII was both a patron and exhibitor at the annual Tring Show. Edward Hyde, the 5th Earl of Clarendon, served as ADC to both Queen Victoria and later Edward VII. Before the First World War, the Third Earl Lord Brownlow's shooting parties at Ashridge often included members of the Royal Family; Queen Mary was also a frequent visitor to the estate. The Shah of Persia also paid a visit to Ashridge. Following her marriage to Thomas Motion, Lady Elizabeth Motion who served as Lady in Waiting to Queen Mary, took up residence on the Serge Hill estate, near Bedmond. In 1935 the Prince of Wales, then the Duke of Windsor, paid an official visit to Berkhamsted Castle. The castle, to this day, is still in the ownership of the Duke of Cornwall, and this was the first time the Ruin had received a visit from its title holder since 1616. At Kings Langley, in respect of its Royal heritage, the village was allowed to fly the Royal Standard from the tower of its Parish Church of All Saints. This privilege was finally withdrawn in the same year as the Duke of Windsor's visit to Berkhamsted.

The 6th Earl of Clarendon, George Herbert Hyde Villiers (1877-1955), held the office of Lord Chamberlain and served in this capacity at the funeral of George VI in 1952. In July 1952 Queen Elizabeth II paid an official visit to Hemel Hempstead, where she laid the foundation stone for St. Barnabas Church in Adeyfield. The shopping precinct of this New Town suburb is now named Queen Square to commemorate her visit. Our final Royal link is provided by the Manor House at Chipperfield which is home to Gerald Legge, the 9th Earl of Dartmouth. His first wife became by her second marriage to Earl Spencer, the stepmother to HRH Diana, Princess of Wales. Diana is now the divorced wife of Prince Charles, himself first in line to succeed Queen Elizabeth II.

Garden scene from Shakespeare's Richard II, featuring the Royal Palace at Kings Langley.

Edward II and Piers Gaveston in the garden of the Royal Palace.

Early engraving of the Dominican Friary.

The tombs of Sir Ralph Verney (centre) and Edmund de Langley in the Parish Church of All Saints, Kings Langley.

Early engraving of Berkhamsted Castle.

Stonework and arch supports of Royal wine cellar.

Site of Royal wine cellar.

Full view of wine cellar excavation, 1970.

View of the Keep at Berkhamsted Castle, 1958.

Agriculture

Hertfordshire summers are warmer than average and have a short, but intense, growing season which favours farmers. Also of particular importance is the number of days when the fields are likely to be full of water or at 'field capacity'. The number of days when this is the case is as low as any other crop growing area in the country and is more favoured than Hertfordshire's chief rival Kent. These two factors together confirm that the county has a very equable climate, particularly for the production of arable crops like wheat and barley. As we have already discussed in the Local Geography chapter (page 7), the composition of local soil is chiefly boulder clay with an underlying strata of chalk. However the soil is also influenced by the last Ice Age which produced additional mixed deposits. These involved large quantities of glacial sand and gravel which contribute to a variety of soil types variously described as comprising 'clay with flint' and 'glacial gravel'. As we will see later, attempts to enhance the fertility of the native soil have a long and successful history. The underlying fertility of the land of the two river valleys, together with their proximity to the major markets of London, ensured long ago that this area would naturally enjoy successful agricultural development.

Agriculture, as distinct from the gathering of wild fruits and small scale domestic provision of daily food, was first introduced to Britain by the people of the Neolithic period, circa 2400 BC. The first light plough, which had no wheels and was drawn by two oxen, came into use from the Continent with the late Bronze Age immigrants of the First Century BC. These Belgic tribes established the first communities in the countryside which could be described as semi-urban and important archaeological evidence of this type of settlement still survives locally at Wheathampstead. Following their invasion of Britain in 55 BC, the Romans recognised both the good agricultural conditions and the strategic importance of the area. This partly prompted them to build the major City of Verulamium nearby. Subsequently a chain of impressive Roman villas were built along the river valleys, in order to manage the various agricultural estates they established there. Archaeological evidence (see Early Settlement, page 12) has already been discovered which locates important Roman villa sites at Northchurch, Boxmoor, Gadebridge and Kings Langley. The demise of these prosperous and well organised farms came almost at the beginning of the Fifth Century, with the general civil disintegration which followed the end of the Roman Empire's influence in Britain. The remaining indigenous farmers soon abandoned the ambitious and larger scale farming of marginal lands which had been introduced by the better organised Romans. Without grazing animals these fields soon returned, within a period of 50 years, to their previous condition of dense scrub mixed birch woods. In the early Saxon times the population declined and settlement retreated so that by the time of the Norman invasion, much of the valley area was again very heavily wooded, especially when compared with other parts of Hertfordshire. An indication of this is the large number of pigs listed by the Domesday Book as being kept locally. Pigs were particularly suited to wooded areas where they could be left to forage for acorns and beech nuts. However when the Anglo-Saxons had settled, they formed the nucleus of what eventually became the modern communities of the Gade and Bulbourne valleys. They built log houses and lived in clans and family groups, clearing the adjacent land for an open field style of agriculture. Under this system large fields, divided into three strips, were cultivated in rotation.

An agricultural feature of the Norman period of the Twelfth and Thirteenth Centuries, was the sheer scale of the wood clearance programmes that were initiated in the local area. As we have already discussed in 'Early Settlement' (page 12), this extensive timber production helped to fund the economies of the Royal Castle at Berkhamsted and also the important monastery which was founded at Ashridge. Medieval farmers were already beginning to use crop rotation in their open field system, whereby areas of pasture, tillage and fallow were rotated. The surrounding woodland and grass areas were set aside for common grazing and the production of nuts, berries, firewood and game. Despite the fact that livestock was still playing a secondary role to crop production, the nation's wool trade was already considerable during the Thirteenth and Fourteenth Centuries. Flemish farmers were encouraged to settle in England, in order that they could pass on their skills. In the reign of Richard III, there was a subsidy of 4 pence per broad cloth produced and in 1387, thirteen producers in Berkhamsted qualified for this subsidy. However, the Fourteenth Century did not herald a bright new dawn for the nation's agriculture which suffered a series of set-backs. Expansion of medieval communities was not as well managed as it would have been had the benefits of the earlier Roman and Norman civilisation been sustained. Consequently there was a period of agricultural decline fuelled both by over-population and soil exhaustion. In addition bad weather, poor health and epidemics of disease amongst the farmed sheep and cattle, added to the general recession. This process of deterioration climaxed with the widespread outbreak of the plague known as the Black Death in 1349. The population decline was now so severe that the extent of arable land contracted, and up to 70 villages in Hertfordshire became deserted. Local evidence of this can be seen at the village of Gubblecote, which is now only a farm and also in the remoteness of the church at Little Gaddesden, which may have been left stranded from its newer, later community by medieval desertion. The tiny hamlet of Nettleden is a fine surviving example of a shrunken village.

As the population recovered and expanded during the Fifteenth Century, so once again woodland was cleared to provide fields for food production. However by Tudor times this was a better managed process, with laws passed to encourage pollarding and coppicing techniques which were designed to help produce renewable supplies of timber. It is worth stressing that, in the two valleys, many of our present fields were taken early from the woodland during the Thirteenth to the Seventeenth Centuries. Because of this, by the time the national programme of enclosures was introduced by Parliament in the early Nineteenth Century, much of the local land had already been enclosed for hundreds of years. Another distinctive characteristic is that this area of West Hertfordshire managed to retain a good proportion of common land. This dates back to medieval times when these slices of territory were designated the wasteland of old manorial estates. This land still belonged, in an absolute sense, to the Lord of the Manor, but his rights were limited by the rights of common folk to use this ground for the grazing of their animals or for collecting wood, gorse, heather and ferns for fuel. It wasn't until the increase in land values, which began in the Seventeenth Century, that major landowners were tempted to try and reclaim some of this land. There has been a strong and successful tradition of resistance to this process locally, best epitomised by what became known as the 'Battle of Berkhamsted Common' (see page 210).

In addition to cereal crops, orchards were another important early agricultural feature of this area. The summer sunshine and the rich soil encouraged hundreds of small orchards within the various local small holdings. As an indication of this, in a survey of 1619, there were as many as 57 orchards listed in the village of Kings Langley. During the Eighteenth Century, most cottagers kept their own cherry trees and grew the famous Hertfordshire black cherry, which was known as the coroon. A typical orchard during the Nineteenth Century ran to three acres. There were over 80 acres of orchards at Bovingdon, where crops of premium cherries were grown specifically for the London market. The people of Potten End became known locally as 'cherry pickers', but the heart of this local industry was at Frithsden, where a Cherry Fair was held annually. To this day a local place name 'Cherry Bounce' has outlived the old Frithsden cherry orchards.

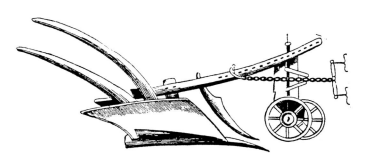

The Great Hertfordshire Plough in the Seventeenth Century.

The successful and increasingly large scale production of the area's principal cereal crops depended on the development of the key tool in the process, which was the plough. The design of what became known as the Hertfordshire Plough had stabilised by the Sixteenth Century as a later version of the early ox-drawn Saxon plough. The length of a furrow, which was 220 yards long, was determined simply by the pulling power of the team of four oxen. Similarly, the width of a day's ploughing of 66ft., was to set the parameter for the standard measurement of an English acre of land. The plough laid the foundations for the success of arable farming in this country and by the 1750's, it had been superseded by an entirely new design which was called the Great Hertfordshire Plough. This consisted of a strong wooden beam, 8ft. long, with a wheel carriage to support its front end. A team of eight oxen was now required to pull this huge tool through the soil. The other key determinant of success was the fertility of the land, and it was in this respect that the valleys were an excellent example of agricultural best practice in the Eighteenth and Nineteenth Centuries. Towards the end of the 1700's, sheep were used, as much for their ability to manure the land as for their wool. The soil was also regularly limed using local supplies of Chiltern chalk. Following the construction of the Grand Junction Canal in 1797, huge quantities of manure, chimney soot, ashes and night soils were brought from the City of London, to be spread on the local fields. Best soot is a natural nitrogenous manure containing ammonia salts and up to 25 bushels were used per acre. At this time Hertfordshire was using more soot than any other county in the land. Underlying layers of chalk were mined from large cavities dug in the landscape to dress the fields; these were known locally as Dene Holes.

By 1822 Cobbett was able to say that the lands of Hertfordshire were "very fine: featuring a red tenacious flinty loam, upon a bed of chalk, which makes it the very best corn land we have in England". The locally established pattern for the rotation of crops was now: turnips, peas or beans, barley or oats, followed by wheat. The Chiltern system of alternating pasture with arable crops was very effective and had impressed the visiting Swedish botanist, Peter Kalm, who visited Little Gaddesden in 1748. He had also taken note of local hay-making practices, whereby hay was hand-cut with scythes and left in the field for four days during fine weather. Some of this hay was then stored in large hay lathes which were square oak boxes 14ft. long and 8ft high. At the corners of these lathes were 30ft. oak posts, set upright to support an adjustable roof, so that as the hay was removed for feeding livestock, the thatched roof could be lowered to protect the hay from the weather.

The development of the land-owning aristocracy in the Georgian period, together with rising prices and the post-war slump which followed the Napoleonic Wars, had gradually begun to squeeze out the smaller local landowner. Throughout the Nineteenth Century, the average farm holding became progressively larger. This was in order to take advantage of the economies of scale and to help meet the growing demands of the new urban food markets. There has always been some small-scale dairy farming and following the general agricultural depression at the end of the Nineteenth Century, cattle began to replace sheep as the principal farmed livestock. By this time barley had become more important than wheat. Mechanisation played an increasing part in the development of the industry, but as late as the 1920's, the corn binders still needed three horses to pull them across the field. The combine harvester, which revolutionised farming by being able to reap and thresh the corn in one process, had evolved in California as early as 1870. However its use was not common in this country until the 1940's. Rapid urban expansion and technological advances have of course helped to redefine the local landscape during the post war period. Arable farming has continued to predominate in the valleys, but hedgerows have been removed, meadows drained and downlands ploughed. The introduction of chemical herbicides and artificial fertilisers poses a threat to the majority of the area's native flora and fauna. Whilst much of Berkhamsted and Northchurch Commons have lost elements of their botanical interest because of a lack of grazing, fine examples of chalk grassland still survive in Tring and Aldbury. The excellent work of the Boxmoor Trust is a fine example of continuing environmental preservation into the Twenty-First Century.

Early reaping machine.

Markets

Given the local emphasis on agricultural development, it is no surprise that historically a strong network of local markets has become established in the valley. These markets allowed farmers to trade their produce and also fuelled the early economic development of the area. Berkhamsted's Monday market dates back to 1217 and enjoyed the early privileges and prosperity that accrued to the town from the fact that Berkhamsted Castle was an important and early Royal residence. A protective charter issued by Edward IV (1442-83) consolidated its dominant position in the local area by stating that no other market could be established within eleven miles of the town. However the importance of the Berkhamsted Market declined in the Fifteenth Century and the town's old Elizabethan Market House burnt down in 1854.

Watford Market.

The market Charter at Tring dates back to 1315 and the presence of a Royal Plantagenet Palace at Kings Langley also granted this smaller village important early market rights and protections during the Fourteenth Century. However by the beginning of the Sixteenth Century, both Kings Langley Palace and Berkhamsted Castle had been abandoned and left to fall into dereliction. The Charter of 1539 awarded to Hemel Hempstead by Henry VIII, which accorded the town Bailiwick status, helped lay the foundation for what was destined to become the principal and most prosperous market town in the area. During the reign of Elizabeth I, a Sheep and Cattle Fair was held in Hemel Hempstead on Holy Thursday. A Charter awarded by Oliver Cromwell granted the town three more fairs in 1656. By 1742 the town was described as having "the greatest corn market in the county, perhaps in the kingdom". The quality of the soil and the agricultural practices used caused Hemel Hempstead to be called 'The very granary of London'. During the Eighteenth Century, a Wool Fair was another annual event in the town, and was held on the last Friday in June; a Sheep Market was also held regularly at the lower end of Hemel Hempstead High Street. Bailiwick records indicate that in 1884 local farmers sold a total of 16,000 fleeces at the Hemel Hempstead market. The success and prosperity of the town's markets allowed for the construction of the fine building we now know as Old Town Hall in the High Street. Here a new Market House, bell turret and giant Corn Loft was built in 1867. It stood on the former site of the old Corn Exchange. Another important local market was held at Tring. This town was well positioned on the junction of early trading routes and was a popular stopping off place for Midlands-based farmers on their way to London. There has always been a strong livestock market at Tring and the traditional market day in the town has always been a Friday. When the old Market House (now the Civic Centre), was rebuilt by Lord Rothschild in 1900, the town's Cattle Market was moved to Brook Street.

The Great Tring Show

In 1840 the Tring Agricultural Association was formed and by December 1842 arrangements for its Annual Meeting included a competition for members, owning or living on land that lay within 10 miles of Tring. The Tring Show, while well supported for its first 40 years, enjoyed a new lease of life when in 1884 Lord Rothschild, who had taken up residence at Tring Park, became a very keen member of the Association. He was later to become its President, whilst his Land Agent, Frank John Brown, held the post of Secretary of Tring Agricultural Association for nearly 50 years. Under their leadership, the Tring Show developed to become one of the most important events in the national agricultural calendar, gaining the reputation of being the best one day show in the country. At the beginning of the Twentieth Century, Tring Show was considered to be "the working dogs Grand National", with shepherds coming from as far afield as North Wales, the Lake District and the Scottish Borders. King Edward VII was both a patron and an exhibitor at the Tring Show and in 1902 the estimated attendance was 20,000.

Mills

In addition to the development of markets, another clear indicator of the agricultural emphasis in the local area was the presence of 17 mills, which were scattered along the river valleys of the Gade and Bulbourne. These were mainly water driven corn mills, although some were also used for the fulling of wool and cloth and a few were later converted into paper making mills during the second half of the Eighteenth Century. Many of these mills were established very early, beside what were then two flourishing and fast-flowing rivers. The Domesday Survey of 1086 noted a total of 13 mills in the two valleys: one at Gubblecote, two at Tring, one at Wigginton, one at Great Gaddesden, two at Berkhamsted, four at Hemel Hempstead and two at Kings Langley. In these early days, the principal function of the water mills was to grind corn for the fairly self-sufficient communities of each individual Manor.

The last flour mill to survive in the area can be found at Tring, run by Heygates Ltd who are the largest private flour miller in the United Kingdom (see Early Industry, page 57). The first mill, here at Gamnel, had been a windmill which was replaced

A water mill near Hemel Hempstead, 1778.

Hay gathering at Hill Farm, Kings Langley, 1930's.

Harvest time at Mansion House Farm, Abbots Langley, 1910.

Horse-drawn hay cart.

Horse-drawn ploughing.

Hay sweeping at Millhouse Farm, Bedmond.

in 1875 by a large mill built by Thomas Mead. Tring is also home to the four storied structure of Goldfield Mill which was the last working windmill in the area. This was being operated by steam as late as the 1920's, its sails having been removed in 1906. Another mill at Tring is Grace's Mill, in Akeman Street. Here Carter Grace (1796-1863) worked as a leading corn merchant and also a maltster, who ground barley for the brewing industry. Upper and Lower Mills at Berkhamsted both feature in the Domesday Book. In 1926 Upper Mill in Castle Street was replaced by the new Music School building, attached to Berkhamsted School, while the old Mill House Hotel still stands today marking the site of Lower Mill. Castle Mill in Berkhamsted is a much later mill and was built near the canal bridge in 1910/11 expressly for the manufacture of animal foodstuffs. A small canal-side wharf was also provided here, but this mill ceased working after World War II and is now used as offices.

Bourne End Mill was mentioned in the Ashridge Charter of 1289 and by 1900 was a roller mill producing $3\frac{1}{2}$ cwt. of flour per hour. The Moat House Hotel now occupies the site which was re-developed in 1972. This new building work incorporated the old mill race into what was then known as the Water Mill Motel. The mill at Two Waters was originally a corn mill, but by 1650 was a fulling mill for cloth. By 1763 it was part corn mill and part paper mill, having been taken over by the Fourdriniers (see page 59). Two Waters Mill was subsequently destroyed by an explosion in 1919. Frogmore Mill was similarly a water driven mill known as Convent Mill in 1650, which by 1803 had also been acquired by the Fourdriniers for paper manufacture. This later became home to the British Paper Making Company at the beginning of the Nineteenth Century. Both Apsley and Nash Mills (see page 59) were similarly converted to paper manufacture by the leading industrialist John Dickinson. Bury Mill at Hemel Hempstead was another corn mill. It was also mentioned in the Ashridge Charter of 1289 and by 1557 was owned by Richard Coombes. This mill, which was owned by Putnam Millers in 1922 and demolished in 1962, stood by the River Gade near the Bury in Queensway. Piccotts End Mill is another early mill, dating probably from Domesday, although the surviving building derives from the Eighteenth Century; its waterwheel was removed in 1963. The main part of this mill was destroyed by fire in April 1991. The nearby mill at Water End, the Noke Mill, has a similar pedigree although its waterwheel still remains. The mill at Kings Langley became Toovey's Flour Mill in 1780 (see page 56) and although the mill at Hunton Bridge has now gone, a fine converted Mill House still stands. There were also charming mills at both the Grove and Cassiobury which serviced the agricultural production of these particular estates.

Straw Plaiting

Straw plaiting was one of the great cottage industries of the area during the Eighteenth and Nineteenth Centuries. A natural by-product of the agricultural emphasis on cereal production, this industry was developed to satisfy what was then a hungry world wide demand for fine straw plaiting. It was the high fashion industry and hat making, in particular, that created this demand. It was an industry which expanded considerably, in direct proportion to growing British involvement overseas. The demand for straw plait was at its peak towards the end of the Eighteenth Century, when the Napoleonic wars stopped the imports of foreign plait and made the local hat manufacturers, both in London and Dunstable,

Straw Plaiting School, 1882.

entirely dependent on local home plaiters. Given the widespread poverty which was endemic among agricultural labourers of the Eighteenth and Nineteenth Centuries, straw plaiting represented an invaluable additional contribution to the average household economy. By the start of the Nineteenth Century a good plaiter could earn up to a £1 a week; women working at home were now earning more than their husbands who laboured all day in the fields. In order to further capitalise on this opportunity, children as young as three years old were taught by the women folk to plait and Plait Schools flourished in most local rural communities. In 1851 straw plaiting was listed as the main occupation of the women of Potten End and, even in larger towns like Berkhamsted, straw plaiting had supplanted lace-making as the key cottage industry of the working folk. An earlier indication of Berkhamsted's importance in the lace-making industry was the issue of a trade token by leading lace merchants Chambers, Langston and Hall of Leighton Buzzard, which bears the inscription "Leighton, Berkhamsted or London".

Straw plaiting, which could easily be done at home, only required three simple tools: a straw splitter, a splint mill and a yard measure. Although there were over 20 different patterns, a straw plait fell into three main forms; plain, pearl or brilliant. Straw plait was made up into a length called a score, which was 20 yards, and this was the unit by which it was then sold at market. A good plaiter could produce four scores a day, which were either sold directly to visiting hat manufacturers, or could be taken to the weekly Plait Market in Hemel Hempstead. The Plait Market was held in Colletts Yard in 1813, before moving to the yard of the Kings Arms in 1832. The enlightened social progress during the latter half of the Nineteenth Century spelt the end of this thriving cottage industry. With the encouragement of Free Trade and the repeal of Protective Duties in 1860, imports of cheap plaits were flooding into this country from Italy and the Far East. The Education Act of 1870 also spelt the end of the Plait Schools, with access to a basic literacy and numeracy now a right for any child in the land.

Watercress

The earliest known reference to cress is by the Swedish botanist Peter Kalm, who visited Hertfordshire in 1748 and noted its use in salads. In 1808 William Bradbury, a very early pioneer of the industry, cultivated watercress at Springhead, near Gravesend in Kent. However he soon moved his business to West Hyde near Rickmansworth, and by 1820

Hertfordshire's watercress was regularly on sale in the London Markets. A key name in the history of Hertfordshire's industry is the Sansom family, who have grown the product for five generations. William Sansom, born in Oxford, first came to this area to grow watercress at Two Waters in Boxmoor, circa 1837. His younger son, Charles, succeeded him here, but the elder son John established a series of larger cress beds at Redbourn. In turn, four of John's sons subsequently became cress growers at various sites in Cassiobury, Rickmansworth, Hitchin, St. Albans and Welwyn. Sansom also owned cress beds at Kings Langley and Apsley. Another principal cress growing family in Hertfordshire was the Payne family, some of whom had initially trained whilst on the staff at Sansoms. Charles H. Sansom of Croxley Hall Farm in Rickmansworth, became the leading national authority on watercress. The formation of the National Watercress Growers Association in 1928 was a key development in the industry. This organisation was part of the National Farmers Union and C. H. Sansom was elected as its first Chairman. Another local cress grower in the valley was the Harrison family, who leased their cress beds in Fishery Lane from the Boxmoor Trust. Joseph Harrison ran the business in 1890; he was succeeded in 1902 by his wife and in 1930 the business was run by his sons, the Harrison brothers. As late as the 1920's watercress, grown by J. P. Sharp at local beds in Bourne End, was taken in baskets by horse-drawn trolleys to Boxmoor Railway Station. 'Gramp' Carter grew watercress at Northchurch in 1935. Another local producer Mr. W. J. Williams, who kept 2 acres under cultivation in the valley near Chaulden, was a founder member of the West Herts. Watercress Growers Ltd. This was a co-operative of 5 local producers, formed in 1964, who decided to build a pack house in Hemel Hempstead in order to streamline and rationalise the packing side of their business. The five growers were all relatively small-scale operators, with combined holdings of no more than 20 acres. Mr. Williams sold his cress under the brand name of 'Gade Spring', whilst others sold under the names of 'Tonic', 'Two Waters', 'Crystowel' and 'Spring Valley'. They also had a joint brand name of cress which was called 'Four Seasons.'

Cress growing requires a mild climate and large quantities of pure water. The water needs to run at an even temperature of 50°-52°F, with a carefully controlled flow through shallow gravel beds. The chalk streams and rivers of the Gade and Bulbourne valleys, with their springs and artesian wells, were ideal for this and the locally grown cress was considered to be of the highest quality. The depth of water in which cress grows is only about two inches and, although there are many varieties of cress, there are two main types. Green cress is the all year round variety and brown cress is a winter only strain. It only takes about six weeks for a bed to reach maturity and it is therefore possible to harvest the crop up to 10 times a year. Originally the cress was cut and packed into large wicker hampers and taken to London by horse and cart, to be sold by hawkers. From the later part of the Nineteenth Century, the railway allowed for faster delivery to the important London markets. Men started work locally at 4.00 a.m., so that the cress could be cut and delivered fresh that morning. Following the First World War, bunched watercress was introduced and the size of the baskets gradually reduced to the non-returnable paper chip basket we know today. In the post-war period, the eastern region of England had 18% of the nation's total area of watercress cultivation and almost all of this production was located within Hertfordshire. The beds just below Two Waters were the most extensive in the Hemel Hempstead locality. In more recent times the London markets were supplied by road at night, using 30 cwt Ford transit vans. There also used to be daily standing orders for rail driven supplies from Hemel Hempstead Station which were required by the Hotels of the major cities like Birmingham, Liverpool and Manchester etc. Most of the Hertfordshire crop however still goes to Covent Garden and represents about one third of the total amount marketed in London. One of the key advantages of watercress, which is a highly nutritious food rich in vitamins, calcium and iron, is that it grows all the year round and is at its best in the Spring when other salads are scarce. Many of the former cress beds of the Gade and Bulbourne valleys are now used as fishing lakes.

Poultry Farming
Thomas William Toovey established his poultry farm at Rectory Farm Kings Langley, in 1889. This was a major undertaking which by 1922 covered around 40 acres. There were six cottages on the farm for married staff, with 20 acres given over to 6,000 laying hens, 2 acres for 2,000 laying ducks and 18 acres for growing stock. Breeding was solely for the maintenance of the flock and the farm was described as semi-intensive. In 1910/11, Toovey's birds produced 130,135 setting eggs in one season. Toovey's Farm employed 10 local people, but had ceased its operations by the early 1960's.

The founder of Berkhamsted Pheasantries, William Dwight, was christened at St. Mary's Church Northchurch in 1843. He had three sons, Percy, Sidney and Arthur, who were all educated at Berkhamsted School. Sidney Dwight lived at The Pheasantries, in Ivyhouse Lane, Berkhamsted, whilst his brothers were based at Little Heath Lane, in Potten End. Their large pheasant farm had up to 3,000 broody hens hatching pheasants eggs in the late 1930's. In 1965 laying pheasants at the Berkhamsted Pheasantries produced over 100,000 eggs in only one season. Another large poultry farm in the valley was created by Wander Ltd on the slopes of Parsonage Farm, overlooking Kings Langley. This Model Farm was one of the finest in the country and had its own laying flock of some 50,000 pullets, bred by the farm from pedigree White Leghorn stock. Wander's Dairy Farm, founded at Parsonage Farm in Abbots Langley, was equally impressive. This farm had its own pedigree stock of Jersey cattle which by the 1960's, had won more than 700 awards at leading agricultural shows around the country.

Early harvest scene at Berkhamsted, circa 1905.

Threshing at Hill Farm, Kings Langley in the 1950's, using a corn elevator.

Corn binding machine, circa 1910.

Farm traction engine.

Tractor ploughing in the 1950's.

Hurdle making at Tring.

Lane's Nursery orchards at Berkhamsted.

Milk delivery cart, Hemel Hempstead.

"Old Shep", local shepherd at Little Gaddesden.

Toovey's Flour Mill in Kings Langley, September 1900.

Prize-winning Jersey cattle at the Ovaltine Farm, Abbots Langley.

Watercress beds at Two Waters, circa 1910.

Toovey's six-wheeled Scammell lorry, 1922.

Road Development

The route through the valley is part of the old road from London to Aylesbury, which followed the line of the River Gade and then the River Bulbourne. It provided an important early route, which linked Berkhamsted Castle to London. This main road, formerly the A41, was recently designated the A4251 following completion of the A41 as a by-pass in 1993. The line of the more northerly section of this old road through the Bulbourne valley, was defined by the earlier presence of the important Roman road of Akeman Street, which was built to link St. Albans with Bicester. This followed a similar line to today's modern road through Bourne End, Berkhamsted, Northchurch and Dudswell. Further to the south, towards the Gade valley area, the former route of Akeman Street is less clear but is still partially defined by property boundaries along Chaulden Lane, Boxmoor and Belswains Lane. Archaeological evidence of this ancient Roman road has also been found near the Booksellers Retreat, close to the railway bridge in Abbots Langley.

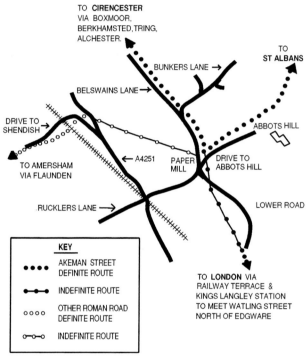

Roman crossroads at Nash Mills, based on the Viatores.

The road network established by the Roman invaders in the First Century BC, helped to define the pattern of national transport links for centuries to come. Another important local Roman road was Watling Street, which ran from Verulamium (St. Albans) to Dunstable and followed a route similar to today's A5 trunk road. The Romans also built a local link road to connect Verulamium with Akeman Street and this ran down the eastern slope of the valley, near Abbots Hill, to join the main route at Nash Mills. To the north of the Bulbourne valley, near Tring, was another important early route which was the pre-Roman Icknield Way. This old trackway dates from Neolithic times and was probably named after the 'Iceni', who were an ancient British tribe. The purpose of this long and ancient track was to link the Bronze Age industrial areas of East Anglia to the religious and cultural centres of activity at Glastonbury and Avebury. At Tring, Akeman Street made an important junction with this early trading route and this meant that the small town enjoyed a key location in terms of trading and transport links. In a similar way the early town of Dunstable grew up, further to the east, at the point where Watling Street made its own junction with the Icknield Way.

Although these Roman roads were not properly maintained following the departure of the Romans in the Fifth Century, the network they left behind was still well used during the Norman and Medieval periods. Certainly from the time of the construction of Berkhamsted Castle until the mid Fifteenth Century, the main road through the valley would have been a busy thoroughfare. It carried a constant stream of visitors and deliveries of Royal supplies to both the Plantagenet Palace and Dominican Friary at Kings Langley. There would also have been similar streams of traffic destined for Berkhamsted Castle and the monastery at Ashridge. However it is worth remembering that, during the medieval period, even what was then considered a main road was little more than a well-trodden right of way linking one town or hamlet to another. Travellers also had the right to diverge from this main track during poor weather. Travel through open countryside and woodland was also at this time unpoliced and often dangerous. To help improve this situation, a Statute issued by Edward I in 1285, decreed that main highways were to be widened and that bordering land should be cleared up to 200ft. on either side. It was thought that this would help reduce the threat of ambush by thieves and brigands. Early medieval carts and carriages were cumbersome contraptions, so travel in this period was very slow and added to the traveller's vulnerability. Most people either journeyed on horse back, or simply walked. Medieval Guilds were involved in helping with the upkeep of some of the important early roads and trackways, although maintenance levels were minimal. The use of such routes continued during the Tudor and Stuart periods, although their condition often left much to be desired. It wasn't until the mid Eighteenth Century that the first stirrings of nationwide industrial development prompted the beginnings of much needed improvements.

Sparrows Herne Turnpike Trust

The Act which established the Sparrows Herne Turnpike Trust was passed in 1762. The main road which this Trust were charged with maintaining followed substantially the route of today's A4251 and ran for about 26 miles. The turnpiked road began at Sparrows Herne, on the south side of Bushey, and travelled through the market towns of Watford, Berkhamsted and Tring to Walton, near Aylesbury. The Sparrows Herne Trustees met annually at the Kings Arms in Berkhamsted, and this group included such local luminaries as the Earls of Bridgewater, Essex and Clarendon and later Sir Astley Paston Cooper. The Chairman at the first meeting was Sir Charles Gore of Tring Park. The first surveyor they appointed was Mr. Jollage, who supervised the initial improvements on all sections of the road. Work was still being completed between Hunton Bridge and Berkhamsted in 1764, prior to the use of the full stretch of the newly improved roadway which began in 1765. Four local toll gates were established: one was built at the bottom end of Chalk Hill near the Watford Bridge, whilst the site of a proposed gate at Hunton Bridge Mill was replaced by an alternative location on the Hempstead Road, near Nascott Farm House. There was a third gate established at Newground, between Berkhamsted and Tring, and a fourth built near New Farm, in Wigginton.

At its first meetings the Trust had decided to mortgage the toll revenues for up to £5000 at 5½% per annum, in order to raise sufficient funds for the initial road improvements. By the Nineteenth Century the business had become profitable and the toll rates were set as follows in 1823: a horse drawn coach 4½d, a laden packhorse 1½d, other beasts (not drawing or laden) 1d, a drove of oxen or cows 10d per score and a drove of sheep, calves or pigs 2½d per score. The appointment of James McAdam, later Sir James McAdam, as the new surveyor of the Trust in 1821, enhanced the efficient management of the business. James McAdam also supervised a new round of road improvements, with the road surface now comprising a compacted layer of small flints which was one foot deep. An Act of Parliament in 1832 raised turnpike tolls and gave further powers to the Trust. From then the toll gates of the Sparrows Herne Turnpike Trust were leased, with the two gates near Watford bringing in an annual income of over £2,500. Road maintenance was now a professional business and the introduction of the General Highways Act in 1835 finally abolished the old system, whereby the local Parish Authorities could demand several days voluntary labour from all able-bodied men to help it maintain the local highways. Because the key economic benefits of good transport links were now beginning to be appreciated, a system of hired labour and paid officials was finally in place. The development of English road construction owes a considerable debt to James Macadam's father, John Loudon McAdam (1756-1836) and the great engineer Thomas Telford (1757-1834). John McAdam's invention of 'macadamising' road surfaces transformed the industry and he was appointed Surveyor General of Metropolitan Roads in 1827. Thomas Telford's contribution to road building centres around his involvement with the London to Holyhead Road. On this project he introduced in 1815 a three layer system which he had derived from Tresaguet's method of road construction.

The Age of the Stagecoach

With much improved road conditions dating from 1780, stagecoach services spread like wildfire along the nation's main routes. In the pre-Railway era, these large stagecoaches were the fastest means of transport in the world and often averaged 12 m.p.h., even on long journeys. Coaching however was an expensive method of travel for most people and as early as 1792, one Coach Company was charging 8 shillings 'inside' and 6 shillings 'outside', as the fare from Berkhamsted to London. This charge amounted to as much as one week's working wage for many of the population. By 1836 the journey from Tring to London is said to have taken 3 hours and the costing structure had changed to 12 shillings (sitting inside the coach) and as low as 2 shillings (sitting on the outside). Another written account of stage coaching prior to the 1830's, tells us that the London to Birmingham mail coach left London at 8.00 a.m. arriving in Kings Langley at 10.30 a.m. The returning coach then passed back through the village at about 5.00 p.m. These mail coaches however did not carry many passengers and, in contrast, the principal passenger coach to London was much slower, leaving Hemel Hempstead at 6.00 a.m. and arriving in London by 10.00 a.m. The terminus for this coach service was near Holborn Viaduct, from where the return journey began at 3.30 p.m., reaching Kings Langley by 7.30 p.m. The outside fare for this service was 4 shillings, with a 1 shilling tip for the driver, so that 10 shillings were needed to afford the return trip to London.

Coaching Inns were an important part of this service and they provided a stopping off place, every ten miles or so, where passengers could relax and take refreshment or stay overnight, if on a long journey. It was also normal practice for at least one of the team of four horses to be changed for a fresh animal when the coach stopped for a break. As you would expect, there were several large Coaching Inns situated along the valley, in order to take advantage of the steady stream of traffic that thundered along the old London to Berkhamsted road. One of the most prestigious was the old Rose and Crown at Tring, rebuilt by the Rothschilds in 1900; at Berkhamsted the Kings Arms had stabling for 40 horses in 1890, with the Bell Inn, in the High Street at Hemel Hempstead, able to cater for 55 horses. The Bell at Two Waters was a Sixteenth Century Coaching Inn and at Kings Langley the Saracen's Head was an official halt for the London to Birmingham stagecoach. Here the Rose and Crown also offered stabling for 10 horses in 1897, whilst the Kings Head at Hunton Bridge was another local Coaching Inn and Post House during the Eighteenth Century.

Stagecoach at the Eagle Inn, near Kings Langley.

Because the stagecoach mainly transported people and perishables, the arrival of the canal in 1797 made little impact on the economic success of the Turnpike system. The key contribution the canal system made towards industrial development was that these new waterways now permitted the cost-effective transport of large quantities of coal and other heavy raw materials that were still impossible to move by road. However the coming of the railway in 1837 transformed the situation, and this new and faster method of transport soon began to deprive stagecoaches of both passengers and the carriage of perishable agricultural products, which needed to get into London as quickly as possible. The effect of the railways can be seen by the reduction of the leasing charges for the Turnpike Gates at Watford, from their peak of £236 in 1837, to only £105 per month by 1857. The Turnpike Trust which had nevertheless succeeded in paying off all its mortgage debts, came to an end on 1st November 1873.

In 1851 Government legislation required four coal posts to be erected at this end of the Gade valley, beside road, river, railway and canal. These posts marked the northern bounds of an

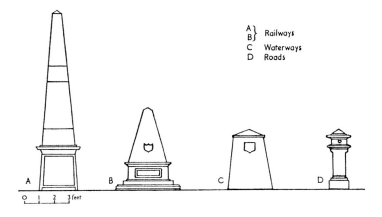

Local coal duty markers.

area, within which duty had to be paid on coal and wine entering London. Prior to this the movement of coal south of the Grove Park near Watford had been forbidden. By 1861 these posts had become redundant, because the boundaries were changed in that year to become co-terminus with the London Metropolitan District. Despite the history of successful transport developments during the Nineteenth Century, it is surprising to realise that some horse-drawn straw and hay carts were still continuing their journey to London into the early 1920's. The slow speeds which resulted from the Red Flag Act of 1865 had done much to discourage the development of steam-powered transport. Mechanical road haulage did not really take hold for another 70 years, because following the First World War there were still severe speed and weight restrictions on motor vehicles. This legislation was designed to protect the existing road surfaces, many of which in the immediate post-war era, were still unable to cope with heavy vehicles and solid tyres.

Local Tramway Projects

By the mid Nineteenth Century, the main railway system was already successful and plans were afoot to extend the benefits of the new technology, by linking smaller towns and villages with routes that extended to the main railway stations. Because steam was also a cheaper motive power than the continuing use of horses, the age of the tram had now arrived. By November 1887 two major local tramway systems were proposed, both these draft projects being engineered by S.P.W. Seldon. The first proposed tramway was to begin at Tring Station and then travel into Tring itself, before moving on to Aylesbury. This tramway had much to gain by linking the town to its railway station and by also providing a direct link with its major neighbouring community in Buckinghamshire. The second scheme of the Chesham, Boxmoor and Hemel Hempstead Steam Tramway, planned to use a smaller 3ft 6in gauge for a 12 mile route, which was to begin at the Midland Railway Station in Hemel Hempstead. This tram trail would have split two ways, one branch travelling through Apsley and terminating at the Red Lion Bridge in Nash Mills. The other fork was planned to head through Boxmoor towards Bourne End, where it would turn south across open fields and climb steeply towards Chesham. The trams on these routes were intended to travel at approximately 8mph on the roads, and up to a speed of 25mph across open fields. A fare structure was planned to charge one penny per mile. Over a period of about four years there were major changes to the plans for the proposed tramway. A switch from narrow gauge to full size railway gauge was considered, as was the use of electric instead of steam traction. The electrification of the tramways would have involved the construction of a large generating station at Two Waters. However the development of the petrol engine, with both the speed and freedom that it offered, spelt the end for tramways anywhere other than in large urban areas, where their economy of operation still offered some advantages. For this reason both the local tramway schemes were still-born and nothing came of Mr. Seldon's ambitious plans. It is worth noting that Lord Rothschild's objection to the proposed new tramway scheme is confused by some writers with what they allege was his rejection of the planned route for the main London to Birmingham Railway. This however is completely fallacious as the Rothschilds did not own Tring Park estate at the time of the railway construction in 1837.

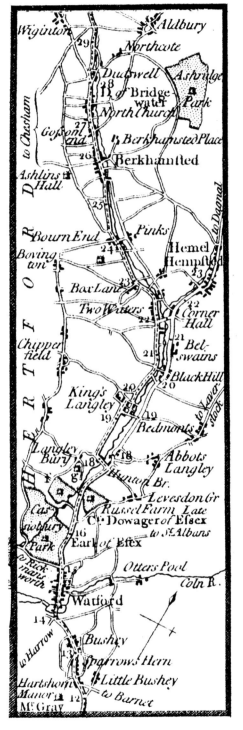

Paterson itinerary road map, 1785.

Early Bus Services

In August 1909 the London and North Western Railway (LNWR) provided a single decker motor bus to operate between Boxmoor Station and the Bury Road (now Queensway). From here it was also possible to extend one's journey to Piccotts End, if required. A small motor shed was constructed for these early buses in the Boxmoor Yard. In September 1913 a new bus route was established along the valley running from Watford through Hunton Bridge, Kings Langley and Apsley to Boxmoor. At Tring the old horse-drawn bus, which linked the town to the railway station, was replaced by a single decker Commer motor bus in March 1914. These early bus services were all owned by the railway companies. There was considerable expansion in the 1920's, following the merger in 1923 which linked the LNWR with the Midland Railway to form the London, Midland and Scottish Railway (LMS). Following the First World War, the gradual replacement of metal wheels with rubber tyres was an important development because it improved the comfort of the ride for passengers and also dramatically reduced the extent of the wear and tear on road surfaces. Consequently an Act of Parliament in 1928 was able to raise the maximum speed of buses with pneumatic tyres from 12 to 20 m.p.h. A later Road Traffic Act of 1930 increased the speed limit still further to 30 m.p.h. The age of the motor bus had now finally arrived with a proliferation of local private operators cashing in on the boom in this new and favoured method of public transport.

B.&B. Coaches, a company run by Mr. Barnard and Mr. Bedford, began to service the route between Potten End and Berkhamsted. The London Passenger Transport Board operated a wide range of local bus services from Two Waters Garage until 1969. The Rover Bus Company, which was established in 1926 by J. R. G. Dell, opened a route between Chesham and Hemel Hempstead, and bus services were also started up to bring workers to the major local factories. Examples of this were the Bream Coaches which started in the 1920's to provide a service for employees at Dickinson's Paper Mill at Apsley and Ronsway Coaches, established in 1948 who also ran buses from Hemel Hempstead to Vauxhall's car factory at Luton. The Two Waters Bus Garage was finally demolished in 1995 and the site has since been redeveloped as home to new Halfords and Tempo retail superstores.

Modern Road Development

The road bridge used by the old A41 road at Hunton Bridge was first built in 1826. By the time this bridge was rebuilt in 1922 most of the traffic heading north was ignoring the earlier routes through Hunton Bridge. The traffic was flowing to the west of the hamlet, directly through Langleybury to Kings Langley and then on to Two Waters. With increasing loads, the A41 was a very busy road and following World War II it was subject to a scheme of major improvements which cost £800,000. As car ownership spread wider in the second half of the Twentieth Century, these old A roads were still the main routes, but they struggled to cope with the increased congestion. Motorways were deemed to be the answer to this problem, and in July 1957 the Minister for Transport confirmed a total expenditure of £204 million on a number of nationwide projects. In June 1958 work started on the local stretch of the M1 London to Yorkshire motorway. This was the first full scale motorway ever to be constructed in this country. As well as providing a fast link to the North, this motorway was also intended to relieve heavy traffic congestion on the A5 and A6 in particular, as well as on the A41 and A414 Hemel Hempstead to Hatfield road. In 1954 daily traffic levels of 10,496 vehicles on the A5 and 6,867 on the A6 had been recorded. This was already causing chaotic conditions in the centre of St. Albans. The construction contract on the local stretch of the M1 motorway was carried out by Cubitts, Fitzpatrick and Shand, with the work supervised by Chief Engineer, Mr. Lindsay Smith. This project was the most highly mechanised construction job in the country; it involved the building of 12 large motorway bridges and used a special £150,000 concrete train to lay the concrete for the road. Many local men were employed on the work force which totalled 600 men; there was also a further group of 100 supervisory staff which included 38 engineers. Together they built this pioneer motorway in only 19 months. The M1 was opened on 2nd November 1959, two months ahead of schedule, by Ernest Marples the Minister for Transport. The local stretch had cost £1,500,000 to construct and had used over a million pounds worth of specialised equipment.

The most significant chapter in the local development of modern road transport links was the completion in 1986 of the M25 motorway. This new six lane road cuts across the Gade valley on a spectacular concrete viaduct which also carries it over the railway and Grand Union Canal. The entire circuit of the M25 motorway was built at a total cost of £1000 million pounds and London's new outer orbital route remains the longest Capital by-pass in the world today. Last minute delays were caused by the additional welding required beneath the Gade valley viaduct near Kings Langley Station. However the full route of the M25 was officially opened by Prime Minister Margaret Thatcher on Wednesday 19th October 1986. Almost immediately, traffic flows exceeded official estimates and currently well in excess of 100,000 vehicles a day stream across the Gade valley viaduct. Despite the obvious environmental threat it poses, the economic and strategic importance to the local area of this motorway is considerable. Junction 20, with its fast access into and around London, its links to both Heathrow and Gatwick Airports and its connections to other major motorway networks, should ensure that the Gade valley continues to enjoy prosperous economic development well into the foreseeable future.

With the opening of the M25, the old problem of traffic congestion through the valley continued. If anything, it was initially exacerbated by additional queues of vehicles attracted by the proximity of the newly provided motorway network. It had long been intended to relieve the town centres of the valley by building a by-pass road on the western slopes of the Gade and Bulbourne valleys. Such a project had already been delayed by decades of environmental concerns. Many years of intense and controversial debate preceded the result of the final Public Enquiry in December 1989. Finally in July 1991 work began on the Kings Langley section, with work starting on the Berkhamsted section in February 1992. By May 1993 the local section of the Kings Langley by-pass was complete and opened to traffic. This was followed by the second section, which ran from Two Waters to Bourne End, opening in August 1993. One month later, the Berkhamsted stretch of the road was complete and this allowed the new road finally to link into the Tring by-pass which had been built 20 years earlier in 1973. This completed bypass then became the A41 trunk road, with the former A41 being redesignated as the A4251. Traffic levels through the main towns of the valley fell initially by around 25% and the general area now had the advantage of a fast link into the M25 orbital motorway system.

Toll gate at Bushey Arches, removed 1872.

Road maintenance outside Tring, circa 1910.

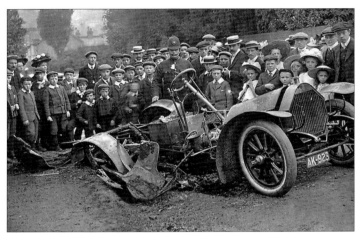

Motor car destroyed by fire at Boxmoor, 1909.

Fallen Elm trees block the Watford Road, 1927.

Local bus service, circa 1925.

The Old Forge in Bovingdon, circa 1908.

Garage in Bovingdon (part of the Old Forge) circa 1920.

Gade valley viaduct under construction, 1985.

Construction difficulties on the M25.

M25 complete, 1986.

Construction work on the A41 By-pass, 1991.

Earth movers on the A41 By-pass, 1991.

Road bridge construction for the A41 By-pass, 1992.

Junction 20, where the A41 By-pass meets the M25, 1994.

Two Waters Bus Garage, demolished 1995.

Double decker leaving Watford Junction railway station, 1995.

View of the Gade valley, looking north-west from Hunton Bridge, 1991.

Illuminated view of the M25 Gade valley viaduct, 1994.

Footbridge on the By-pass at Tring, 1994.

History of the Canal

The invention of James Watt's steam engine in 1763 was the key to the birth of the Industrial Revolution. It meant that factories could be located wherever manpower, raw materials and coal could be assembled. Bulk supplies of raw materials and fuel therefore needed to be delivered cheaply and easily to these new industrial centres. Even the best of the turnpike roads of the late Eighteenth Century were still unsuitable for the carriage of heavy freight, so inland waterways were devised as the first principal method of providing industrial transportation. The so called 'Father of Inland Navigation' was Francis Henry Egerton (1736-1803), the Third Duke of Bridgewater. He used James Brindley (1716-1772) as his main engineer and Brindley went on to plan over 400 miles of canals and act as consultant on many more schemes. Another famous name in national canal development was Thomas Telford (1757-1834) who was involved in the building of several important aqueducts, the Caledonian Canal and most of the Shropshire Union Canal. Francis Egerton's first project was to build the Bridgewater Canal to link his Worsley coal mines to Salford and Manchester, in the east and to Hollin Ferry on the Mersey, in the west. By achieving this, he guaranteed to deliver coal to Manchester at half the previous rate. In return the canal could also be used to carry large quantities of finished industrial products like iron, bricks and tiles which needed to be taken from the great cities and transported to the towns, markets and sea ports for export. A rapidly expanding population also meant that there was now a need to deliver large quantities of agricultural produce to the newly developing urban areas.

Although many questioned Francis Egerton's sanity, because of the initial expense involved in the construction of his canal, it was not long before the advantages of this new form of transport were obvious to everyone. Britain's new wealthy entrepreneurs, together with many of the land-owning aristocracy, soon clamoured to invest in this new and excitingly prosperous business. By 1780, over two thousand miles of new canal had been constructed across the country at a cost of £3,323 per mile; the initial return on shares was an impressive 48%. 'Canal Mania' reached its peak in March 1793 when 48 new canal schemes were put before Parliament. The plan for the Grand Junction Canal, was one of these and was sanctioned by an Act of Parliament dated 30th April 1793. By 1800 the total length of the canal system had risen to 3,066 miles.

It is interesting to note that the southern end of the first proposed route for the local stretch of the Grand Junction Canal was quite different from that eventually built. The original intention was for this canal to cross the River Gade on an embankment aqueduct to the south of Kings Langley. It was then planned to build a 900 yard tunnel through the high ground at Langleybury and provide a flight of locks down to the Colne, to the north of Rickmansworth. An amended route was sanctioned by a further Act of Parliament, dated 24th December 1795. At the end of the day, it had proved considerably cheaper to pay compensation to the Earl of Essex (£15,000) and the Earl of Clarendon (£5,000). These payments secured an easier line for the canal along the valley floor, which ran through their private estates. However conditions were also imposed by these two Lords to ensure that the Canal Company made the waterway as attractive as possible on its journey through their estates. Hence the charming decorative bridge at the Grove and the wide stretch of water running through Cassiobury Park. The co-operative attitude of the local aristocracy contrasts sharply with their much more vehement objections to the far noisier and more intrusive steam trains, which were to arrive some 40 years later.

The initial capital raised for the Grand Junction Canal project was £350,000 and when the route was re-assessed by the appointed surveyor William Jessop, he estimated a total construction cost of £372,275. Work began on the local stretch in May 1793 and by the end of that year there were over 3000 men on the payroll, working simultaneously on different sections. When completed the entire Grand Junction Canal was 137 miles long, with a total of 101 locks. The canal now provided a direct and cost effective transport route from the Midlands to London, and was used principally to transport coal south to the Capital. The previous water-borne route from Birmingham to London, via the Oxford Canal, had been over 100 miles longer.

The canal had taken twelve years to complete and an important feature of the Grand Junction was that it was made broad enough to accommodate two narrow boats, side by side. It was also capable of taking 70 ton barges that were 70 ft. long and 14 ft. wide. The highest section of the Grand Junction Canal, between London and Birmingham, is the Tring Summit which is over 390ft. above sea level. This required the making of an

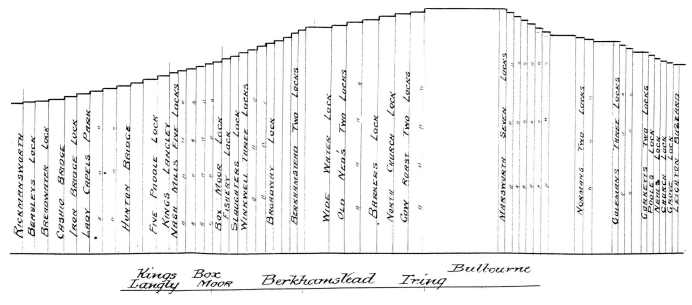

Rise and fall of the canal, showing individual locks, 1900.

impressive cutting which was one and a half miles long and over 30ft. deep in places. This was an outstanding engineering feat when one considers that this cutting was dug using only picks and shovels. In several areas clay dug from pits close to the canal was used to 'puddle' or line the bottom and sides in order to help waterproof the canal.

To the north of the Tring Summit, the canal crosses into Buckinghamshire at Bulbourne, where British Waterways later established its Repair Depot. The canal begins its southerly descent from Tring at the Cow Roast lock, near Dudswell. It then follows the line of the Bulbourne valley down through Northchurch, Berkhamsted, Bourne End, Winkwell and Boxmoor, before arriving at Two Waters where it joins the River Gade. The canal's further descent continues along the Gade valley through Apsley, Kings Langley, Hunton Bridge and Watford to Croxley Green. Shortly after this the waters of the canal are joined by the River Gade and then later by the Rivers Colne and Chess at Batchworth, Rickmansworth. The construction of this impressive canal was achieved in phases: Kings Langley was reached from the Thames by 1797, Berkhamsted by 1798 and the canal was running through the Tring Summit by 1799. Work on the summit itself had begun back in 1793 and it was completed in March 1797, together with its feeder branch from Wendover. Every boat crossing the Tring Summit uses 200,000 gallons of water and this feeder branch was therefore an essential feature of the canal, designed to keep the summit fed with water. However periods of drought soon meant that the meagre supplies of water from local streams became insufficient to top up this busy canal system. The solution was to build a series of large reservoirs in the Tring area: Wilstone (1802), Marsworth (1806), Tringford (1816) and Startopsend (1817). The canal was very thirsty for supplies of water and this led to several disputes with local millers, like T. W. Toovey at Kings Langley, who used steam and river power to drive their flour mills. An important dispute between John Dickinson and the Canal Company was resolved in March 1818. This involved the closure of the canal from Frogmore to the tail of the four Kings Langley locks. A new line for the canal was created here, nearer the river. This cut out the stretch of old waterway from Two Waters that had leaked so consistently. However, in the process, the original Kings Langley locks were replaced and an extra lock added. In order to avoid renumbering all the locks southward, the new Kings Langley lock No.69 was renumbered No.69A.

As soon as they were opened, the canals proved an immediate success. Heavy goods could now be moved around the country with a cheapness and speed never known before. The industrial transformation encouraged by this cost effective haulage of freight was considerable. Positive effects on the local economy were also felt immediately; farmers were now able to receive double the price for their premium produce by sending it to London. Local blacksmiths prospered, helping to maintain the early fleet of horse-drawn wideboats, as did the local publicans at establishments like the Fishery Inn at Boxmoor, who provided stabling for these working horses. For the first time cheaply priced coal was reaching the area and the Grand Junction Canal was able to deliver raw materials in bulk, to local canal-side factories such as the Dickinson Paper Mills at Apsley and Toovey's Flour Mill in Kings Langley.

A horse-drawn fly boat, with a picked crew of three men and a 20 ton load, could do the entire canal journey from Birmingham to Paddington Basin in 36 hours. A pair of narrow boats could

Working boats at Nash Mills, 1859.

carry up to 60 tons which was far more than any other method of transport. In addition to grain and forage, these barges began to take away flour and malt from the local mills, returning with soot and dung from London to manure the local fields. Supplies of coal and building materials also came in by canal boat and stone blocks, imported brick and slate roofs could now more easily be used in the local construction industry.

The Grand Junction Canal first managed to pay a dividend in 1803 and this rose to a peak of 13% in 1825. At this time £100 shares in the canal were changing hands at £350 each. Commercial receipts totalled £147,857 in 1815 and the best year for the canal was 1836, the year of the railway's construction, when income reached £198,086. It is not an exaggeration to say that the construction of the London to Birmingham Railway spelt the beginning of the end of the commercial success of the canal system, but it was a gradual process. Although the new railway almost immediately became the preferred method of transport for both passengers and perishable goods, this type of traffic had nearly always used the road system prior to the 1840's. For much of the Nineteenth Century, the canal was still able to compete successfully with the railways, by slashing its toll charges on the transport of heavy freight. Total tonnages carried on the canal system continued to increase until they reached their peak of 1,404,012 tons in 1868. Ironically had the canal not been close to the eventual London to Birmingham Railway route, this later project would have cost more, given the previously prohibitive cost of transporting stone for building purposes.

Much of this growth in freight business was confined to the southern end of the canal, from Berkhamsted to London, where barges up to 14ft. wide could operate. However, given much reduced charges, revenues were already dropping sharply, falling to a total of £68,531. As an example of this, peak toll rates of 42d in 1839 had fallen to a mere 5d per ton in 1851. Despite price cutting it became impossible to reverse what was an inevitable decline and by the end of the Nineteenth Century, the railways were delivering ten times more freight than the canal system.

Local Industrial Use

Several local gas works used the canal. The "Berkhampstead Gas Company" opened in 1849 to the north of the town, and was situated between the canal and the railway. Some coal was delivered by canal boat to a wharf at these gas works, and in return crude tar was dispatched by wide boat for distribution in the London area. A similar gas works opened at Rickmansworth in 1854, close to the town's wharf, at the end of the Rickmansworth branch of the canal. Another industry which used the canal was the sand and gravel industry. There was a gravel pit at Winkwell, linked to the canal, and a similar one at Primrose Hill, near Kings Langley. There were also major timber merchants using the canal in both the Hemel Hempstead and Berkhamsted areas. In Hemel Hempstead Joseph Lavers began his business at Fishery Wharf in 1869, later moving to a larger wharf at Corner Hall. Another timber merchant, Job East, had a wharf and a large warehouse at Gossoms End, near Northchurch. The wharf at Two Waters Bridge was built by the Boxmoor Trust and became the main coal wharf for the town of Hemel Hempstead. From 1864 Henry Balderson ran this wharf which now dealt in coal, coke, stone and corn, together with imported wine and spirits. From 1947 Boxmoor Wharf was used to bring in barrels of lime juice pulp from Dominica for Roses Lime Juice (see page 62). William Cooper's agricultural chemical business also had its own wharf at his Ravens Lane factory in Berkhamsted. The canal was essential for the prosperity of John Dickinson's extensive Paper Mills in Apsley, Kings Langley and Croxley. Toovey's Flour Mill and the Ovaltine factory in Kings Langley, were both examples of other important local customers for the canal system. (for more details on these aspects please refer to the Early Industry chapter on page 56).

Stephenson's skew-bridge at Nash Mills, 1859.

Given all this industrial traffic, it is not surprising that there were three local boat building yards to service and supply the transport fleets required. As early as 1802 William Butler owned the barge 'Berkhamsted Castle' which was built in the town in 1801 by Peacock and Willets. In 1826 their boatyard was owned by John Halton and in 1882 it was taken over by William Edmund Costin. Another local boatyard was established later at New Mill in Tring, and this was run by the wheelwright John Bushell in 1881. Later the business was run by Charles and Joseph Bushell until it closed in 1948. Bushells built boats for Meads Flour Mill at Tring, for Toovey's Flour Millers, and also provided some of the fleet belonging to the John Dickinson Paper Mills. The third local boat yard was situated at Frogmore, Rickmansworth and this business was established by William Henry Walker in 1905. Walkers boatyards were best known locally for the Ovaltine boats they built during the 1920's. However many of the commercial boats

working in this area were operated by private contractors like Pickfords, who maintained their own storage warehouse in London. Companies of this size soon transferred their business to the railways from 1847 and much of their fleet was then taken over by the Grand Junction Canal Company. These boats were subsequently purchased by two newly formed canal companies which merged in 1889 to become Fellows, Morton and Clayton, perhaps the best known of all canal carrying companies. They in turn sold out to the British Transport Commission in January 1949. At this time they were running up to 100 boats carrying various cargoes of coal, timber, grain, tea, sugar and spices along the canal. Another popular firm of canal carriers were the Willow Wren boats that operated on the Grand Junction Canal during the 1950's.

The Decline of the Canal

During the First World War, canals had come under the control of the Board of Trade. Following this conflict the Grand Junction Canal, suffering increasing competition from the railways, was still struggling financially and it was thought that the acquisition of the Warwick Canal might improve the situation. The eventual outcome of this proposal was that the Regents Canal and Dock Company was merged with the Grand Junction Canal, who also purchased the Warwick Canal. From 1st January 1929, this new concern became known as the Grand Union Canal. In another attempt to compete with the railways, steam boats were tried on the canal, but were soon supplanted by diesel engine powered boats in the early 1930's. Further improvements were financed in 1934 when all bridges to Birmingham were widened to 14ft. However these efforts were all to no avail and with ever dwindling levels of freight, the hard winters of 1962 and 63 were the final blow, because they caused the canal to freeze up altogether. The canal system had been nationalised in 1948 and had only just come under the management of the British Transport Commission in that fateful year of 1962. The Transport Act of 1968 subsequently classified the Grand Union Canal as a recreational cruiseway. From this time it ceased to be considered principally as a commercial waterway. The last major haulage contracts on the Grand Union Canal, were for the carriage of cement to Birmingham and these lasted until April 1969. Another smaller contract was operated by T. D. Murrell and involved the deliveries of lime juice pulp to Boxmoor Wharf. Surprisingly this business lasted until October 1981 when the final load of 33 tons was delivered.

Canal Revival

It is alarming to consider that during the 1960's complete closure of the canal system was once considered, but happily the canals have enjoyed a strong revival during the last twenty years. The canals provide a superb habitat for many species of plants and wildlife and the current upsurge in environmental interest has contributed to their protection. However the key catalyst for survival has been the growing interest in leisure boating holidays and several local businesses now cater for this demand. In 1978 Goodwill Cruisers were established at Watford, followed by Ensign Carriers in 1979 and the town now has its own marina above Cassio Bridge. In 1971 Bridgewater Boats began their business at Castle Wharf in Berkhamsted and a large marina was built at Cowroast in 1980. The pleasure cruising industry suffered a setback in 1980 when the long Blisworth Tunnel had to be closed for repair. However its overhauled structure was re-opened in August 1984 and this restored the Grand Union Canal as the important through route north in the nation's canal network.

Queue of working boats at Cassio bridge.

Canal at Cassiobury.

Cassiobury Lock, 1916.

Lady Capel's Wharf at the Grove, 1928.

Horse-drawn wide boat nearing Lady Capel's Wharf, 1916.

Hunton Bridge Lock, 1897.

The steam boat 'President' beneath Hunton Bridge, 1995.

Rebuilding of Hunton Bridge, 1904.

Gas and oil carrying boat at Home Park Lock, 1955.

Coal barges approaching Home Park Lock, circa 1958.

Ovaltine working boats unloading coal, 1955.

Dutch barge passing through Kings Langley, 1995.

Working boat at Toovey's Flour Mill, circa 1950.

Boat at Dickinson's Mill, Apsley.

Working boats at Nash Mills in the 1960's.

The Dickinson barge, Lord Nelson, waiting by Red Lion Lane bridge, 1895.

The canal at Boxmoor, circa 1910.

Canal boats passing the Fishery Inn, 1954.

Horse-drawn boats passing under old Fishery Bridge, Boxmoor 1925.

View from the bridge at Billet Lane, looking towards Northchurch, 1993.

Canal by the Crystal Palace at Berkhamsted, circa 1893.

Ravens Lane Lock, Berkhamsted.

The bridge at Dudswell, 1935.

Cow Roast Locks, 1935.

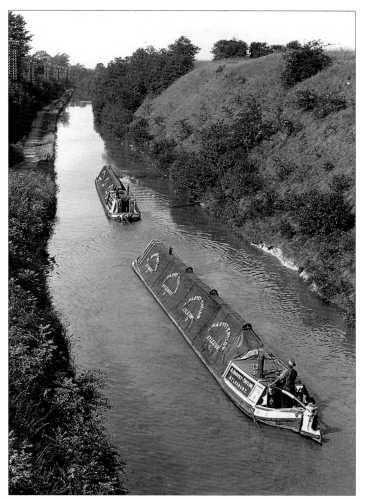

Boats passing through Tring cutting, 1925.

Bushell's Boat-building Yard.

History of the Railway

The route for the London to Birmingham Railway was surveyed by the father and son team, George and Robert Stephenson. Robert was subsequently appointed sole engineer for the project in September 1833 and the first construction work began in the Spring of 1834. The original intention was to adopt the most straightforward route north. It was planned to lay a track from Watford, along the floor of the valley to the west of the Grand Junction Canal. The plan was then to continue the railway line down to the end of the Gade valley, and this would still have involved some deep cuttings to the north of Hemel Hempstead. However the eventual route settled upon was even more challenging and was forced upon the Railway Company by the vehement and powerful objections from nearly all of the major landowners in the valley. As a result of their intervention it was finally agreed that the railway, like the main road and the canal, was instead to veer westwards down the Bulbourne valley, bringing new economic benefits to Boxmoor, Berkhamsted and Tring. One can only imagine what developments might have occurred within the communities of the old Hemel Hempstead High Street, Water End and Great Gaddesden had the plans stayed in their original form. The new route, which lay narrowly to the east of the canal, was fraught with engineering challenges. It required extensive tunnelling work, the construction of deep cuttings and raised embankments some 30-40ft. high.

Leading opponents of the original London to Birmingham Railway scheme were the Lords of Essex and Clarendon. Their objections to the disturbance of their Watford estates required the construction of both the Watford Tunnel and the Oxhey Cutting, together with a huge embankment and viaduct to enable the railway to cross the River Colne. In a similar way, the even more vigorous representations of Sir Astley Paston Cooper and Lord Brownlow at the southern end of the valley, ensured that the Bulbourne valley would eventually be chosen. These two influential men simply refused to countenance the more easterly route, which would have so seriously disrupted the tranquillity of their country estates at Gadebridge and Ashridge. This Gade valley route was originally chosen to avoid the summit of the Chiltern Hills at Tring, which would now require a major cutting to allow the railway to pass through. Thirty years earlier the local aristocracy had been more welcoming, when the far gentler and more pastoral canal system had been built through the valley. By the 1830's many of them were now shareholders in the Canal Company and because they were markedly less co-operative to this new and competing mode of transport, the terms of the final settlement laid down by the Railway Act were much stricter. Affected landowners were now only allowed interest relief on land purchased in lieu of that sold to the Railway Company, so most failed to make any serious profit from the railway's arrival.

The construction of the London to Birmingham Railway was a massive undertaking, but work proceeded at an impressive rate from the Spring of 1834. This was because the Railway Company managed the process effectively, by awarding contracts for various sections of the line to smaller contractors on a competitive basis. 112 miles of railway construction was shared by 29 different contractors and consequently construction work occurred all along the route simultaneously. W. & L. Cubbitt secured three contracts to lay just over 9 miles of track from Kings Langley to Tring Station. The more dangerous job of digging the Tring Cutting was awarded to Mr. Townsend, an engineer from Smethwick who brought in his own army of labourers. By August 1835 the construction of 86 miles of

railway line had been contracted out and the purchase of two thirds of the required land was already secure. During 1836 the average number of workmen employed on the project was 10,000, most of whom were then earning a wage of between 18 and 24 shillings per week. By March 1837, when all the remaining contracts had been issued and the project was nearing completion, the total work force had reached 12,000. Following the construction of the Grand Junction Canal (1793-97) it was the second time in less than 40 years that the local area had been invaded by a huge influx of contract labourers. Accommodation and refreshment for these gangs of tough navies certainly fed the local economy, but during this period tales of civil disobedience and late night rowdiness are not uncommon.

At the southern end of the valley 482,113 cubic feet of soil was excavated for the Oxhey Cutting and the viaduct built here across the River Gade cost over £10,000 to construct. The Watford Tunnel was one mile and thirty one yards long. It was dug, using only picks and shovels, through a solid stratum of chalk which was interspersed with intervals of loose sand and gravel. This was very difficult and dangerous work and in one accident in 1835, 10 men were buried alive in a sudden rush of sand and gravel. The Railway Company had to sink a large shaft down into the tunnel, in order to remove the bodies, and this rescue operation cost them £140,000. However the largest undertaking of all on the local stretch of line was the construction of Tring Cutting which was 2½ miles long. This required the excavation of up to one and a half million cubic yards of chalk and soil to carry the railway through the Chiltern Hills. It took 400 men, using only spades, picks and horse-drawn barrows, 3½ years to dig this cutting. As we can see from the illustration on page 47, horses were used to help drag the men and their wheelbarrows up the inclined plane, at an angle of not less than 45 degrees. On the descent back down the slope, the men and the horses who were backing down, were helped by the pulley's cable taking the strain. The ambitious nature of the railway's construction, which often operated on slopes some 60 to 70 ft. high, meant that this was taxing and dangerous work. In addition to the lives lost in the Watford Tunnel accident, seven men were killed at Berkhamsted and a further four perished at Northchurch. The digging of the Tring Cutting cost a further six lives and 37 other men suffered serious injuries, as loads fell on them when ropes broke or the horses became restive. It is difficult to overstate the scale of the work involved during the construction of the London to Birmingham Railway. Estimates indicate that the total amount of earth moved in only one three mile stretch of the embankment, running from Watford to Nash Mills, was equivalent to the building of the Great Pyramids in Ancient Egypt. For at least one year of the project, all activity depended entirely on human and horse labour. However in 1835 the first steam locomotive, called the 'Harvey Combe', arrived in the valley. Ironically it was delivered in sections by canal boat. The Harvey Combe was assembled in a barn at Pix Farm in Bourne End. When the first rails had been laid, this engine was then able to make a valuable contribution by drawing heavy truckfuls of earth and chalk from the cuttings to help build up the embankments.

The London to Boxmoor stretch of the line was finally opened on 20th July 1837 and one year later on 17th September 1838, the line was clear for through traffic from Euston to Birmingham. The total cost of the London to Birmingham Railway had been £2,500,000. The new service proved to be an immediate success and in the first year of operation trains

Construction work on the Watford Tunnel, 1857.

Construction work at Berkhamsted, 1858.

Embankments at Boxmoor, 1857.

Tring Cutting, 1857.

carried 39,855 passengers. From London, the trains entered the Gade valley via the Watford Tunnel and travelled along a high embankment to Nash Mills where they crossed the canal on a skew bridge, designed by Robert Stephenson. The journey then proceeded through cuttings to Boxmoor Station, from where a substantial 'oblique arch bridge' carried the railway line across the main road and on to another high embankment, across Boxmoor. Here the line crosses over the canal again on another skew bridge. The onward journey on embankments along the Bulbourne valley was relatively straightforward through to Berkhamsted. Here the railway line travelled through a short tunnel to Northchurch, before preparing to leave the valley via the Tring Cutting.

In 1829 tests had been arranged to determine the speed of the first railway engines and the best of the early steam trains successfully demonstrated that they could pull 12 trucks full of coal, at an average speed of 20 m.p.h. Once established the first class Mail Train left London at 11.00 a.m., reaching Watford at 11.35 a.m. and Tring by 12.35 p.m. At this period an early mixed-class passenger train, which left Euston at 9.00 a.m., would reach Harrow at 9.38 a.m., Boxmoor at 10.22 a.m., Berkhamsted at 10.33 a.m. and Tring at 10.46 a.m. The fare for a journey from Kings Langley Station to Euston was then about 3 shillings. However the comfort of passengers in those days left a lot to be desired, with some carriages being open-topped. It was also soon necessary to replace granite sleepers with timber , in order to help improve the smoothness of the ride. The original rails of the London to Birmingham railway were between 12ft. and 18ft. in length and made of malleable iron, although steel rails were introduced in 1857. Two hotels were built specifically to meet the

needs of the new breed of train travellers. These were the Railway Hotel at Boxmoor, now the site of La Mirage Night Club, and the Harcourt Arms at Tring Station (later called the Royal Hotel).

In 1846 the London to Birmingham Railway was taken over by the London and North Western Railway (LNWR) as part of an amalgamation with four other railway companies. The rapid expansion of freight traffic on the local stretch of the railway soon meant that a third line needed to be added in 1858, to prevent disruption to passenger services. As the demand for passenger services continued to grow, new branch lines were built to St. Albans in 1858 and to Rickmansworth in 1862. These additions now required a bigger and more suitable station site, so Watford Junction was built. The demands for increased capacity seemed insatiable. A fourth line was added in 1875 and this then required a doubling of the tunnel to the north of Watford. Now that there were four lines, the faster traffic was confined to the western tracks, with the slower freight traffic to the eastern tracks that ran alongside the goods sheds and sidings. The annual passenger bookings at Watford Junction had now reached 100,000, a level of traffic which had more than trebled in 30 years. The sheer number of trains required to cope with demand was creating a bottleneck in the London area. To help solve this problem a double tunnel was constructed at Primrose Hill, ahead of Euston Station. This allowed a regular hourly passenger service between Watford and London to be established.

The London and North Western Railway (LNWR) became part of the London, Midland and Scottish Railway Company (LMS) in 1923. Following the railways' important contribution

Watford Junction steam sheds in the 1950's.

First Deltic diesel on trial passing Watford, 1957.

Goods train approaching Watford tunnel in 1952.

Rebuilt Patriot hauling express passing Hunton Bridge in 1955.

LMS Compound hauling express passing Gypsy Lane Bridge in the 1950's.

to the war effort during 1939-45 (see page 87) the Railway Company was nationalised, becoming British Railways in 1948. In the 1950's Government policy began to favour the development of diesel and electric locomotives and the phasing out of steam on the local section through the valley began in 1961. By this time 705 of the trains departing daily from Euston were diesel. When the programme of electrification commenced, the work proceeded from north to south down the line. By September 1964 the old LMS steam express locomotives were banned south of Crewe, because there was now insufficient clearance for these engines under the new electric catenary. The overhead supply for the new electric engines operated at 2,500 volts AC, drawn from the National Grid. A full electric service from London commenced in January 1966. This began a period which was known as a 'commuter paradise', when these faster trains were operating on both the main and suburban lines. Although the old steam expresses travelled at speeds of 60 to 80 m.p.h., the new electric locomotives had much greater acceleration, and were designed to run continuously at 100 m.p.h. if required. The local stretch of the line was now part of the important west coast line to Glasgow, as well as a very busy commuter route into London. By 1970 the west coast route was the busiest trunk route in the country. Given the introduction of four aspect colour signalling, clear headways of 3 minutes were now safely established between successive trains, each travelling at 100 m.p.h.. The end result of all this modernisation is that today, the journey time from Hemel Hempstead to the Capital has been reduced to 30 minutes.

Local Railway Stations

A railway station at Kings Langley was operational from 1841, although not officially opened until 1842. A substantial brick-built Victorian frontage was provided in 1896 for this small station. It had previously been a wooden structure known as Home Park Halt in the first days of the railway. This old station building was sadly demolished in 1991. The construction of the modern station and booking office formed part of a rolling programme of modernisation which was instigated on this line by Network South East and completed in 1992. A passenger station first opened at Apsley on 22nd September 1938. It was provided by the LMS Railway Company, working in association with John Dickinson. It was designed principally for the use of the thousands of employees who then worked at the Apsley Paper Mills. Hemel Hempstead Station in Boxmoor was already a two storey structure by 1837, consisting of a booking office, waiting rooms and a departure yard. Boxmoor Station developed a very busy goods yard which, for example, later dealt with daily supplies of watercress to London and the nationwide dispatch of products made by G. B. Kent at Apsley.

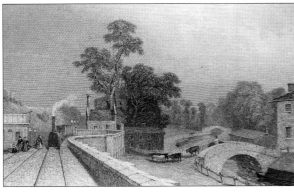

Early engraving of Berkhamsted Station, circa 1858.

This station which from 1964 became known as Hemel Hempstead Station was modernised and substantially rebuilt in the same year.

The first station at Berkhamsted was a charming structure, built in the Elizabethan style close to Berkhamsted Castle. However it had been something of an archaeological tragedy that the railway's construction at Berkhamsted required the demolition of part of the Barbican and entrance to this ancient Norman Castle. As early as 1875, a new larger station, was built only a 100 yards away from the original site. The railway station at Tring was designed by the Architect George Aitcheson (1792-1861) and his plans for the building were first exhibited at the Royal Academy. The cost of this station was £1885 and the contract included the provision of a locomotive and engine shed. Tring station is situated some two miles from the principal town it serves and this was certainly a factor behind the construction of the adjacent Royal Hotel. It is worth stressing at this point however, that the station at Tring was built where the people of the town wanted it. Despite the objections of the Comte d'Harcourt at Pendley, a deputation of the town's traders, led by Mr. Kay the silk manufacturer, offered to make up any difference required in land compensation so that it could pass, as planned, through Pendley lands.

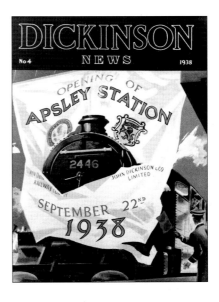

The Hemel Hempstead to Harpenden Railway

In economic terms it was unfortunate that, as a direct consequence of the opposition of the local landowners, the growing and important town of Hemel Hempstead had been by-passed by both the Grand Junction Canal and the main London to Birmingham Railway. In the decades which preceded the age of the petrol engine, this was a serious economic disadvantage. Consequently in July 1863 the Hemel Hempstead Railway Company was formed to build a line which would link Boxmoor Station to Hemel Hempstead. Another important role for this new branch line was to carry supplies of coal and coke to the local Gas Works. With the involvement of the Midland Railway Company, a branch extension to a Junction just north of Harpenden was also authorised in 1866 and the new line finally opened on 16th July 1877. This service, which has since become known as the 'Nicky Line', ran a single-track passenger service to and from Luton, as well as carrying goods traffic. At this time the first passenger train of the day left Hemel Hempstead at 9.00 a.m.,

Local passenger train passing Kings Langley goods sheds circa 1958.

Parcels train leaving Kings Langley Station, 1948.

LMS Pacific express passing through Kings Langley, 1947.

Goods train passing the Ovaltine factory, 1947.

Nicky Line engine in the sidings at the Cotterells, 1958.

Austerity engine passing northbound through Apsley, circa 1945.

City of Birmingham LMS Streamliner express passing Shendish estate, 1959.

Parcel train leaving Hemel Hempstead at Boxmoor Station, 1958.

calling at Redbourn, which was the only intermediate station. The train arrived at Chiltern Green, Harpenden only 25 minutes later. This was the Midland Railway's junction point, where passengers could either switch to a main line train into St. Pancras, or stay on and travel through to Luton with a total journey time of 40 minutes. The railway was focused towards Luton initially to service the straw plait industry. However in the time that elapsed between planning and opening the new railway the straw plait trade had unfortunately collapsed.

By 1886 the Hemel Hempstead Railway Company had been dissolved and the Midland Railway took over the entire operation. In 1888 Harpenden became a junction with a large bay that could hold branch line trains. In addition to the three stations, four halts were now added to the line, in order to encourage more traffic and the number of trains was increased to nine per day. At Hemel Hempstead the passenger service was extended to a new terminus at Heath Park Halt but, as the roads began to improve, the volume of custom for the Nicky Line fell into a slump. The regular bus services established by the end of the 1920's were the beginning of the end for the Nicky Line's passenger trains, which were withdrawn in 1947. This only left freight services, with a daily freight train now leaving Harpenden for Hemel Hempstead at 9.00 p.m. each night. All traffic finally ceased in 1963, but several years later the Nicky Line was reopened as a private mineral railway operated by Hemelite Ltd. Hemelite, which was based at Cupid Green from 1958, had always been a major user of the Nicky Line. This Company's brick making factory required up to 8 wagons of ash daily. When British Rail decided to shift all its remaining goods traffic to other lines, Hemelite was allowed to operate its own train on the line from 30th April 1968. However eleven years later, when the controlling signal box at Harpenden was closed in September 1979, the Company had no option but to resort to road transport.

All trace of the old Hemel Hempstead to Harpenden Railway has been removed from Hemel Hempstead. It is now difficult to imagine it was ever there running along the Cotterells. The old bridge which was built in 1870 to carry the Nicky Line across the Marlowes was demolished in July 1959. Its former site at the entrance to the town's main shopping area is now dominated instead by the modern office blocks of the New Town development.

The Ro-Railer
The introduction of this curious vehicle in 1931 was prompted by diminishing passenger levels caused by the increasing competition from local bus services. The Ro-Railer provided a type of bus, which was designed to run on its railway lines as well as the roads. This new vehicle had the advantage of being able to reach right into the town centres. In addition petrol consumption on the rails was approximately half that used when travelling by road. There was therefore some realistic expectation that this innovation could be the answer to the declining profitability on the smaller rural railway lines. By the beginning of 1932 the Ro-Railer was operating with some success locally and the railway company was on the point of ordering more vehicles, when substantial mergers affecting bus services around London brought its road operations to an end. Government regulations were then introduced preventing the Railway Company from running road services. The result was that this ambitious experiment was immediately shelved by the new London Passenger Transport Board, which had absorbed the former LMS's commitments in the local area.

0-6-0 tank engine at Hemel Hempstead Midland Station in 1929.

LMS City of Bradford Streamliner passing Berkhamsted Station in the 1930's.

Passenger express approaching Berkhamsted Station in 1959.

Tank engine hauling a goods train through Berkhamsted in 1959.

Local passenger train at Berkhamsted Station, 1955.

Passenger train to Tring emerging from Northchurch Tunnel, 1951.

Southbound Mancunian express approaching Northchurch Tunnel, 1956.

Passenger express, bound for London, leaving Tring Station, 1950.

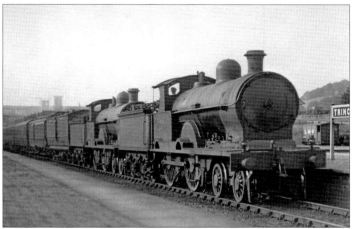

Double headed passenger train in Tring Station in the 1950's.

Mixed goods train northbound through Tring Cutting, 1959.

Coronation 'Scot' passenger express at Tring Summit, 1938.

Local Railway Accidents

An early serious accident on the local line was the Watford Tunnel accident which occurred on 21st May 1866. It involved a combined excursion train which came from Northampton. By the time this huge train had reached the Watford area it consisted of two locomotives pulling 44 carriages which were carrying 2000 passengers! The weight of this train proved too much when the engine driver tried to brake ahead of the Watford Tunnel. As a result his train crashed through a dead end siding and into Gypsy Lane bridge, near Hunton Bridge, some 500 yards from the tunnel itself. No one was killed in the accident but some 30 people were injured in the crash, which happened at a speed of around 8-10 m.p.h. A more spectacular train derailment occurred by the railway bridge at Hunton Bridge in October 1922. An engine and tender on a journey from Crewe to London slid into buffers near the bridge and tumbled over, blocking the road up to Abbots Langley. Luckily both the driver and the fireman escaped unhurt. This was followed by a more serious incident on 13th March 1935, when there was a series of major goods train collisions, involving four separate freight trains. The accident occurred when the first goods train broke down on the track behind the Railway Arms at Primrose Hill, near Kings Langley. Unwarned by signals, the second train crashed into the back of the stationary train; this was followed by the third and fourth trains crashing into the wreckage. The combined weight of the meat, milk, general freight and coal trains involved was some 2730 tons. The wreckage blocked all the main lines in and out of Euston and the driver of the milk train was killed in the second of the three collisions.

A more disasterous accident took place at Bourne End on Sunday 30th September 1945. It was reported, as he saw it happen, by an American pilot from USAF Bovingdon who was flying overhead. The Perth to London express train had plunged over the railway embankment at high speed and the first five coaches were piled up some 30 feet in the air. The train, which was packed with over 700 service men and women, had shot the points. The incident occurred when it was passing at an estimated speed of some 60-70 m.p.h.. Thirty nine people were killed and a further 94 were injured in what was nationally the worst rail disaster for 30 years. At least the pilot's instant action in reporting the incident on his radio ensured that the emergency services arrived at the scene quickly. One of the worst ever national rail disasters occurred near Harrow in October 1952. This was when a major collision involving three trains killed 112 people. Thirty-seven of the fatalities were local people. The accident was caused when the Perth to London Express crashed into a stationary local passenger train. This first collision was soon followed by the London to Manchester Express crashing into the resulting wreckage.

A later incident happened on 21st April 1963 when there was a collision between the Holyhead to Euston diesel express passenger train and a rail-mounted engineering crane. Despite braking from 80 to 20 m.p.h. the driver of the diesel electric locomotive was unable to avoid striking the tail end of the crane. This had been hanging over the 'up' fast line as it was manoeuvering to perform its duties on the slow 'down' line. The crane was badly damaged and the passenger train derailed, but there were no serious injuries.

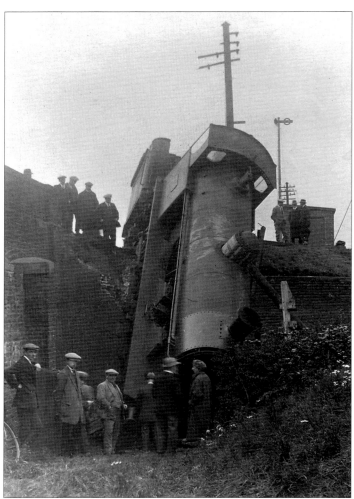

Derailment at Hunton Bridge, 1922.

Collision of goods trains at Kings Langley, 1935.

Diesel express crash near Kings Langley, 1963.

Scenes showing major railway accident at Bourne End, 1945.

Prior to the beginning of the Nineteenth Century most industrial activity in England was closely allied to its already well established agricultural traditions. As we have already discussed in the earlier chapter on agriculture (page 22), a profusion of water mills were built in the local area, specifically to harness the power of the Rivers Gade and Bulbourne. These early mills were used for the wholesale grinding of both corn and barley and also the fulling of wool and cloth. The clearance of local woodland and the use of timber, not just for fuel, but for furniture and general construction purposes also engaged and developed the skills of local craftsmen. Tanning, malting and brewing are further excellent examples of activities closely allied to agriculture. Each community also had its own collection of village wheat traders, shop and inn keepers, blacksmiths, farriers, tailors, shoe and rope makers, all of whom concentrated on servicing a local need. During the Eighteenth Century, thriving cottage industries such as lace making and straw plaiting enabled both the womenfolk and the children to make a significant contribution to the family economy. Dating from the Georgian period, many fine houses had been built in the pleasant countryside which was relatively close to London. Their occupants were wealthy land owners who could offer new sources of local employment in the form of vacancies for domestic staff, gamekeepers and agricultural labourers to work on their lands and estates. In the Nineteenth Century it was not uncommon for some of the finer houses such as the Grove in Watford or Tring Park to employ a domestic staff of over 20, although many were not always recruited locally. At this time, it was not unusual for the more modest dwellings of professional men, traders and innkeepers also to employ several domestic staff of their own.

What we today recognise as industrial manufacture did not become properly established in this county until the beginning of the Nineteenth Century. It was then that the new and vastly improved methods of transport that we have discussed in previous chapters, became the catalyst for this next phase in the nation's history. At the dawn of the Industrial Revolution, it was possible to obtain raw materials and transport finished goods much more cheaply and quickly than ever before. This meant that large-scale and specialised industrial manufacture, geared to national and international markets, was now a practical proposition. Furthermore the very arteries of communication that made this transportation possible ran right through our local valley. The Grand Junction Canal (constructed 1797) and the London to Birmingham Railway (constructed 1837), both followed the Gade and the Bulbourne valleys, directly linking the industrial Midlands and the North to the thriving Port of London. Once it gathered momentum, this constant stream of new commercial traffic quickly brought improved levels of trade and prosperity to this part of Hertfordshire. It also began to encourage some of the new industrialists to set up businesses in this area, in order to take advantage of these economically important transport links. As local employment opportunities blossomed, so the population of the area expanded quite rapidly. One indication of this is that between 1801 and 1841 the population of towns in this area grew by 120% as compared to only 60% in the rest of Hertfordshire. In order to understand this process of early industrial development, it is helpful to look in more detail at some of the principal industries established in the local area.

Flour Milling

Although we listed most of the local mills in some detail in our earlier chapter on agriculture, there still seems some point in specifically featuring flour milling as a good example of an early industry which immediately benefited from the improvements made during the Industrial Revolution. This was also an industry which made good use, in particular, of the newly provided canal system. Toovey's Flour Mill began in 1780 when Thomas Toovey married into the Surrey family who were the existing millers in Kings Langley. By 1846 his son, Thomas Toovey II, had sold the mill to the Grand Junction Canal Company for £15,000, with a 21 year lease which was granted back to him at £300 per annum. By 1898 the mill at Kings Langley had passed to his grandson, Thomas William Toovey, and by 1915 T. W. Toovey was established. In 1894 a steam engine and new steam roller had been installed and in 1913 Foden steam lorries began to replace the old wagon and horses that had been used for road deliveries. By 1914 production capacity at Toovey's Mill was 8 sacks an hour, with each sack weighing 2.5 cwt and 'Golden Spray' was the brand name of Toovey's top grade flour. The main raw material for the Kings Langley millers were sacks of wheat delivered to the mill on the canal by wide boats from Brentford. Toovey's relied on outside canal carriers until 1916, when they acquired two wide boats of their own. Both these vessels were of 11ft. beam and each was capable of carrying a load of 45 tons; the first boat 'Langley' was built by Bushell Brothers of Tring, whilst the second boat 'Betty' was a second hand purchase. 'Betty' was subsequently replaced in 1922 by a second new boat called 'Golden Spray' also built by the Bushell Brothers of Tring. These boats only enjoyed a short working life at Toovey's Mill, both being sold off in 1930. They then worked for a company which was involved in waste disposal carriage.

The old iron breast water wheel, which was 12ft. in diameter, was removed from the mill in 1921 and replaced by two Swiss turbines to produce electricity for the mill. Toovey's flour was delivered within a 25 mile radius. This included London and major industrial bakers like Peak Freans and McVities and Price Ltd, who were important customers. Significant by-products of milling at Toovey's were toppings and bran, which were sold on a commercial basis as animal foodstuffs. In 1935 a huge 1000 ton capacity grain silo was built on the mill's canal side site at a cost of £8,000. However by 1939, flour milling had ceased at Toovey's and the company's name was changed to Kings Langley Mills Ltd. The firm's principal brand was sold to Spillers who continued to make Golden Spray flour until the 1950's. In 1946 the mill was bought back from the Canal Company and the business now concentrated on the manufacture of animal foodstuffs, trading as Kings Langley Mills Ltd. Eventually in 1978 this company went into voluntary liquidation. The old mill house still survives, but all the working buildings, including the giant grain silo, were demolished in 1980.

Also important was the Tring flour mill which was situated much further north on the Wendover arm of the canal. In 1875 Thomas Mead built a five storey tower mill, close to the old windmill at Gamnel. This new mill was powered by a beam engine and following the old windmill's demolition in 1910, William Mead had erected a silo which was capable of holding 2000 quarters of grain. William Mead died in 1941 and in 1944 Heygates, a national milling company, acquired the Tring flour mill. Heygates who became the largest private flour miller in England, funded a continual programme of modernisation which ensured that the mill at Tring became the only surviving late Twentieth Century flour mill in the valley. Another flour mill worthy of note was the mill at Bourne End which was working until the Second World War. In 1900 J. Goodall Knowles of Broadway Farm installed a roller mill at Bourne End which was capable of producing 3½ cwt of flour per hour.

Brewing

Malting is one of the first industries mentioned in the history of the district, like milling, and dates back to the Thirteenth Century. It was in the early 1600's, that London brewers discovered that the waters in this area were much purer than those of the Thames. Consequently it is no surprise to find plenty of documentation of local breweries operating in most of the towns and larger villages of the Gade and Bulbourne valleys during the Seventeenth Century. Groomes Brewery thrived at Kings Langley and, in common with the Swan Brewery at Berkhamsted, remained in business until 1897. In 1664 William Fuller was a brewer at the Bell Inn in the old High Street of Hemel Hempstead, whilst at Tring, the Tring Brewery operated opposite the Bell Inn until 1900. In addition to these larger firms, many of which were related to principal Inns, most local communities also had several beer houses. These operated from more modest cottages where ordinary folk could fill up a jug or a flagon to re-stock their own supply on a daily basis.

The principal industrial brewer established locally in the Nineteenth Century was Joseph Benskin, who began his business in Watford in 1867. By 1800 a great deal of ale and beer was already being brewed at Watford, exploiting the ready supplies of pure water available from the River Gade and the River Colne. In 1835 there were eight malt kilns and three breweries in the town and by 1891 these had grown to ten malt

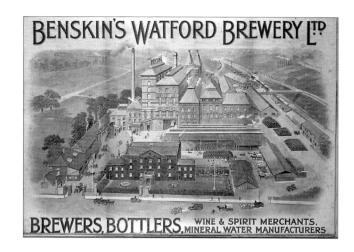

kilns and five breweries, whose combined output was said "to exceed that of all others in the country put together!". The first Watford brewery to be taken over by Joseph Benskin was the Dysons Cannon Brewery which had been active in the town since 1750. By 1885 one of the Benskin family formed a partnership with Panton's Wareham Brewery to develop the Cannon Brewery, under the name of Benskin & Co. By 1897 the business became the Benskins Watford Brewery Ltd and expanded to include Groomes Brewery at Kings Langley, the Kingsbury Brewery at St. Albans, Healeys Brewery in Watford and another at Woburn Sands.

Prior to Joseph Benskin's arrival, a major Nineteenth Century brewer in Watford was Edmund Fearnley Whittingstall who died in 1856. The Brewery he owned eventually became Sedgewicks Brewery, but by 1924 this too had been absorbed into the Benskins Company. Sedgewicks were important in the brewing industry because they were one of the first to introduce bottled beer in 1892. Before this innovation, all English beer was drawn from the wood. By 1911 Sedgewicks were selling more than three million bottles a year. By the time Benskins had acquired Sedgewicks, the company had swallowed up all the smaller breweries in Watford, with only one remaining independent. This was the Wells Brewery, sometimes known as the Lion Brewery, a much newer business started by Alderman Thorpe who was Mayor of Watford in 1923. However the share capital of Wells Watford brewery was eventually purchased by Benskins.

The most famous Benskins beer was the potent Colne Spring Ale, which was matured in casks for up to one year. Benskins successfully expanded into a national business and by 1931 were employing up to 350 local people. In 1957 the company became part of Ind Coope Ltd. and in 1958 Benskins built a giant bottling store in Watford, with a floor area of 13,000 sq.ft. At this time Ind Coope also established a large distribution depot in Hunton Bridge which had been formerly owned by the Taylor Walker Brewery and then Grants of St James, the wine and spirit merchants. Our story ends with a company rationalisation which closed the old Benskins Brewery building at 194 High Street. Happily this impressive structure became the ideal site for Watford's new Town Museum which opened in the converted building on 11th March 1981.

Silk Mills

By 1792 silk throwing (spinning) had become one of the principal manufacturing industries in Watford where there were at least three silk mills operating. The town's principal silk mill was at the Rookery and this continued to produce silk until 1881, when the premises was taken over by the Watford Steam Laundry. Another local town which played an important role in this industry was Tring where, towards the end of the Eighteenth Century, there were so many small canvas making factories that the town had become known as 'Little Manchester'. In 1824 an industrialist from Macclesfield, Mr. William Kay, established a large Silk Mill at Tring. He built his 'silk throwing' mill in Brook Street where he diverted the nearby Miswell and Dundale Springs into a mill pond in order to provide sufficient head of water to drive his mill engines. By 1836 the mill employed 600 local people, a work force which was supplemented by a small army of girl apprentices from London who lodged in a large house in Brook Street, near the Cattle Market. Weekly wages at the silk mill were then 15 pence for a child and 75 pence for a man. In the latter part of the Nineteenth Century cheap foreign imports began to cut into the market for English silk and by 1879 the number of silk mill employees had fallen to 400. When the Rothschild family purchased Tring Park from William Kay's estate in 1872, the silk mill was leased to Messrs. Evans, of Wood Street in London. Soon after this, the business really began to struggle and the Rothschilds initially took over the silk mill to help cushion the economic effects for many of the local employees in Tring. However, given the flood of cheap foreign imports, the silk manufacturing industry in this country was effectively over by the dawn of the Twentieth Century.

Timber

We have already discussed the wholesale clearance of local woodland for building purposes dating back to Medieval times. Although the felling of local timber was never again to be so widespread or dramatic, wood remained an important construction material and was used domestically, both as fuel and for furniture production. The development of improved transport systems transformed the situation and now meant that large quantities of wood could be moved around more easily. One of the first industrialists to exploit this situation was Job East, who used the canal to import timber to the saw mill which he established at Gossoms End, near Berkhamsted in 1840. This business, which later became East & Son, had a modest beginning. It began its operations in a small saw mill with horse-driven gearing and initially employed no more than 10 people. However the Crimean War (1854-56) brought the company its first large contracts for the production of lance poles, rammers and tent poles which were used in the conflict. This allowed East & Son to provide work for up to one hundred new employees. In the 1930's East & Son manufactured all 202 wooden lock gates required for the widening of the Warwick section of the Grand Junction Canal. Another early timber merchants founded in Berkhamsted was established by William Kay who had previously worked locally as a fencing contractor for the London and Birmingham Railway. It was this company which continued trading into the modern day as J. Alsford Ltd. By the late Nineteenth Century Berkhamsted had become famous for its thriving local wood working industry. By 1880 a total of over 200 men were employed at Easts, Kays and other smaller timber yards in the town.

These timber merchants were also closely linked to the brush making industry, which in late Victorian times employed a further 100 local people. This brush making tradition is still sustained by the Kent Brush Factory in Apsley which was first established in 1901. William Kent originally founded his brush making business in London in 1777. His son moved the business from its factory in Westminster to Great Marlborough Street. One hundred years later, the Apsley factory was built by G. B. Kent. It included two houses in the grounds, with five

cottages built for employees in Kent Avenue. G. B. Kent was a successful national manufacturer who was a major client of the railway system. The greater part of the company's output was retailed via some 6000 High Street Chemists, so most of the goods were packed into individual 8lb parcels and collected daily by van to be delivered to the railway station for despatch. This was the main trading pattern at Kents, persisting until the mid-sixties. The dominating presence of the old Kent factory was removed and replaced by today's smaller modern company premises, which were built as part of the Texas Homecare development, which opened in November 1984.

Another significant local timber merchant trading to this day is W. H. Lavers & Sons in Hemel Hempstead. In 1869 W. H. Lavers leased land at Fishery Wharf, situated just below Fishery Lock. The business thrived immediately and he first leased and then purchased a much larger wharf at Corner Hall, which was 100 yards down stream from Two Waters Bridge. This wharf had the advantage of its own canal dock which Lavers used to land large quantities of imported timber which were delivered by canal boat. In 1927 the business was incorporated to become W. H. Laver & Sons Ltd. By this time however the importance of the canal, as a key means of transport, had declined. In 1931 the dock area was filled in to increase the capacity of the timber storing area. Another local timber yard was the Foster Saw Mill, established in Boxmoor during the early 1900's. This business concentrated upon supplying building and fencing material, joinery and best timber for musical instruments. Here was another local employer whose business thrived, allowing for extensive enlargement and modernisation of the original mill. However, following a disastrous fire, Fosters Saw Mill was demolished in 1965. This spelt the end for its prominent 100ft. chimney, which had become something of a local landmark.

Paper Making

The Gade valley provided perfect conditions for the early paper making industry to flourish. The River Gade offered the ready supplies of clear running water that were required to turn the mills' water wheels and were necessary for the paper production process. Later the construction of the canal in 1797 enabled easy and economic transit of goods and raw materials to and from London. Paper manufacture in England began in 1496 when John Tate was making the first white printing paper at Sele Mill in Hertford. It is surprising to realise that paper continued to be made by hand, and in single sheets, for a further three centuries. Eventually in 1798 a Frenchman devised a process for making paper in continuous lengths. This invention by Nicholas Louis Robert was developed in England by two London stationers, Henry and Sealy Fourdrinier. In 1803 the first paper to be made by machine, in this country, was produced at Frogmore Mills, Apsley. Unfortunately the enormous cost of turning Robert's inventions into a commercial success bankrupted the Fourdriniers in 1810. Eventually in 1890 the mills were acquired by the British Paper Company, their present owners.

The great local success of the paper-making industry was founded when a London stationer, John Dickinson (1782-1869) bought Apsley Mill in 1809. He went on to build a business which became the area's most important employer in the Nineteenth Century. Dickinson had invented and patented his own idea, known as the cylinder mould machine. Using a combination of these machines and the Fourdrinier technology, his business expanded rapidly. He acquired Nash Mills in 1811 and built Home Park Mill at Kings Langley in 1820 and Croxley Mills in 1829. The impressive early development of his business was supported financially by George Longman, a member of the wealthy Longman publishing dynasty. Together they traded as Longman and Dickinson until George Longman died in November 1822. The successful industrial production of paper, initiated by the Fourdriniers and later realised by John Dickinson, represented a quantum leap for the industry. Instead of small quantities of hand-made material, it was now possible to mass produce paper on huge reels. These developments at Two Waters and Apsley led the world, creating vast new markets for affordable paper which gave birth to the development of the printing industry.

The success of John Dickinson's business relied not only on efficient mechanisation of paper manufacture, but also his constant inventive ability. He produced a non-smouldering cartridge paper for cannon ammunition which proved invaluable during the Peninsula War and the Waterloo Campaign. In 1824 he invented a card cutting machine and a paper pasting process which was to manufacture pasteboard. In 1830 a machine which he installed at Nash Mills, to make fine plate papers for printing, broke the French monopoly. In 1829 he patented a security paper with silk threads running through it which was used by Rowland Hill for the uniform Penny Post covers and envelopes. In more recent times this innovation has also become important for the development of forgery-proof currency notes. In 1843 John Dickinson introduced the production of coloured coated papers at Home Park Mill and installed the first colouring machine in 1878. Gummed paper and adhesive tape were later added to the Home Park range. John Dickinson's envelope production, which started around 1850, had reached three million per week by 1887 and in 1894 Croxley Mill's weekly output of paper was 140 tons. An indication of the company's rapid development is that in 1838 Nash Mills had been producing 8 tons of paper per week and this level of production had risen to 50 tons by 1900. By 1911 Nash Mills had become the largest producer of white and tinted pulp board in the country. The story of Dickinsons throughout the Nineteenth Century was one of constant expansion. In this period compulsory education had transformed the standards of literacy and the newly developed postal system had prompted an exponential growth in the levels of correspondence. These factors, combined with rapid technological growth, meant that the English paper and stationery manufacturing industry was now poised to enjoy vast international markets.

The canal played its part in servicing this impressive industrial development, carrying finished paper products to London and returning loaded with the raw materials for paper production. The company had always maintained some boats of its own: The Lord Nelson (1870), Lord Howe (1884) and the Hero of the Nile (1891). In February 1926 a new motorised narrow boat was launched at Tring to provide a link with the Dickinsons major depot at Paddington. However the company traditionally relied mainly on outside carriers for most of this work. This was organised, under contract, by Fellows, Morton and Clayton, one of the leading canal carrying companies. Nevertheless their working boats were still painted up in Dickinson's colours. The old steamers 'Countess' and 'Princess', with their butties 'Alice' and 'Kate', worked on the run for many years until they were replaced in 1927 by the motor boats 'Jackal' and 'Jaguar', with their butties 'Helen' and 'Hettie'. The raw materials brought to the Dickinson factories included rags from Paddington, and wood pulp, chemicals, china clay and esparto grass from Brentford. Between 1904-28 the average annual tonnages delivered by canal boat are an impressive indication of the scale of

Early drawing of Home Park Mill, 1842.

Dickinson's industrial production. Paper delivered from the mills totalled 7,225 tons. Some 38,540 tons of coal were required as fuel for the factories whilst 20,985 tons of raw materials from both Paddington and Brentford were used in the various production processes.

As the company developed during the Twentieth Century, John Dickinson & Co. became established as a clear market leader, with brand names such as Lion Brand, Basildon Bond and Croxley Script becoming popular and well known stationery products throughout the world. At Apsley the emphasis was now on large scale card and envelope production and the company had become the major local employer. Back in 1881 the company had employed an already impressive work force of 722, but by the time of the Great War (1914-18) a total of 1604 Dickinson's workers enlisted to fight for their country. Dickinsons made a key contribution to this war effort by producing trench mortar bombs and during the Second World War, Apsley Mills became an important munitions factory, also manufacturing paper-based auxiliary fuel tanks for long range aeroplanes. Further expansion took place between the two wars when a new card development building was added at Apsley in 1935; this was followed by the new envelope department in 1937. The company's work force had now swollen to 5,000, a figure which was sustained throughout the 1960's. Dickinson's business had gone from strength to strength and the sheer scale of production can be judged by the fact that by then the company was manufacturing the staggering total of 135 million envelopes per week.

The company name of Dickinson was temporarily lost when the firm changed its title to the Dickinson Robinson Group (DRG) in 1966, following a merger with E. S. & A. Robinson Holdings Ltd. Increased mechanisation had begun to reduce the work force from its peak of 5,000 to well under 2000 employees by the time that a giant 'remote control' warehouse was built for the company in 1989. This provided 80,000 square feet of storage space with a capacity of 15,000 loaded pallets, all operated by computer controlled automatic stacker cranes. The old factories at Home Park and Croxley Mill had already been demolished in 1982, by the time that the remaining stationery business in Apsley was taken over by the Swiss firm Biber Holdings A.G. in 1989. This new company re-introduced the original company name of John Dickinson and rationalised all the remaining business operations. The previous D.R.G. paper and board operation at Nash Mills now became SAPPI Graphics, a division of the South African Paper and Pulp Industries (Europe) Ltd. In 1992 work began to clear the Apsley site and demolish all the old factory buildings. These have now been replaced by a modern Dickinson warehouse built nearby and an extensive 'out of town' shopping centre featuring a Sainsburys supermarket, opened in the Summer of 1993.

Printing

Given that, by the early Nineteenth Century, the greater Watford area was already an established base for paper manufacture, it can be no surprise that the town developed in the Twentieth Century as a major national centre for the printing industry. Watford was close to London with excellent transport links and also had the advantage of four river valleys in its neighbouring area. The rivers of the Colne, Chess, Ver and Gade had given rise to the establishment of up to 24 mills in the area by the early 1800's. An early pioneer of the printing industry was John Peacock who had moved from the West

Country to establish a business in Watford in 1823. He set up his first printers shop in what is now the Lower High Street, approximately where the Bakerloo Line station now stands. Peacock's activities flourished and he quickly established himself as an important local printer, bookbinder and card maker.

Another key name in the development of printing in Watford was David Greenhill, who in 1903 helped establish a four-colour French press operating under the trading name of Bemrose-Daziel Ltd. This firm became the very first in the country to turn out multi-colour printing on a large scale. Because of their early success they were incorporated into the business of Waterlow, Brothers and Layton in 1908. By now Watford was already established as the leading centre in the country for colour printing and a new phase was about to begin with the development of photogravure in colour. Richard André and his two nephews had used the engraving techniques they learnt in Meisenbach, Munich, to create a process engraving business in Bushey Grove Road. In 1909 David Greenhill became Manager of this business which was then called André and Sleigh. In 1914 this firm was taken over by the Anglo Engraving Company to form André, Sleigh and Anglo and subsequently bought up by another local concern called Menpes Printing Company, which had premises in Whippendell Road. In 1918 the entire business moved into the Whippendell Road buildings and the new combined operation traded under the name of Sun Engraving Company.

Following the First World War, Watford was home to the Sun Engraving, Odhams and Rembrandt printing businesses which made it easily the largest and most important centre for Gravure Printing in Europe. This industry flourished during the 1930's and local letterpress printers were now producing work of the highest quality. The process engraving carried out in Watford, especially in colour blocks, was of a standard comparable to any in the world. In 1936 the largest photogravure works ever seen were established in Watford by Odhams. At this time Sun Engraving were also producing a total output in excess of 1,000 tons of printed matter per week. By 1940 over 5,000 local people were employed in the Print Industry which had become Watford's major industry. By 1963 this figure had risen to 10,000 operatives employed by 39 different firms of printers.

Iron Working

In 1798, Joseph Cranstone came from Horsham and opened an Ironmongers Shop in Hemel Hempstead. Joseph died in 1811 but his second son, Joseph Cranstone Junior, added an iron foundry to the business in 1818. The first company premises were on the east side of the old High Street, behind the shops, and their trade soon prospered. By 1867 Joseph Cranstone was placing advertisements, stating that he was ready to accept orders to manufacture engines, agricultural equipment, and machinery of every description, using his new and powerful steam driven equipment. In the same year Joseph Cranstone enjoyed the distinction of building the first steam powered 'road motor' to travel from Hemel Hempstead to London. He handed over the business to his son William Henry Cranstone, who soon extended his father's workshops and built a new warehouse in the yard. During the Nineteenth Century Cranstones did not employ many people, but in 1897 when their foundry won an important contract to make two ton bearings for the Admiralty, the business was able to take on a further 120 men. Another example of their industrial work was the construction of a large three hundred horsepower engine for a gold mine in Johannesburg, South Africa.

Cranstones were also responsible for the building of the town's first gas works back in 1835. Local gas works were another Victorian industrial development which used the canal system. The gas works at Berkhamsted were opened in 1849, to the north of the town and were usefully situated between the canal and the railway. Coal was delivered by boat to the gas works wharf which also dealt with the traffic of crude tar, delivered back by wide boat for distribution in London. A gas works was opened in Rickmansworth in 1849, close to the town's main canal wharf. There were also several smaller works at Kings Langley and Tring, which made little use of the canal system. One industry which did was the sand and gravel industry. There were gravel workings at Kings Langley, close to the canal by Primrose Hill and a gravel pit at Winkwell which was operated by Cranstones in 1893. However, the main local centre for the sand and gravel industry was at Rickmansworth.

The Hemel Hempstead firm of Cranstones, which subsequently became known as the Hemel Hempstead Engineering Company, was one of the first companies to move to the New Town's Industrial area, occupying premises in Cupid Green from 1949. There are several fine examples of Cranstone's decorative iron work which have been well maintained and can still be admired in Hemel Hempstead today. A Cranstone iron water fountain stands outside the Heath Park Hotel. This was erected in October 1835 to commemorate the 'third centenary of the first printing of the English Bible'. In the old High Street you can also still see a fine old cast iron water pump which was erected by public subscription in 1848. This was subsequently converted into a gas, and then later an electric street light. The beautiful old iron bridge in Gadebridge Park was also erected in 1840 by Joseph Cranstone and on the splendid wrought iron gates at the entrance to the old Town Hall is the inscription "Erected W. H. Cranstone, High Bailiff AD 1872".

Another local iron worker was James Davis, who established an iron foundry in the Marlowes in 1855. His firm quickly developed a successful specialisation in producing agricultural implements. James Davis's son, William Davis, travelled extensively as a representative of his father's company, which was now called Davis & Son. Unfortunately William met with an early death in 1871, aged 27. One of James Davis's daughters, Emma, then married local farmer Joseph Bailey of Chambersbury Farm, which proved to be a good match for the business. The company became Davis & Bailey. Joseph Bailey, who was a local farmer on a large scale himself, was already conversant with the problems and challenges that faced the majority of their prospective customers. The business, which had a tradition of employing the best local craftsmen, soon enjoyed an excellent reputation for the design and manufacture of top class agricultural machinery and equipment. The Iron Works were situated approximately where Bank Court is today and the Davis and Bailey premises had a large yard which faced on to the Marlowes and backed on to the River Gade. Facilities here included carpentry workshops, blacksmiths and machine shops, as well as the foundry and smelting furnace which were located close to the river. By 1929 the work force comprised 30 men, together with several young apprentices. However following the Second World War, with the advent of the economies of scale available from much larger scale production and the development of even more sophisticated machinery, the firm became less competitive and was gradually run down. The business was finally closed on the death of Joseph Bailey in 1949, and the company's old beam engine was taken into store at the Science Museum.

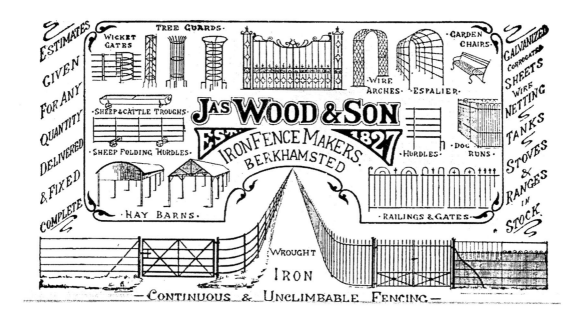

In 1826 James Wood began his business in the High Street at Berkhamsted, making and repairing iron fencing and wirework. As his reputation grew, Wood secured contracts to make estate gates, fire guards, rat traps and candle snuffers for many of the large houses in the area. He produced work for the Ashridge, Gadebridge and Cassiobury estates. He also made pipes for the early supply of gas to individual houses. In 1974 a serious fire destroyed Wood's original glass and ironwork showroom, which had been built over 100 years previously. However the business is still growing strong and recently the company celebrated 170 years of continuous trading in Berkhamsted.

Coopers

William Cooper arrived in Berkhamsted, in 1843, some ten years before the birth of Henry Wellcome who was later to found a rival business to his own. William Cooper was one of the first veterinary surgeons to qualify from the newly established Royal College of Veterinary Surgeons. He had made an important breakthrough in veterinary care, by developing the first effective sheep dip in 1843. This innovation was destined to become the foundation stone for one of the world's great veterinary and agricultural businesses. Cooper's first factory was built in Ravens Lane and because his initial product was in such demand, the business expanded rapidly. By 1885 he had over 120 employees. In 1925 the company was amalgamated with Macdougall and Robertson to become Cooper, Macdougall and Robertson Ltd. Wellcome became Cooper's chief competitor, although the two firms' activities were to some extent complementary. Both shared a common interest in the development of foot and mouth vaccines, although Wellcome's principal interest was in the biological field, whereas Coopers concentrated on chemical dips and dressings. These became the basis for many modern

insecticides. Where as Wellcome were dominant in the animal health business in the United Kingdom with little export activity, Coopers had been operating successfully in Argentina, Africa and Australia since the end of the Nineteenth Century.

Conditions became ripe for a merger of the two companies and in 1959 Cooper, Macdougall and Robertson was acquired by the Wellcome Foundation. The Cooper Technical Bureau had been formed in 1919 and was acknowledged as the world's centre of expertise in the development and field use of cattle and sheep dips. This became a key responsibility, because without these chemicals the agricultural economy of the

modern world would be in danger of collapse. Following the merger, there was a rationalisation of all the research effort within the Group. This culminated in 1973 with the amalgamation of the veterinary research staff of the two organisations into the Wellcome Research Laboratories. This process incorporated the former Cooper Technical Bureau and the Cooper Research Station, near the Golf Club at Berkhamsted. Prior to this merger, Cooper also used to run a programme of top quality stock breeding at Home Farm in Little Gaddesden. More recently the company has enjoyed further important success with the development of its anti-bacterial drugs for animals. In 1995 the Wellcome Group of companies was acquired by Glaxo and together they now form Britain's largest industrial concern.

Roses Lime Juice

The business of L. Rose & Company and their barrel run to Boxmoor wharf is an interesting example of another local industry which exploited the canal system for the transportation of its raw materials. In fact, its activity represented the very last commercial deliveries on this stretch of the Grand Union Canal. The roots of this industry stretch back to the Eighteenth Century when the firm of Rose who were Ships Chandlers, supplied the Royal Navy with lime juice, which helped combat scurvy amongst sailors. This part of their business became so profitable that a junior member of the family, Lauchlan Rose, began to concentrate his activities on the production of lime juice from his own estates in Dominica. He then realised that, by sweetening the juice and presenting it in attractive bottles, he could popularise it as a refreshing drink for the domestic market. Other by-products were created as alternative uses for the lime harvest with the development of lime marmalade and lime oil for use in soap and perfumes. Lime was also sold to confectioners as a flavouring for sweets and jellies. Helped by such innovations, the company grew rapidly during the 1920's and 30's. However its Headquarters in Worship Street, London were badly damaged during the war by an evening air raid in 1940. As a result of this damage, the second Lauchlan Rose, grandson of the founder, transferred all his staff and equipment to a new manufacturing base in St. Albans.

From 1947 the lime juice, destined for St. Albans, arrived by canal boat at Boxmoor wharf in large oak casks, which were then drained and stacked for return to Dominica on the next shipment. In Dominica there are two lime harvests, one in the Spring and one in the Autumn. The lime pulp was extracted locally from the fruit and then left to settle in huge vats. It was then racked off and dispatched to England by deep sea vessels, which was capable of taking it across the Atlantic to the London Docks. From the docks it was then transferred to Brentford using Thames barges, from where canal barges transported it along the Grand Union Canal to Boxmoor. The last working run of these canal boats for Roses Lime Juice was in 1981.

Boxmoor wharf was built by the Boxmoor Trust with monies they received in 1799 from the sale of land to the Grand Junction Canal Company. Boxmoor wharf, situated by Two Waters bridge, became the main coal wharf for the town of Hemel Hempstead and, from 1864, it was managed by Henry Balderson. Mr. Balderson was a dealer in coal, coke, stone and corn and also handled imported wines and spirits, which were delivered to the wharf by canal boat. In 1892 he ran two boats of his own, the Mildred and the Ellen, from Boxmoor wharf.

"O Mister Moon, these Rusks are fine,
They're crisp and crunchy all the time.
Good for health and for your teeth,
Enjoyed by all the World beneath."

Wander

In 1865 a Swiss chemist, Dr. George Wander, established the high nutritional value of barley malt. With this knowledge he began to manufacture malt extract and launched a food drink called Ovaltine, which was destined to become world famous. In 1900 George was succeeded by his son Albert, export markets quickly followed and a British company was founded first to sell, and then to manufacture Ovaltine in England. Production at Wander's canal-side factory in Kings Langley began in 1913 and, with the business expanding rapidly, an impressive new factory was built between 1924-29. This work was supervised by Sir Harry Hague, then Managing Director of Wander Ltd.

In 1929 Wander bought two local farms; Numbers Farm at Kings Langley and Parsonage Farm at Abbots Langley. Together these 460 acres became an important part of the company's marketing strategy and were also capable of producing the eggs, milk and barley for malt, required to process Ovaltine. These two farms became known as the Model Poultry and Dairy Farm and were designed as an exact replica of the farm created by King Louis XVI for his Queen, Marie Antoinette. The impressive dairy buildings of Parsonage Farm, near the Bedmond Road, have now been converted into a private residential complex known as Antoinette Court. Wander used to maintain a large laying flock of at least 50,000 pullets in free range conditions on the slopes of Numbers Farm, whilst the Dairy Farm also kept its own prize-winning herd of pedigree Jersey cattle.

In common with Dickinson Paper Mills, Wander also had its own fleet of narrow boats. The motor boat Albert and its butty Georgette were in service from January 1926. At its maximum, the Wander fleet comprised seven pairs of narrow boats. The final canal side delivery of coal to the factory was completed on 14th April 1959 by Wander's last pair of working boats Minas and Enid. In the 1950's business had expanded to the extent that the Wander factory at Kings Langley employed up to 1,400 local people. However the constant updating and automation of production processes has meant that this figure has now been reduced to a modern work force of around 400. Modern production statistics are nevertheless impressive. The company's automated brew house processes 30 million kilos of grain and 20,000 tons of malt extract are produced annually. Wander's modern product range includes Ovaltine Light and Ovaltine Options, which are popular flavoured chocolate drinks. Annual production of these is a staggering 175,000,000 sachets. Every week 15,000 cases of Wander products leave the Kings Langley factory, with over half this output being exported overseas.

Brocks Fireworks

On 5th November 1720 John Brock, who was described as an 'artist in fireworks', was buried at St. James Church in Clerkenwell. John Brock's early interest in his art was destined to develop into the nationally famous Brocks Firework Company which continues trading to this day. Brocks moved out of London to Hemel Hempstead in 1933, because the company was running out of space in Sutton where it was no longer possible to expand its production capacity safely. The Brocks factory at Hemel Hempstead was purpose built on a 207 acre site at Woodhall Farm and accommodated more than 200 separate buildings. It was claimed to be the largest firework factory in the world with 60 magazines and drying rooms, capable of storing up to 1,300,000 lbs of fireworks and 5 tons of gunpowder. In 1935, when King George V's Jubilee was celebrated, fireworks were made at Hemel Hempstead, on Royal instruction. They were sent all over the world, including the colonies. Brocks eventually moved out of Hemel Hempstead and transferred all their production to Scotland in the early 1960's.

Tring Flour Mill

Kay's Silk Mill, leased by David Evans in 1872.

A timber yard in Berkhamsted at the turn of the century.

G. B. Kent & Sons Ltd., brush factory at Apsley.

Bushell Brothers Boat-building yard at New Mill, Tring, circa 1920.

W. H. Cranstone's trade fair stand.

The Grove Mill, circa 1907.

Frogmore Mill, 1905.

Home Park Mill, 1929.

View of Apsley Mills.

Croxley Mill, 1920.

Nash Mill, 1988.

Dickinson's paper stores at Apsley Mill, 1925.

Loading Dickinson's barges at Apsley Mill, 1916.

First fleet of Dickinson's delivery vans in the 1920's.

Workforce emerging from Apsley Mill during the 1920's.

Aerial view of Boxmoor wharf.

View of Rose's Lime Juice Wharf (now B&Q), 1962.

Rose's Lime Juice processing plant at Two Waters.

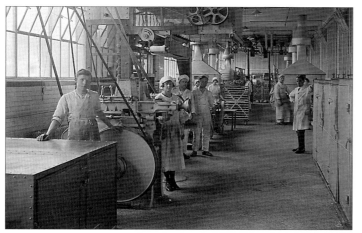

Early production at Wander factory.

Ovaltine canning plant.

Malt extract production.

Ovaltine packing area.

View of Wander factory in the 1950's.

On the outbreak of the First World War there was a rush of volunteers to serve in the London Territorial Force. The initial call for 30,000 men was satisfied within one week during August 1914 and a 2nd London (Reserve) Division was created in September. When the 2nd London Division left for France in March 1915, the Reserve Division took their place. The Artillery Brigades moved out from London to Hemel Hempstead, whilst the rest of the Division moved to the St. Albans and Watford area, from their initial base in Surrey. Squadron headquarters for the Hertfordshire Yeomanry was in Watford and, in common with many of the smaller urban communities to the north of London, Hemel Hempstead was about to become a Garrison town.

Many of the troops stationed locally enjoyed morale boosting visits from the nation's leaders. In September 1914 King George V paid a surprise visit to inspect the Territorials and, in the same year, Lord Kitchener inspected the Queens Westminster Rifles at Leverstock Green. Princess Louise also attended a Parade of the 1st 13th Kensington Battalion at Cecil Lodge, Abbots Langley. By November 1914 work was underway on a large military camp in Gadebridge Park, which consisted of 34 substantial timber huts, each 120ft. by 20ft. This new army camp became the centre of military activity in the area and, with the influx of thousands of service men, many local shops and restaurants enjoyed a boom in their business. Despite the number of volunteers joining up, the garrisoned

WE'RE DOING OUR DUTY

Parish Church.

FOR KING AND COUNTRY AT TRING

With Hemel Hempstead now established as the base for the Royal Artillery, the 5th Company of the London Brigade was based in Gadebridge Park with its headquarters in the Town Hall. The 6th Brigade's headquarters was at St. Paul's Church School; the 7th Brigade were camped, with horse lines, at Boxmoor and the 8th Brigade at Apsley. The 18th Battery were based near Heath Park, the 19th at Bovingdon and the 21st were quartered at Shendish. By September 1914, four of the first Kitchener battalions had arrived in Berkhamsted, whilst the Queens Westminster Rifles established a base at Leverstock Green. At Hemel Hempstead there were also large army camps on the Highfield estate and along the old Redbourn Road; there were other camps at Langleybury, Hazelwood House and Gaddesden Place. There were over 100 tents in the Park at Berkhamsted with more troops based along the valley at Hudnall, Dagnall, Gossoms End and Tring. The 1st 13th Kensington Battalion were camped near Abbots Langley whilst the London Scottish Regiment had a Battalion headquarters at Bucknalls House, in Garston. This is now part of the Building Research Station. The 1st Battalion of Princess Alexandra's Post Office Rifles were also stationed in Abbots Langley, until they left for France in March 1915, whilst the Royal Army Medical Corps. (East Anglian Regiment) were based at Kings Langley, until they left for the Dardanelles in that same year.

troops had actually increased the overall population in most local communities.

The first unit from the 2nd London Division to see action was the 2nd London Heavy Battery, which left Kings Langley and sailed to France on 15th March 1915. On 19th March they went into action behind Neuve Chapelle, before being ordered north to Ypres on 1st April to assist the Indian Corps. The first major action for the men of 'F' Company Hertfordshire Regiment was on the Somme, during the Battle of Ancre on 13th November 1916. This was a successful action and many of these soldiers were later involved in the Battle of Passchendael, in the Ypres Salient where they attacked strongly on the Picklem Ridge.

Back at home blackout instructions were issued in November 1914. In October a Zeppelin had flown over West Hertfordshire for the first time. On the night of 13th October 1915 five German naval airships raided south east England, leaving 48 people dead and a further 64 injured. The biggest raid of the war was on 2nd September 1916 when 14 airships crossed the coast, with three Zeppelins passing close to Hemel Hempstead. The nation also suffered from enemy submarine action. This culminated in February 1917 with an unrestricted German submarine campaign against our merchant vessels.

Prior to the Great War Britain was heavily dependent on foreign imports for its food supply, with 40% of her meat and 80% of her wheat coming from overseas. On the outbreak of war, hoarding of food began immediately with a tariff issued in August 1914 which set firm prices. Clearly a key priority was to increase home food production and, by December 1915, the Town Council at Hemel Hempstead had set up a War Agricultural Sub Committee. However by the end of 1916, the situation had begun to deteriorate and a National Food Controller was appointed by the Prime Minister, Lloyd George. In 1917, with a shortage of men to work the fields, there were plans to use German prisoners of war, with 10,000 prisoners being made available. By June 1918, 565 prisoners of war were working in Hertfordshire with a further 255 placements planned. Some refugees from the conflict in Europe were also being accommodated locally. Many of these had come from Belgium and a Relief Committee was set up in 1915 to help plan their care.

Dickinsons, the area's largest employer, initially encouraged their staff to enlist with promises of partial pay during the conflict. By the end of the war over 130 employees from Apsley and Nash Mills had perished in the fighting. Part of Apsley Mills was commandeered for Government supplies and from 1st June 1917, it became a controlled establishment of the Ministry of Munitions. Here they manufactured three inch bombs for mortars and copper bands for 4½, 14 and 18 pounder shells. Nash Mills also produced some mortar bombs and small shells for the conflict, whilst G. B. Kent contributed large quantities of brushes of every description. The British Paper Company at Frogmore Mills made fuse boxes, food containers and cigarette boxes for the Army and Navy Canteen Board, whilst Cranstone Engineering at Hemel Hempstead, made sinkers for Mark 12 sea mines. Fosters Saw Mills produced wooden ammunition holders called 'ditty boxes'. 'Tank Week' of 4th March 1918 was well supported locally and, in recognition of Hemel Hempstead's contribution, a British heavy Mark IV tank was displayed for some 20 years after the conflict, outside the Heath Park Hotel.

The training of troops at Gadebridge Park ceased in the autumn of 1917. This was in readiness for the camp's new role as a military hospital treating the war wounded. Many of the huts were converted into wards for 40 men and the hospital opened on 15th August 1918, with local rumours rife that it was to be used primarily for the treatment of returning soldiers with venereal disease. Earlier in the conflict there had been 20 hospital beds made available for soldiers at the West Herts Infirmary, with a further 36 beds added in the new temporary Windsor Ward. This new Infirmary was built in 1917,

following a public appeal. Hemel Hempstead had also set up its own Volunteer Training Corps in January 1915. This catered for the local men who could not join up because they were either too old or in key occupations. By the end of that year there were 123 members in service locally. In 1916 the various Voluntary Training Corps around the country were re-organised into a national force. Most of the peace time Police Constables had joined the military forces, so there was also a need for Special Constables to serve at home. On average there were 185 'Specials' locally enrolled at any one time during the conflict. These men played a key role patrolling the streets during air raids and guarding key installations such as water reservoirs.

News of the Armistice reached Hemel Hempstead at midday on 11th November 1918 and this meant that some wartime regulations began to be relaxed. Unfortunately the suffering did not stop here, because a virulent form of influenza swept across Europe at the end of 1918. This resulted in many fatalities, particularly amongst the often poorly fed and dispirited populations of the countries involved in the conflict. Because the war had ended, food was a little easier to obtain, although problems of food supply continued and 12,600 new ration cards were issued from Hemel Hempstead. Although the war had been won, the cost had been terrible. The local communities had to slowly recover and adjust to the awful reality of the casualties which had touched virtually every family in the nation. Of the 12,000 men garrisoned in the Berkhamsted area, over 2,000 did not return; an historical fact commemorated by the striking War Memorial on Berkhamsted Common, where many of them had trained. Tring unveiled its War Memorial on 27th November 1918 in remembrance of 93 local soldiers who perished in the conflict. In Apsley a building was erected in Orchard Street, in memory of villagers who had died and Abbots Langley's Memorial to their loss of 81 men was unveiled by Violet Henderson in 1919. Kings Langley's War Memorial was unveiled on 1st October 1920 by Sir Frederick Halsey and on 26th June 1921, at Hemel Hempstead, Lt. Colonel L. F. Smeathman unveiled the War Memorial at Moor End, upon which are carved 387 names.

Peace Day on Saturday 19th July 1919, was a wonderfully happy summer's day with special processions, celebrations and parties in all the local communities. Teams of Boy Scouts delivered copies of a Souvenir Programme to every house on the electoral register. Another local highlight at the end of the Great War was the triumphant return to Kings Langley of Private Christopher Cox, who was awarded the Victoria Cross for his bravery in rescuing the wounded under fire.

Troops riding through Tring.

Cavalry at Hemel Hempstead.

Soldiers at Balls Pond Farm, Kings Langley.

Soldiers of the Hertfordshire Regiment at Shendish.

Off-duty soldiers drying their uniforms.

Army field kitchen.

Medical Corps. outside Abbots Langley School.

Village blacksmith and troops outside the Kings Head at Abbots Langley.

1st/13th Kensington Battalion marching through Kings Langley, September 1914.

Earl of Clarendon (right) waits to greet Christopher Cox V.C.

Christopher Cox's triumphant return to Kings Langley.

Peace Day celebrations in Hunton Bridge, 1919.

Inauguration of Tring War Memorial, 1918.

In May 1939 the Military Training Bill legislated for the registration for service of all males aged 20 and 21 of British nationality. Registration was later extended to all men aged 18-41, with the proviso that employers must reinstate men on completion of their military service. However everyone had the opportunity, when registering, to state whether they had any conscientious objections to military service and had a chance of their views being upheld by a tribunal. If approved as conscientious objectors they had to register for full time work in agriculture, forestry or ARP ambulance work. Given the evident terrors of the Great War, feelings were not as strong against non-participants in the Second World War. Thousands of troops were billeted in the Dacorum area, with American, Dutch and Polish troops also training in the district. In 1940, following Dunkirk, men from the British Expeditionary Force and from the 51st Highland Division were stationed at Ashridge and Polish soldiers bivouacked near the Bridgewater Monument.

On the Home Front, petrol soon became scarce and food rationing was introduced in January 1940. There was also a great focus on salvage, with paper carefully recycled and all food refuse used for feeding pigs and poultry. As the war developed the need for metals intensified and this resulted in park gates and iron railings being dismantled and melted down. People were also encouraged to hand in pots and pans made of aluminium which was invaluable when recycled in aircraft construction. Another feature of the Home Front was the 'Dig for Victory' campaign, which encouraged people to dig up their lawns and gardens in order to increase vegetable production.

Sponsorship
Community led sponsorship of the military effort was common during the Second World War. The town of Hemel Hempstead first sponsored a Spitfire at a cost of £5,000, a sum easily raised during Wings Week in 1941. This plane, No. 8787, joined 602 Squadron on 3rd August 1941 and made 21 operational flights before failing to return from escorting Blenheim bombers over Abbeville. Warship Weeks were also organised by the National War Savings Committee and the local communities of Berkhamsted, Potten End and Little Gaddesden exceeded their target of £175,000 to provide a new submarine hull for the war effort. Their adopted vessel was completed in April 1942 as HM Submarine P.44 and given its official name of HM Submarine United on 31st January 1943. Hemel Hempstead also sponsored HMS Berkeley, a Type 1 'Hunt Class' Destroyer, raising a total of over £286,000, whilst Tring adopted FY 1614 which was a requisitioned trawler used for mine sweeping. The local regiment of the area was the Hertfordshire and Bedfordshire Regiment and its men saw

action in Europe, North Africa, the Middle East and Malaya. The Herts. and Beds. were involved in the Anzio landing in Italy, with others unfortunately landing in Singapore just before it fell to the Japanese. Later the Regiment was involved in the capture of Monte Cassino, whilst another group was fighting with the Chindits in the Arakan.

The Home Guard
On the Home Front an important feature were the three Observer Posts in the Dacorum area located at Kings Langley, Berkhamsted and Markyate. Post L2 was at Markyate, with Post C1 at Kings Langley feeding information, by telephone, direct to Watford Centre at Cassiobury Drive. Post F3 at Berkhamsted was situated outside the town, overlooking Ashridge and Berkhamsted Commons. In the early days there were frequent scares concerning parachutists and these observer posts were fully occupied monitoring the movement of enemy aircraft. Later in the conflict they helped regulate the American bombing raids launched from Bovingdon Airfield and also helped plot the movement of gliders sent to Arnhem.

Once the Blitz had begun in June 1940, the evening skies of the valley were busy with enemy aircraft. Many of these used the area, which was only five minutes flying time from London, as a turning point for their bombing raids over the capital. Given this fact, war time casualties and damage suffered locally were mercifully light. It is interesting to note that this area was considered safe enough for great statues from the streets of London to be brought out for storage within the grounds of Berkhamsted Castle. The worst period for local bombing was between September and October 1940, with bombs falling virtually every day. Most of these mercifully landed on open ground. On 20th October 1940, a string of 10 bombs was dropped, in intervals, over the village of Kings Langley. One of these bombs demolished the Griffin public house, on the Water Lane bridge, killing publican Mr. Edward Carter. Another tragedy occurred in January 1941 when a bomb fell on Long Marston School House killing the Headmistress, Miss Ruth Whelan. By far the worst incident in the area occurred on 1st May 1941, in Belswains Lane, where a bombing raid killed nine people. The fatalities included one child and two ARP Wardens on patrol. Several houses were destroyed and many other buildings were damaged in the extensive blast. In Felden an important water tower was threatened by fire following a bombing raid, whilst in Berkhamsted a house in Shootersway was badly damaged. Sunnyside railway bridge was also blown up by a high explosive bomb in the summer of 1941. In November 1940, another bomb had dropped near the main railway line at Folly Bridge, derailing the London to Glasgow Express; there were 20 casualties from this incident but none were fatal. In the Hemel Hempstead area there were two fatalities, with three seriously and forty slightly injured by bombing. In the Berkhamsted area, one person was killed, with five seriously and one slightly injured. The parish of Abbots Langley was hit by a total of 76 high explosive bombs and 10 incendiaries, with the most damage being sustained in the Hazelwood Lane and Gallows Hill areas. In Bovingdon, 14 high explosive bombs and 15 incendiaries landed, the most serious incident occurring when three bombs landed in Hogs Pit Bottom.

Civil Defence

Throughout the conflict there was frantic activity on the ground and a great deal of organisation was required to help minimise the damage and protect the civilian population. Very soon after the outbreak of the war, the Civil Defence Organisation within the Hemel Hempstead Rural District Area was declared to be at full strength. Control centres in the Town Halls at Berkhamsted, Hemel Hempstead and Tring were manned 24 hours a day and First Aid posts were established. Elephant Farm, in Hemel Hempstead, was scheduled to be a mortuary if required. By October 1939 there were 600 people enrolled in Air Raid Precaution (ARP) in the Hemel Hempstead area. The Dickinsons factories at Apsley had 400 people involved in both ARP and fire fighting work and had invested £25,000 to help pay for 100 local bomb shelters. Trench shelters were dug in many parts of Dacorum, but these were designed for people caught in the streets. Encouragement

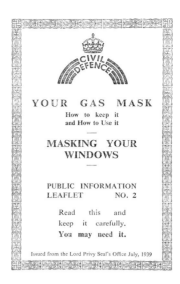

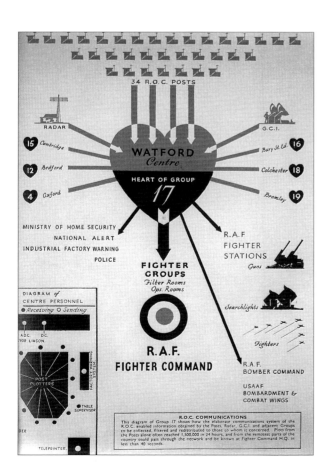

was given to householders to construct their own Anderson shelters. Fire watching was an important contribution which helped to reduce bomb damage and elaborate schemes were set up in the local area. There were 500 volunteer fire watchers in Hemel Hempstead and district, with a further 200 volunteers in the Kings Langley area.

On 16th May 1940 it was announced that battalions of Local Defence Volunteers (LDV) should be organised and effective immediately Their early duties included the regulation of petrol use and the manning of road blocks. The 7th Battalion, which covered the Dacorum area, fell in a National Zone under Eastern Command and its headquarters were initially at 41 High Street in Tring. LDV observation posts were set up in most communities and the Battalion was commanded by Captain G. M. Brown, with Major P. de Soissons as second in command. By September 1940 this LDV force had become known as the Home Guard and the 7th Battalion was moved to the Rothschild Estate Office at 20 High Street. In December 1941 a large scale invasion practice simulated fierce fighting around Tring and Berkhamsted, with the Home Guard responsible for defence. Men aged between 18 and 51, and not already involved in Civil Defence, could now be forced into the Home Guard, in areas where numbers were low. Invasion Committees were formed in local towns and where men were in both the Home Guard and the ARP, the ARP was to have priority unless the enemy were in the vicinity. Another important duty for the Home Guard was to help protect road and rail communications to ensure a smooth flow of troops through the area to the assembly points for the D Day landings. A new but short-lived menace occurred, following the D Day Invasion of 6th June 1944. This was Hitler's V1 Rocket, or flying bomb, whose buzzing flight above signalled terror. One recorded incident was when a V1 crashed at Scatterdells Woods in Chipperfield and another rocket destroyed a barn at Langley Lodge Farm in Kings Langley. Fortunately only a few such rockets fell locally, causing only minor casualties and little damage to property.

The Railway

The railway played a vital role during the conflict, helping to move essential supplies throughout the nation. The local line through the valley was part of the Midland and Scottish Railway which was co-ordinated from its wartime headquarters at the Grove, near Watford. During September 1939, 1,450 special trains evacuated half a million children from major cities into the country without a single casualty. Later in the war, over 200 special trains were run on six consecutive days from Liverpool and other ports, bringing in American service men and their equipment. Some of the airmen were destined for RAF Bovingdon. The climax of the railway's wartime effort were the D Day preparations when all previous records were exceeded as 25,000 trains were run to the south coast during the eleven weeks which preceded the Invasion of Europe.

CHRISTMAS FESTIVITIES
FOR
EVACUEE CHILDREN

It is on the generosity and goodwill of the public ot Berkhamsted and district that the success of this scheme will :—: depend. :—:

Please Send **YOUR** Contribution To-day

Forward to the Hon. Treasurer, Rotarian S. D. SHORTELL. Westminster Bank, Berkhamsted, or hand it in at any local Bank or to any member of the Rotary Club, of Berkhamsted.

The use of this space has been kindly granted by Messrs. Cooper, Mc Dougall and Robertson, Ltd.

Evacuees

The presence of evacuees made a considerable impact on the daily life of most towns and villages in the area. Plans had been drawn up in 1938 to move up to four million people in England, Wales and Scotland. As part of this effort, most of the communities in Dacorum were designated reception areas to receive evacuees from London. Initial surveys indicated that up to 6,777 rooms were available locally with accommodation for up to 2,405 people. The ARP Officer anticipated coping with a total of 7,400 people arriving at Hemel Hempstead Station, with 5000 of these to be placed in the Urban Area and a further 2,400 to be found homes in the Rural District. Berkhamsted Urban and Rural Districts expected to receive a further 2,466 children and adults. With so many children arriving, education was an important issue and a shift system was devised. This involved local children using school facilities in the morning and evacuee children occupying the buildings in the afternoon. By August 1939 the Government had decided to evacuate all expectant mothers from London, within one week of their confinement. It was estimated that 540 mothers would initially travel into Hertfordshire from the London County Council area. Three maternity homes were established locally at Home Farm, Tring, Grimsdyke in Berkhamsted, and at The Hoo in Great Gaddesden. The smaller villages were also playing their part in coping with the influx of evacuees, with the populations of Kings Langley and Little Gaddesden each swollen by several hundred. Chipperfield and Bovingdon also received 120 and 160 evacuees respectively. By Christmas 1939 the first wave of evacuation had subsided and during what became known as the 'Phoney War', over half the evacuees had returned to London by early 1940. The second phase of evacuation was prompted by the start of the London Blitz in 1940 and some of these evacuated children did not return home until 1942. Germany's fearsome bombing of the Capital had caused the population of Hertfordshire to increase by 150,000 in the space

of a few weeks. The final phase of evacuation, 2 years later, was prompted by the arrival overhead of the V1 flying bombs. Between June and September 1944, some 2000 Londoners were officially billeted in the Borough of Hemel Hempstead.

One of the leading organisations responsible for facilitating the evacuation was the Womens Voluntary Service (now the WRVS), which had been officially launched in June 1938. By 1945 membership of the service in Hemel Hempstead stood at around 1000 volunteers. All women, especially those under the age of 40, were expected to make a contribution to the war effort. In addition to helping war production in the local factories, another possible contribution was through agriculture. By June 1944 the Women's Land Army had become active, tending farms throughout the valley. Towards the end of the conflict, prisoners of war were also used to work the fields; Italians worked at Coxpond Farm in Hemel Hempstead, whilst there were Germans labouring on at least one farm in Gaddesden Row. There was also a camp for German prisoners of war on land between Whippendell Woods and the Grove, near Watford.

Industrial Production

The area's major employers were keen to make an industrial contribution to the war effort and they took on a large number of women to be trained in war work. Production continued round the clock, in both day and night shifts. Brocks, the Hemel Hempstead manufacturer of fireworks, switched their production facilities to signal rockets, parachute flares and Verey lights. Kent Brushes at Apsley made special hollow cased brushes designed to help with escape attempts by our prisoners of war. Production output was greatest at the Dickinson factories, where by 1938 large quantities of gas masks were already being assembled. As the conflict developed, Apsley Mills became a key wartime installation. As a result the factory was extensively camouflaged from both land and air and blacked out at a cost of £8,800. During the war Apsley produced a total of eighteen million bullets, seventeen million mortar shells and three thousand tons of 'window', which was an anti-radar product. Dickinsons also produced ten thousand disposable paper petrol tanks for long range fighter bomber attacks and manufactured many other tubes and containers for the range of explosives and munitions used in the fighting.

Airfields

Two large airfields were built locally as part of the Allied war effort against Nazi Germany. In 1940 the Ministry of Aircraft Production made land on Hunters Farm, near Hunton Bridge, the subject of a compulsory purchase order. A runway 150ft. wide was immediately constructed and two separate factory areas were built. In No.1 Factory the London Aircraft Production Group built two variants of the Halifax bomber and the total wartime output here was 450 of the Halifax II, with Rolls Royce Merlin XX engines and 260 of the Halifax B, powered by the Bristol Hercules radial engine. In No.2 Factory the de Havilland Aircraft Company formed the Second Aircraft Group to organise the manufacture of Mosquitos, which reached the staggering total of 1390 fighters completed by the end of the war. This war time production facility became known locally as Leavesden Aerodrome and later from 1966-92 it was home to the Small Engine Division of Rolls Royce employing over 3,500 people. Much more recently the now deserted factories and aerodrome were used as a principal location for the latest James Bond movie, Golden Eye, which starred Pierce Brosnan and was released in 1995.

Work on the much larger Bovingdon Airfield, built by John Laing & Son Ltd., began in 1941. This involved the construction of a main runway of 1500 metres and two further intersecting runways of 1300 metres. A perimeter track was also established at Bovingdon with 27 dispersal pans extending into Strawberry Woods, to the north. The new airfield's technical site and four hangers were in the south east corner, close to the village. In August the U.S. Air Force began to arrive to take over what was later to become U.S. Air Station 112. The first B17 Flying Fortresses flew in to Bovingdon from America on August 18th 1942. This incoming 92nd Bomb Group was part of the U.S. 8th Air Force and was commanded by Colonel Sutton. The B.17's first mission from Bovingdon was flown on 6th September 1942, with one plane lost on a bombing raid over a French aircraft factory. However Bovingdon's role as a combat air field was short lived, and it soon became the major training base for B.17 crews arriving in Europe from the U.S.A. When General Eisenhower was appointed Supreme Commander, his private plane was kept at Bovingdon. In December 1943 one Flying Fortress crashed and caught fire in Bourne Grove Wood, killing 10 flying personnel. In September 1944 the Combat Crew Replacement Centre was disbanded and the U.S. Air Transport Command (Europe) moved into Bovingdon. This was the organisation which was later to coordinate the G.I.'s return to America following V.E. Day. In October 1945, the first Super Fortress ever to be seen in Europe landed at Bovingdon. After the war in April 1946, Bovingdon Airfield reverted to the control of the RAF and it remained a service installation until the Ministry of Defence closed the Airfield in 1968.

Ashridge

Ashridge was commandeered on the outbreak of the War as an Emergency Hospital. Large huts were built on the open park land to the north and the first patients were 500 of the wounded brought in from the Dunkirk Landings in May 1940. However the majority of the 20,000 patients treated at Ashridge were civilians, transferred out from the London Hospitals of Charing Cross, University College and Queen Elizabeth. Over 12,000 operations were performed and 3,000 births were recorded at Ashridge between 1940 and 1946. At one time two wards were occupied by German prisoners of war, survivors of submarine warfare. In 1945 the last patients at Ashridge were our own returned prisoners of war who had been held in German camps and were all suffering from malnutrition. Further to the south, Leavesden Hospital was used as another Emergency Hospital which helped cope with French casualties from the D Day Landings.

The Ashridge estate, with its rich woodland, also provided cover for several large army camps, as well as the Home Guard, during the hostilities. The XIth Hussars and Highland Division were camped in readiness on the Ashridge estate; the XIth Dragoon Guards were at Hudnall, and Polish and Dutch army personnel were based near Ringshall. On 24th February 1945 General Eisenhower arrived on a visit to Ashridge, accompanied by General Montgomery. After the war Ashridge was restored to its trustees by the Ministry of Health in June 1946 and by 1951 the army hospital huts had become part of the Public Record Office. Records were kept here until 1978/79 when they were moved to Kew and these old buildings were finally demolished in 1980. This allowed the through road, past the front of Ashridge House, to be restored to its old pre-war route.

The End of the War

Preparations for the successful 'final push' of the D Day invasion caused a significant build up of troops in the district. In February 1944 General Montgomery had inspected troops who were assembled on the school playing fields at Berkhamsted. Shortly after this, King George VI paused to inspect troops lining the road in Boxmoor as he passed through the area. After D Day, the danger of Germany invading Britain disappeared and a stand down of the Home Guard started on 1st November 1944. A relaxation in the black out regulations had begun in September 1944 and there was also a reduction in the hours of duty required from the volunteer firemen and fire watchers. The Civil Defence Organisation officially ceased to be needed for purposes of war on Wednesday, 2nd May 1945. At 7.45 p.m. on Monday 7th May a news flash from the BBC proclaimed Victory in Europe and late that evening two days of national holiday were announced. Thanksgiving services were held and bells were rung at all the Parish Churches. In Berkhamsted a large Nazi flag was spread across the road for traffic and pedestrians to use as a carpet. Many street parties were organised for local children in all the towns and villages of the Gade and Bulbourne valleys. This round of celebrations lasted from the initial VE Day right through until the second weekend.

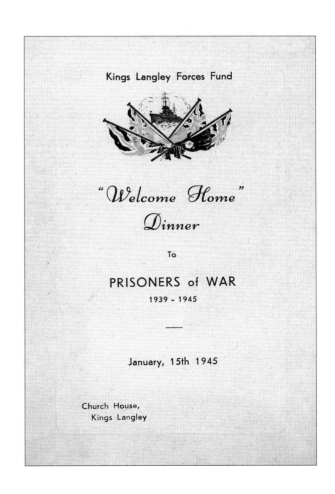

Kings Langley Forces Fund

"Welcome Home"
Dinner

To

PRISONERS of WAR

1939 - 1945

January, 15th 1945

Church House,
Kings Langley

Home Guard on the roof of Dickinson's Apsley Mill factory.

7th Platoon 'A' Company on guard at Apsley Mill.

Aircraft fuel tank production at Dickinson's.

Land Army girls at Water End.

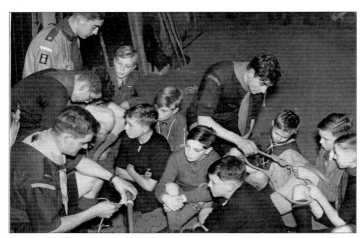

Kings Langley Scouts with London evacuees, 1959.

Bomb damage at Nash Mills, May 11th 1941.

Kings Langley Home Guard on parade in Love Lane, 1942.

General Eisenhower reviews the XIth Hussars at Ashridge in 1944.

Bomber crews at U.S.A.F. Bovingdon.

Bovingdon's P.C. Lord with American Military Police.

Mosquito workforce at Leavesden.

Mosquito production at Leavesden Aerodrome.

American Airmen host Christmas party for war-time orphans in 1943.

V.J. Day celebrations in Bedmond Village Hall, 1946.

New Town Development

One of the most urgent post war issues was to tackle the crisis of homelessness caused by the bombing of major cities, especially London. Lord Abercrombie had suggested in the Greater London Plan which was published in 1944, that several satellite towns should be built around the Capital. In this area, Redbourn was the initial choice for development, but soon rejected as unsuitable. In October 1945, there were already 1000 families in the Hemel Hempstead area who wanted a home. Hemel Hempstead was soon identified as an alternative location which it was thought could be later successfully re-developed to accommodate an influx of up to 30,000 Londoners. Initially there was considerable reluctance and some fear of such a drastic change being proposed for the locality. However by mid May 1946, the Hemel Hempstead Borough Council had proposed a resolution to allow for an expansion of the town's population from some 22,000 to 50,000 inhabitants. The Government moved quickly once this local decision had been taken and by the end of July 1946, it was officially announced that Hemel Hempstead was to be a New Town, under the New Towns Act. Its population was now set to increase from 20,000 to 60,000 in an identified area of 5,470 acres. Hemel Hempstead had now become the first and most important of the new towns which had earlier been specified in the Greater London Plan.

The plan was that this New Town would be developed in six distinct neighbourhoods and these initially were to be at Belswains, Adeyfield, the Redbourn Road, Gadebridge, Boxmoor and Felden. A brand new road system would also be built to provide easy access from these neighbourhoods into the town centre. The commercial trading area would be extended from the old High Street into a completely re-developed Marlowes. The early industrial areas which were already established at Nash Mills and Apsley, would now be joined by a brand new industrial estate at Cupid Green. The Development Corporation required to oversee the project was formally established under the Chairmanship of Lord Reith on March 6th 1947. In October 1946, G. A. Jellicoe had been appointed as General Planning Consultant and he produced a plan for the New Town which was available by June 1947.

These initial ideas were rather more ambitious than the subsequent reality. There were plans to redevelop some of the old High Street into secluded squares and terraces and the Marlowes was to be completely redesigned as a modern boulevard in the tradition of Princes Street, Edinburgh! The water gardens were a key feature of the plan, but a more complex early design foresaw the new Civic Centre constructed on an island in a lake created near to the Bury. Here the water's edge would also run up to the side of other splendid buildings such as an Art Gallery and Theatre. The 1947 plan also envisaged provision of an Assembly Hall and the removal of the West Herts. Hospital to an out of town site, so that its land could be used to house the New Town's Market. This first plan also specified the closure of both railway stations at Apsley and Boxmoor and their replacement with a new station at Two Waters. By 1948 the New Town Development Corporation had acquired the old Manor House at Westbrook Hay for use as its Offices. It had also secured the land required at Cupid Green to establish a camp for the construction workers. The original intention for the industrial area at Cupid Green was to allocate 200 acres, with an additional 100 acres held in reserve for expansion. The first plans for the industrial estate allowed for the provision of works canteens, playing fields and pavilions, with an adjacent sports stadium and arena for the town.

The construction contract which was awarded to Mowlem, began on March 1st 1948. An amended plan issued by the Minister of Town and Country Planning on August 25th 1949 reclassified the location of the new residential areas. These were now to be at Adeyfield, Apsley, Bennetts End, Boxmoor, Highfield, Leverstock Green and Warners End; with Chaulden being retained as a reserve area for later development if required. These seven designated neighbourhoods were each to have their own shopping centre and public buildings including junior and infant schools. There was also to be land left 'spare' to serve as public gardens, games and recreational areas, and allotments. Adeyfield was to be the largest of these developments, with a planned population of 10,500, whilst every effort was going to be made to retain the existing village atmosphere of Leverstock Green. The housing mix was carefully specified with property being of four basic types. Two of these types were to account for 90% of all the housing and, of these, approximately half were to be for sale and the rest were to be council housing for rental. One third of the houses were to have two bedrooms and just over half the housing stock would be provided with three. There was a detailed building programme established for the first five years with a further outline plan which covered the next fifteen years.

In 1949 work began on 415 houses, 14 shops and one school; the first factory was also built in the new industrial area for the Hemel Hempstead Engineering Company. By 1951, 292 houses had been finished and a further 54 were under construction; the Primary School at Adeyfield was open and its shopping centre was nearly completed. In the industrial area, the Central Tool and Equipment Company Ltd. now occupied their new 16,000 sq.ft. factory and, close by, a much larger factory of 92,000 sq.ft. was already under construction for Alford and Adler. Five miles of new roads had already been provided and work on a further 12 miles of sewers was well underway. Progress in the building work was accelerating rapidly and, by the end of 1951, the set target of 750 houses had been exceeded; the 1000th new house was completed in Hemel Hempstead on 23rd April 1952. In that year the industrial estate also began to take shape with the completion of new premises for major concerns such as Multicore Solders, London Ferro-Concrete, Rolls Royce, Addressograph-Multigraph and Rotax. By now the Development Corporation had made a film called 'Home of Your Own', which was first shown at the Festival of Britain and later at over 250 cinemas in the Greater London area. On Sunday July 20th 1952, Her Majesty Queen Elizabeth II visited Hemel Hempstead. She toured the industrial area, Bennetts End and Adeyfield, where she laid the foundation stone for St. Barnabas Church. Permission was later sought and granted to name the shopping centre at Adeyfield the 'Queens Square' to commemorate this Royal visit. By June 1952, the Development Corporation were able to state that three new families were moving into Hemel Hempstead every day and there were already between 6-7,000 new inhabitants.

Two years later Adeyfield had been completed and the average daily intake for the town had now risen to 10 new inhabitants. The total growth to date, of some eleven thousand new inhabitants, was approximately one quarter of the final number. By 1954 the first new shops had opened in the

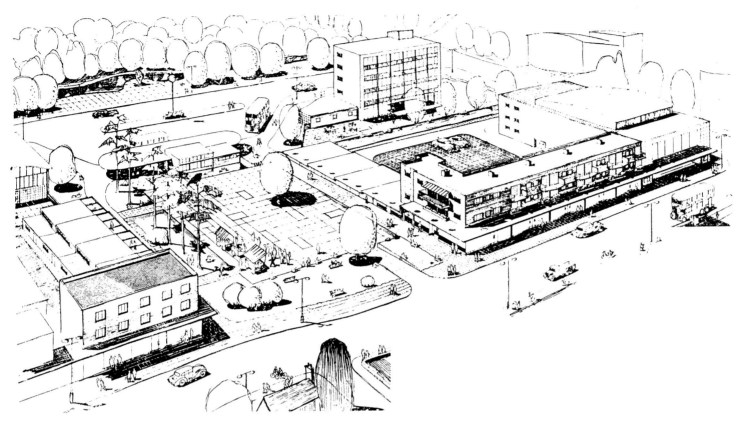

New town plans for remodelled town centre, 1952.

Marlowes and the town's main market was now established there. The total population of Hemel Hempstead had risen to 38,000 and 22 new factories, with a combined floor area of 700,000 sq.ft., had already created some 4000 new jobs locally. There were already 55 shops in the various neighbourhoods and a further 100 were either established or under construction in the Marlowes. During 1957 the Ministry announced that new development at Hemel Hempstead would continue until the resident population had reached 60,000. Importantly the line of the M1 motorway had now been agreed and this would provide a modern high speed link for Hemel Hempstead to both London and the North. Encouraged by this, a further industrial area was established in the north eastern section of the town, ready to accommodate major new commercial arrivals such as Atlas Copco and Kodak Ltd. Kodak first came to Hemel Hempstead in 1957, when they moved their Colour Processing Plant from Harrow to new premises in Maylands Avenue. No doubt encouraged by the presence of the M1 Motorway, built in 1959, the company then established a major Distribution Department at Swallowdale. At the peak of its operations, Kodak's Colour Processing Plant offered employment to around 1700 local people.

The New Towns Act was passed in 1959. This was designed to lead to the eventual disbanding of the Development Corporation, with its powers and responsibilities given to the New Towns Commission. It was the Government's intention that this Commission would also plan for the development of several other new towns. In 1959 the viaduct, which carried the Nicky railway line over the southern end of the Marlowes, was removed and the foundation stone of the new Odeon Cinema was laid by the famous film actress Lauren Bacall.

The last report of the Development Corporation was published in 1962 and it revealed that the social mix of the New Town had been carefully and successfully planned. By 1960 the percentage of the New Town's population involved in either skilled, professional or intermediate occupations was already above the national average. The corresponding proportion of unskilled labour at Hemel Hempstead was already smaller than in most equivalent sized communities. The enlarged Plough roundabout, at the southern end of the Marlowes, had been completed by 1962 and Dacorum College of Further Education was built between 1961-63. The Odeon Cinema, with seats for an audience of over 1100 people, had already opened in August 1960 and architects Clifford Culpin and Partners had designed the new Civic Centre which was constructed between 1962-66. On the front of the building a roundel can still be seen showing a bas-relief of Henry VIII to commemorate the award of a Royal Charter in 1539. The famous Water Gardens were finally constructed in 1962-63, to an amended design by G. A. Jellicoe. Between 1961-63 B.P. House was constructed, featuring an unusual linear office block. This spanned the Marlowes and allowed traffic coming into the town from the Plough roundabout to flow beneath it. This building subsequently suffered serious structural problems which required its demolition in the winter of 1988/89. In 1962 the Development Corporation was finally replaced by the Commission for New Towns. Development continued, but was now fuelled by natural growth, rather than artificially planned expansion. Homes in the Grove Hill area were being occupied by 1967, but building work was not completed there until 1977. The role of the Commission was now more a supervisory one as landlord of a housing stock of nearly 10,000 houses, featuring up to 200 different designs.

Considerable care was taken to provide a variety of houses and flats, which were constructed using different materials to avoid monotony. Each new neighbourhood enjoyed its own unique design and layout, with plenty of open space provided to help keep each community distinct from the next.

One principal effect of the New Town development had been the transformation of the Marlowes which, before the war, had been a poorer and rather shabby part of Hemel Hempstead. There were already quite a number of old shop premises in the Marlowes, but they were swept away as the road was widened and new outlets were created by the Development Corporation. One survivor of this change was the town's post office, which was built in the 1930's and retained its charm until a modernisation in 1988. Another significant development in Hemel Hempstead was the construction in 1971 of the impressive skyscraper to serve as offices and national headquarters of Kodak Ltd. Built at a cost of £4.4 million, this new office block has accommodation for up to 1000 employees. In April 1973, close by this new office block, the town's Plough roundabout became known locally as the 'magic roundabout'. This was when it was selected as one of several experimental roundabouts established around the country by the Road Research Laboratory. This unusual system, which today uniquely survives in Hemel Hempstead, provides a series of mini-roundabouts which allow for a more efficient two-way flow around the main central roundabout. The increasing number of functions required of the Borough Council, together with the creation of the Dacorum District Council in the local government re-organisation of 1974 necessitated extension work to the Civic Centre which began in 1981. A major overhaul of the Marlowes, focused around the provision of a

brand new Shopping Mall was announced in 1987. This impressive upgrading of the town centre's facilities, which included the pedestrianisation of the Marlowes, was completed in 1990.

Whilst the architecture of Hemel Hempstead New Town may be modern, the fine history of this old community is still celebrated in some of the names used in the town centre. The King Harry pub, by the bus station, recalls the town's Tudor patron, Henry VIII. Waterhouse Street remembers Thomas Waterhouse, the King's favourite priest and last Rector of the Monastery at Ashridge, whilst Combe Street reminds us of Thomas Waterhouse's brother-in-law, Richard Combe, who succeeded him at the Bury in 1540. The post-war creation of Hemel Hempstead New Town is an obvious success of economic and social planning. The continuing development of Hemel Hempstead with its excellent transport links, the prosperity of its current population of 79,463 and the variety of opportunities offered by major industrial employers, such as B.P. and Kodak, all offer evidence that this town will continue to thrive in the Twenty-First Century.

View of the Marlowes, 1912.

Marlowes showing Nicky Line bridge, demolished 1959.

The Cotterells in the 1950's.

Plough roundabout showing the War Memorial in its original position in the 1950's.

New Town house construction, 1950.

Queen Elizabeth II visits Adeyfield, July 20th 1952.

New Town industrial estate.

Queens Square in Adeyfield, newly completed.

The Water Gardens looking north, 1971.

View of the Marlowes, 1971.

View of BP House, 1971.

View of the Kodak building, 1991.

Cassiobury

Cassiobury was the family seat of the Earls of Essex for over 250 years (1668-1922). In 1546 Cassio was granted by the Crown to Sir Richard Morison, who began building a Manor House which was completed by his son Charles. By December 1559, an inventory specifies an extensive property of 56 rooms and out-buildings. Lady Bridget, widow of Sir Richard Morison, was responsible for the building of the Essex Chapel in the Parish Church of St. Mary, Watford, which holds the tomb of her husband. In 1580 Charles Morison acquired the Manor of Kings Langley and he also maintained a house there, close to the former Royal Palace. Some ruins of this structure still remain in the front garden of a house on Langley Hill. The only surviving child of Sir Charles Morison was Elizabeth, who married Arthur Capel in November 1627. In his will of 1633, he left the bulk of his estate to her and their son Arthur. This effectively severed the link between the Morisons and Cassiobury and began the tenure of the Capel family.

Arthur Capel, who as a loyal supporter of Charles I was beheaded on 9th March 1649, had always preferred his own seat in Hadham Hall, near Bishop Stortford. Consequently, Lady Capel and her family lived on at Hadham until the restoration of Charles II in 1660. In 1661 Arthur Capel, eldest son and heir to the Capel estate, was awarded the title of Viscount Malden and Earl of Essex by the King and in 1668 he moved his family seat to Cassiobury. Between 1674 and 1680, the house was extensively re-built by Hugh May, architect to Charles II, with only the west wing of the original Morison house retained. The gardens were also laid out in a spectacular formal style, identical to those at the Palace of Versailles. Cassiobury was visited by Elizabeth I, who planted an oak tree by the main drive, half way between the lodge and the mansion.

Algernon, the 2nd Earl of Essex (1657-1710), was succeeded by his eldest son William (1697-1743). The 3rd Earl was Gentleman of the Bedchamber to George II when he was Prince of Wales. He later became Knight Companion of the Garter, a member of the Privy Council and Keeper of St. James and Hyde Parks for the King. By this time the Capel family had become leading members of the nation's aristocracy and the 4th Earl, served as Lord Lieutenant of Hertfordshire and one of the Lords of the Bedchamber to George II.

George Capel Coningsby (1757-1839), the 5th Earl, was chosen as M.P. for Westminster in 1779. He was a staunch Whig supporter and Member of Parliament for various constituencies throughout his Parliamentary career. In 1805 he commissioned the noted architect James Wyatt, who was also involved at both Ashridge and Gaddesden Place, to re-model Cassiobury. Wyatt retained ten reception rooms of the old house, demolishing two front wings of the 'H' shaped structure and adding portions of his own to enclose a courtyard. Humphrey Repton was commissioned to re-plan the grounds in 1800. The lavish interiors at Cassiobury featured spectacular carvings by Grindling Gibbons, the most notable of which was the grand staircase. By the Twentieth Century this was the only surviving example of a significant staircase by Gibbons and when the house was dismantled in the 1920's, it was sold at auction to an American and is now in the Metropolitan Museum of New York. During this period several lodge houses were built on the estate, the prettiest of which was Swiss Cottage, for many years home to the daughters of the 6th Earl.

The 6th Earl, Arthur Algernon, was the eldest son of the 5th Earl's half-brother and he succeeded in 1839. Cassiobury was used by Queen Adelaide as her Royal residence from 1846-48 and subsequent monarchs, Queen Victoria and King Edward VII, both paid regular visits to the Earls of Essex. Arthur Algernon re-assumed the old spelling of the family name, Capell and in 1892 was himself succeeded by George Devereux de Vere. The Capel family has an impressive tradition as patron of the arts and has owned many important paintings. The 1st Earl's collection of 34 pictures included work by Van Dyck and the famous Kit Kat series by Sir Peter Lely includes a portrait of the 2nd Earl of Essex. The 4th Earl commissioned portraits by Thomas Gainsborough and Sir Joshua Reynolds, while the 5th Earl was an exceptional patron who owned works by Hogarth, Henry Edridge, Henry Hunt, Sir Edwin Landseer and not least J.M.V. Turner. In 1893 Christies of London sold nine pictures owned by the family, which included a Landseer and three Turners for the sum of 15,670 guineas. Another sale of some of the family's porcelain and furniture raised a further £24,402.

The 7th Earl was Aide de camp to the King, and Vice Lieutenant of Hertfordshire. He had one son, Algernon George de Vere, who succeeded as the 8th Earl on his death in 1916. The 7th Earls second wife, Adele, was dowager Countess of Essex in June 1922 when the house at Cassiobury was sold. Earlier in 1908 and 1912, parts of the park had been purchased by Watford Borough Council and sadly the old house itself was demolished in 1927. Most other reminders of the great estate; the Swiss Cottage, the Mill, the Essex Alms-houses and the Park Gates no longer survive. Only one small lodge house, Cassiobury Cottage, remains together with 'Little Cassiobury' which stands behind the Town Hall on the Hempstead Road. Russells, a more substantial dower house of the Essex estate, built in 1718, also still survives as a home for the elderly. It was here that the mother of the 3rd Earl of Essex and her unmarried daughters lived out their lives. Russells was later home to Maharajah Gaekwar of Baroda, during his pre-war visits to England. In 1932 a further 261 acres of Cassiobury estate land were bought by the Watford Borough Council and leased to the West Herts Golf Club. This land, together with the public park at Whippendell Woods, is all now owned by the town and remains the outstanding legacy of the Earls of Essex to the town of Watford.

Carved staircase by Grindling Gibbons.

An engraving of Cassiobury viewed from the south-west, 1837.

The Great Library at Cassiobury.

Swiss Cottage.

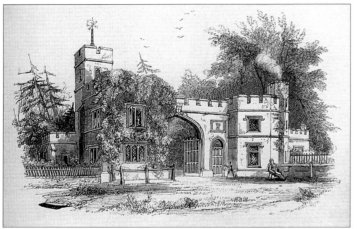

Entrance lodge and gates to the Cassiobury estate.

Cassiobury viewed from the south-west.

Cassiobury, prior to the First World War.

Gates to Cassiobury Park, 1957.

Cassiobury Mill.

8th Earl of Essex.

Essex Almshouses.

The town of Watford celebrates the marriage of the 8th Earl of Essex, 1893.

Swiss Cottage, 1916.

View of Cassiobury from the canal, circa 1914.

The Grove

The house known as the Grove was the family seat of the Earls of Clarendon for two hundred years (1735-1935). There was a house on the site as early as 1400, when John Heydon "owned that part of the Manor of Cassiobury which is known as the Grove". The estate stayed in the Heydon family until 1602 when Francis Heydon, who was then High Sheriff of Hertfordshire, conveyed it to Sir Clement Scudamore.

At the beginning of the Eighteenth Century, the Grove Estate was in the possession of Arthur Mohan St Ledger, the 3rd Lord Doneraile. Eventually in 1753 it was sold by trustees of his cousin, Elizabeth St Ledger, to the Hon. Thomas Villiers, second son of the Earl of Jersey, who became Earl of Clarendon in 1776. The very first Earl of Clarendon, Edward Hyde (1608-1674), was an ardent Royalist who had been made Lord Chancellor by King Charles in 1658 and later became the King's Chief Advisor following the Restoration. The title of Clarendon remained in the Hyde family until 1753 when the 4th Earl died. Because the 4th Earl's son had died as a young man in Paris, the title could not be passed on.

Thomas Villiers, the purchaser of the Grove, had married the heiress of the Hyde family and initially held the title Baron Hyde of Hindon. However in 1776, in recognition of his diplomatic work in Dresden, Vienna and Berlin, he was raised to the dignity of the Earl of Clarendon and the family crest became the Eagle of Prussia. Thomas Villiers commissioned an architect, likely to have been Matthew Brettingham, to build a new house for him on the Grove estate in 1756. This initial structure was subsequently enlarged in 1780 and 1786. Further additions and enlargements to the house were made in 1875 by architect Edmund Blore (1787-1879) who created the house we know today. A Lodge was provided on the Hempstead Road and in the Nineteenth Century, the main drive to the house ran from Grove Mill Lane, due south of the main entrance. The picturesque canal bridge built circa 1795 is itself Grade 2 listed.

Following the death of the First Earl in 1786, the Grove was inherited by Thomas Villiers (2nd Earl born 1753). He produced no heir and on his death the title passed to his brother, the 3rd Earl, John Charles Villiers (1757-1838). John Charles Villiers had been made King's Consul in the Duchy of Lancaster by his father, who was Chancellor of the Duchy, and also sat in Parliament from 1790-1802 as M.P. for Portsmouth. George III, his Queen and Court were regular visitors at the Grove during the latter part of the Eighteenth Century. The 4th Earl, George William Frederick Villiers (1800-1875) enjoyed an outstanding political career. He served as Lord Lieutenant of Ireland and was awarded the Order of the Garter and the Insignia of the Bath by Queen Victoria. He also held the position of Foreign Secretary three times serving between 1853-58, 1865-66 and 1868-70.

During the time of the 4th Earl, the Grove became one of the most fashionable houses in the country and lavish weekend parties catered to the best of London society. In December 1827, the Duke of Wellington stayed at the Grove as a house guest. A large domestic staff, which then included four 'figure footmen', tended to the needs of the family and their guests. At this time the gardens were also some of the finest in the country. At the Grove there was a walled garden of four acres, along one wall of which ran the extensive greenhouses, which were used for growing grapes, nectarines, figs and other exotic fruits. On the death of his father, Edward Hyde became the 5th Earl of Clarendon. Edward Hyde served as ADC to Queen Victoria and later to King Edward VII who visited him at the Grove in 1909. He also served as Lord Chamberlain 1900-1905. There is a monument to the 5th Earl in the woods near the gardens of the Grove.

The 6th Earl, George Herbert Hyde Villiers (1877-1955), enjoyed a highly distinguished career. He was Chief Government Whip in the House of Lords from 1922-25 and Chairman of the BBC from 1927-30. George Herbert was made Governor General of South Africa 1931-39 and following this he was honoured as Knight of the Garter. He was subsequently made Lord Chamberlain and served in this capacity at the funeral of King George VI. Of more local interest, the 6th Earl was also the first 'Charter' Mayor of Watford 1922-23. In 1922 the 6th Earl vacated the Grove and moved to Hampstead in London.

The Inner Library at the Grove.

The Grove in the 1950's.

Ornamental bridge at the Grove, 1928.

6th Earl of Clarendon.

Rare photograph of the Grove in the 1880's.

ARMS OF THE EARLS OF CLARENDON.*

At first the house remained in the ownership of the Clarendons and during this time it first became a gardening school and then a hotel and health centre rather grandly known as 'The National Institute of Nutrition and College of Dietetics' or 'The London Spa'. Following this, the Grove also enjoyed a brief spell as a girls boarding school. When the Grove was finally put up for sale, 'The Times' lamented "the passing of one of the great political houses of the Nineteenth Century". The house was first owned by 'Equity and Law Life Assurance' from whom it was purchased by the London, Midland and Scottish Railway Company in May 1939. The purchase remained subject to protecting a right of way to the Clarendon family vault.

Under the code name 'Project X', the Grove was speedily converted into the war time operational headquarters of Britain's largest railway company. By 4th September 1939, three thousand staff were at work at the Grove, many in temporary huts in the grounds. The strategic importance of war time work at the Grove is difficult to over-estimate, given that it involved the planning of the nation-wide movement of vital supplies under the constant threat of attack from enemy aircraft. Concrete air raid shelters were built and, following 'Dunkirk' when the threat of invasion seemed most likely, the Grove was constantly patrolled by the Home Guard with loaded rifles.

Following the war most of the LMS staff moved back to Euston House and, following nationalisation of the railways in 1948, the Grove came under the control of the British Transport Commission. In 1957 it became their Work Study Training Centre and reverted to railway ownership when the British Railways Board was formed. To the west of the estate, behind the house, the Civil Engineering Training Centre was set up in 1968. By the mid 1970's the need for centralised work study and computer training courses had ebbed within the organisation, and the Grove became a Management Training Centre. Only recently this year, the house has been sold to the Hotel Group who already own the exclusive Athenaeum Club in Piccadilly. If full planning permissions are granted, this company hope to redevelop the property into a luxury hotel with conference facilities and its own golf course.

The Grove in 1861.

Langleybury

The estate of Langleybury dates back to 1545 when Henry VIII granted it to Sir Richard Lee, one of his most distinguished and loyal military commanders. In 1575 Sir Richard sold Langleybury back to Elizabeth I and it remained in the Sovereign's ownership until 1616. James I then allowed the first Prince Charles the use of the estate under the care of several trustees, which included Francis Bacon. When Prince Charles became King Charles I, he instructed these trustees to convey the Manor of Langleybury to Thomas Child in 1626, and the Child family then remained in occupation until 1711.

The next owner of the Langleybury Estate was Sir Robert Raymond, who commissioned the building of the impressive Georgian structure which survives today. It is thought that this mansion house was built over the demolished remains of the earlier Manor House and farm buildings. Sir Robert Raymond, a lawyer, was a leading figure of his day who benefited from a close friendship with Sir Robert Walpole, England's first Prime Minister. Raymond's political career flourished and he was first appointed Solicitor-General before becoming Attorney-General. Sir Robert served as Lord Chief Justice of England 1724-32 and was made Baron Raymond in 1731. A large and impressive marble memorial to Robert Raymond can still be found in St. Lawrence Parish Church at Abbots Langley.

The 2nd Baron Raymond died childless and the house and estate passed to a Kent family, the Filmers, in 1756. Although the Filmer family owned the house for 82 years, they did not often live at Langleybury and leased the house to a succession of residents. From a local perspective, the most notable member of this family was Sir John Filmer who was appointed Vicar of St. Lawrence, Abbots Langley in 1785. Although John Filmer left the area in 1810 when he became a 7th Baronet, a charity was founded in his will of 1834 which left £100 in trust to the Vicar and Churchwardens for the poor of the Parish.

Early engraving of Langleybury House.

In 1836 the house and some 600 acres of land at Langleybury were sold to Edmund Fearnley Whittingstall, a leading brewer based in Watford. He in turn passed the property to a London banker, William Jones Loyd in 1856. W. J. Loyd then substantially renovated what was a typical early Georgian house. He reversed the alignment of the building, so that what had been the rear of the house became, instead, the front entrance. He also added large porches and bay windows which somewhat detracted from the classic simplicity of the original Georgian design. At this time the interior of the house was also completely gutted and replaced with Victorian features, some of which survive to this day.

Arms of Baron Raymond.

W. J. Loyd then settled down to become the local squire of the area, in the great Victorian tradition. His house, estate and farmlands were the principal employer in the area and he readily accepted paternal responsibility for the population in the hamlet of Hunton Bridge. In 1858 he built St. Paul's, a small infant and girls school, at his own expense and this building still survives as the carefully restored offices of the architects Wakelin Associates. He followed this act of charity by commissioning the construction of St. Paul's Church in 1864, built by George Myers and Sons of Lambeth, to a design by the architect Mr. Woodham.

St. Paul's is a small but impressive church, whose principal feature is an oak shingled spire which is 130ft. high. W. J. Loyd (born 1821) is buried in the churchyard of St. Paul's and his grave is marked by a large marble cross which was carved by the Florentine sculptor Romanelli. The churchyard at Langleybury also houses an impressive tomb belonging to Ocean and Forest, the unusually named sons of the intrepid writer and explorer Violet Olivia Cressy-Marcks who, as Mrs. Fisher, lived at Hazelwood House from 1932-70. (see page 96). The bell tower of St. Paul's at Langleybury houses a fine ship's bell which was taken from a convent during the Crimean War. This was presented to the church by Lord Rokeby of Hazelwood House.

The last and longest owner occupier at Langleybury House was the second son of W. J. Loyd. This was E. Henry Loyd, who inherited the house in 1885. Henry Loyd continued his father's tradition of benefaction and support to the village of Hunton Bridge. When he died in 1938 his coffin was carried, by eight of his employees, through the grounds of Langleybury House to the funeral service at St. Paul's and the entire community came to pay their respects.

On the death of E. H. Loyd, the property of Langleybury then passed to his eldest son, William Lewis Brownlow Loyd. During the Second World War he allowed the house to be leased to the Equity and Law Insurance Company. In 1947 Langleybury was finally sold to Hertfordshire County Council who used the house and grounds to establish Langleybury Secondary School, which opened in September 1949. A feature of Langleybury is the School Farm which is still an important public attraction and currently enjoys some 8,000 visitors a year.

Portrait of E.H. Loyd.

Langleybury in the Nineteenth Century.

Langleybury Mansion, 1897.

St. Paul's Churchyard, 1990.

Hunton Bridge

In the Fourteenth Century, the small hamlet of Hunton Bridge stood at the southern end of a lush wooded river valley. This part of the valley was used as a Royal hunting park and estate by the Plantagenet Kings who were resident at the nearby Royal Palace which had been built in Kings Langley for Edward I in 1276. The Anglo-Saxon 'Hunta-tun' means 'town of hunters', whilst the bridge which gives Hunton Bridge its name would have been built as an early crossing point over the River Gade. This Royal hunting connection survived unbroken into the Seventeenth Century when Prince Charles, later King Charles I, was Lord of the Langleybury estates. It is said that the hunting lodge used by Prince Charles stood where today we find the King's Lodge licensed restaurant. To support this claim, a room in the building does have a fireplace with the date 1642 and the Royal Arms set in plaster above it.

View of the railway bridge at Hunton Bridge, 1840.

The original bridge at Hunton Bridge, which would have been a wooden ford, was rebuilt in brick by local bricklayer Luke Lewin of Abbots Langley. The Sparrows Herne Turnpike Trust paid for its construction. Following a fatal stagecoach accident, caused by the severe camber of the bridge, the wall of the bridge was altered in 1808. The bridge was subsequently re-built in 1904, and again in 1922 with reinforced concrete. The other important bridge in the village is the railway bridge, which was erected in 1836 by the London and Birmingham Railway Company.

Hunton Bridge has always occupied a strategically important location at the southern entrance to the Gade valley. As late as the Seventeenth Century, the valley's through traffic was made to divert its journey through Hunton Bridge to avoid trespassing in the Royal parklands. In these early days the hamlet of Hunton Bridge was also a crossing point on the route which linked St. Albans to Rickmansworth. It is easy to imagine that all this passing traffic brought bustling trade to the tiny hamlet of Hunton Bridge which grew up round its old corn mill on the River Gade. This early economic activity increased when a wharf was built to cope with the additional commercial traffic brought by the Grand Junction Canal from the turn of the Nineteenth Century.

The mill at Hunton Bridge was owned by Sir Richard Lee in

1544. The firm of Puttnams, who also kept the mill in Grove Mill Lane, operated flour mills here into the 1920's. During the Second World War, the mill at Hunton Bridge was used as a small munitions factory, although after the war the building became dangerously derelict and so was pulled down. Only the waterway from the canal and the old water wheel remain from the mill itself, although an impressive mill house still survives. Though much altered, the mill house is over 200 years old and was home to Sir Roland Hodge during the 1930's. It still has highly attractive landscaped gardens running down to the canal.

The most important of the Hunton Bridge public houses is the Kings Head, because it was the local Posting Inn during the stagecoach era of the Eighteenth Century. During the Nineteenth Century, successive landlords of the Kings Head also managed the commercial business generated by the Hunton Bridge wharf. Obadiah Oldfield was landlord of the Kings Head 1832-46 and in 1839 he is also listed as the local coal merchant and butcher. Coal was sent down on the canal from Midlands coalfields in Leicestershire and Warwickshire. In addition to coal, Hunton Bridge wharf also handled timber and building materials dispatched from Watford and London.

Beyond the Kings Head is the local hall, known as the 'Village Institute'. This was formerly called Ivy House and was converted into a large hall with a public bathroom; from 1914 it was also used as a Sunday School. Hunton Bridge's former Baptist Chapel, built in 1851, is now home to Chapel Studios, a stained glass workshop established by Alfred Fisher. Opposite the Baptist Chapel is a substantial Nineteenth Century house which used to have extensive gardens. This was known as 'The Limes' and was home to Ada and Lilian Bickersteth, ladies of considerable means who enjoyed a position of importance in the local community between 1910 and 1940. It was the Bickersteths who financed the construction of the Village Hall and also provided three pairs of 'cottages for the needy' in Old Mill Road. Now known as Brookside, these houses are still managed by the Hunton Bridge Cottage Trust. During the first half of this century, the local Hunt, led by Mr. and Mrs. Barrat of Great Westwood House, used to meet regularly under the chestnut trees of The Limes. This house, which was later owned by the Taylor Walker Brewery, was used as a Home Guard School and canteen during the Second World War. In 1960 the buildings were used by Grants of St. James, the wine and spirit merchants, before becoming the property of Ind Coope Breweries. In 1974 Ind Coope were absorbed into the major firm of local brewers Benskins, Watford.

The Farriers Arms, demolished in 1965, stood next to the general store at the corner with Old Mill Road. The village forge stood next to the Farriers Arms and this later became the site for a taxi business and Garage, established by Jim Quelch in 1919. Beyond the forge, next to the Dog and Partridge, on old Mill Road, was the Hunton Bridge Stores run by Mr. G. Roberts from 1919-1940. This stood here, together with a small sub-post office, kept by Frank Young from 1924. Another historic pub in the village, the Maltsters, was used to house German prisoners of war during the First World War. The Maltsters was adjoined either side by two Seventeenth Century cottages and stood close to the entrance to the Ind Coope Brewery distribution yard. There was a large malt-house to the rear of the Inn, but all these structures were pulled down when the Maltsters was demolished in 1963.

Hunton Bridge village in the 1920's.

Hunton Bridge Stores in the 1930's.

The Maltsters Arms, 1916, also showing the Farriers Arms (right).

The Maltsters Arms in the 1950's.

View of cottages and Baptist Chapel from the canal bridge, circa 1910.

Looking towards the Kings Head, 1919.

Hunton Bridge post office and baker's store in the 1920's.

Old Mill Road showing the Dog and Partridge, circa 1920.

Hunton Bridge Mill, 1890.

Hunton Bridge, 1904.

Hunton Bridge Mill.

Hunton Bridge Wharf, circa 1925.

Lady Capel's road bridge approaching Hunton Bridge, circa 1924.

Riverside cottages in Old Mill Road.

Hunton Bridge petrol station in the 1920's.

Hazelwood

Hidden away behind Hunton Bridge, towards the bottom of Southway, one magnificent mansion still graces the local area. In 1812 Henry Botham arrived in Abbots Langley, determined to build an impressive country seat for himself. The estate he purchased was initially 42 acres which he subsequently extended to 72 acres by securing some of the adjacent land from the Earl of Essex. Henry Botham's widow, Lydia, then bequeathed Hazelwood to one of her nephews, Samuel George Gambier. He promptly sold it to another nephew Henry Robinson Montagu.

In 1847 Henry Montagu became a very wealthy man when he inherited over 5,000 acres of land and the title of 6th Baron Rokeby. At this time he enjoyed an annual income of £9,000 and employed a domestic staff of 21 at Hazelwood. Lord Rokeby was a professional soldier who had fought as a 16 year old ensign at the Battle of Waterloo. By 1854 a distinguished military career had seen him rise to the rank of Major General, fighting at the Battle of Sebastopol in the Crimean War. He was subsequently decorated by the Monarchs of three allied powers.

Henry Montagu, 6th Baron Rokeby.

Following the death of his wife in 1868, he spent his declining years with his daughter Elizabeth, improving the Hazelwood estate and laying out the impressive gardens. Lord Rokeby died in 1886. After his death, the house belonged to Admiral Ralph Cator for the next ten years, before he was succeeded at Hazelwood by the Rev. Henry Stuart Gladstone, a relation of the famous politician. At first the Rev. Gladstone leased out the house to various members of the London aristocracy, until in 1907 he decided to live there himself. He spent over £1000 on renovations only to see the house destroyed by a huge fire on the 8th March 1908. Ironically, given the Prudential's current ownership of Hazelwood, he collected a handsome insurance payment of £10,500 and immediately set about re-building the house. The second Hazelwood was very similar to the first house, but it was now set at a slightly different and improved angle to the ornamental grounds.

In 1930 Hazelwood was sold to Violet Olivia Cressy-Marcks who was virtually unique, at the time, as an intrepid female explorer. In 1932 she married Mr. Francis Fisher, a meat wholesaler from Watford. As Mrs. Fisher, she was employed by the Daily Express as their special war correspondent and she later became the first English person to be allowed an audience with Mao Tse Tung at the Chinese war front. Emperor Haile Selassie of Ethiopia lived in some secrecy, as a war time exile, at Hazelwood, following the Italian invasion of his country in 1935.

During the Second World War some of the lands of the Hazelwood Estate were taken over by the Ministry of Defence for aircraft manufacture. This wartime work created the factories and airstrip of Leavesden Aerodrome which was later to become the famous Rolls Royce plant for small aero engines. Much of the rest of Hazelwood's lands were used for the Hillside Estate, part of a massive council house building programme in Abbots Langley during the 1950's. Following the death of Mrs. Fisher in 1970, the house became rather run down and during this time was owned by a property company and used regularly for film location work. The major feature film, 'Raging Moon' directed by Brian Forbes, used the house as its principal location. Sam Wanamaker shot a film called 'The Executioner' at Hazelwood, starring Joan Collins and George Peppard. Hammer Productions also regularly used the house to film some of their popular horror movies.

In 1979 the house was sold to the 'Dexion' group of companies and became their corporate headquarters. In 1986 Hazelwood was acquired from Dexion by Prudential Assurance who began a careful two year programme of restoration and additional building work. Today Hazelwood has become the impressive Hunton Park Prudential Management Centre, set in its own attractive grounds of 22 acres. The centre is run by a management team led by Director, Mr. Clive Peacock and currently grounds staff are working to restore some of the original garden features of the former Hazelwood House.

Mrs. Fisher, née Violet Olivia Cressy-Marcks.

Mrs. Fisher meets Mao Tse Tung.

The tomb of Ocean and Forest, sons of Mrs. Fisher.

Hazelwood House and gardens before the fire of 1908.

Hazelwood House after the fire of 1908.

Morgan rally at Hunton Park Management Centre, June 1994.

As its name suggests, the early development and prosperity of Abbots Langley is inextricably linked to the wealth and political power of the monastery, established at nearby St. Albans in the Eight Century. One surviving manuscript of the monastery, written in the Thirteenth Century by monk Matthew Paris, tells us that "in 1045 Ethelwine the Black, a Saxon, and his wife, Wynfleda, have given 'Langelei' forever to the Abbot and the monks of St. Albans". The word 'langelei' denotes a long meadow or clearing. In the wake of the Norman invasion, Paul de Caen, became Abbot of St. Albans. Over the next hundred years, the position of Abbot of St. Albans soon developed to the point where his influence and power was rivalled only by the Monarch himself. The agricultural community of Abbots Langley prospered, encouraged by his important patronage, until the Reformation in 1539. At this time the monastery at St. Albans was torn down by Henry VIII, with only the nave of the Abbey Church surviving. Abbots Langley became one of the many manors awarded by the King to his distinguished military commander, Sir Richard Lee.

Parish Church of St. Lawrence, Abbots Langley.

The Parish Church of St. Lawrence

The Parish Church of St. Lawrence the Martyr dates from the Twelfth Century being dedicated to St. Lawrence in 1154. Domesday records tell us that there was a resident priest in Abbots Langley, so it is quite likely that a Saxon church preceded the Norman building. However the oldest parts of the building are the fine Norman arches of the north and south arcades. The church tower was also built in the Twelfth Century and is now supported by two large, but unequal buttresses, which are Fifteenth Century additions. The top of the 60ft. tower was once adorned by a short spire or 'Hertfordshire spike' which was removed in 1853. The tower's embattled surround was replaced with brick in 1935. The six bells in the tower date from 1734, though some have since been re-cast. Prior to a disastrous fire in 1969, the entire roof of the church was over 500 years old. The corbels of St. Lawrence depict friars in grotesque attitudes and the church boasts an outstanding example of a Fourteenth Century stone font.

There is a surviving fragment of English glass, showing the patron saint St. Lawrence, in a window to the east of the chancel. On the wall, to each side of the chapel's east window, can be seen the faint outline of rare Medieval wall paintings which were uncovered during restoration work in 1935. The two figures depicted are St. Thomas of Canterbury (left) and St. Lawrence (right). The church also has several fine monuments and memorials, of which the 'Kneeling Lady' memorial to Anne Combe, the wife of Francis Combe, the tribute to his son by celebrated sculptor Sir Thomas Armstrong, and the marble monument to the 1st Baron Raymond and his son are the most remarkable. From Stuart times, The Church of St. Lawrence has a fine brass, dated 1607, mounted on the north wall and a coat-of-arms dated 1678. The house to the rear of the church is still in use and is a superb example of an Eighteenth Century vicarage. However the small house built for the Curate no longer survives. It was called Glebe Cottage and used to stand in ground now occupied by St. Lawrence Close. Outside the church, the distinctive Lych Gate is also worthy of note. This was built in 1902, by a local craftsman Edwin Glenister, as a memorial to Queen Victoria.

Abbots House

The elegant Queen Anne frontage of Abbots house, which stands just beyond the church, conceals elements of a much earlier structure. This is likely to have been a large Medieval open hall where the Abbot would have held local court and stored his share of the manor's produce. A Seventeenth Century barn, stables and oast house still survive on the site. At the turn of the century the house was home to Thomas Armstrong C.B., an eminent Victorian artist and sculptor who was Director of the South Kensington Museum, later to become the Victoria and Albert Museum. Abbots House was bought by Professor Laski in 1937 and it became home to the authoress and broadcaster Margharita Laski, who lived there until after the war. From 1954 it became the family home of the local doctor, Dr. P.R.V. Tomson who ran his village surgeries from the house between 1955 and 1963.

Kings Head

Opposite Abbots House stood the Kings Head, an Inn owned in 1779 by Stephen Salter. Beside the old Kings Head, was a yard containing the village forge where William King was blacksmith in 1839. Unfortunately this charming Eighteenth Century building was demolished and replaced by the modern Kings Head in 1965.

Old Cottage

Further beyond the church, almost opposite the village's modern library, is No. 9 High Street, which is one of the oldest surviving buildings in the village. Recently restored, it was a half-timbered house with jetted front and original doorways and dates from the Sixteenth Century.

Manor House

At the other end of the village, opposite Kitters Green, once stood a superb, Seventeenth Century house with three gables

Manor House, circa 1850.

Cecil Lodge, circa 1850.

and magnificent tall chimneys. From 1641, until its demolition in 1953, this house was owned jointly by Sidney Sussex College, Cambridge, and Trinity College, Oxford. The Manor House had been left to both universities by the village's leading benefactor Francis Combe, who was a wealthy landowner from Hemel Hempstead. His wife was Ann Greenhill and several generations of the Greenhill family lived at the Manor House until 1820. Mr. J. Inett-Ward lived at the Manor House between 1892 and 1922. His daughter, who became Mrs. Faulkner by marriage, was a talented wood sculptor whose work can still be found in the Parish Church. The last resident at the Manor House before the war, was Major J. H. Drake who lived there from 1922-38. All that remains on the site is the small Manor Lodge building. This was the former snooker room for the old estate, which is now run by the Parish Council as a Day Centre for the elderly.

Kitters Green

Opposite the Manor House grounds was a large pond at Kitters Green which survived until the village's water table lowered in the 1930's. This was the site of the village green, the laundry and also the village pound which was reconstructed by the Parish Council in 1984. Behind the pound stands Pound Cottage, originally a mid to late Seventeenth Century building and several low flinted brick built estate workers' cottages which formerly belonged to the Manor House. Close to the site of the old village laundry is picturesque Yew Tree Cottage, also dating from the Seventeenth Century.

Cecil Lodge

This house used to stand at the top end of the village, close to the 'T' junction with the Bedmond Road. Cecil Lodge is likely to have been built in the early 1760's and presented to Lord Cranborne upon his marriage. It is thought that he lived at Cecil Lodge until he succeeded to the Earldom of Salisbury in 1780 and took up the family seat at Hatfield House. Cecil Lodge grew to be a very impressive mansion which featured an onion domed tower and fine balustrade, added to the main house by the 1840's. Between 1832 and 1848 the house was home to Mr. J. Muir. One of Mr. Muir's daughters, Eleanor Muir, was an author of childrens' stories and her book 'The Three Bears' features Cecil Lodge. A notable resident of Cecil Lodge was the Right Hon. W. H. Smith, who was a leading Hertfordshire magistrate. He lived at the house from 1864-70 and it was his father who founded the highly successful nation-wide chain of newsagents and booksellers. From 1896-1919, Cecil Lodge was home to important village benefactors Mr & Mrs R. D. Cleasby. The house was then bought by Mr. A. J. Wall, an importer of Portuguese wines, who lived there until 1933. Unfortunately Cecil Lodge was badly damaged by fire in the mid 1930's and, in common with the Abbots Langley Manor House, fell into disrepair during the Second World War. Cecil Lodge was eventually bought by the Watford District Council and demolished to make way for housing development in 1953.

Langley House

Situated directly across the road from the modern library, Langley House was built in the 1750's by Sir John Cope Freeman, County Sheriff of Hertfordshire. He built the house for his retirement, using wealth accrued from his former ownership of a large and lucrative slave plantation in Jamaica. From 1886 to 1905, the house was home to Mr. Robert Henty, brother of the celebrated author G. A. Henty. Langley House was then purchased by Sir Robert Molesworth Kindersley. Lord Kindersley, who was knighted in 1917, served as Governor of the Bank of England between 1906 and 1923. In 1929 Langley House was bought by the Salvatorian Fathers of Wealdstone to serve as their novitiate. The billiard room of the house also served as the Catholic Church for the district. Mass for the villagers of Abbots Langley continued to be conducted at Langley House until the adjacent Catholic Church of St. Saviours was opened in 1963. Named after the only English Pope, Nicholas Breakspear who was born at nearby Bedmond, Langley House became known as Breakspear College, an internationally significant Roman Catholic Seminary. In 1986 Langley House was sold by the church and converted into Breakspeare Hospital specialising in environmental medicine and the treatment of allergies.

Troley House

The oldest part of this impressive house dates back to the Queen Anne period. Troley House was renovated and extended circa 1820 and its estate occupied ground where Follett Drive is today. From 1832-51 Troley House was home to Robert H. Atkinson and between 1886-1928 Samuel Sharrock was resident at the house. The Sharrock family used the grounds of Troley House as a market garden and the estate featured three large greenhouses, an orchard and about one third of an acre of peonies. In 1928 Troley House was purchased by Mr J.C.N. Heather who lived there with his family until 1948. In its heyday Troley House enjoyed the distinction of having the only swimming pool in Abbots Langley. During the Second World War the Heather family held regular fetes in the grounds to help raise funds for the war effort. It is worth noting that, at least until 1948, the house name was always spelt Troley and not Trowley. Troley House was eventually demolished in 1958.

In the dip of Tibbs Hill Road is 'Trowley Bottom', a local place name which dates back to Medieval times and derives from 'Trolls' ley', meaning fairies' meadow. At right angles to the main road, there are four houses called Kingsfield Cottages which date from the Seventeenth Century. When first built they are likely to have been one single timber framed dwelling and were converted and re-fronted in red brick during the Eighteenth Century.

Model Cottages

An architectural curiosity still survives in the village at Tibbs Hill Road. At the Great Exhibition, held in Hyde Park in 1851, the architect Henry Roberts designed some model cottages at Prince Albert's request. His brief was to produce accommodation which would 'improve the conditions of the labouring classes' and in 1856, an example of these houses was erected here in Abbots Langley. Their rather austere Victorian facades now conceal three separate residences facing the main road.

Booksellers Retreat

The attractive house called the Booksellers Retreat is rather hidden away, near the railway line at the bottom of Kindersley Way. In 1842 John Dickinson of Apsley Mills gave three acres of land to the newly-founded Booksellers Provident Society, so that they could build local accommodation for their members. The foundation stone for the original building was laid on 3rd September 1845, by the 6th Earl of Clarendon. The architect responsible for the attractive design of the house was W. H. Cooper of Grays Inn, London. The purpose of this project was to provide a retirement retreat for those members, or their widows, who were receiving annuities from the Booksellers' Society. This noble purpose still continues and in 1965, the first of 24 modern bungalows was added to the accommodation on the site. The original Provident Society has now become the Book Trade Benevolent Society and this body remains responsible for the institution. The main house still provides seven individual flats and, as befits its trade connection, has a splendid library. This is presided over by a bust of the original patron, John Dickinson which was sculpted by the noted Italian sculptor Carlo Marchetti. In 1979 the original Booksellers Retreat was re-named Dickinson House.

Booksellers Provident Retreat, 1846.

View of old Abbots Langley High Street, 1959.

Church of St. Lawrence, Abbots Langley, 1916.

Abbots House, 1995.

Langley House, 1897.

The old Abbots Langley School, 1976.

Cecil Lodge, 1897.

Wall family wedding 1925.

The Compasses at Trowley Bottom, circa 1900.

Troley House in the 1920's.

Model cottages in Tibbs Hill Road.

Entrance gates to Cecil Lodge, now part of Summerhouse Way.

High Street view, looking west 1935.

Abbots Langley High Street looking east in the 1940's.

Kitters Green, 1916.

Manor House, 1897.

Leavesden Hospital

The 76 acre site for Leavesden Hospital was purchased by the London Metropolitan Asylums Board for a sum not exceeding £7,600. The final cost of the construction of the imposing Victorian structure of this asylum for the "sick, insane and other classes of the poor of London" was £145,600. The foundation stone of the building was laid on 31st October 1868 and the first patients were admitted to the new Leavesden Asylum on 9th October 1870. When first built, the wards of the Asylum comprised five blocks for male and six blocks for female patients. Each block accommodated up to 160 people and was three storeys high. The buildings were a miracle of grandiose Victorian planning with the ground floor of each block taken up by a large day-room together with lavatories and storage, whilst the upper floors provided the dormitories. Long corridors provided access to these blocks and infirmaries were placed at the southern end of each corridor. In these early days the sexes were strictly segregated, with the female wards to the west and the male accommodation to the east of the central block. The Asylum's central block featured a magnificent hall with the boardroom and offices to the right of the main entrance, off College Road. There was also a chapel and from the time of the hospital's construction, the road beside the site became known as Asylum Road.

By 14th April 1871 all the beds on the female side were occupied and one year after the first admission, there were 739 male and 899 female patients in residence. Most staff were expected to live in, with differing standards of accommodation allocated to the various grades of staff. By November 1876 the total number of patients had increased to 2118. Unfortunately, because of a patient's escape, iron bars were put on all the windows between 1880-81. Following the First World War the Asylum was officially re-named the Leavesden Mental Hospital, and its business clarified as "care of the mentally deficient". The assistant medical officers at Leavesden were now training up to 122 nurses at a time. Occupational therapy was also being developed at Leavesden and by 1933 the female bath block had been converted into a occupational centre and gymnasium. During the 1930's, when unemployment was particularly high, the hospital was receiving up to 200 applications for work per week. In common with the Dickinson paper mills at Apsley, and the Ovaltine factory at Kings Langley, Leavesden Hospital was now one of the area's largest and most important employers.

Situated opposite Leavesden Hospital was the St. Pancras Industrial School, designed by the same architect as the Asylum building. Opened in 1870, this was another impressive Victorian edifice established by the St. Pancras Guardians specifically to house and train orphan children as apprentices and domestic servants. When these buildings were no longer needed, the London County Council proposed that they should be used as an annexe for Leavesden Hospital. During the Second World War, this hospital annexe was used as an emergency hospital which later catered for some of the wounded French survivors of the Dunkirk landings. In 1943 the hospital annexe was used as a base for the Royal Canadian Military Air Force. Following their departure it eventually became an English teacher training college, which explains the change of local street name from Asylum to College Road. This training college subsequently left the annexe in 1950 and all the buildings were returned to hospital use. Elderly psychotic patients were now transferred there to relieve congestion on the main hospital site, whilst the former military huts became the Abbots Langley Hospital for geriatric patients.

Architect's drawing of Leavesden Asylum.

By 1957 patient numbers at Leavesden had risen to 2,266; a nursery unit was established in 1967 and a boys unit was added in 1969. On 19th April 1966 a new school for children and adolescents had been opened at the hospital by H.R.H. Princess Marina, the Duchess of Kent. In 1974 a brand new social club for patients, called "Friendly Leaves", opened on part of the annexe site. However by the late 1960's patient numbers had begun to decline, falling to a total of 1356, in 1981. Dr. Eric Shepherd who had been Physician Superintendent of the hospital since 1963, retired in 1981. Plaques in the hospital chapel commemorate the work of both Dr. Shepherd and his predecessor, Dr. Hewlitt. The publication of the Government Community Care legislation in 1990 signalled the beginning of the end of Leavesden Hospital, which was gradually run down during the first half of the current decade. The hospital closed in 1993, bringing to an end over 120 years of hospitalised care of the mentally handicapped at Leavesden. Many of the old buildings have already been demolished and large parts of the hospital site are being re-developed to provide a substantial amount of new housing for the local area.

BATHING RULES

1. The following rules apply to the ordinary cleansing bath and no other kind of bath is to be given without specific order by the Medical Officer.

2. Every patient shall be bathed once a week (unless there is a special medical order to the contrary) and as much more often as is necessary. Every patient shall be bathed immediately on admission, unless the Medical Officer orders otherwise.

3. Under no circumstances is a patient to be bathed unless two nurses are present.

4. Fresh water must be prepared in the bath for each patient.

5. In preparing a Bath the cold water is to be turned on first.

6. The height of the water in the bath is never to exceed 7 inches and this can be measured with the bath thermometer.

7. Care is to be taken that the hot water and the cold water are thoroughly mixed before the patient enters the bath, and no additional hot or cold water is to be added to the bath while the patient is in it.

8. Before the patient enters the bath, the temperature must be ascertained by the thermometer, and is not to be less than 90 degrees, nor above 98 degrees Fahr. unless specially ordered. In case of the thermometer becoming inefficient, all bathing operations are to be suspended until another is obtained. The Chief Charge Nurse or Charge Nurse is responsible for the temperature of the water.

9. In the bath each patient is to be well cleansed with soap. After coming out of the bath care must be taken to dry those patients who are feeble and helpless, and to clothe them as rapidly as possible.

10. On no account is the patient's head to be put under water.

11. Keys of the bath taps are to be kept inaccessible to the patients and are on no account to be left on the taps.

12. Except during the use of the bath the door of the room is to remain locked and the floor to be kept dry.

13. The waste valve is always to be left open while the bath is not in use.

14. It is the duty of one of the Head Nurses to be present at all baths given under medical order, and to take care that the duration does not exceed the time specified in such order.

15. The presence of any bruises, sores or other eruptions, upon the person of any patient when bathed is to be reported to a Medical Officer.

16. A Head Nurse is always to be present in the General Bath Room during the time the patients are being bathed (also at such other places and times as may be required by the Medical Superintendent) in order to supervise all bathing operations and to ensure that the rules are rigidly observed.

Leavesden Hospital, circa 1920.

Recreation Hall, 1937.

Aerial view of Leavesden Hospital and St. Pancras School.

St. Pancras School, 1920.

Orphan nursery in the 1950's.

Bedmond

As we approach the next Millennium, the historical significance of Bedmond is secure. This village can confidently lay claim to have been the birth place of the only Englishman ever to have been elected as Supreme Pontiff of the Roman Catholic Church. It is believed that Nicholas Breakspear, who was destined to be Pope Adrian IV, was born circa 1100 at Breakspear Farm, in Bedmond. Sadly, and rather surprisingly perhaps, the farmhouse itself was demolished in the early 1960's to make way for a small crescent of modern houses. Today only a concrete plaque commemorates the site's importance. Behind the farmhouse there used to be a natural spring which produced an abundance of water with a bluish tinge. This was said to be 'holy water' and to have special curative powers, especially for the healing of the eyes. Throughout the years Breakspear Farm became the site of regular religious pilgrimages and celebrations which continued into the Twentieth Century.

Pope Adrian IV

Pope Adrian IV
Nicholas Breakspear was first refused admission to the monastery at St. Albans and went instead to France to study near Paris. He was later admitted to the Abbey of St. Rufus, near Avignon, where he became Abbot in 1139. He quickly developed a reputation as a rather stern leader, with very high standards. When he was summoned to the court of Pope Eugenius, he made such a positive impression that he was promptly promoted to the post of Cardinal of Albano in 1146. Nicholas was also an excellent preacher and was therefore deemed to possess all the necessary qualities for the ultimate promotion. Consequently, following the death of Anastasius II on 5th December 1154, he was appointed Pope Adrian IV. Unfortunately Pope Adrian's reign was short and problematic, dominated in particular by a protracted power struggle with the Holy Roman Emperor, Frederick Barbarossa. Eventually the Pope's supremacy was directly challenged, when in order to assert his right to collect taxes in Italy, the Emperor marched south and laid siege to Milan. However before this conflict was resolved, Pope Adrian died suddenly in Anagni, on 1st September 1159. His death remains shrouded in mystery; the official historical record says that he choked on a fly whilst drinking! However it seems more likely, given the circumstances, that he was poisoned by some of his political enemies. In 1886 three new residential roads, constructed in the neighbouring village of Abbots Langley, were named in tribute to this Papal connection; these were Popes Road, Adrian Road and Breakspear Road.

The name of Bedmond derives from the old English 'byde', meaning depression or hollow and 'mont', meaning on a hill. Thus we have a site for a village which is near to a hollow on a hill. The hollow referred to is almost certainly the spectacular dip which remains today behind the White Hart Inn.

Bedmond Pond
Well into the Twentieth Century, this hollow was in fact a very large and deep pond, jokingly referred to as 'Bedmond Docks' by the local people. It is likely that when Leavesden Hospital sank an artesian well in its grounds, all the Bedmond ponds and wells began to lose their water. Today the pond has completely disappeared and some of the land has been filled in and planted with Poplar trees. The area has become known as the Plantation and part of the site is now dominated by a modern structure. This is a neo-classical villa, designed by architect James Gorst, which is currently the family home of Mr. and Mrs. Jeremy Stewart-Smith.

White Hart
The White Hart is an attractive old Inn, parts of which date from the Seventeenth Century. In 1779 the White Hart was owned by Watford brewer, William Smith. In 1844 it was kept by another leading local brewer, Edward Fearnley Whittingstall, who lived nearby at Langleybury House. During the Eighteenth and Nineteenth Centuries both local hunts, the Hertfordshire Hunt and the old Berkeley, would often meet at the White Hart Inn.

Holy Well at Breakspear Farm, Bedmond.

Serge Hill

Just past the White Hart, in Serge Hill Lane, is the Lodge for the Serge Hill estate. At this point there used to be impressive wrought iron gates at the front of the half-mile carriageway which led up to the mansion. Serge Hill was built circa 1720 and for over 250 years the house has been home to the local squire of Bedmond. At its peak the Serge Hill estate covered over 3000 acres and nearly everyone in the village would have been employed there in one capacity or another. In 1900 the population of Bedmond was 500 and the community was essentially a collection of modest outlying farms and cottages mostly owned by the Serge Hill estate. The dominant family in the history of Bedmond is the Solly family and we know that Isaac Solly was resident at Serge Hill in 1804. He was succeeded by Samuel Reynolds Solly (born 1814), who in turn was succeeded by his son William Hammond Solly in 1866. W. H. Solly died on 23rd June 1897 and his grave can be found in the churchyard of St. Lawrence, Abbots Langley. From 1901 until 1919, Major Thomas Aubrey Shepherd-Cross leased the property to a leading light of the Abbots Langley community, Mr. W. H. Henderson. Major Shepherd-Cross then sold Serge Hill to Major Thomas and Lady Elizabeth Motion, who came to live in Bedmond following their marriage in 1927. Lady Elizabeth was distinguished by becoming Lady-in-Waiting to Queen Mary. The present residents of Serge Hill are Lady Joan Stewart-Smith, daughter of Major Thomas and Lady Elizabeth, and her husband Rt. Hon. Sir Murray Stewart-Smith who is currently a Lord Justice of Appeal and also a Privy Councillor.

Church of Ascension

At Church Hill, (formerly Porridge Pot Hill), we find Bedmond's own unique church. This was provided for the village in 1880, by Mr. Solly of Serge Hill and built at a cost of £80. This quaint and unusually small structure is an early example of the use of corrugated iron in building work. Traditionally the responsibility of Abbots Langley Parish Church, the Anglican services of the Church of Ascension survived until its closure in 1974. The building was then taken over by an independent evangelical group known as the Bedmond Fellowship. However in 1983 the church re-opened, under the care of St. Lawrence, and there is now one service per fortnight on Sunday mornings at Bedmond. The Solly family were generous benefactors to the local community. They also provided the original village school which sustained the infant education of Bedmond children until the construction of a modern Junior School in 1968. The family also made significant contributions to the local fund-raising efforts which led to the construction of Bedmond Village Hall in 1930.

Cottages in Porridge Pot Hill

Opposite the church, on the other side of Church Hill (formerly called Porridge Pot Hill) was an old cottage facing the main road. In its south facing garden, three yew trees were planted by Mr. John Botwright who was resident here at the turn of the century. It was his intention to grow them into the likeness of the 'Prince of Wales Feathers', but remarkably they instead grew into the shape of a cross and became a famous landmark thereafter. Next to Mr. Botwright's cottage, further down Porridge Pot Hill, on the west side, stood another three half-timbered cottages. These were some of the oldest surviving buildings in Bedmond and dated from the Sixteenth Century. During the Eighteenth Century, the houses formed an old tavern known as the Travellers Rest. Local legend has it that

1850's drawing of Dick Turpin.

the Travellers Rest was a regular bolt-hole for famous highwayman, Dick Turpin, when he was in the area. This is not as fanciful as it sounds given that we know Turpin's first recorded crime was a robbery conducted at a Chandlers Shop in Watford. Available information on the life of Dick Turpin also tells us that when he was a wanted man, he arranged secret meetings with his wife in Hertfordshire. Allegedly, he would disappear by hiding in the very large chimney above the fireplace! During their time as part of the Travellers Rest Inn, the cellars of these cottages were converted to stables, but they were so small that the horses had to be led out backwards. Despite being protected buildings, all these cottages disappeared in the 1960's, having been rather controversially demolished as part of a road widening scheme.

High Street

At the southern end of the village the Bell Inn still dominates the view. This is a very old Inn, formerly called the Blue Bell, which was kept by Christopher Newman in 1618. Beyond the Bell, nearer the Breakspear Farm site is a house which was formerly another old Bedmond Inn. This was the Green Man which finally closed its doors in 1942. Opposite the Green Man, Frederick Sherfield local blacksmith 1906-42, worked at the village forge. Further into the village, beyond the Bell, by one of four Sixteenth Century cottages, was the village wood yard. Across the road from the wood yard, there were allotments leading to Lyme Tree Cottages and the village well; these have now all been replaced by modern housing. Opposite the top of Toms Lane is No. 52 High Street, a house that was occupied until 1919 by Mr. Walter Gentle, who worked as the Estate Agent to the Solly family of Serge Hill. Further down the High Street, on the west side, prior to the construction of the modern council houses and shopping precinct, there used to be a corn chandlers, the village Reading Room (also provided by the Solly family), a wheelwrights shop and Bedmond's old Baptist Chapel. The old Baptist Chapel was recently demolished in 1995 to make way for new housing in the village.

Rear view of Serge Hill, 1897.

Serge Hill, 1897.

The White Hart, 1908.

Cottages on Church Hill, 1908.

Church of Ascension circa 1950.

Bedmond Pond circa 1910.

Looking towards Church Hill, 1908.

Bedmond High Street looking south towards the Bell, 1908.

The Woodyard, circa 1912.

The Bell Inn in the 1930's.

Village Stores, 1951.

The Green Man.

Breakspear Farm circa 1910.

Annual pilgrimage to Breakspear Farm in the 1950's.

Kings Langley

Kings Langley, as the name suggests, is a village with a history of significant Royal patronage. In 1045 'Langelei', which then included the lands of both Abbots and Kings Langley, was given to the Abbot of St. Albans by the Saxon, Ethelwine the Black. However by 1276 the western part of Langley had been acquired by Eleanor of Castile, the wife of Edward I (1272-1307) and she used the lands to create a Royal hunting park of 128 acres. Under Eleanor's personal supervision, a Royal residence was built in the form of a magnificent Palace, which was situated at the top of Langley Hill. Excavations in 1970, during building work in the grounds of Rudolf Steiner School, gave some indication of the likely grandeur of the Palace, when an impressive 100ft. wine cellar was uncovered. In 1302 Edward I granted Langley to his son and heir Edward, the first Prince of Wales. In 1308, under the patronage of Edward II (1302-27), an important Dominican Friary was established on land to the north of the Royal Palace. The church of the Friary was consecrated in the summer of 1312, and in 1315 the murdered body of Piers Gaveston, favourite and likely lover of Edward II, was buried in this church.

During the 'Black Death' of 1349, the Royal Palace at Kings Langley was used as the Seat of Government by Edward III (1327-77). Of particular interest to Kings Langley is Edmund, the fourth son of Edward III, who was made the first Duke of York. Edmund was born at the Palace in Kings Langley in 1341 and died there in 1402. Edmund and his first wife, Isabel of Castile, were originally buried in the Friary Church. However in 1574, by order of Elizabeth I, their bodies were moved to the Parish Church of All Saints, in Kings Langley, where their impressive tomb remains to this day. The Black Prince, eldest surviving brother of Edmund, was a key member of the Plantagenet Royal Court. Although he spent most of his energies in the wars with France and in the overhaul of the castle at Berkhamsted; he was also the founder of the monastery of Bonhommes at Ashridge. However the Black Prince's eldest surviving son, who became Richard II (1377-99), grew up at the Palace and like Edmund became very attached to Langley. Richard was also first buried in the Friary Church at Langley, following his assassination at Pontefract Castle. His body was later moved to Westminster Abbey, by order of the young Henry V, who had fond childhood memories of the betrayed King. Shakespeare recalls Royal days at Kings Langley in his play 'Richard II', which features one scene set in the Palace itself and another in the garden at Langley.

King Henry V spent some time at the Palace in 1414, though the last member of the Royal family to use Kings Langley as a Royal residence was, Queen Joan of Navarre. Subsequently there was a disastrous fire in 1431, following which the Palace began to sink into gradual decay. Later three of Henry VIII's six wives were, in turn, granted the Royal Palace at Langley, but none of them chose to live there. In 1580 the lease of the Manor of Kings Langley was assigned to Charles Morison, who had already inherited the Manor of Cassiobury from his father, Sir Richard Morison. Charles nevertheless built a sizeable house in Kings Langley, the surviving ruins of which can still be found in the garden of No. 80 Langley Hill. Finally in 1630, most of the Royal estate was sold to settle, in part, the debt King Charles I owed to the City of London. In respect of its history, as home to a Royal residence for over 350 years, Kings Langley held a rare honour. This was the right to fly the Royal Standard from the tower of the Parish Church of All Saints; a privilege finally withdrawn in 1935.

Given that so little survives today, it is difficult to imagine the sheer scale of the Royal site. Suffice it to say that the Friary blossomed to become the richest Dominican house in all England and at its peak accommodated as many as 100 friars. One can only guess at the magnificence of the Royal Palace itself, when one reads that the chapel of the adjacent Friary, rivalled Westminster Abbey both in its scale and its splendour! No trace of the Palace survives today above ground level, and all that remains of the 'Finest Friary in England', is the locutorium, a long narrow building which served as the friars parlour and conversation room. This building has been considerably extended and is now known, rather confusingly, as the Priory. Here Miss Cross founded the Priory School in 1910. This school was later absorbed into one of the educationally distinctive Rudolf Steiner Schools, which became successfully established on the adjacent Royal Palace site in 1949.

Engraving of the Friary, 1819.

Parish Church of All Saints, Kings Langley.

Interior of All Saints.

Tomb of Edmund de Langley.

Essex Cottage

This historic two storey timber framed building, which is now 'La Casetta' the Italian Restaurant, retains its original ground floor chimney and lies within a conservation area. It is one of the oldest buildings in the High Street and dates from the Sixteenth Century; the date 1509 can be found inscribed on one of its upstairs walls. However most of the present building, visible from the High Street, dates from the Seventeenth Century. In the 1890's the house was known as Essex Cottage, but by the 1920's had become the Village Tea Rooms, a popular meeting place for many years. It was formerly the Old Cottage Restaurant, offering English/French cuisine, before becoming an Italian restaurant in 1985.

Cooks Yard

Cooks Yard stood where Sadlers Walk sheltered housing development is today. It was here that George Cook began business as the village wheelwright in 1886. Between 1913-20, the yard also housed a blacksmith's forge, a cobbler and farrier. In modern times Cooks Yard developed into a garage business with petrol pumps and workshops. To the rear of Sadlers Walk housing development, which replaced the garage business, is one remaining older structure which was the Cook's family home. Part of the structure of this house dates back to 1700 and it is now a protected building.

The Fisheries

This Seventeenth Century building was the Vicarage and belonged to All Saints Church until 1934. Renovated by John Kingston, founder of the Kings Langley Players, the building then served as a local doctor's surgery, and fish shop until 1983. It has now been converted into modern office accommodation.

Water Lane Lock.

Waterside

In the pre-industrial age the people of Waterside enjoyed easy access to supplies of fresh water from wells of only 6ft. deep. Lying just below the main thoroughfare and market place of Kings Langley, the community of Waterside was very much the heart of the village for the average working man. For over 150 years, the centre of economic activity at Waterside was Toovey's Mill which had been established in 1780 by Thomas Toovey. Situated close to the canal, Toovey's 1000 ton grain silo (built in 1935), was a familiar Kings Langley land-mark until its demolition in 1980. Several shops and three pubs, the Red Lion, King William IV and the Lamb, tended the daily needs of the mill workers and canal trade of Waterside. Of the three Inns, only the structure of the Red Lion survives today as a private residence. The last of the old Sixteenth and Seventeenth Century cottages of Waterside were demolished in the course of a road widening scheme in 1967-68, and also provided the site for council-run sheltered housing for the elderly at Willow Edge. The mill at Waterside ceased trading in 1978, but is commemorated by the name of the modern housing development later built on the site. This new housing estate which incorporates the original mill-race, surrounds the attractive late Eighteenth Century Mill House, which remains on the corner of Water Lane. This Mill House, built circa 1788 for Thomas Toovey, is a two storey red brick building with a fine doorcase and is Grade II listed.

Local Inns

Standing opposite Blue Court, the Rose and Crown is an Eighteenth Century Coaching Inn and Post House which is listed as having stabling for 10 horses in 1897. This Inn, notable for its distinctive veranda frontage, was originally a small wine tavern kept by James Goodwin in 1635. The Saracens Head is certainly the oldest surviving public house in the area. A timber-framed building which dates from the Sixteenth Century, it has Tudor and crown badges set in the plaster of one of its upstairs ceilings. In the Eighteenth Century it also was an important Coaching Inn which acted as a halt for the London to Birmingham stage coach. The Langleys is a large structure set back from the main road at the northern entrance to the village and was originally a Seventeenth Century timber framed building. It was built as a dower house of the Shendish estate and was home to two daughters of Thomas Norton Longman who died in 1930. Until the end of the Second World War it remained a substantial private house known as Whitlars. In 1947 it became the Whitlars Hotel and in 1967 was extensively re-modelled by the Scottish and Newcastle Breweries. From this time it became known as the Young Pretender before it was again re-developed in the 1980's as the Langleys public house and restaurant that we know today.

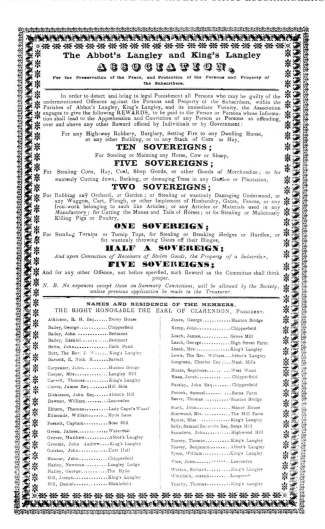

All Saints Parish Church

Although founded in the second half of the Twelfth Century, the structure of All Saints Parish Church dates substantially from the Fourteenth and Fifteenth Centuries. Its most important relic, housed in the Memorial Chapel, is the tomb of Edmund de Langley, the first Duke of York. Kings Langley's privilege of being able to fly the Royal Standard was renewed by Queen Victoria in 1878, when the Royal Chapel was dedicated. The Queen also donated the stained glass herald window which was installed in the chapel. Her Majesty Queen Elizabeth II headed the subscription list when funds were raised to recast the ring of eight bells at All Saints in 1958. The oldest of these bells was made during the Commonwealth in 1657. All Saints Church still has an exceptional wooden carved chanticleer pulpit dating from 1600 and a fine reredos, carved in Derby alabaster, which was presented to the church in 1873 in memory of Charles Longman by his son, Arthur Hampton Longman of Shendish House.

Village School

The first Village School was an attractive Victorian building which stood in Church Lane, just below the grounds of All Saints Church. The original structure was built of flint and brick, at a cost of £288. It was provided for the village in 1838 by the wealthy local employer John Dickinson of Apsley Mill, and was initially designed in two parts with separate rooms for boys and girls. Mr. Edward Toms served as village headmaster of Kings Langley from 1886-1926 and during his tenure, additional buildings were provided in Alexandra Road. The original school was demolished in 1987, having been replaced by the modern purpose-built secondary and junior schools in Love Lane and Common Lane respectively. The Cloisters, a sheltered housing development, now stands on the old school site.

Rudolf Steiner School

This school, originally known as the New School, began in 1949 with 100 pupils. Both Priory House and Friarswood were used as accommodation for the school which in 1975 also purchased the former Priory School which had been run by Miss Cross from 1910-55. It was Miss Cross who first adopted the Waldorf principles of education, following a Christmas visit in 1922 from Rudolf Steiner, the Austrian philosopher and educationalist. The Rudolf Steiner School now has an impressive array of modern buildings on a ten acre site, which was formerly home to the Plantagenet Royal Palace at Kings Langley. The school's distinctive kindergarten building was opened on 24th May 1968 by the Poet Laureate, C. Day Lewis.

Manor House and Manor Lodge

The Manor House of Kings Langley used to sit in the middle of Kings Langley High Street, approximately on the site of the Royal Mail Sorting Office. Built in 1580 by the Kettell family, it had a brick walled garden and was in use as the Manor House until 1745. From this time the structure deteriorated until it was pulled down by Robert Blackwell in 1848. He built a new Manor House at Chipperfield which incorporated the arms of the Kettell family rescued from the old house. In its place at Kings Langley, he built Manor Lodge, which in the early part of the Twentieth Century became known as 'The Villa'. During this time it was home to Christopher Beaton, a cousin of Cecil Beaton, the well known high society photographer. Manor Lodge was demolished in 1969.

Kings Langley Manor House, demolished 1848.

Langley House

Langley House is scheduled as an ancient monument and is thought by many historians to be the probable site of the first Medieval Manor House of Langley. The present house, which is screened from the road at the southern end of the High Street by a high brick wall, was described as 'newly built' in 1784. Formerly owned by His Honour Sir William Stabb (retired judge), who now lives at Pale Farm in Chipperfield, since 1968 Langley House has been the family home of Benny Green, writer, musician and broadcaster.

Red House

Originally two cottages which were re-fronted in the early Eighteenth Century, this imposing house still survives in the High Street. It was home to surgeon Charles Wotton and the son of a later Sir Richard Wotton (1811-93), before becoming for several years both the practice and family home for village Doctor, Dr. F. C. Fisher (1881-1918). Dr. Fisher later built an impressive family home in the High Street, called Little Hayes. This also served as the village's main Doctor's Surgery from 1908 until 1963. It was eventually demolished to make way for today's flats of the same name. Continuing its medical tradition, the Red House currently houses the dental practice of Grace McKeown.

Blue Court

At the southern end of the village, opposite the Rose and Crown, is the house known as Blue Court. Formerly known as the Pole House, it was built in 1830 for the Groome family, who ran the local brewery on a site behind their new house. At its peak Groomes Brewery had 32 outlets, but was bought out by Benskins in 1897. The malt-house, which stood opposite the church in Church Lane, was given to the Parish in 1904, by the wife of John Edward Groome in his memory. Refurbished by public subscription, this became known as Church House, though the building has since been sold by the Church and converted into offices. Blue Court became a hotel from 1931-66 and was the premier venue in the village for weddings, dances and dinner parties. It was also a popular night-spot for American airmen stationed at Bovingdon Airfield during World War II. Although it fell into considerable disrepair, the house was carefully restored in 1980, at a cost of £330,000, by the Finlinson Construction Group. It then became their business headquarters before it was sold in 1990 to become a base for the Engineering Industry Training Board.

High Street, Kings Langley 1907.

Funeral procession through Kings Langley High Street, 1915.

Essex Cottage, circa 1911.

View of the High Street looking north, 1909.

May Fair Procession, 1922.

Toovey's Mill and Silo, 1958.

High Street, showing Rose and Crown, 1900.

Saracen's Head and Crown Post Office (extreme left) circa 1910.

Waterside 1963.

Demolition of Toovey's Mill Silo, 1980.

Rear view of Langley House, 1988.

View of Little Hayes, 1896.

Church Lane in the 1950's.

Blue Court 1958.

Langley Hill, 1906.

Kings Langley Common circa 1898.

Pound and Pound Cottage, 1909.

The Nap and Wesleyan Chapel, 1937.

Kings Langley Priory, circa 1910.

Priory School buildings.

Kindergarten at Rudolph Steiner School.

Rudolph Steiner.

Chipperfield

Today the village of Chipperfield still enjoys a favoured and historic setting. Its ancient Common is overlooked by the old village Inn, Parish Church, original school buildings, vicarage and Manor House. This spread of open land at Chipperfield was originally bequeathed by Edward II to the Dominican brotherhood of the Friary, which he helped to establish next to his Royal Palace at Kings Langley. A large fish pool, which survives to this day in the woods, was regularly stocked and fished by these Dominican monks. From 1714 it became known as Apostles Pond, when a circle of twelve lime trees (whose leaves would help to keep the water sweet) were planted around it by John and Mary Marriott of Pinglesgate House. By 1983 these lime trees had grown too large and were pollarded and twelve new lime trees were also planted which will eventually replace the originals.

Two barrows, which are Anglo-Saxon burial mounds, are also to be found in Chipperfield woods and it has been speculated that these were subsequently used for target practice by Royal archers in the time of Richard II. The Common woods are also home to some magnificent trees; it is said that some of the sweet chestnuts are over 700 years old and were planted by returning Crusaders. Local legend also tells how Richard III sat beneath one, having fallen from his horse, whilst the village women laughed at his humped back.

The name Chipperfield derives from the old English word 'ceapere', meaning trader, hence trader's field. Chipperfield has always been an agricultural community, fortunate to be surrounded by fertile farmland. Until well into the Twentieth Century, extensive fruit orchards were prevalent in the area.

Seal of the Dominican Friary.

Carters of Chipperfield

During the Sixteenth Century there were two wealthy farmers in Chipperfield, both called Thomas Carter. One farmed at Pinglesgate Farm, whilst the other owned both the local mill and windmill and lived at Pale Farm, where an impressive farmhouse survives to this day. Two of the Carter family emigrated to America, where a John Carter secured some very rich farmland. His son, Robert Carter, built up an eventual holding of over 3,000 acres and employed as many as 1,000 slaves on his estates. Robert became known as 'King Carter', wisely investing his profits in an emerging merchant banking empire. He became one of America's first millionaires. In 1977 Robert's settler father, John, was proved by Debretts to have been the direct ancestor of Jimmy Carter, the 39th President of the U.S.A.

Manor House

Thomas Gulston built the original structure of the Sixteenth Century Manor House which overlooks the southern end of the Common. Surviving indications of Tudor architecture, together with six small gables, timbering and typical chimneys, can still be seen at the back of the house. By 1711 this structure was known as Pinglesgate House and had been re-fronted in Queen Anne style by John and Mary Marriott. In 1850 Robert Blackwell inherited the Manor House together with land and three farms from his uncle John Parsley. Robert Blackwell also owned a Manor House at Kings Langley which had fallen into disrepair. When this old house was demolished the wooden panelling, together with the coat of arms of the Kettell family (previous owners of Kings Langley Manor House 1559-1663), were rescued. These were subsequently installed at the Manor House in Chipperfield, which then became his principal residence.

On the death of Robert Blackwell's wife in 1910, the house was left to Samuel John Blackwell, who enlarged it by adding wings at either end. The Manor House now had an impressive frontage extended from seven to eleven windows. In October 1936, the sons of Samuel John Blackwell presented the Commons of both Kings Langley and Chipperfield to the Hemel Hempstead Rural District Council, for the nominal sum of ten shillings. There was a specific proviso that no trees were to be felled. Later from 1959-61, the Manor House became home to the famous actor and comedian Peter Sellers, and it is currently the principal residence of Gerald Humphrey Legge, the 9th Earl of Dartmouth. The Earl's first wife, by her second marriage to Earl Spencer, is now step-mother to Her Royal Highness Diana, Princess of Wales.

St. Paul's Church

The Church of St. Paul, Chipperfield was built in 1837, by public subscription, and consecrated on 10th October 1838 by the Bishop of Lincoln. The attractive Victorian vicarage, itself a substantial structure, was built in 1848 for the first Vicar of Chipperfield, the Rev. Henry Dennis (1838-60). In that same year, the Ecclesiastical Parish of Chipperfield was created and made distinct from that of Kings Langley. The village school, another superb example of Victorian architecture, was also built in 1848, although later extended in 1880. It served as Chipperfield Primary School until 1973, when it was replaced by today's modern circular buildings.

Consecration of the Church of St. Paul, Chipperfield, 1848.

The Street, circa 1910.

Two Brewers and Bunyan's Corner

The Two Brewers Inn dates from the Sixteenth Century and was built on land belonging to John Carter of Pinglesgate. In 1878 this old Inn had attached to it a corner shop where grocer Joseph Bunyan ran his business. Other shops on this corner included, at the turn of the century, a tailors, a post office and a cycle shop. This community focal point became known as 'Bunyan's Corner'. It has been claimed that the Two Brewers was a regular training camp for Britain's most celebrated boxer, Bob Fitzsimmons. He held the world heavyweight, light-heavyweight and middleweight championships concurrently in 1903. What is more certain is that Chipperfield was one of the last places in England where cock-fighting was practised. The remains of these well-used cock pits can still be found further down Common Lane.

The Windmill was already a beer-house by 1838. It was named after a four storey stock windmill which stood close by and was re-built circa 1820. We know that the windmill at Chipperfield, now demolished, was still working as late as 1877, but by 1881 it was idle. Running towards Bunyan's Corner, from the cross-roads at the bottom of Tower Hill, was the other main thoroughfare. This was known as 'The Street' and in the latter half of the Nineteenth Century, it contained several shops, as well as a bakery, a blacksmith and an undertaker's yard behind the Royal Oak public house. Chipperfield Baptist Chapel was built in The Street in 1837, whilst another building of note is the modern Catholic Church, Our Lady Mother of the Saviour, in Dunny Lane. This was built on land given by Sir Charles Forte and the first Catholic service in Chipperfield was held there in December 1989.

Bunyans Corner, 1908.

Locals at the Two Brewers Inn.

The village forge at the turn of the century.

Chipperfield Common at the turn of the century.

Chipperfield Village.

St. Paul's Church, Chipperfield, in the 1890's.

The Vicarage, Chipperfield.

Apostles Pond, circa 1960.

Chipperfield House, circa 1910.

The Manor House, Chipperfield, 1935.

Tower Hill near Chipperfield, circa 1908.

The Dell, Chipperfield, 1927.

Shendish

The Shendish estate has a considerable lineage and dates from 1086 when Ralf, as Sergeant at Berkhamsted Castle was given by his Lord, Robert Count de Mortain, "land of the capital Manor of Langley called Chenduit". Ralf's probable descendents, the Chenduit family, held this manor until 1276. It was in this year that Eleanor of Castile, the wife of Edward I, acquired most of the lands of Langley for the Royal park and Palace she intended to found in Kings Langley. By 1364 the remains of the Shendish estate had passed to the Parker family and Edmund Parker is listed as Court Baron of this Manor in 1427. By now Shendish was a much reduced estate or sub-manor, with lands which did not extend much further southwards than Rucklers Lane. Unfortunately any traces of the early manorial building and farmstead were demolished in the course of building the present structure.

Arthur Hampton Longman.

The present attractive and imposing Shendish house sits within its old estate lands on the west side of the Gade valley, to the north of Kings Langley. The house we know today was built in an Elizabethan style for Charles Longman and was constructed between 1854 and 1856. In 1853 Charles Longman had inherited a considerable fortune from his father, publisher Thomas Norton Longman III (1771-1842) and he used some of this windfall to purchase the Shendish estate. It was Charles' uncle, George Longman M.P., who had been John Dickinson's original financial partner.

When Charles Longman died in 1873, he was succeeded at Shendish by Arthur Longman who was a very different character. He was a keen sportsman who had very little interest in or involvement with the paper making business at Apsley. When Arthur died in 1908, his cousin Thomas Norton Longman V lived at Shendish until his death in 1930. Thomas Norton had been one-time Master of the old Berkeley Hunt and during his tenure a full pack of hunting hounds was kept at Shendish. After the death of Thomas Norton Longman, the house and the entire estate were put up for auction in 1931. Shendish was then still a very grand property, listed as having an impressive hall, 4 reception rooms, billiards room, 18

bedrooms and 4 bathrooms. The entire estate still ran to over 1300 acres of land and the auction on 15th September 1931, offered an option to buy the main house itself, either with 92 or 523 acres. Included in the sale of the entire Shendish estate were two other 'gentlemen's residences', 22 cottages, the Home Farm and four other local farms. Between 1932 and 1936, Shendish became a preparatory school, but by March 1936 the house itself and its remaining lands had been acquired by Dickinsons Ltd. This well established paper and stationery manufacturer then formed a committee to oversee Shendish's development as a Sports and Social Club for its employees. The company invested £15,000 in Shendish, and in May 1937 the 'Dickinson Guild of Sport' was officially opened by the company's Chairman, Mr. Reginald Bonsor. More recently Shendish became used more commercially as a conference centre and venue for training and management courses. In 1994 Shendish was privately purchased and has now become 'Shendish Manor', one of Hertfordshire's leading conference and banqueting venues. Eight conference suites, together with an eighteen hole golf course, are now offered by this elegant house which still has an estate of 140 acres of parkland and formal gardens.

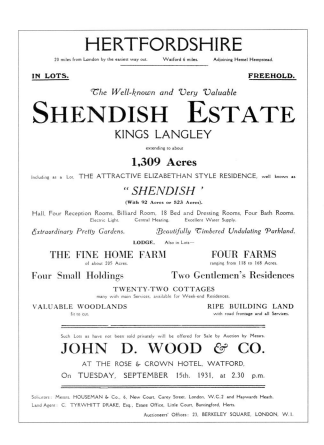

Barnes Lodge

The impressive early Nineteenth Century structure of Barnes Lodge occupied a site on the slope of the valley, to the north west of Kings Langley. This location was close to the Shendish estate, for which Barnes Lodge acted as a dower house during the late Nineteenth Century and early Twentieth Century. Between 1899-1902 Barnes Lodge was home to Lewis Evans, a Director at Dickinson's Mills. Mrs. Arthur Longman lived at the house from 1909-14, following the death of her husband. After the 2nd world war Barnes Lodge was home to a preparatory school which was run by Mr. M. Hayward until 1968. This fine old house was demolished in 1975.

Shendish House, 1912.

Hunt led by Thomas Norton Longman, Barnes Farm, 1923.

Golden Wedding Celebrations of Thomas Norton Longman, Shendish House, 1922.

Shendish as Dickinson's Sports and Social Club in the 1950's.

Barnes Lodge, circa 1951.

Apsley

Apsley is essentially a community with an industrial heritage. In particular, its role as a centre for the paper-manufacture industry over the last two hundred years, has defined the character and development of the original hamlet. Certainly until the post-war changes inspired by the New Towns Act of 1946, Apsley was considered to be the principal industrial suburb of Hemel Hempstead. This role began to be superseded by the provision, for Hemel Hempstead New Town, of the new industrial estates in Cupid Green and Maylands Avenue; a process which has been completed by the demolition of the old Dickinsons factories in 1992. With the arrival of various superstore developments in the last two decades, (Texas Homecare in 1984 followed by the Sainsburys supermarket in 1993), the economic function of Apsley has now become predominately retail. This retail emphasis has been reinforced by Apsley's interesting mix of specialist shopping outlets.

The history of the area itself dates back to the early Twelfth Century, when there were said to be two mills: one at Apsleymille (Apsley Mill) and the other at Ashemille (Nash Mill). The word Apsley derives from aspen tree; similarly the word Nash comes from ash tree, and these two terms were therefore used to distinguish between two early mills which stood geographically quite close to one another. Until the second half of the Eighteenth Century, both these mills were working corn mills standing on the River Gade.

Manor House
We know that there was an ancient Manor House site which stood on the corner of Featherbed Lane and the London Road. Written records tell us that the very last manorial court in the sub-manor of 'Buers' was held here in 1805. A later version of this building, Manor Farm House, survived on this corner until it was demolished after the war and replaced by commercial premises as part of the New Town Plan.

Dickinsons
The introduction of paper-making to Apsley was of national significance as a starting point for modern paper manufacturing processes. It began when the two London stationers Henry and Sealy Fourdrinier started producing machine-made paper at Frogmore Mill in 1803. Although the Fourdrinier brothers went bankrupt in 1810, their activities at Frogmore Mill were eventually taken over by the British Paper Company. However the key moment in the history of Apsley was the arrival in 1809 of John Dickinson. He was the founder of John Dickinson & Co. Ltd., a company which grew rapidly to make Apsley the centre of the largest paper-making and converting industry in the world. As we will see later it was John Dickinson and the family of Sir John Evans, who married his daughter Harriett, together with members of the Longman family at Shendish, who defined the shape of the community which grew naturally around this fast developing industrial base at Apsley.

One year after the acquisition of Apsley Mill in 1809, John Dickinson bought Nash Mill. He subsequently established further factories for his business at Home Park Mills at Kings Langley in 1826 and Croxley Mills in 1829. As the paper trade expanded, John Dickinson soon became a wealthy man and in 1836, he began building himself the fine family home of Abbots Hill. This new house lay on the eastern side of the valley, just to the south of Apsley. The arrival of the Grand Junction Canal in 1797, and particularly the diversion he achieved for the benefit of his factories in 1818, provided John Dickinson with

a key transport link. His business was now expanding so rapidly that by 1904, the company was receiving an average of 38,540 tons of coal annually, delivered by canal boat. In the great Victorian tradition, some of the family's commercial wealth did flow back in to the local community and it was these endowments that helped create much of the Apsley infrastructure known today.

John Evans in the library at Nash Mills House.

Nash Mills House
Nash Mills House was built in 1790 and was the first family home to John Dickinson FRS (1782-1869) following his marriage to Ann Grover in 1810. Prior to the construction of Abbots Hill, when John Dickinson moved to London temporarily in 1834, Nash Mills was home to Mr. and Mrs. Charles Longman, until their own Shendish estate was built in 1856. Nash Mills then became home to John Dickinson's daughter Harriett and her husband John Evans, later Sir John Evans KCB (1823-1903). John Evans lived there until they moved to Britwell, by Berkhamsted Common. Another family member, Charles's brother William Longman, also moved to Berkhamsted where he lived at Ashlyns Hall from 1863 until his death in 1877. William Longman had married the daughter of John Dickinson's son-in-law, Emma Pratt Barlow. Her father, Frederick Pratt Barlow a solicitor, had become a business partner of John Dickinson upon his marriage to his elder daughter, Frances.

Do Little Cottages
John Dickinson's first investment in the community of Apsley was the construction of Do Little Cottages. These were built on ground close to the canal, between the Red Lion and the main Apsley Mill factories, and comprised two rows of six cottages built around a square. In the centre of the square stood a communal water pump which survived until all these houses were demolished in 1934. It has been speculated that the name Do Little Meadows derives from the days when the Abbot of St. Albans would send some of his monks to the corn mills of Apsley, to enjoy a break from monastic life.

Nash Mills School
Nash Mills School was built in 1847 by John Dickinson in order to provide a basic education for the local children, most of whom were destined to become apprentices at his factories. This Victorian school building, which survives today with modern additions, was designed by John Dickinson himself

and constructed on land between the Old George and the Three Tuns public houses. By a deed dated June 1861, it became a "School for Poor Persons" and by 1870 the school was managed by a committee which included both John Evans and Charles Longman. In 1876 the school was also being used for church services on alternate weeks and as a village Sunday School. By 1891, ninety children were regularly attending.

Apsley Manor School

Following the construction of Nash Mills School, Apsley Manor School was built in 1857. It stood in Thorpe Street which has since been re-named Avia Close. Although this school did not flourish to the extent of Nash Mills, closing in March 1939, it did re-open in September of that year to help accommodate the flood of young war evacuees from London. Following the war an overflow of children from Nash Mills went to Apsley Manor School before its successor, Belswains School opened. Apsley Manor School finally closed its doors in 1949.

St. Mary's Church

The Church of St. Mary at Apsley End was opened for public worship in 1871. It was consecrated at a ceremony on 31st August 1871, by the Bishop of Rochester. The first Vicar of St. Mary's was Rev. D. Ingles M.A. John Evans served as vicar's warden of St. Mary from 1871-1896 and was followed in this role by his son, Lewis Evans, between 1887-1894 and 1899-1902. The Church of St. Mary's was built by Messrs. Bell and Son of Saffron Walden, to a design by Diocesan architect Joseph Clarke F.S.A. The main structure of St. Mary's has rough flint walls and quoins with dressings of Ancaster stone. To this day, its impressively proportioned shingled spire dominates the surroundings. The tower of the church has six bells with a combined weight of 53 cwt. The donor list for these bells reads like a who's who of the leading lights of Victorian Apsley. The tenor bell was the gift of Charles Longman (1809-1873), the High Sheriff of Hertfordshire, the second bell was given by the first vicar, Rev. Ingles, the third was the gift of John Evans FRS (1823-1908), the fourth donated by Frederick Pratt Barlow (1815-1883), who had married John Dickinson's eldest daughter Frances in 1840, and the fifth was the gift of John Dickinson Junior (1815-1876) the only surviving son of the founder of Apsley Mills.

The Church of St. Mary owes its life more to Charles Longman than anyone else. It was he who, on the death of his wife in 1860, declared his ambition to build a church in her memory to serve "the people of Two Waters and Nash Mills". This however was not a scheme favoured by John Dickinson, whose death in 1869 cleared the way to proceed. Undoubtedly, the outstanding feature of St. Mary's is the beautiful reredos, which was presented in 1915 by the Longman family in memory of Mr. & Mrs. Arthur Hampton Longman. The screen depicts Christ as the Priest King and has extensive gilding. The church's internal War Memorial to those who died in both wars is also notable and was carved in oak by Gertrude White.

Non-Conformist Churches

The former Baptist Chapel in Featherbed Lane was established in 1818. It is now home to a Maranatha Christian Church. The present Community Centre was converted from Apsley's second Methodist Church which opened on 5th February 1908. Today's Methodist Church at Apsley was formerly the schoolroom of this church.

Village Club

Apsley Village Club was founded in 1874 with A. H. Longman as Patron and John Evans as its first President. Early in 1899 the club became a member of the Working Men's Club and Institute Union and is still a thriving organisation today.

Fire Brigade

As a small community, Apsley enjoyed excellent protection from a Fire Brigade which was first established at John Dickinson's Nash Mills in 1883. The Captain of this Fire Brigade until 1920 was Lewis Evans. Although active throughout the area, the Brigade's primary purpose was to protect the Dickinson's factories and as the production levels at Apsley Mills rose, the various engines and appliances were moved there in 1897. During the war the Brigade became part of the National Fire Service, which was itself disbanded in 1948. Since then, with the formation of the County Fire Service, private fire brigades were restricted to servicing only their own premises.

Apsley and Nash Mills Nursing Association

This was another key institution of benefit to the local community founded in 1911 by Mr. A. H. Longman of Shendish House. By 1912 the first District Nurse, Miss Martin, had been appointed. For the payment of sixpence a month one could claim her services, if medical attention was required. She was supplied with a bike and her work continued until the National Health Service assumed responsibility in 1948.

Kent Brushes

The history of Apsley would not be complete without a mention of the other principal employer into modern times, Kent Brushes. Between 1901 and 1905 the London firm of brush-makers G. B. Kent and Sons Ltd. (established 1777), built a new factory in Apsley. They also purchased five in a row of ten houses that were built at the end of Weymouth Street; this became known locally as Kent Avenue. At their peak, Kent Brushes were employing 200 people in Apsley during the 1960's. The five acre site of Kent's old factory has recently been re-developed and a modern office for Kent Brushes was built when the Texas Homecare and Bulk DIY Stores were opened in November 1984.

It is worth stressing that the industrial role of Apsley was very much respected in the first half of the Twentieth Century. When the Prince of Wales paid a visit to Salmon Meadow, after laying the foundation stone of West Herts Hospital on 20th July 1926, he was presented to the Directors of John Dickinson & Co. Ltd., the British Paper Co. Ltd. and G. B. Kent & Sons Ltd. He later addressed a large group of workers who had gathered to meet him in the meadow.

The Bell Inn at Two Waters

The Bell at Two Waters, which started life as a Sixteenth Century coaching Inn, is one of the oldest public houses in the area. Stagecoaches travelling between London and Aylesbury stopped at the Bell to allow passengers for Hemel Hempstead to disembark at Two Waters. A Seventeenth Century structure, altered in the Nineteenth Century, survives with timber frame exposed on the south side gable. As late as 1907, horse and carts would stop for refreshment at this old Inn, which stands close to the point where the River Bulbourne meets the River Gade. The Bell Inn's position denotes the southern end of Boxmoor and the beginning of the community of Apsley.

Empire Day procession at Apsley, 1918.

St. Mary's Church in the 1960's.

Opening of the Methodist Chapel, February 1908.

Two Waters, 1960.

A view of the Bell in Two Waters, circa 1910.

Apsley Village and Church, 1957.

Apsley, circa 1920.

Apsley Manor School.

Early school group at Apsley Manor.

Nash Mills School.

Belswains Lane in the 1920's.

Do Little Cottages, built 1826.

Nash Mills House, home of John Evans until 1905.

View of Apsley Mill, circa 1910.

Sir John Evans.

Engineers and millwrights employed at Dickinson's, 1874.

Lunchtime at Apsley Mills in the 1930's.

Inauguration of the Dickinson's War Memorial, 1919.

Dickinson's plant at Belswains Lane.

Nash Mills 1991.

Demolition of old Apsley Mill buildings, showing new automated warehouse in the background.

Aerial view of Apsley in the Gade valley, featuring the Dickinson factories, 1991.

Abbots Hill

By 1837 John Dickinson, who had bought Apsley Mill in 1809, was already a very wealthy paper manufacturer. He now set about building himself a fine house to the south of the mill at Nash Mills, on the eastern side of the Gade valley. The western side was already occupied by the Shendish estate. The site John Dickinson chose was high on a spur of land that had previously been occupied by Black Hill Farm. It has often been asserted, but never verified, that John Dickinson utilised surplus building materials from the local stretch of the London to Birmingham Railway in the construction of Abbots Hill. These are most likely to have been some of the thousands of discarded stone sleepers that were soon replaced by timber, offering railway passengers a more comfortable ride. Some of these may have been added to a later extension to the house. Although the rear of the house has a pleasing line, the front of Abbots Hill is rather plain and austere, perhaps reflecting the man himself. On this note, it has also been said that Charles Dickens used Abbots Hill as a model for the creation of the formidable Bleak House, in one of his most successful novels. For a house of its size, Abbots Hill is probably unique in having been built with only one entrance, this being the front door. It is said that John Dickinson wished to scrutinise every visitor to his house, another detail which perhaps paints a picture of the man. However the Dickinson family certainly lived very well at Abbots Hill and their beloved daughter, Harriet Ann was fond of holding dances and fine dinner parties at the big house.

John Dickinson

Abbots Hill, Herts.

When Abbots Hill was sold in 1912, it was bought by the two Miss Bairds who used it to found a private, fee-paying school for girls. Abbots Hill School continues to prosper to this day, under the direction of the present headmistress, Mrs. J. S. Kingsley. This well-known private school is set in 70 acres of park-land and caters for up to 180 girls aged between 11 and 16. The junior school to Abbots Hill, St. Nicholas House, caters for a further 100 younger pupils and moved to the site in 1968. Prior to its amalgamation with Abbots Hill, St. Nicholas House had been an independent school based at the Hollies in Green Lane, Hemel Hempstead. This junior school moved to Abbots Hill when its former home was demolished by the New Towns Commission.

By 1859 John Dickinson had handed over the running of his paper manufacturing business to his son-in-law and nephew John Evans (1823-1903) who had married John Dickinson's daughter, Harriet Ann. He later became Sir John Evans, developing an international reputation as an archaeologist and numismatist. Sadly Harriet Ann, who was the first of John Evan's three wives, died at the early age of 35. Sir John's eldest son, Arthur Evans, achieved even greater fame than his father. Like Arthur Longman, his contemporary at the Shendish estate, he showed little interest in the paper mills which had founded the family's wealth. Instead he travelled extensively, developing his passion for archaeology, which was no doubt inherited from his father. Arthur Evans (1851-1941) will always be remembered for his stunning archaeological discovery of the Minoan civilisation at Knossos, Crete. In contrast, Sir John's second son Lewis Evans (1853-1930), was actively involved in the business and became a full partner in the firm of Dickinsons.

Sir Arthur Evans

Abbots Hill, 1897.

The Drawing room at Abbots Hill.

Front view of Abbots Hill, 1897.

The library at Abbots Hill.

Stable block at Abbots Hill, 1991.

Headmistress, Mrs. J. S. Kingsley and senior girls, 1996.

Commemoration Day 1995.

St. Nicholas House School, Boxmoor, in the 1960's.

St. Nicholas House School, 1995.

Boxmoor

In 1650 Two Water Moor and Box Moor were said to comprise 120 acres, but prior to the Eighteenth Century, Boxmoor barely existed as a separate settlement. The identity of Boxmoor really begins with the coming of the canal (built 1793-97) and was cemented by the arrival of the railway some 40 years later. These two events were catalysts that spurred on the development of the Victorian village of Boxmoor. Historically the word 'moor' denoted marshland, which was the prevailing condition of this area close to a much more vigorous River Bulbourne in earlier times. In addition box trees are very likely to have grown wild in the prevailing chalky soil above the river, so the place name Boxmoor has a fairly straightforward derivation. In simple terms, the area today known as Boxmoor stretches along the main road from the Bell Inn at Two Waters, in the south, to the junction with Box Lane in the north.

The story of Boxmoor has to begin with the story of the moor itself. This land was first given by Elizabeth I to the Earl of Leicester. By 1577 Peter Grey owned the moor, but several years later he signed an agreement, dated 26th May 1581, to sell the moorland and water meadows to three Hemel Hempstead men: John Rolfe, Richard Pope and William Gladman. A further deed of 26th April 1594, makes it clear that the purpose of this purchase was to secure the land for the public benefit of the inhabitants of Hemel Hempstead and Bovingdon. The money for this transaction seems to have been raised by public subscription, and the deed was witnessed by Francis Combe the younger and 66 other trustees.

On September 14th 1799, a committee of seven Boxmoor trustees was formed to oversee the compulsory sale of 25 acres of trust land to the Grand Junction Canal Company and the sum of £900 was eventually obtained. The Boxmoor Trust had previously lost some of its water meadows to improvements made on the London Road, which formed part of the Sparrows Herne Turnpike Trust (1762-1873). Arising from the difficulties concerning this land transaction with the Canal Company, an Act of Parliament dated 10th June 1809, formally established a Board of twelve trustees, to allow the future transactions of the Boxmoor Trust to be conducted on a more secure legal and business-like footing. Subsequently on 16th September 1836, a further 12 acres of land was sold by the trustees to the London and Birmingham Railway. Some of the monies from these sales were used to purchase Blackbirds Moor and also allowed the trustees to construct Boxmoor wharf. The Trust subsequently gained most of its income from the lease of this new wharf, for which it charged a full commercial rent. Boxmoor wharf will always be remembered for its role as the Rose's Lime Juice Depot. The wharf stood where we now find the B & Q Superstore.

Another matter formalised by the appointment of the twelve trustees in 1809, was the rights of pasture or grazing, which were now controlled by the issue of pasture tickets. For example in 1842, six tickets were required for one horse, four for a cow or ass and two for a hog. The purchased 'rights of pasturage' were assigned to the inhabitants of local houses by means of a small circular metal plaque, bearing a particular number. From 1833, eight hundred of these plaques were made by the local ironfounder Joseph Cranstone.

Although there is an on-going need for horse pastures, the demand for livestock grazing has now declined. However because local people still wished the moor to be grazed, the trustees have established their own pedigree herd of Belted Galloway cattle. In 1982 Howe's Retreat at Felden was purchased to help the Trust with its breeding programmes of Shetland cattle and Soay sheep. Latterly some Norfolk Horns have also been introduced onto the Boxmoor estate. The Trust's property portfolio at one time included five pubs no longer in existence: the Friend at Hand, the Boatman, the Star, the Crown and the Artichoke (currently a pet shop on the main road). Throughout its history, the Trust has always been active in supporting the local community by providing monies or land for public buildings such as St. John's Church and the former Town Hall.

In order to protect the green space for the Hemel Hempstead area the Trust cannot, by law, decrease its size and it has continued to try to increase the acreage under its protection and environmental care. In 1886 the Trust bought two pieces of land which are of great beauty and historical interest. These are Sheethanger Common, home to Boxmoor Golf Club, and Roughdown Common which is classed by the Trust as a Conservation Area. Since 1886 Trust lands have comprised approximately 240 acres and the moor itself has been planted with attractive varieties of horse chestnut trees. The area of Roughdown Common is of particular botanical interest, hosting several rare species of wild plants. Recently the Trust completed another important acquisition when, in 1995, it obtained 160 acres of Westbrook Hay Farm on a 125 year lease. This takes the total acreage under its control to 400.

To local people specific areas of the moor have their own special names. Box Moor itself lies to the west of St. John's Church, whilst Heath Park Moor is to the east. Two Waters Moor lies along Two Waters Road; then there is Station Moor, followed by Fishery Moor and just beyond the railway, opposite Box Lane junction, are Snoxall's Moor and Snook's Moor. In the earlier part of this century, there was also a Cotterell's Moor, but that vanished with the coming of Leighton Buzzard Road and the roundabout.

Snook The Highwayman

People who visit Boxmoor are usually intrigued by the story of the highwayman James Snook who was born in Hungerford in 1761. By 1800 Snook was a wanted man with a string of highway robberies to his name. On 17th May 1801 he robbed the mounted post boy, John Stevens, who was carrying the mail between Tring and Hemel Hempstead. Following this incident Snook fled to Southwark in London, with a haul of letters that contained between them a sum of money variously recorded at between £150 and £550. The crime was reported to the local Postmaster John Page of the Kings Arms in Berkhamsted. John Page was also the High Constable and a huge reward of £300 was promptly posted for the capture of the highwayman. Snook managed to remain at liberty until 5th December when he was captured in Marlborough Forest. Subsequently he was charged with robbery at Bow Street on December 9th and committed to Newgate Gaol. Later on 8th March 1802, James Snook was tried at Hertford Assizes, found guilty and sentenced to death. Constable Page of Berkhamsted stipulated that he should be executed as near as possible to the scene of the crime. Consequently three days later, James Snook was both hung and buried on Boxmoor, close to where the robbery took place. Thousands of people came to witness the execution. One hundred years later in 1904, the Boxmoor Trustees provided some small grave stones on the moor to commemorate the event. It is thought likely that James Snook holds the macabre distinction of being the last highwayman in England to be hanged at the scene of his crime. Confusingly, this grave bears the name Robert Snooks presumably recorded by oral tradition and corrupted from 'Robber'.

Box Lane Chapel.

Box Lane Chapel
The Church of England's grip on the faith of the nation, tightened by the Conventicle Act of 1664, ushered in a more hostile environment for non-conformists everywhere. The Gade and Bulbourne valleys were an area rich in dissenters (see Tring in particular on page 232), many of whom practised their Baptist faith secretly in local cottages and barns. One of the first local chapels was built in Box Lane in the early 1600's. This boasted the special feature of a hatched doorway, at the back of the pulpit, to enable the preacher to make a quick escape if threatened. Tradition has it that Oliver Cromwell once worshipped at Box Lane Chapel. The chapel, officially founded in 1668, was re-built in 1690 and subsequently altered in 1836 and again in 1876. Its survival as an early chapel is owed, at least in part, to the protection and patronage it received from the nearby estate of Westbrook, which was leased by Henry Mayne. Henry and his son James Mayne, who bought the manor in 1592, were both leading Puritans of their day. During the Nineteenth Century, some Roman funeral remains were found in the graveyard of the chapel at Box Lane (see page 14). The doors of Box Lane Chapel closed finally on 29th June 1969, ending well over 300 years of worship on this site. It was subsequently converted into a private house, at which time an upper floor was added.

Boxmoor
Beginning in the 1850's, several large houses were constructed in the area. These belonged to the earliest commuters, most of whom were wealthy professional men who worked in London but preferred to live in the country. The Nineteenth Century also saw the beginning of genuine residential development in Boxmoor, which sprang up to provide accommodation for the rapidly expanding number of people employed by the larger local factories, such as Dickinson's Mills at Apsley. As part of this process, Horsecroft, Kingsland and Moorland Roads were developed by local builders.

Boxmoor House
Built in the mid Nineteenth Century for wealthy surgeon Thomas Davis, from 1873 Boxmoor House became the residence of the Rev. James Blackwood and his wife Alicia. The Rev. Blackwell died in 1882, but Lady Alicia lived on at Boxmoor House for over twenty years. The house served as a hospital in the First World War and during the 1930's was the Arniston School for the Imbecile Children of Gentle Folk, run by the two Misses Isbister. The house was bought by Hertfordshire County Council in 1942 to become Boxmoor House School. Box Lane Farm was formerly part of the estate of Boxmoor House. The small building standing beside the Eighteenth Century Swan Inn, at the junction of Box Lane and London Road, used to be the Lodge to Boxmoor House.

Box Lane House
This estate, with buildings dating from the Eleventh Century, originally formed part of the Manor of Westbrook Hay. The charming house, which survived into the Twentieth Century, was set in two acres and was finally demolished in the 1960's to make way for Copper Beech Close.

Churchill
This imposing house, formerly known as The Heath, was built by William Hammond in 1830. It was later home to Mr. E. A. Mitchell-Innes and family, whose son Gilbert's unusual Medieval-style memorial can still be found in St. John's Church. The property was auctioned on 4th July 1934 and bought by the local authority for £3,500. The house was used for family welfare clinics and a public open-air swimming pool was built in the grounds. The Churchill site is now home to the Dacorum Sports Centre.

Lockers Park School
In 1872 H. Montague Draper started his preparatory school at Hillside in Heath Lane, before moving it to the purpose-built Lockers Park which he founded in 1874. This impressive building was designed by leading architect Sidney Smith. Admiral of the Fleet Earl Mountbatten of Burma was a notable former pupil of Lockers Park (1910-1913). Hillside School later became known as Heathbrow School, amalgamating with Shirley House School, Watford in 1964. This school then moved to the impressive house at Beechwood Park in Markyate, the former home of the Sebright family.

Hammerfield
This distinctive housing estate was built on a hammer-shaped piece of land, formerly belonging to Ebenezer John Collett, whose 'gentleman's residence' was Lockers, a Sixteenth Century house, altered in the Eighteenth Century. This is not to be confused with Lockers Park, but is an entirely different building still situated on Bury Hill. This building has now been converted into residential flats, after serving for several years as the sixth form annexe of Cavendish School. Hammerfield was another example of a speculative development, started during Boxmoor's development at the turn of the century. The estate was abandoned for a time when the developer went out of business. Prompted by the planting of thousands of conifers, in the late 1800's, this area became known as 'Little Switzerland', a name echoed by the architecture of some of its houses.

Fishery Inn
Established in the early part of the Nineteenth Century, the Fishery Inn was a popular canal-side tavern, which offered stabling for horses and a resident blacksmith at the Fishery Forge. An attractive stone balustrade bridge replaced the Nineteenth Century bridge in 1922, but sadly this has now been spoilt by a modern reinforced concrete structure. Another of Boxmoor's oldest pubs is the Three Blackbirds in St. Johns Road. This dates from 1760 and sits opposite the Roman

Churchill, Boxmoor.

Lockers, circa 1910.

Heath Park Hotel and Halt.

Heath Park Hotel in the 1890's.

Boxmoor Hall at the turn of the century.

First World War tank on display at Heath Park.

View of Hammerfield, circa 1935.

Catholic Church of St. Mary and St. Joseph which was built in 1898. Another local pub, the Steamcoach, further down St. Johns Road near the church, may have been named after Joseph Cranstone's partly successful road steam carriage experiment of 1867. The painting on the Inn sign is however of another vehicle and the name of the pub may therefore have more to do with the proximity of the railway.

Boxmoor Hall

Founded by the Boxmoor Trust, Boxmoor Hall was constructed in 1889-90 for the sum of £1300. It was built in the Flemish style of the Seventeenth Century from designs by W. A. Fisher. It has served as a Court House and main venue for most of the public meetings in Boxmoor. It has for many years served as the local Youth Arts Centre. A public water pump and drinking fountain, made by local ironfounder William Cranstone, still stands outside Boxmoor Hall. Later this was converted for use as a gas standard lamp. It was erected in October 1835 "For the public benefit and to commemorate the 300th anniversary of the first printing of the English Bible".

St. John's Church

Prior to the establishment of St. John's, the main village area of Boxmoor was known as Crouchfield; 'Crouche' being old English for cross, no doubt denoting a cross-roads. The parish of Boxmoor was formed in 1844 and the Church of St. John, Boxmoor was erected on the site of a former Chapel-of-Ease to the Parish Church of St. Mary, Hemel Hempstead which had been established in 1829. The opening service at St. John's was held on 7th April 1874 with a sermon by the Bishop of Rochester. The building, in Gothic style designed by the architect Norman Shaw R.A., was constructed at an approximate cost of £4250 and provided seating for 700 persons. The church features an octagonal bellcote on the nave roof and a five-light west window with geometrical tracery. The first incumbent at St. John's was the Rev. A. C. Richings of Christ College, Cambridge (1865-99). He built the rambling vicarage in Heath Lane, at his own expense, but this house has since been demolished. The church and churchyard were enlarged in 1893 and a new vestry added in 1909. From 1974, the Vicar of St. John's, Boxmoor was also Chaplain to West Herts. Hospital. The War Memorial, now situated by the church, in St. Johns Road was initially erected at the Plough roundabout. St. John's School was first opened in 1842 as a National School, and was later transferred to the County Education Authority. St. John's Hall was officially opened on 30th April 1932 by the Bishop of St. Albans. It has recently been purchased from the Ecclesiastical Authorities and is now owned by the Hemel Hempstead Operatic and Dramatic Society.

Heath Park

On the north side of St. Johns Road, Heath Farmhouse together with its barn and cottage, are early timber-framed buildings dating from the Sixteenth Century. The nearby hotel takes its name from this district and was built primarily to service the passenger trade first brought by the London and Birmingham Railway in 1837. The Heath Park Hotel was described in 1869 as a first-class hotel for gentlemen and their families. The Heath Park, now a modernised building of the same name, sits next to Boxmoor Hall. A First World War tank used to stand on the Green in front of Heath Park and was a gift to the Borough in recognition of its record war savings. It was removed from public view shortly before World War II.

View from Roughdown Common, Boxmoor, 1910.

Fishery Road, Boxmoor, circa 1912.

The grave of James Snook, 1905.

Boxmoor, looking towards the railway station, circa 1908.

Swan Inn at the junction of London Road and Box Lane, circa 1914.

Sheethanger Common.

St. John's Church, Boxmoor.

St. Johns Road in Boxmoor, circa 1910.

Bovingdon

Despite the fact that the population of the village has more than quadrupled during the last 100 years, for most of its life, Bovingdon has been a modest but thriving agricultural community. One of the most important phases in its history has been this recent rapid expansion of its population; in particular the post-war growth of the community. The population of Bovingdon showed only minimal increase throughout the Nineteenth Century, when a total of 799 people in 1801 had grown to only 1056 by 1891. In contrast, the 1047 people present in 1901 showed a marked increase towards the total of 4491 persons recorded in the census of 1991. This population growth, combined with its role as USAF Bovingdon during the Second World War and the later arrival of the Mount Prison in 1988, has given the village of Bovingdon greater significance in the Twentieth Century.

Situated some 500ft. above sea level in the Chiltern Hills, three miles to the south-west of Hemel Hempstead, Bovingdon began its life as a small clearing in the extensive forest that once covered this side of the Bulbourne valley. There were originally two hamlets: one clustered around the church and possible old Manor House (Bury Farm), and another approximately half a mile to the south around a triangular area of Green or common land beside which now stands the Royal Oak public house. There is no specific mention of Bovingdon in the Domesday Book. The earliest record of Bovingdon dates from 1200, when the village name is likely to have been derived from the old English 'bufan dune', meaning a settlement 'above the down'.

In 1290 the Bonhommes monks from the monastery at Ashridge, were granted all the woodland in the Bovingdon area. They soon set about converting this gift into cash by clearing the forests, with much of the timber being used for the substantial repairs that were required at Berkhamsted Castle. In common with much of the rest of the Hemel Hempstead area, there is very little surviving woodland at Bovingdon. Later tree planting seems to have been restricted to small copses established in hollows to provide timber for fuel, building and fences. We can safely assume that the beginnings of a community at Bovingdon sprang from the creation of Medieval farms established in the wake of the woodland clearance. A tax roll of 1295 lists 74 people in the area, but this probably also includes the population of Flaunden.

Local Farms

As would be expected, there are many examples of nearby farms and homesteads, which date back to the Sixteenth and Seventeenth Centuries. Of these, the most notable are the attractive Sixteenth Century farmhouse of Rent Street Farm, on the Chipperfield Road and the Seventeenth Century Bury Farm, built on an earlier manorial site. Green Farm was originally a Fifteenth Century open hall house and Water Lane Farm is a Seventeenth Century house with Sixteenth Century barn. Yew Tree Farm dates from the Seventeenth Century and Marchants Farm at Pudds Cross is a very early farmstead site, with surviving buildings also dating from the Seventeenth Century. The 'Parish Guides' village walk leaflet, obtainable from Bovingdon library, will help to locate all these old farm buildings.

Church of St. Lawrence

It is thought that a church or chapel has stood on this site since 1200. We certainly know that there was religious activity in Bovingdon from 1235. This was the year when the Vicar of Hemel Hempstead, Bernard de Graveleigh, appointed two curates, one each for Bovingdon and Flaunden. In 1290 the religious care of Bovingdon was transferred to the monastery at Ashridge and there it remained until the Dissolution in 1539. There is little surviving record of the first church, but it is thought that the church which pre-dated the present one was built around 1320. The only remaining artefact of this period in the Church of St. Lawrence is the chest tomb with a stone effigy of an unknown knight. Local legend has it that this knight was responsible for building the first Bovingdon church.

Early drawing of Bovingdon Church.

Until the Nineteenth Century, Bovingdon was a chapelry of St. Mary's, Hemel Hempstead and was served by a resident curate, with the exception of the period 1760-1834. Eventually in 1834 Bovingdon became a separate Parish, independent of Hemel Hempstead, and Granville Ryder paid for the patronage of Bovingdon Church. He also gave a plot of land opposite the Church of St. Lawrence, so that a parsonage could be built. Bovingdon's first Vicar, the Rev. Arthur Brooking, married into the Ryder family. The first vicarage of St. Lawrence was built in Vicarage Lane and is now known as Church Lane House. By 1844 the church was in such a poor state of repair that it had to be demolished. With the help of Granville Ryder, the Rev. Arthur Brooking managed a major re-build of the church by 1846; this work excluded the tower. During this building work, it is said that some Anglo-Saxon remains were discovered in the foundations which could have dated from the first church at Bovingdon. During the 1880's two rows of yew trees were planted alongside the churchyard path. In 1884 the Lych Gate of St. Lawrence was built in memory of Granville Ryder's daughter, Isabel Moore. The old curate's house, in the churchyard, was considered too small and pulled down in 1886, whilst in the 1930's the parsonage was sold as being too large!

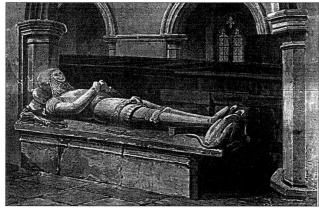

Knight's tomb in Bovingdon Church, 1852.

A new vicarage was built on part of the vicarage glebe and the Parish Room was moved about 150 yards up the road from the old vicarage. St. Lawrence can be described as a Victorian vernacular church. It features a five bay nave with an embattled west tower and a lean-to vestry to the north east. St. Lawrence features a total of 15 memorials to the Ryder family of Westbrook Hay and there are some early brasses to the memory of the Mayne family in the chancel which are now partially covered.

It is worth mentioning that, perhaps encouraged by the lowly status of the village church, many of the villagers of Bovingdon were keen non-conformists. During the Sixteenth and Seventeenth Centuries, this local tradition of faith was encouraged by both the Mayne and Lomax families. These successive Lords of the Manor of Westbrook Hay both helped to sustain the local non-conformist chapel in Box Lane. One of the country's leading non-conformists during this time was Dr. Edmund Staunton. He spent the last ten years of his life in Bovingdon and ironically was buried at the local Parish Church; there is a memorial tablet in the chancel floor of St. Lawrence.

Village School
The original Bovingdon School was the building now known as The Close, off the Chipperfield Road. This was partly destroyed by a fire in the 1930's. The oldest surviving log book from Bovingdon School is dated 1890, though the school was probably founded several decades earlier. The present school was built on land adjacent to the Bovingdon Memorial Hall and was officially opened on 28th March 1927. Since then the junior school, joined by an infant school which opened in the 1960's, has been significantly expanded to cope with the rapid post-war growth of the Bovingdon population. Since 1991 the Bovingdon Primary School site has been shared by a modern purpose built Public Library, specifically designed by Hertfordshire County Council to be a dual-use facility linked to the school.

The Ryder Memorial
This attractive memorial is Bovingdon's best known landmark and stands on the cross-roads at the south end of the High Street. Built in 1881 this timber framed structure, on a red brick plinth with blue brick chamfered offsets, suggests a well-head, but is not a well. Erected to honour the village's principal benefactor, Granville Dudley Ryder (1799-1879), the memorial's design also recalls the Ryder family's vital role in supplying the village with water, when droughts in the early 1800's dried up most of the Bovingdon wells. The site of the main well in the village lies further up the Chipperfield Road, with the remains of its railings visible behind the pond area, known by villagers as the 'Bovingdon Docks'.

Bovingdon Revels 1980

The Bell
Bovingdon

Local Inns
The most important surviving hostelry is the Wheatsheaf, which is a heavily timbered structure, likely to date from the Fifteenth Century. This building has played a full part in village life, also serving as the slaughterhouse during the Eighteenth and Nineteenth Centuries. More recently part of the building was used as a barber's shop and also as the village post office. Opposite the Wheatsheaf is the Bell, an Eighteenth Century Inn which was kept by Elizabeth Bingham in 1756. The Bull, which stands at the cross-roads in the village centre, is less than 200 years old and was kept by Thomas Austin in 1826. An interesting discovery was made at the Bull when, during renovation work in 1985, a secret room was found in the attic. This room still contained an old camp bed and a radio transmitter, together with pens and newspapers dating from 1939. It was clearly the secret lair of a war-time spy who was ideally positioned to monitor the activities of the local military command posts and the later activities of the Americans, based at Bovingdon Airfield. It is perhaps also worth noting that the family of the infamous Lord Haw Haw, William Thorpe, lived at nearby Sarratt. His wartime broadcasts often commented upon the accuracy of the Watford Town Hall clock. Halfway House, formerly the Rose and Crown, is a significant landmark on the Hempstead Road, so named because in Victorian times it was considered to lie exactly half-way between Chesham and old Hemel Hempstead.

RAF Bovingdon
The three runways of Bovingdon Airfield were constructed in 1941 by John Laing & Son, on a site which is 535ft. above sea level. The main runway was built 4,950ft. long with two intersecting runways, each 4,300ft. long. By 15th June 1942 the Airfield was ready to be handed over to the R.A.F. and it was originally earmarked for the use of the No. 7 Bomber Group. However this plan did not materialise and in August 1942, the United States Army Air Force turned Bovingdon Airfield into the U.S. Air Station Base 112. The troop ship 'West Point' had brought the necessary ground personnel of the 92nd Bomb Group across the Atlantic to Liverpool. These men were soon joined by squadrons of Boeing B-17 Flying Fortresses which started flying in between the 18th and 26th August. However the newer B-17 F's were soon transferred out and replaced by the older B-17 E's, and it was these planes that began the first local combat missions of the war, from 6th September 1942.

The operations of this part of the U.S. 8th Air Force soon settled down under Commanding Officer Colonel Sutton and at one stage these four-engine bombers would leave for Germany at the rate of one every two minutes. The 8th Air Force sustained its first bomber fatality on the 21st August and the first Flying Fortress to be lost from Bovingdon was on a mission to Meaulte, France on 6th September 1942. With the Luftwaffe waiting in strength, and the Americans attacking mainly in daylight, the casualty rate soon became heavy for the allies all over occupied Europe. With replacements arriving in large numbers from the U.S.A., Bovingdon became a key airfield for training new crews up to squadron standard on the B-17 heavy bombers. On 4th January 1944, the 92nd Bomb Group began moving to Alconbury, where it reformed as a Combat Group. The remaining servicemen at Bovingdon then formed the nucleus of the 11th Combat Crew Replacement Centre under Director of Training, Major John P. Dwyer.

In its war-time role Bovingdon Air Base had many celebrated visitors from across the Atlantic. Mrs. Eleanor Roosevelt visited her son, who spent several weeks here with the student detachment of the 15th Photo Mapping Squadron. When General Eisenhower came to England, in order to help plan the allied invasion of Europe, his personal B-17 was kept at Bovingdon. Film stars Clark Gable, James Stewart and William Holden were all serving airmen who spent some time at U.S.A.F. Bovingdon, whilst Glen Miller, Bob Hope and Merle Oberon visited to entertain the troops. With the Allied victory in sight, the Combat Crew Replacement Unit moved out in September 1944. In its place, the U.S. Air Transport Service (Europe) arrived with their Douglas C47 and C53 carriers. After VE Day Bovingdon became a major base for the return of American servicemen to the U.S.A. It has been said that during this time, Bovingdon was busier than London's International Airports.

Following a brief stay by the R.A.F. in 1946, the Ministry of Civil Aviation took over Bovingdon. The Airfield was then used by independent airlines and also by B.E.A. as a diversion airport, when either Heathrow or Northolt was closed due to poor weather. Many V.I.P.'s were flown in and out of the country here, during the post-war years. At this time Bovingdon was also home to the Communication Units of both the Fighter and Coastal Commands of the R.A.F. Following the Berlin air lift of 1948/49, and the uneasy peace that followed, the 3rd U.S. Air Force came to Bovingdon in 1951. The 7531st Air Base Squadron remained here for 15 years with their C47 'Gooney Bird' transports. During this time, with R.A.F. Coastal Command based at Northwood and the U.S. 3rd Air Division H.Q. at Ruislip, Bovingdon was an obvious choice of location for military planning. A fantastic variety of aircraft now paid regular visits for joint conferences. The airfield was also the backdrop for a series of war-time epic feature films such as 'War Lover' starring Steve McQueen and '633 Squadron'. During the 1960's episodes of the T.V. series Z Cars were also made at Bovingdon. In 1968 a Defence White Paper included R.A.F. Bovingdon as one of the airfields to be given up and all the Ministry of Defence property at Bovingdon, except the married quarters, had been disposed of by 1976. Bovingdon Airfield is now the venue for a variety of different events such as markets, go-carts and stock car racing.

Bovingdon Poisoner

In 1972 the village of Bovingdon received unwanted national attention as the scene of two particularly unpleasant murders by the infamous serial poisoner Graham Young. In 1971 Graham Young had obtained a job as storeman at the small factory of John Hadland, a specialist manufacturer of optical and photographic equipment based in Bovingdon. Shortly after he joined the company, the firm's staff gradually began to suffer from what became known as the 'Bovingdon Bug'. As a friendly and helpful young storeman, Graham Young was always ready to make drinks for his colleagues and it is said that the tea soon began to taste bitter. Two members of staff eventually died, Bob Egle in July 1971 and Frederick Biggs in September. After Young had boasted to the firm's medical officer, Dr. Iain Anderson, of his knowledge of poisons, the police were alerted and arrested him on suspicion of murder. He was subsequently found to have been slowly poisoning his victims with thallium. Graham Young was tried for murder at St. Albans in July 1972, found guilty and jailed for life. He was initially held in a top security hospital. 18 years later Graham Young died of natural causes at Parkhurst Prison on the Isle of Wight.

Bovingdon Prison

In November 1970 the Home Office announced that they planned to site a new prison at Bovingdon. By May 1971 it was known that this was intended to be a Category 'C' Prison, designed to hold up to 500 inmates. By November both Hertfordshire County Council and Hemel Hempstead Rural District Council had decided to fight the plans and a Public Enquiry opened at Hemel Hempstead Civic Centre on 26th April 1972. However in September 1972, the Home Office announced the go-ahead for the prison which was to comprise five cell blocks, together with a sports hall, workshops, library, car park and outdoor games area, all surrounded by a security fence 5.2 metres high. There were to be 140 houses built for prison staff and it was expected that approximately 230 jobs would be created. Due to many changes in the plans, work did not begin until the summer of 1984. The contract for the building work was awarded to Wimpey at a cost of £18 million. In August 1987 the Home Office announced that the prison was going to be a youth prison called The Mount, which finally opened its doors in March 1988. The Mount's official opening, as a Youth Custody Centre, was attended by H.R.H. Princess Anne in November 1988. The Mount has since become a H.M. Prison Category 'C' housing adult offenders.

View of Bovingdon from the Chipperfield Road, circa 1906.

Crossroads at Bovingdon showing the Halfway House in the 1920's.

Ryder Memorial in the 1950's.

Southern end of Bovingdon village in the 1920's.

Church of St. Lawrence, Bovingdon, in the 1950's.

The Bell Inn, 1912.

Flood at Bovingdon in the 1950's.

Bovingdon Post Office, 1910.

Bovingdon Green.

Rickett's Family Butchers.

Pudds Cross Farm, Bovingdon.

Mr. F.E. Bryant of Water Lane Farm, circa1930.

Flag Ceremony, U.S.A.F. Bovingdon.

R.A.F. Bovingdon, derelict in the 1970's.

Flight of Avro Anson aircraft over Bovingdon.

Bovingdon Prison.

Princess Anne opens the Mount on Tuesday, October 25th, 1988.

Westbrook Hay

The main structure of this substantial house dates from the Eighteenth Century, although there may be traces of several earlier buildings within the fabric of its foundations. By the beginning of the Nineteenth Century, this two storey red brick house had an impressive seven bay frontage, with parapet, and a three bay projecting centre. Westbrook Hay's role as a preparatory school for boys and girls dates back to 1963 when the school was transferred from its previous home at Gadebridge House, the former residence of Sir Astley Paston Cooper 1768-1841. The estate's early Nineteenth Century Lodge survives close to the main A4251 road, to the north of the main house. This is a charming single storey cottage, built in orné style and currently undergoing extensive renovation.

The estate itself dates back to the Thirteenth Century, when it is mentioned as early as 1204 in grants of land to Queen Eleanor. The first structure on the site was a hall built in 1238 and we know that this building then included a small chapel. In 1312 John de la Hay received a grant for life of all lands at La Hay: John de La Hay later became Sheriff for Hertfordshire 1331-32. By 1442 the Manors of both Westbrokehay and Eastbrokehay had been settled on Richard de la Hay and his wife Margaret. Both manors were then conveyed to their son Matthew and his male heirs. The last De la Hay recorded locally is Edward de la Hay who was a man of considerable wealth and influence. He was a close friend of Cecily, Duchess of York, who paid him frequent visits at Westbrook Hay, from her quarters at nearby Berkhamsted Castle. When Cecily died, her will of 1495 included a substantial bequest to Edward de la Hay. On Edward's death the Manors of Eastbrook and Westbrook were left in two parts to his surviving daughters.

During the late 1580's the house at Westbrook had been let to Henry Mayne and by 1592 the Westbrook part of the estate had been sold to his son James Mayne. The Mayne family lived at Westbrook Hay until 1667, when the manor was sold by James Mayne's two grand daughters, Mary and Sarah, to a Joshua Lomax. Joshua Lomax, who came from Bolton in Lancashire, had bought three substantial country estates in Hertfordshire and he gave Westbrook to his youngest son Thomas. Thomas Lomax then set about re-building the house, which by 1700 was described by Chauncy as a "very fair mansion house of brick". Thomas was succeeded at Westbrook by his daughter Ann, who married Richard Ryder. The Ryders then became an important local family. Sir Dudley Ryder was Attorney General 1737-57, later becoming Chief Justice of the Kings Bench. The Westbrook Hay estate then passed first to his son Lomax, who died childless and intestate in 1779, and then to Lomax's younger brother Thomas. Thomas Ryder died in 1821 and bequeathed the manor to a distinguished relative, the Rt. Hon. Richard Ryder, Judge Advocate General and Secretary of State 1809-12. Richard Ryder also died without issue and Westbrook Hay was then left to his nephew, the Hon. Granville Dudley Ryder, who was son of Dudley, the 1st Earl of Harrowby. As we will read later, Granville Dudley Ryder took an active interest in the surrounding community, both in the village of Bovingdon and also at Bourne End where he paid for the establishment of the School/Church House in 1843. When Granville Dudley Ryder died in 1879, he was succeeded at Westbrook Hay by his son Dudley Henry Ryder who continued his father's tradition of public benefaction.

The Ryders were a very wealthy family who at the end of the Nineteenth Century employed a domestic staff of 24 at the big house and remained very involved in the life of the community.

Granville Dudley Ryder.

Most local people benefited at some time or another from the generosity of the family, who were regular patrons of Bovingdon Parish Church. The Ryders had become very much the local squires to the communities of both Bovingdon and Bourne End, employing many villagers on their farm estates. Dudley H. Ryder died in 1911 and, following the death of his widow in 1915, Westbrook Hay was let. The last member of the Ryder family to own Westbrook was Frederick Granville Ryder who held the property from 1933, until it was acquired by the Hemel Hempstead Development Corporation in 1948 and used as their local offices. The school that eventually came to Westbrook Hay in 1963 began life as Rye House School, Bedford and was established in 1892 by Augustus Scobell Orlebar. This school was purchased by Mr. G. W. Gruggen in 1902 and moved to Gadebridge Park in January 1914. It may interest many to know that the school's founder, the Rev. Augustus Orlebar was, as a boy, used by Thomas Hughes as the principal inspiration for the character of Tom Brown in his classic childrens' novel Tom Brown's Schooldays. Also of interest at Westbrook Hay is the house on the estate known as Puddingstone House. This is built entirely of Hertfordshire puddingstone. The fascinating geological story behind this unusual substance is told in more detail on page 7.

Westbrook Hay.

Westbrook Hay Preparatory School, 1996.

Frontage of Westbrook Hay, 1996.

Puddingstone House at Westbrook Hay, 1996.

Dudley Henry Ryder.

Bourne End

The name Bourne End comes from the old English 'burna', meaning stream. It is in common use, especially in the chalk districts of England, where it is not unusual for small streams to appear following periods of abnormally high rainfall. The suffix 'end' is a very popular term throughout Hertfordshire and denotes a small village or hamlet. One can now see that the name of Bourne End tells the story of how this small hamlet became established by the banks of the River Bulbourne. The community grew up close to where one of its feeder streams, the Bourne Gutter, used to swell the River's flow until the lowering of the water table during the Twentieth Century. There is no longer much evidence of the vigorous River Bulbourne that was once the very artery of life in Medieval Bourne End. As for the Bourne Gutter, it has long since become an intermittent stream, only flowing when the rainfall exceeds 32 inches in a period of twelve months. Records indicate that in 1860, it overflowed its banks into the garden opposite Bourne End Mill for the first time in 30 years; and at the beginning of March 1926, it was a continuous stream for about 400 yards above the junction of the lanes from Bottom and Lower Farms. The spring of 1951 was also one of the Bourne Gutter's fuller years. Local tradition has it that the flow of the Bourne Gutter was "woe water" and its rising was a sure sign of impending pestilence, disaster or war.

The discovery of various pre-historic implements in ground near Bottom Farm suggests that there was an early settlement beside the Bourne Gutter. Historians have also suggested that, given the even distribution of Roman farming villas already discovered along the valley (at approx. two mile intervals), there are remaining Roman foundations yet to be found in the Bourne End area. Bourne End is certainly mentioned in documents dated 1357, (referred to as 'le Bournend'), and as early as 1296 reference is made to an Emma de la Bourne as "tenant in this place".

Haxters End Farm, 1858.

The Mill
The economy of the hamlet of Bourne End has always been entirely agricultural, centred on the old water mill powered by the River Bulbourne. Some Bourne Enders would have worked on land belonging to the estate of Westbrook Hay and the substantial Nineteenth Century Saw Mill, later established in Bourne End Lane, would also have provided employment. The water mill at Bourne End was one of five listed in the Charter of Ashridge 1289, when the monastery was founded. A directory of 1832 lists a William Littleboy at the mill which had various tenants, until J. Goodall Knowles of Broadway Farm

took over Bourne End Mill on a long lease in 1893. He replaced the existing three pairs of mill stones with a new roller mill in 1900. He also added an oil engine to the power already provided by the nine foot overshot water wheel. This increased the production rate to one and a half sacks (3½ cwt) of flour per hour. By 1901 J. Goodall Knowles' son, Alfred, was resident at the mill house in Bourne End. The mill ceased operation soon after the Second World War, although the site remained undeveloped until after bad damage by fire on 5th November 1970. The building lost in the fire was an early Nineteenth Century, two storey structure with a three storied gabled weather-boarded central block.

Bourne End School and Churchroom.

In December 1972 the modern 40 bedroom Water Mill Hotel opened on the site of the mill, the remains of which had been scheduled as a listed building. The hotel's architects were therefore careful to incorporate elements of the Nineteenth Century mill and mill race into the new design. This historic link, created for the modern motel building, was lost when the property was subsequently bought by the Queens Moat House Group and re-named the Hemel Hempstead Moat House. Opposite the hotel, the White Horse which is a charming Seventeenth Century Inn, still survives by the main road. In 1756 it is listed as being kept by George Paine. Bourne End's other pub, the Anchor, is probably older than the White Horse, with its timber framed structure dating from the Sixteenth Century. In 1838 William Saunders is listed as the licensee at the Anchor.

Local Farms
Pix Farm is listed as occupied by Robert Pick in 1304, though by 1603 the variant spelling of Pixe had been introduced. The first locomotive seen in the area was assembled in a barn at Pix Farm. This was the 'Harvey Coombe', brought to Bourne End in its component parts by canal boat in 1835. Its purpose was to help with the construction of the London to Birmingham Railway. Haxters End Farm was owned in 1314 by William Heckesault and by 1565 his surname had evolved into the place name Hark Salt End. Haxters End Lane was re-named Little Heath Lane following the demolition of the old farmhouse. Bourne End Farmhouse dates from the Seventeenth Century and has a timber frame visible in two east gables. This two

storey building, with modern casement windows, shows a cross gable to the road. On the north western side of Bourne End (towards Berkhamsted), was a large unfenced field known as Broadway Common. It was here in 1867, that a late Celtic sword was found in the watercress beds. This impressive weapon, still in its scabbard, is now held by the British Museum. The lands of Broadway Farm were on the western side of Bourne End, whilst Pix Farm occupied the fields lying to the east of the River Bulbourne and the Grand Junction Canal (constructed in 1797). Although the curious story of Peter the Wild Boy is told in the history of Northchurch where he was buried (see page 221), he spent much of his time at Broadway Farm in Bourne End, where he died on 22nd February 1785 at the supposed age of 72. Peter had earlier spent many happy years at Haxters End Farm, in Bourne End, under the care of yeoman farmer James Fenn. When he died, Peter the Wild Boy was moved to Broadway Farm under the care of James Fenn's brother Thomas. The lands of Moor End Farm mark the southern territory of Bourne End, extending towards Boxmoor.

Bourne End School/Church Room

Historically the inhabitants of Bourne End fell within the widely scattered parish of St. Mary's, Northchurch. Principally because of its position on the border of three different parishes, (Boxmoor, Bovingdon and Hemel Hempstead), Bourne End had no religious centre of its own until the middle of the Nineteenth Century. In 1843 a school building was provided in Bourne End by local squire Granville Dudley Ryder, to ensure elementary education for the children of the district. On Sundays this school became the local church, with services on Sunday mornings and evenings; it was also home to two Sunday Schools held in the morning and afternoon. During the time of Dudley Ryder at Westbrook Hay (1879-1911), the entire family would attend the morning service, via the gravel path which ran down the hill from the big house. As late as 1935, there were 57 scholars at Bourne End School, but by 1937 there were only 25 children attending. The school did not open again following the Second World War and was later converted into a private dwelling. The house retains its patterned tiled roof with two gabled dormers.

St. John's Church, Broadway

No doubt spurred on by the Ryder's gift of a school room at Bourne End, this attractive little Church was built as a Chapel-of-Ease to Northchurch in 1854-55. Canon Sir John Hobart Culme Seymour, who was Rector there for 50 years, bore much of the expense of the construction. St. John's, which was dedicated on 23rd May 1855, has an interesting fresco above the sanctuary, which represents Dante's vision. Designed by Sir Giles Gilbert Scott, the church also displays a charming spirelet on the roof, which is a perfect example of a feature known as the small "Hertfordshire spike" or "snuffer". To perpetuate the memory of his wife Elca Rose, who died in 1889, Edward Curtis of the Hall in Berkhamsted paid for the decorations in the church and the creation of a new altar for St. John's. In 1913 the new Parish of Bourne End was finally established with St. John's as its Parish Church. From this date the old school building was no longer used as a place of worship.

Winkwell

The name 'Winkwell' probably comes from the old English 'wincel', meaning a corner and weil (a spring or well). The area is referred to in local documents dated 1623; this being the approximate date of the construction of the building which is now the Three Horseshoes Inn. Although the Seventeenth Century Three Horseshoes has been much altered, it still has an old gabled tiled roof and the later Nineteenth Century addition of a veranda. In 1838 Benjamin Glenister is listed as the beer retailer at the Winkwell Inn. Situated in one of the Seventeenth Century cottages beyond his Inn, was the blacksmith's home and this house was also called Winkwell. The swing bridge at Winkwell was replaced in 1865 and subject to further overhaul in November 1878. By this time a second swing bridge had been installed at Bourne End in 1868, this was situated further up stream at Bourne End Mill.

Although plagued by current day traffic levels on the A4251 (the former A41) main road, Bourne End's survival as a small hamlet has enjoyed something of a charmed life. Its rural environment has enjoyed two fortunate escapes in its history, the first when the tramway proposed in 1887 was cancelled. This noisy tramway would have sliced through Bourne End on its main route intended to link Hemel Hempstead to Chesham. The more recent escape took place when Bourne End, which is within the Municipal Borough of Hemel Hempstead, was placed outside the designated area of the New Town in the plans prepared by G. A. Jellicoe in 1947. However the recently constructed A41 by-pass now slices through some of Bourne End's farmland, separating Bottom Farm from the Bourne Gutter.

PETER the WILD BOY.
Brought to England by
King George I.

Bourne End, 1921.

White Horse at Bourne End, circa 1908.

Bourne End Lane.

St. John's Church, Bourne End, in the 1940's.

Bourne End Post Office at the turn of the century.

Bourne End Mill in the 1970's.

The Three Horseshoes, circa 1920.

The Three Horseshoes and swing bridge, circa 1925.

Winkwell in the 1970's.

Winkwell swing bridge.

Hemel Hempstead

Hemel Hempstead is notable for the superb surviving Norman architecture of its Parish Church of St. Mary's. The other key building in the town's history is represented by the elements of a Sixteenth Century structure known as The Bury. However only some parts of the surrounding walls and the gatehouse of this old mansion house survive today. The Charter Gate, with the landscaped Charter Gardens beyond leading towards Gadebridge Park, commemorate a charter which was awarded to the town by Henry VIII in 1539. This Charter granted the status of Bailiwick to Hemel Hempstead and permitted an annual fair and a weekly market with its own Court of Piepowder. Nearly one thousand years earlier the Domesday Book recorded that Hemel Hempstead was relatively unimportant. The name 'Hamelhamstede' is of Saxon origin, meaning 'homestead of Hamel' and is therefore likely to have been land belonging to Heamele, Bishop of Mercia in the Eighth Century. We do know that 'Hamele' was granted to the Bishop of London in AD 705 by Offa, King of Essex.

Early settlement is indicated by Roman finds in the Gadebridge and Boxmoor areas (see Early Settlement chapter on page 12). However Hemel Hempstead's development throughout the Medieval period suffered from competition, with economic activity generated by Royal patronage in two neighbouring communities. To the north at Berkhamsted, the Norman castle was a centre of great power and early prosperity, whilst to the south of Hemel Hempstead at Kings Langley, the Plantagenet Kings erected a splendid Royal Palace and founded a Royal hunting estate. However as the nation's economy began to develop, Royal residences closer to the Capital became more favoured and, by Tudor times, both these Royal establishments had fallen into disuse.

By the Fourteenth Century 200 able bodied persons were needed to reap the harvest in the Hemel Hempstead area. Already a busy agricultural community, the demise of the neighbouring Royal estates, together with the seal of approval denoted by Henry VIII's award of Bailiwick status in 1539 laid important foundations. Following the Dissolution of the Monasteries, the King had again become Lord of the Manor and now had a clear financial incentive to expand the prosperity of the area. Specifically this gave Hemel Hempstead clear licence to develop its principal role as a thriving market for the local area, throughout the next four centuries. Similarly by the Nineteenth Century Hemel Hempstead's long running success as a market town paved the way for its contemporary position of local industrial dominance.

Despite the heritage of this area, there was still a danger that the post-war arrival of such a massive New Town development in Hemel Hempstead would distort the true historic perspective of this early community. The story of this development is dealt with in an earlier chapter of this book (see page 78). However by focusing now on the early settlement which developed into the old High Street, close to the mills and the River Gade, one has a better chance of envisaging Hemel Hempstead as it had been for most of its life. We find that until the Twentieth Century, Hemel Hempstead fitted neatly into the pattern of most of the other communities discussed in this book. The historic buildings of the old High Street, together with the Gadebridge Park Estate, tell a story of a particularly successful market town growing up in attractive rural Hertfordshire.

St. Mary's Church.

Early drawing of Hemel Hempstead Market House.

St. Mary's Parish Church

The Parish Church of St. Mary dates from 1140-80 and is one of the oldest and very finest churches in Hertfordshire. To support the early date of its foundation, there is surviving flint rubble and Roman bricks which belong to the first church building. St. Mary's Hemel Hempstead is the best Norman church in the county and, indeed, there are few comparable examples of Norman architecture in England. The aisled and clerestoried parochial nave, dating from the Twelfth Century, has remained almost entirely as the original and the central tower with four stilted arches to nave, chancel and transepts, is also of Twelfth Century construction up to the base of the tower. The top of the church's 70ft. tower was once embattled in the Fourteenth Century, when the magnificent timber framed spire was added. This spire, which rises a further 130ft. above the parapet, is a beautiful example of an early, fluted timber spire covered with lead.

The Bury

Thomas Waterhouse, the fifteenth and last rector of the monastery at Ashridge (1529-36), was known by Henry VIII as his own "gentleman priest". Although he at first retired to Castle Street in Berkhamsted, following the dissolution of the monasteries, both he and his family came into the possession of the Bury estate in Hemel Hempstead. In 1540 his brother-in-law, Richard Combe, bought the Bury from the Crown, together with "its fields, gardens, fishery, dovecote, meadows, brew house, bake house and mill", for the princely sum of £108. What we refer to as the old Bury was built on the site of an earlier mansion, by Sir Richard Coombe circa 1595. When completed this fine old Elizabethan house offered "fourteen rooms all finely furnished". A later Richard Combe acquired part of the manor in 1650, although following the Restoration of Charles II, it reverted to the Crown and Combe was then appointed Steward of the Estate. In 1702 the manor was leased to the Halsey family and subsequently purchased by them in 1815. The Bury stayed in the ownership of the Halseys until it was eventually acquired by the Hemel Hempstead Development Corporation.

Henry VIII visited Anne Boleyn at Lockers Park House in 1535. Local tradition has it that the King conducted some of his courtship of Anne in the attractive environs of Gadebridge Park. It also dubiously alleges that on 29th December 1539, when he granted his Charter to the town, he did so from the window of a porchway in the Charter Tower, which was not then built! This Sixteenth Century gatehouse, together with some contemporary walling from the old Manor House, is all that remains of the old Bury structure which was pulled down in 1791 by William Ginger. His replacement is an Eighteenth Century structure also called the Bury, which was built circa 1790, and survives to this day, off the link road between the Leighton Buzzard road and Queensway. It has been used as offices for the Hemel Hempstead Rural District Council and the Divisional Education Service, it now houses the Registry Office. The mill at the Bury was one of the five listed in a charter originally granted to the Monks of Ashridge in 1289. These were all early corn mills, powered by the flow of the River Gade. In addition to the two more distant mills at Two Waters and at Frogmore, near Apsley, there were two other mills close by: one at Piccotts End and the other at Water End which are discussed in the later chapters of the book (see page 164 & 168). The mill at the Bury survived until its demolition in 1962.

At the extreme north-west corner, the aisle wall is founded on a large boulder that may be of pre-Christian origin. The west doorway is a splendid example of both Norman design and sculpture work, with rich mouldings in the arches and capitals which depict Adam and Eve and the serpent. Eleven of the twelve clerestory windows are original, the twelfth (second from the east on the south side) was altered in the Fifteenth Century. The font is Norman in style, but was completely re-cut and embellished with Biblical scenes during the Nineteenth Century. The Royal Arms, dated 1763, are on the wall of the north transept, whilst the south transept windows are in memory of the Godwin and Grover families. The south aisle windows honour the Paston Cooper family of Gadebridge, amongst others. Thomas Waterhouse of the Bury requested that he should be buried in the chancel of the Parish Church of St. Mary, but there does not seem to be any burial space marked. However the church does hold the vault of the Combe family, Thomas's surviving family relatives. Important structural repairs were made to St. Mary's in 1846 and the principal restoration in the last century was carried out from 1879-88. Recently the fabric of the impressive spire was given a major overhaul in a process which lasted several years and was carried out from 1985.

The Bury

Hemel Hempstead, Herts.

Market Town

As we have already discussed, the early village of Hemel Hempstead, clustered around its Norman church, the River Gade with its corn mills and surrounded by hundreds of acres of fertile land, was in an ideal position to develop considerable agricultural prosperity. Henry VIII's Bailiwick Charter allowed Hemel Hempstead to hold a weekly market every Thursday. During the reign of Elizabeth I, Holy Thursday saw a sheep and cattle fair in the town and an annual 'pleasure fair' was held on the feast day of Corpus Christi. A Charter given by Oliver Cromwell granted the town a further three fairs in 1656. Hemel Hempstead was the trading centre for all the cereals produced by local farmers, who would come with their carts and tip their corn and barley into what are now the Town Hall cellars. As early as 1742 the journal of the unknown traveller can describe the town confidently as having "the greatest corn market in the county or perhaps in England". Prompted by this activity and passing traffic, traders and Inns sprang up all along what we now term the High Street. It is interesting to note though, that by 1851, the number of local agricultural labourers listed in the census, had been eclipsed by straw plaiters who were mainly women and children. This was a key cottage industry (see page 26) and merchants representing Luton and Dunstable hat-makers would visit the old plait market held in a yard, in a narrow passageway off the High Street (now Austins Place by the Bell Inn).

Some older structures survive behind newer frontages, but as a direct consequence of a disastrous fire in 1749, most of the buildings in the old High Street now date from the mid Eighteenth to late Nineteenth Century. The High Street is now one of Dacorum Borough Council's Conservation Areas and, seen in isolation, is one of the more attractive town centres in Hertfordshire. An interesting feature at the edge of the lower sunken side of the High Street is one of local ironfounder Joseph Cranstone's water pumps, which used to be surmounted by a working gas lamp. Gas lighting was first introduced to the High Street in 1835 and the town's first gas-works in Bury Road were also built by the Cranstones.

Although the attractive landscape and agricultural prosperity of the Hemel Hempstead area, had led to the founding of estates in Georgian times, the first sign of investment in the civic grandeur and infrastructure of Hemel Hempstead was the laying of the foundation stone for the Town Hall in 1851. Constructed on the site of the old Corn Exchange, and adjacent to the old market place, this building was designed by George Lowe of Clements Inn of Lombard Street in London. The Jacobean style structure was developed as funds became available during 1851-88. The market house, bell turret and corn loft were erected in 1867, the corn loft being later converted into a Municipal Council Chamber or Town Hall, when the corn trade declined. The last Council meeting in this handsome Council Chamber with panelled walls, was held in February 1966. A likeness of Henry VIII, the founding father of prosperous Hemel Hempstead, is carved in stone on the Town Hall, which is now the Old Town Arts Centre.

Hemel Hempstead's ancient Bailiwick status survived until 13 July 1898, when a Charter granted by Queen Victoria established a new Corporation. From this date, the Borough of Hemel Hempstead was created with its own Mayor, Aldermen and Burgesses. In recognition of its previous history, the

Mayor of Hemel Hempstead was entitled to add the honorary office of Bailiff to his official title. The first Mayor of Hemel Hempstead was Sir Astley Paston Cooper, a later relation of the famous, but childless, surgeon of the same name who lived at Gadebridge (1811-1841). The stone fountain which stood in the Broadway, at the entrance to Gadebridge Park, was presented to the town in 1898 by the Misses Ann and Helen Varney, to commemorate the creation of Hemel Hempstead as a Borough.

The coming of the canal in 1797, and the arrival of the railway in 1837, signalled the beginning of the Industrial Revolution which was to stimulate the eventual shift in emphasis for the town of Hemel Hempstead. Local land-owners, like Sir Astley Paston Cooper at Gadebridge, were vehement in their opposition to the noisy railways in particular, and their displeasure ensured that this artery of communication was kept well away from the old town centre. However this meant that Hemel Hempstead's development westwards to meet it, together with the expansion of both Boxmoor and the industrial suburb of Apsley, was inevitable. This growth of the town along the Marlowes is a process that would have evolved, without the further stimulation of New Town Development, which made a brand new design for the Marlowes the centre of its plans.

Local Inns
It is interesting to note that the 'Register for Licences' in 1900, lists the amazing number of 28 public houses and 43 beer houses for Hemel Hempstead. Pleasingly some of these old Inns still survive in the High Street; while two of the oldest, the Cock Inn and the Meremayde, have gone. Most notable of the survivors are the Bell (The Old Bell), the Kings Arms (Old King's Arms), the White Hart and the Rose and Crown. The Bell's first known registration as an Inn was 1603. In 1664 it was owned by William Fuller, who in addition to being an Innkeeper, also practised as a surgeon here, storing his drugs in the cellar! Following his death in 1671 his daughter managed this pub, together with another Inn, 'The Leg', which stood next door. In 1756 the Bell is listed as the best appointed Inn in Hemel Hempstead, offering nine beds and stabling for up to 55 horses. The Kings Arms is another listed early Seventeenth Century, timber-framed building, first mentioned in 1660 when it was kept by Abraham Crawley. Like the Bell Inn it merged with a neighbour, the Black Lion, to create a larger Inn sometime between 1785 and 1790. For a period after 1756, it had been known as the Prince's Arms, named after the Prince of Wales who later became George III. In 1826 the Kings Arms was used as the local Excise Office and in 1845 its yard regularly hosted the straw plait market. The Inn with the earliest documentation is the Rose and Crown. It is first mentioned as the Crown in 1523, when it was kept by William Patewyn, who was also a local butcher. Deeds still exist for the Rose and Crown dating from 1545. This Inn is mentioned in the Bailiwick minute book of 1629 which states that "no smiths' stalls shall be erected between the Cock door and the Crown door". In 1756 this Inn is listed as having stabling for up to twenty horses. The White Hart Inn in the High Street can be traced back to 1625 and is another typically attractive early Seventeenth Century Inn with timber framing and old tiled roofs.

The Anglican Church of St. Paul
This Victorian church used to stand on the crest of the hill in Queen Street on the site given by Sir Astley Cooper. It was built by public subscription at a cost of £3000 and consecrated on June 22nd 1869. The ecclesiastical parish of St. Paul, which was formed in 1878, was absorbed into the parish of Hemel Hempstead when the Church of St. Paul was closed for re-development in June 1961. The handsome red bricked Vicarage was also demolished at this time. The Parish Room was re-named Davidson House and became the headquarters of the local Conservative Constituency Association. The vicarage site became the base for the Royal British Legion Club, whilst new flats were built on the former church site. As part of the New Town plan, a new church, dedicated to St. Paul was built in the Highfield neighbourhood. Some pews and memorial windows were transferred to it from the old church of St. Paul, in order to create a link with the past. Other churches of historical note, in Hemel Hempstead, are the stylish mock gothic Baptist Church built in the Marlowes in 1860, and the imposing Congregational Church in Alexandra Road, which dates from 1890. This substantial structure stands on the site of a temporary Iron Chapel which had been donated by local ironfounder Joseph Cranstone in 1880.

Corner Hall House.

Corner Hall
Situated at the southern end of Hemel Hempstead, it would be an omission not to mention the aptly named Corner Hall. This house is a late Fifteenth, early Sixteenth Century timber-framed house whose drive began on ground which is now occupied by Cedar Walk. It was the main structure in a hamlet which occupied the end of the road linking Frogmore End to Two Waters. At one time this building was said to have been a hospice and resting place for pilgrims, with a resident warden, who was a member of the Pearson family. As far back as 1637, we find records of a Thomas Deacon of Corner Hall who was Bailiff of Hemel Hempstead. He is buried in the chancel of St. Mary's Parish Church. A later Thomas Deacon, who was also Bailiff of the town in 1823, sold the house to the Woodman family in 1850. There is still a stone high up on the wall of the Town Hall commemorating a son, Thomas Woodman, who was Bailiff of Hemel Hempstead during the construction of the Town Hall in 1861. Corner Hall later became the residence of the well known Edwardian author, William John Locke (1863-1930). Also at Corner Hall was Three Gables, an attractive house which became home to Mr. A. J. Sanguinetti who was owner of the British Paper Company from 1890.

St. Mary's Parish Church, 1996.

West door of St. Mary's Church, 1930.

The Bury Gatehouse, circa 1934.

Broadway and the entrance to Gadebridge Park, circa 1910.

Early view of the Marlowes at the turn of the century showing the Baptist Church (left).

The Marlowes looking north, circa 1910.

Hemel Hempstead High Street, 1881.

Peace Day, Hemel Hempstead, 1919.

View of old High Street showing the Town Hall and Market Square, 1919.

High Street showing Cranstone gas lamp, circa 1910.

High Street looking towards Piccotts End, circa 1910.

View of Hemel Hempstead circa 1921.

View of Hemel Hempstead from Midland Hill, circa 1919.

Aerial view of Hemel Hempstead in the mid 1950's showing Nicky Line viaduct.

Gadebridge House, first known simply as Gadebridge, was built for the Combe family in the Seventeenth Century. It was constructed on land which then formed part of the estate belonging to their principal mansion house at the Bury. The house that survived into the Twentieth Century featured an impressively formal ten bay frontage in the Georgian style. There was also a colonnade attached to the east side of the house which led towards the principal entrance. An early Nineteenth Century bridge survives in Gadebridge Park as an attractive and stylish reminder of the old estate. The bridge has a cast iron single segmented span with geometric pattern railings. In 1811 the estate of Gadebridge was purchased by Astley Paston Cooper (1768-1841) who was the leading surgeon of his day. A pupil of the distinguished surgeon Henry Clive, he was himself to serve as Professor of Anatomy to Surgeons Hall from 1794-96. Professor Cooper was heavily involved in private practice, whilst still lecturing at St. Thomas' on surgery and anatomy and also attending as surgeon at Guys Hospital. Pressure of work eventually took its toll and he resigned his Professorship in 1815, four years after moving to Gadebridge.

Directly because of his profession, Astley Cooper became a very wealthy man; it is difficult to overstate the social importance enjoyed by a leading doctor at the beginning of the Nineteenth Century. It has been said that in 1815 Cooper's annual income reached the staggering total of £21,000, easily exceeded the income of any other physician in the country. He was attending many of the nation's nobility with patients who included Lord Chatham, Lord Liverpool, Sir Robert Peel and the Duke of Wellington. In 1817 his position of eminence in the history of medicine became secure when he performed an operation which became a landmark in surgery. This breakthrough was achieved when in operating for an aneurysm, Cooper saved the life of his patient by tying the abdominal aorta. This successful intervention, accomplished before the days of antiseptic surgery, was hailed as a medical triumph.

Another spectacular career development for Astley Paston Cooper, took place when he was summoned somewhat reluctantly, to treat King George IV in 1821. He did however successfully remove a tumour from the King's head, for which he was created a Baronet in the same year. In 1827 he was elected President of the Royal College of Surgeons and the following year was appointed Surgeon General to King George IV. This was a post he continued to hold during the reign of King William IV and also when Queen Victoria first came to the throne. Sir Astley Paston Cooper died on the 12th February 1841, at the age of 73, and was buried beneath the chapel at Guys Hospital. The family hatchment was carried at the head of the funeral procession and subsequently fixed to the north wall of the south transept of St. Mary's Church. A statue to his memory was placed in St. Paul's Cathedral and a further monument created in St. Mary's Parish Church. An entry from the Dictionary of National Biography states that "No surgeon before or since has filled so large a place in the public eye as Cooper". His name is still remembered today, with the award of a triennial prize for a medical essay, given by the physicians and surgeons of Guys Hospital. Sir Astley Paston Cooper's abiding local legacy is twofold: firstly the foundation of hospital care, (the development of which is discussed overleaf), and secondly his fierce opposition to the railway! He teamed up with Earl Brownlow of Ashridge and persuaded many more of his more aristocratic patients to

ensure that the original plan was blocked in the House of Lords. He was simply not prepared to have his fine lawns and trout stream carved up by what he considered to be a noisy and unnecessary inconvenience. He was eventually successful in achieving a re-routing of the railway through the Bulbourne valley at Berkhamsted, instead of following the Gade through Hemel Hempstead.

Astley Paston Cooper.

Because Sir Astley Paston Cooper was childless, despite two marriages, the award of Baronetcy in 1828 specially allowed him to appoint a successor. He named his nephew Astley, who was adopted and lived with him as a son, to become Baronet. A later Astley Paston Cooper who is said to have owned over 1000 acres of land in Hemel Hempstead, was made first Mayor of the Town in 1898. Gadebridge House subsequently housed a leading preparatory school in January 1914. This school was originally established in 1897 as Rye House School in Bedford by Augustus Scobell Orlebar. It thrived at Gadebridge until it moved to Westbrook Hay in 1963, where it continues as a successful preparatory school today. Gadebridge House was then occupied by the Commission for New Towns until it was demolished to provide a site for the Marketing Education Centre built by Kodak Ltd in 1973. These impressive modern buildings were in their turn demolished during 1994 to make way for new housing development.

Gadebridge, circa 1905.

Gadebridge Park, circa 1912.

White bridge in Gadebridge Park, 1983.

Gadebridge Lane, circa 1910.

Piccotts End Road, circa 1910.

Hospital Development

As well as being one of the nation's leading doctors attending aristocracy, Astley Cooper was also inundated by the health problems of local people when he was resident at Gadebridge. He was sufficiently concerned by their plight to persuade some of his land-owning friends to help him provide money for the conversion of a group of cottages, at Piccotts End, into a small local hospital. This Cottage Hospital opened in January 1827 and soon dealt with patients who came from many miles around. In its first seven months of operation it dealt with a total of eleven in-patients and 336 out-patients. Piccotts End Cottage Hospital (see also page 164) was such a success that it soon proved too small. Sir John Sebright of Beechwood Park at Markyate was then prompted to build in 1831 a new infirmary for Hemel Hempstead at his own expense. It remained the principal hospital for the area until it was replaced by the adjacent West Herts Infirmary in 1877. The building provided by Sir John Sebright served a wide area, including Watford, and patients came from as far away as Northampton. When it closed as a hospital in 1877, the building was taken over by Kings College Hospital in London and used as a Convalescent Home. They re-named the building Cheere House, in memory of a long standing benefactor and secretary of Kings College Hospital. Later in its history the house was used as a Nurses' Home and a Medical Training School.

The West Herts Infirmary, which was opened in 1877 by the Duchess of Teck, became the first hospital in the county to have X-ray equipment installed in 1899. Further developments occurred when the foundation stone of the new maternity block of St. Paul's was laid on 21st July 1926 by H.R.H. Prince of Wales. Hemel Hempstead's first workhouse had been established in 1724 on the summit of Queen Street (now Queensway Hill). A second building, 'Hempstead House', under the care of the Dacorum Board of Guardians, replaced it around 1837 and St. Paul's Hospital was built on the site of this second workhouse. The building was originally designated as the Marnham Maternity Ward, when it was opened by the Marchioness of Salisbury, on 20th July 1927. Its name was given in memory of the late Miss Marnham and the Marnham Trust which had for many years been very generous in its support of the West Herts Infirmary. The Marnhams were local land-owners who lived in a pleasant country house called 'Hollies' in Green End, Boxmoor. This was the house that later became home to St. Nicholas Preparatory School, which transferred to Abbots Hill when the 'Hollies' was demolished for re-development. Our story of the local hospital is brought fully up to date with the opening of the modern buildings of West Herts Hospital in 1987. By the early 1990's all patients had been moved out of St. Paul's and the old infirmary building.

Beechwood Park in the early 1800's.

Beechwood Park School, 1995.

Sir John Sebright, 1852.

St. Paul's Church, circa 1910.

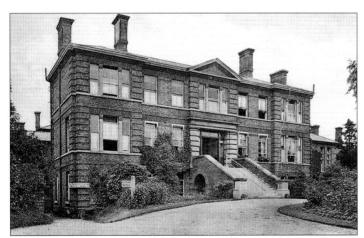

West Herts. Infirmary, 1909.

Cheere House, circa 1912.

Children's Ward at West Herts. Hospital.

Dr. F. C. Fisher outside West Herts. Infirmary, 1908.

Piccotts End

Throughout history the most significant feature of Piccotts End has been its superb water supply. It is perhaps difficult for Twentieth Century observers to imagine the strength and flow of the River Gade, as it was several hundred years ago. In the time of William the Conqueror there was an annual royal tithe placed on the River Gade to produce a healthy crop of eels for sale in London and this clearly indicates a river much deeper and wider than we know today. The cause of the river's diminution is however no mystery, given that a post-war geographical survey identified Piccotts End as an optimum site for the extraction of pure water. This investigation was to help find a sufficient supply for the expanding population planned for Hemel Hempstead New Town and the extraction of water was initially limited to the staggering total of four and a half million gallons per day, by a Ministry Order dated 1947. It was not just a question of the quantity of the water at Piccotts End, but also its quality. A sale notice dated 3rd July 1840 proclaimed, boldly, that the waters both at Piccotts End and Water End were "Saline and Chalybeate springs, the water of which is said to be similar to Cheltenham".

Piccotts End Mill

Given the ready water supply, it is no surprise that we find an ancient mill, listed in the Domesday Book, at Piccotts End. In a survey of 1700 it was recorded as being one of four mills on the River Gade at Hemel Hempstead, that between them "do grind upwards of ten thousand bushels of wheat every week". The structure of the three storey mill which survived into modern times, was unfortunately badly damaged by fire in April 1991. It was a weather-boarded building on a brick base dating from the Eighteenth Century. The mill was provided with an attractive, adjoining mill house of red brick which dates from 1873. This house has a Welsh slate roof and a doorway, (left of centre), with attached Doric columns. During the Twentieth Century the focus of activity at the mill increasingly became the production of animal foodstuffs by Piccotts Kingmill Ltd. The water wheel at Piccotts End Mill was removed in 1963 and milling activity at Piccotts End ceased when both the mill itself and the mill house were re-developed as residential accommodation.

Piccotts End Murals

There is no doubt concerning the most significant historical feature to be found at Piccotts End; these are the magnificent Fifteenth Century wall paintings adorning the walls of one (No. 132) in a row of four old Elizabethan cottages that sit back from the main road. These four dwellings were originally one structure which is likely to have been a long low medieval hall, originally built in flint and oak, with wattle and daub walls and a thatched roof. It is believed by most local historians that this early building served as a meeting place and hostel for pilgrims on their journeys to and from the great Monastery of Bonhommes at Ashridge. The tradition of painting on walls, particularly in churches and monastic establishments, has been strong since the Middle Ages, but surviving examples from this period are rare in England. The wall paintings at Piccotts End were discovered by Mr. Arthur Lindley in 1953, during renovation work on the cottages. To his astonishment, these pre-Reformation Catholic wall paintings were revealed beneath six layers of ageing wall paper on a wall 17ft. in length. The paintings are difficult to date precisely, but certainly fall within the period 1450-1550 and it is probable that they derive from the earlier of these two dates. The images on the Piccotts End murals, which depict Christ and a number of saints, are far from straightforward interpretations. The depicted Christ is a rather strange Buddha-like figure and the central images are entwined in a large vine-like scroll, which has hidden within it many mystical symbols. Experts who have studied the work are persuaded there may be a link here with a heretical sect of Cathars, established in southern France during the Thirteenth Century. The cottage has been graded as an Ancient Monument and the preservation of these specimens is considered as a matter of national importance. Since the first find, some similar traces of wall paintings have also been discovered in a first floor room at nearby Piccotts End Farm, which has surviving timber-framed buildings dating from the late Sixteenth Century. The existence of such paintings in an English domestic building was described by Sir Albert Richardson, President of the Royal Academy, as unique. Curiously the same group of cottages also has Elizabethan decorations in an upstairs room.

Piccotts End Infirmary

The four Fifteenth Century timber-framed cottages which house the famous murals, do have a second claim to historical significance as Hemel Hempstead's Nineteenth Century cottage hospital. It was these same cottages that were used by Sir Astley Paston Cooper (1768-1841) to establish Hemel Hempstead's very first hospital. The small infirmary, established by this distinguished surgeon who lived nearby at Gadebridge, was opened in January 1827. It catered as best it could to the local population's medical needs until 1831, when a larger infirmary was built to replace it by Sir John Sebright. The infirmary yard at Piccotts End today however bears no trace of this early cottage hospital.

All Saints Church

All Saints Church at Piccotts End was founded on a site near the infirmary yard of the old cottage hospital. This small church, built in the decorated style with chancel and nave, was consecrated on All Saints Day 1907. It was constructed with funds left by Nathaniel Wishart Robinson (of Robinson and Mead, the local Estate Agents). The family partners in the firm provided the church clock in memory of Edward Mead. However the hamlet of Piccotts End has never been a separate ecclesiastical parish, always falling within the pastoral care of its mother church of St. Mary's, Hemel Hempstead. The Church of All Saints, Piccotts End was seldom used and, despite a brief revival after the Second World War, public worship at Piccotts End church ceased and the building has now been converted into a private house.

Full view of Piccotts End murals.

Old cottages at Piccotts End, which house the medieval murals discovered by Mr. A.C. Lindley (left).

Piccotts End School

Piccotts End School was built on a site at the bottom of Piccotts End Lane which leads off the main through road and eastwards up to Grove Hill and Cupid Green. This school was established in 1872 and catered for the educational needs of children from distant farmsteads, as well as those local to the hamlet of Piccotts End. At first there was sufficient demand for the school to flourish and additional classroom accommodation was built in 1906. However, in common with many of the smallest rural schools, the Second World War heralded closure. Education at Piccotts End School ceased in 1939. The buildings were subsequently demolished and the site sold for re-development.

Piccotts End

Until the mid Twentieth Century, there was no Leighton Buzzard Road running through the Gadebridge meadow below Piccotts End. The main through route north was the extension of the Hemel Hempstead High Street that still dissects this tiny hamlet. The old wall on the west side of this road marked the boundary of Paston Cooper's Gadebridge estate, leading up to the flint and brick Lodge and entrance gates to Gadebridge Park. An indication of the agricultural activity centred on the mill at Piccotts End is that there were once three public houses in Piccotts End, which are all now private cottages. The first of these was the Partridge (formerly the Crown) which stood on the corner, near the alley leading to Piccotts End Lane. The second and principal pub in Piccotts End was the Boars Head and it dated from 1736 when Daniel Baxter, a victualler, kept the Inn. In 1756 it had stabling for two horses. This old pub was later home to the local coal merchant, before serving as

Piccotts End's General Store and Post Office. True to Piccotts End rural traditions, opposite the site of the Church of All Saints is a carefully restored Tudor farm house. There was once also a beautiful old flint barn which stood on the corner of Dodds Lane, but sadly this has since been demolished. Piccotts End's third pub, the Windmill, was one of two cottages standing beside the fine Georgian house that overlooks Gadebridge meadow.

Marchmont House

The most impressive building in Piccotts End is Marchmont House, a substantial mansion which was built by Hugh, Lord Polwarth of Polwarth, the Third and last Earl of Marchmont. This house, with Georgian entrance, was constructed between 1771 and 1772 and served as the Earl's family home until his death in 1794. It is a good example of an English county house, built in the neo-classical style and features a recessed porch with Doric columns. Hugh Polwarth had a great interest in literature and was an avid collector of rare books and manuscripts. He delighted in the friendship of the celebrated essayist, Alexander Pope, who would often visit him at Piccotts End. In 1873, as the Third Earl of Marchmont, he donated the clock which sits on the base of the spire of the Parish Church of St. Mary's. The Polwarth hatchments can still be found lodged in the north transept of St. Mary's, hidden by the organ casings. Marchmont House later became the dower house of the Gadebridge estate to which the Dowager Lady Cooper retired in 1841 following the death of Sir Astley. The exterior fabric of the house survives to this day as the Marchmont Arms, a popular and substantial public house offering full restaurant facilities.

Piccotts End Mill in the 1930's.

Mill Pond at Piccotts End in the early 1890's.

All Saints Church, Piccotts End, 1956.

Blacksmith's at Piccotts End, 1921.

Piccotts End village, 1921.

Piccotts End, 1996.

Marchmont Arms, 1996.

Water End

North bridge at Water End, 1928.

Lying to the north of Piccotts End is Water End, another riverside hamlet which owes its existence to the power of the River Gade. Water End however is a more low lying settlement than its near neighbour, which accounts for the water-logged meadows that provided such perfect conditions for the watercress beds which used to flourish here on the western side of the Leighton Buzzard Road. As one might expect, Water End was also home to an ancient mill; Noke Mill being the earliest of the five corn mills mentioned in the Ashridge Charter of 1289. The name Noke or Noake is actually a corruption of Oak Mill and documents dated 1369 list 'Oke Mill' as one of the properties of the Manor of Southall; Southall being at that time a sub-manor of the Manor of Great Gaddesden. A later mill building was erected in 1850 and the mill house was described by W. Branch Johnston, earlier this century, as a "Seventeenth Century timber-framed building, carefully restored as a private dwelling". The mill which can be reached by a narrow lane, close by the Grist House, has long since fallen into disuse, although the water wheel and much of the equipment are still in place within the building. It was used as a Youth Hostel from 1933 until 1951.

Close by the mill, Gaddesden Hall was the Manor House and farmstead to the sub-manor of Southall which is first recorded in 1200. In the Fifteenth Century the property was known as Oliver's Place, after Robert Oliver who was the holder in 1448. In 1792 Gaddesden Hall was sold by Thomas Osman and Thomas Kellam, to William Hulme. The hall served as a farmhouse into the 1920's when it was converted into a private residence. During the Nineteenth Century, Water End was a favourite overnight resting place for carters delivering hay to the Haymarket in London. Among the services available were those of a blacksmith, sadler, wheelwright, corn chandler and shoe maker; whilst the village shop at Water End at this time incorporated an ale house, reading room and some accommodation.

The first listed reference to the Red Lion at Water End dates from 1736. This attractive old Inn which sits near the bottom of Potten End Hill used to hold one of Cranstone's iron plaques (No. 537) which conferred rights of pasturage on the moor at Boxmoor. The public house has now been radically altered by modern extensions in the 1990's in order to provide enlarged restaurant facilities. At Water End, the main Leighton Buzzard Road crosses the River Gade twice within a quarter of a mile. At one of the bridges there are two very sharp bends and historians have speculated that this was an Eighteenth Century adjustment, designed to provide the newly built Gaddesden Place with an unbroken stretch of parkland, leading down to the water's edge. Although only dating from the Nineteenth Century, the bridges at Water End are particularly attractive. They were built with pointed arches, in Medieval fashion, which nicely reflect the peaceful style of this riverside hamlet. In fact the pleasant rural atmosphere of Water End has survived the Twentieth Century expansion of Hemel Hempstead remarkably well. The narrow bends of its through road require little further traffic calming measures to tame the speed of cars, and its picturesque cluster of Sixteenth and Seventeenth Century cottages remain particularly well restored. One of these half timbered structures has crucked timbers, an architectural feature uncommon in Hertfordshire.

Another delightful Sixteenth Century cottage, set in an acre of ground, is home to a man whose vigilance and environmental concern has done much to help retain the natural environment at Water End. This is the acclaimed watercolour artist Gordon Beningfield, who draws much of his inspiration from the local countryside. Several books have been published which aptly illustrate Mr. Beningfield's sensitive and accurate portrayal of the natural world. He has designed sets of stamps for the Royal Mail and in 1994, was awarded the Silver Cross of St. George for his work as a countryside artist. One mile to the north of Water End is the village of Great Gaddesden, the historic Manor of Gaddesden being the key influence on the life of the surrounding area.

Noke Mill, 1937.

Noke Mill Cottages, 1921.

Gaddesden Hall, 1923.

Footbridge at Water End, 1937.

South bridge, Water End, 1921.

Water End village, 1937.

Looking towards Hemel Hempstead from the north bridge, 1921.

The Red Lion, Water End, 1996.

The Manor of Gatesden, which has a complex history, was bequeathed to the Abbey of St. Albans by Ethelgifu sometime between 942 and 946. This arrangement was brusquely ignored by William the Conqueror who promptly granted the manor to Edward of Salisbury, Sheriff of Wiltshire, in 1086. By 1261 the manor was in the possession of the Earl of Lincoln, transferring to the ownership of the Earl of Huntingdon exactly one hundred years later. By 1485 the Earl of Derby was Lord of the Manor and his family held it until it fell, because of a lack of male heirs, to Robert Cecil, later Earl of Salisbury. He sold it in 1602 for the sum of £3000, and by 1604 the Manor of Great Gaddesden was owned by Sir Thomas Egerton, Lord Keeper to Queen Elizabeth I. All the surrounding manorial lands (the Little Gaddesden lands formerly owned by the monks at Ashridge, the Manor of Lucies and the sub-manor of Southall) were at this point unified under the ownership of Sir Thomas. From him, this enlarged manor passed to successive Earls and Dukes of Bridgewater and then, through the female line, to the Earls Brownlow until the Ashridge estate was sold on the death of Ethelbert, the 3rd Earl. Sir Walter Halsey of Gaddesden Place purchased the manor from Lord Brownlow's trustees in 1928 and today it remains with his descendants.

The Rectory lands of Great Gaddesden which formed the separate estate centred on the Golden Parsonage have a more straightforward early history that falls neatly into two distinct phases. The Rectory and Advowson was attached to the manor until 1382 when these particular lands were given to help support the Dominican Friary at Kings Langley, being held in trust by the Prioress of Dartford. However in 1544 the Golden Parsonage, together with its Home Farm and the Rectory and Advowson of Great Gaddesden, were granted to William

Halsey by Henry VIII. The Halsey family are recorded in the village during the reign of Henry VI and had been renting the Rectory since 1520.

Golden Parsonage

A large Tudor mansion was built by the Halsey family on what were Medieval foundations. The size of this earlier structure is indicated by the fact that, in the time of Charles II, Sir John Halsey was paying tax on 15 hearths or fireplaces. The ancient manorial site of the Parsonage also features a deep well of considerable antiquity. The present Golden Parsonage dates from 1706, when elements of the earlier structure were re-modelled to serve as the west wing of what was intended to be a great mansion. This building project was probably never completed, because this branch of the Halsey family suddenly decided to move to Hamburg to pursue commercial interests, where they remained for much of the Eighteenth Century. The Golden Parsonage however remained the principal local home of the Halsey family until 1774. There has been speculation concerning the origin of the house's name, all of which is unproven, although some writers have suggested it derives from the carpet of daffodils surrounding this delightful house every Spring. Towards the end of the Nineteenth Century, the house was occupied by a preparatory school for 40 boys run by a Mr. Tylecote. Later the Golden Parsonage became once again the home of the Halsey family when Sir Thomas Halsey returned to it from Gaddesden Place in 1950. The present occupants of the Golden Parsonage are Mr. & Mrs Nicholas Halsey and their family who have lived in the house since 1980. Nicholas Halsey served as the High Sheriff of Hertfordshire in 1995. Mr. Halsey is currently the Manager of the 2000 acre Gaddesden estate and also Chairman of the Ashridge Estate Management Committee.

Golden Parsonage.

Gaddesden Place

Throughout the middle years of the Eighteenth Century the Halseys traded in Hamburg, retaining their links with Great Gaddesden. Thomas Halsey was Comptroller to the Allied Forces of Germany during the Seven Years' War and A.D.L. to the Duke of Brunswick. On his return to England in 1768, he employed the young architect James Wyatt to build an impressive Palladian villa, which was to become the new family seat for the Halsey family. The result was Gaddesden Place, occupying a magnificent site on top of the hill that overlooks the Gade valley and the village of Great Gaddesden. Gaddesden Place is a particularly important building because it is reputed to be Wyatt's first country house and reminds us of his adherence to the English Palladian tradition at the beginning of what became a very successful architectural career. There is a point on the lane between Frithsden and Nettleden, where one can view the style of Wyatt's first country house, Gaddesden Place, and contrast it with the Gothic style of his final commission, Ashridge House, some 40 years later. Unfortunately it was necessary to rebuild the original Gaddesden Place, following a disastrous fire on February 1st 1905. However the architect in charge of its restoration, Cole A. Adams, successfully managed to retain its Eighteenth Century splendour. The new house was now part of an impressive estate surrounding a park of 150 acres, running down to the banks of the River Gade at Water End. The imposing entrance of Gaddesden Place is still dominated by four full height Ionic columns and an impresssive sweep of sixteen steps.

The Halseys are an historically notable family who have always played a significant part in local and national life. Sir Thomas Halsey achieved distinction as a Judge during the reign of Charles II. From the date of Sir Thomas's son's election to the House of Commons in 1685, until 1906, there was hardly a year when a Halsey did not represent Hertfordshire in Parliament. A branch of the family emigrated to New England in 1630 and descendants of this early pioneer, another Thomas Halsey, have lived in Long Island, New York, ever since. One of these is Fleet Admiral William F. Halsey who achieved great naval success in the Pacific campaign of the Second World War. In 1984 a long lease of Gaddesden Place was sold to the Moir family who immediately undertook further meticulous restoration work on this fine old country house.

The Hoo

There has been a house on the site of Gaddesden Hoo since the Fourteenth Century. This attractive mansion house once boasted its own lodge, and part of the existing structure dates from circa 1690. In 1907 a new larger house was built on the estate and it was this Hoo which was used as a war time maternity hospital. Over two thousand babies of different nationalities were born at the Hoo during World War II. This later structure proved too expensive to maintain and consequently was demolished in 1949/50. The surviving Hoo has been home to the Wood family for three generations and it now has some Twentieth Century additions and extension work.

The age of many of the existing buildings in the parish of Great Gaddesden is worth stressing. Of the other houses in the Parish, Six Tunnels Farm is a fine example of an Elizabethan house and there are several other half-timbered cottages in the vicinity; at least one of which has some wattle-and-daub in an internal wall. Bunkers is an example of a cottage that has kept its name since the Sixteenth Century.

Church of John the Baptist

The Church of St. John the Baptist sits nicely on a slight hill in the heart of the village of Great Gaddesden. It is a superb example of a small Norman church which uniquely boasts flat red Roman bricks standing in the heavy buttress supporting its Twelfth Century chancel. The nave is Thirteenth Century work and the plain north arcade is a Fourteenth Century addition. Prominent gargoyles are set high on the tower and inside the church there are beautiful Thirteenth Century carvings. The north window depicts St. Francis and the church also contains the Halsey Chapel, which was built in 1730 by Henshaw Halsey, and houses many of the family's memorials. The earliest of these is a marble and alabaster monument erected by John Halsey in 1650 in memory of his parents, William and Lettice. On the north wall of the chancel is a richly carved monument in bath stone which recalls the saddest incident to befall the Halsey dynasty. This happened during the night of 24th April 1854, when Thomas Plumer Halsey his wife and son all died when their ship was lost on its voyage from Genoa to Marseilles.

Gaddesden Place.

The Cock and Bottle

The earliest known reference to this Inn at Great Gaddesden is 1734, when it was kept by James Hall and subsequently taken over by his widow. In 1756 it is listed as having stabling for four horses and accommodation for passing coach travellers. By 1839 the Cock and Bottle was owned, together with all the surrounding cottages, by Hannah Chennels although the Inn itself was kept by her husband George Chennels.

Barn

Situated on the north side of Pipers Hill, Great Gaddesden has a fine late Medieval barn which dates from the Fifteenth Century. This building, which historically has belonged to Church Farm, was extended into an 'L' shaped roadside range during the Seventeenth Century. The fine timbered structure of this superb barn retains four of its five original cruck frames and is currently undergoing an extensive programme of restoration.

Gaddesden Row and Jockey End

Just as the domestic community of Little Gaddesden sprang up to service the Ashridge estate, so was Gaddesden Row home to the estate workers and tenant farmers who owed their living to the Halsey estate of the Golden Parsonage and Gaddesden Place. However it is worth noting that the area has a much older history, as evidenced by the discovery of Stone Age tools, weapons and flints at Gaddesden Row. Jockey End, to the north of Gaddesden Row, has also yielded implements from the mid Palaeolithic period. The straight line of Gaddesden Row is a clue to the fact that it was an early Roman road; this later became part of a Medieval trackway to St. Albans However there has as yet been no evidence discovered which links the road to the place name of nearby Bridens Camp, where it would be nice to imagine there could have been a local Roman encampment. All that remains at Bridens Camp is the old Inn and early Freehouse, the Crown and Sceptre, which dates from 1839 and was once used as a tap house for the Halsey estate.

A building of note at Jockey End is the Sixteenth Century timber-framed cottage which stands beside the Green at the northern end of Gaddesden Row. The earliest known occupant of this cottage was John Ringshall who inherited the property in 1595. By 1763 the cottage, in common with most others, was owned by the Halsey family who let it. In 1880 this house served as the local straw plaiting school and was later the village Post Office and home to a leading member of the Suffragette movement, Miss Postlethwaite. In 1928 Miss Postlethwaite collected 75 names on a petition to the Rural District Council to supply Gaddesden Row with water; the hamlet's inhabitants also asked for a telephone. However it was not until 1955 that the outlying hamlet of Gaddesden Row was supplied with mains water. At the turn of the century Miss Postlethwaite's property had been known as Puzzle Cottage, although later the name Yew Tree Cottage and then The Yews became adopted for this historic structure. The local Inn, the Horse and Jockey, which stood nearby, was burnt down in 1919.

St. Margaret's Nunnery

This ancient Nunnery stood on a site approximately half way between the village of Great Gaddesden and the Ashridge estate, close to the parish border of Little Gaddesden. Nowadays all trace of these religious buildings has disappeared; the only surviving indication being grass which grows with a shaded demarcation along the lines of early medieval foundations which are on land occupied by a modern house and garden. The Nunnery's place in local history survives in the name of a nearby copse and farm hamlet; also St. Margaret's Lane and the later buildings of St. Margaret's which is now an Amaravati Buddhist Retreat. The present farm buildings of St. Margaret's are for the most part Nineteenth Century and were erected about 300 metres to the south-west of the old Nunnery site and original farm buildings. The original Medieval structure certainly survived as late as 1740 when the Nunnery was described as "entirely standing, though it was only small'. At this time the Parlour and Hall were said to be 'well wrought in Totternhoe stone' and behind these buildings stood a small chapel, with a square tower that only ten feet high.

The Nunnery was officially founded by Henry de Bois, Bishop of Winchester about 1160. However, an earlier charter of protection from Archbishop Becket names the lands as already given to the nuns by Bishop William Grifford who died in 1129. The foundation was Benedictine and by 1260 there was a modest resident community of eight nuns, five professed and three novices, which was called St. Margaret de Gatesden. Local Benedictine Nuns received a gift of lands from Edward I, issued by Royal Grant in 1280 from the Palace at Kings Langley. There was a larger house of the same order based nearby at Ivinghoe and which acted as the Mother House to St. Margaret's at Gaddesden. For several centuries this small community of nuns "gave all their devotion to God and to their neighbouring brothers in the great monastery of Bonhomme at Ashridge, which was only a few fields away". At the time of the Dissolution there were 'nine religious' when the lands and property of the Nunnery, together with the manor of Meuresley, were granted to Sir John Dance of Dauncey. The site eventually became part of the Ashridge Estate and when the Nunnery bell was rescued from the ruins, it was given by Lady Bridgewater to the Parish Church of St. Lawrence, Nettleden where it remains to this day.

Local legend tells of a ghostly voice still haunting the former grounds of St. Margarets. It is said that these belong to a wayward nun who fell in love with a local herdsman. The two lovers were discovered by the Mother Superior and, following an elopement, the guilty nun was forced to return to the Nunnery where she was tried and sentenced to death for adultery. As for the herdsman, he had to earn his pardon by undertaking a long pilgrimage to distant lands before he was allowed to return to his community.

The penitent nun of St. Margaret's.

Gaddesden Place, circa 1906.

Gaddesden Place overlooking the Gade valley, 1996.

Halsey family in 1915.

Mr. & Mrs. T. F. Halsey at their Golden Wedding celebrations, 1915.

Mr. Nicholas Halsey at the Golden Parsonage, 1995.

View of Great Gaddesden.

Church of St. John the Baptist and Village School (right), 1921.

The Hoo, 1996.

Cottages at Great Gaddesden, 1921.

Church of St. John the Baptist, Great Gaddesden, 1921.

Village School and War Memorial, 1994.

Great Gaddesden Junior School, 1956.

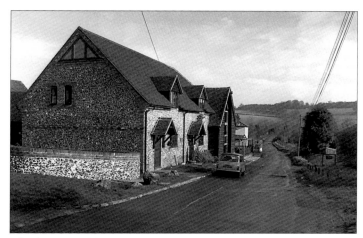

Church cottages and barn, 1994.

Interior of cruck barn, 1994.

Church Farm, 1957.

Wood End Farm, Gaddesden Row, 1956.

Gaddesden Row, near White House Farm, 1955.

Potten End

Until the middle of the Nineteenth Century the word 'Potten' was only applied to the lower part of the village, i.e. the area of Little Potten End which lies closer to Water End. The inhabitants who lived further up were considered to be living at Martins Pond. Despite local finds of Medieval pottery, the name 'Potters End' had never been used. The place name 'Pottern End' however, first appears in a document dated 1726; the old English 'pottern' meaning a building which was used for storage, often containing a hoard of pots, jars and other similar vessels. Historically the lands of Potten End have straddled the boundaries of the three much earlier Saxon communities of Gaddesden, Berkhamsted and Hemel Hempstead. The ancient Iron Age/Saxon boundary marker Grims Dyke intrudes into what we know as Potten End. Surviving traces of this ditch run parallel to Vicarage Road before it turns west towards the club house of Ashridge Golf Club.

It may be surprising to know that Potten End as a recognisable community dates from no earlier than the beginning of the Nineteenth Century and Kelly's Directory did not award the village a separate entry until 1874. In all the manorial surveys most of the land in Potten End, to the north of the pond, lay outside the Manor of Berkhamsted and belonged instead to Frithsden. Frithsden itself was part of the lands of Little Gaddesden granted to the monks of Ashridge by Edmund, Earl of Cornwall in 1285. Within the Manor of Great Gaddesden there was a sub-manor of Southall whose grounds extended up from Water End and included the remaining lands of Little Potten End. During these earlier centuries the lands of Potten End would simply have been part of the unenclosed common land belonging to these manors. Such manorial waste was then used for grazing pigs and the cutting of both fern (bracken) for animal bedding and furze (gorse) for fuel. The cutting of ferns was a practice which continued at Potten End until the end of the Nineteenth Century.

A key moment for the future development of Potten End occurred in 1604 when all the nearby manors and sub-manors were unified under the ownership of the first Duke of Bridgewater at Ashridge. Some small and scattered tenanted homesteads had begun to spring up in the area during the Sixteenth and Seventeenth Centuries. In 1607 these tenants had the right to dig the land for chalk, clay and sand. The earliest settlements in Potten End with surviving documentation, are small homesteads like the cottages and farm of Five Acres, which was owned by John Dearmer until his death in 1742. In 1751 another five acre farm was New Barns, owned by the Blackwell family. Their descendants later became tenants of Potten End Farm, off the Water End Road. An Eighteenth Century map of the area also shows a windmill at Heath End, to the north of Potten End Road.

The Pond and Village Green
The earliest record of the village pond being known as Martins Pond dates from 1607, when the pond would have certainly been much larger than it is today. There has only been one structure built close to the village pond and this was the Seventeenth Century cottage with three acres, still known today as 'Martins'. Deeds still exist relevant to this property dating from 1669, when it was described as 'lying against the pond'! As late as 1840 there was still only 'Martins' and one other cottage called 'Evergreens' by the pond. Evergreens cottage, with its garden and orchard, belonged to a Hemel Hempstead butcher who was then renting it out to Luke Foskett, a local carpenter. At this time there was still no pub, no Parish Church or school in Potten End and the remaining land around the pond was just open ground. What one recognises today as the centre of Potten End, did not acquire its village green status until 1933. The original and much older village green (Ingram Green) still exists at the earlier village centre, a quarter of a mile to the east, closer to Water End.

Potteries and Brickworks
Broken pieces of Medieval pottery have been found on two sites at Potten End; one at Binghams Park and another near Potten End Farm. In the 1950's an early clay walled kiln was found in the garden of a house in Rambling Way. In 1933 a similar Twelfth Century kiln had been discovered in the neighbouring village of Nettleden. It is important to realise that these Medieval kilns did not just produce decorative domestic ware, but also bricks and tiles for building. These early kilns were therefore the forerunners of Potten End's Nineteenth Century brickworks. These were established by John Hare Nash and were run from a site, which is now home to 'The Warren', at 19 Hempstead Road. Potten End's first industry flourished for nearly 100 years and when John Nash's son inherited the business in 1871, it employed seven men and three boys. However, reduced transport costs and the economies of scale achieved by larger producers, killed off the local Brickworks at Potten End before the turn of the century.

Lane's Nurseries
Potten End's largest and most important employer became established in 1840 soon after the brickworks began. John Edward Lane was living at 'Martins' and held a 21 year lease for Martins Farm. John Lane was the grandson of Henry Lane who had founded a very early nursery garden in Berkhamsted in 1777. The latter half of the Eighteenth Century saw a surge of interest in gardening throughout England, which this new

John E. Lane (1808-1889)

business was able to capitalise upon. Throughout the next hundred years, Henry Lane and Son expanded into three major holdings: Home Nursery at Berkhamsted, Broadway Nurseries at Bourne End and Balshaw Nurseries at Potten End. In 1880, eighty of the 140 acres owned by the Lane's business was in Potten End. Half of this ground was given to mixed farming and the remainder to specialist nursery work. By 1892 the business had a staff of 100 men, with a further 100 people employed at fruit-picking time. Many of these nursery workers were now tenants of Frederick Quincy Lane who inherited the business from his father. They lived in local cottages, many of which were newly built in the Nineteenth Century by John Costin, a builder from Berkhamsted. Lane & Son created two famous apples, the Oakland Seedling and the better known Prince Albert. They were also one of the first nurseries to make a general garden fertiliser and the Potten End Nurseries became famous for their collection of ornamental trees and shrubs. Lanes were also keen pioneers who supported the introduction of rhododendrons and azaleas to England. Several species were first imported into this country from the Himalayas in 1847, and many remain today growing on their original sites around the village. Although Lanes nursery business survived in Potten End until the 1950's, the Depression of the 1920's and 30's began the decline in its prosperity.

Village School

In the early Nineteenth Century, there were three straw plaiting schools in Potten End. The first proper village school was provided for the community in 1856 by the Hon. John Finch of Berkhamsted Place (1793-1861). This was an immediate success and a second classroom was soon added, courtesy of Lady Alford and Lord Brownlow of Ashridge. Between 1864-73 the number of children had grown from 30 to nearly 70, and by the end of the century there were well over 100 pupils at Potten End School. Following the Education Act of 1944, it became a primary school with a reduced roll of 45 children. However the post-war baby boom eventually created a need for a new school building. Work began on this in 1959 and by 1965 pupil numbers at Potten End had increased to 122. In 1968 further new classrooms were added.

Church and Parish

Between 1840 and the end of the century, the population of Potten End doubled to over 400 inhabitants. The Ecclesiastical Parish of Potten End was founded in 1895, and at this time a vicar was shared with Nettleden. Potten End first received a piped water supply in 1889, but had to wait until 1963 for mains sewerage. In terms of civic boundaries, Potten End only achieved its independence in 1985. The bakery was the earliest shop in Little Potten End and was operational by 1854. There have only been two families of bakers in the village during the last 125 years. Two or three small shops functioned in the row of cottages called The Front from the 1860's. The Post Office opened at No.1 The Front in 1910 with a local girl as postmistress. It later moved to a modern building on the opposite corner. The shop in Church Road, which is now the Village Stores, was established in 1926. Electricity first came to the village in 1928 and gas followed in 1932. The recent timings of these developments are a reflection of the relative youth of Potten End as a village community.

The non-conformist Chapel in Potten End was established well before the Parish Church. The present chapel, registered on 1st January 1836, was originally a 40ft. by 20ft. structure. This chapel had never had a resident minister until the appointment of Pastor John Lewin in 1974. Holy Trinity Church, at Potten End, originally a chapel-of-ease under the Rector of Berkhamsted, opened in 1865 and was consecrated on 11th January 1868. Its status as a Parish Church was confirmed on 11th June 1895, when the Curate, Rev. Sydney Summers, became the first vicar appointed to Nettleden and Potten End. This church building was designed in an Italian Norman style by the architect F. C. Penrose who was surveyor of the fabric of St. Paul's Cathedral (1862-97). The Holy Trinity Church was built at a cost of £858 on one acre of allotment ground provided by Earl Brownlow who also paid the sum of £350 towards its construction. The Rev. Summers then oversaw the

Potten End Village School.

building of the church room which was formally opened in July 1896. This was erected in the northern part of the original acre given by Lord Brownlow. Until the Village Hall opened in 1927, it was home to all the principal meetings and social events in Potten End. The White House in Vicarage Road became the old vicarage and was subsequently extended by the Rev. J. L. Rhys (1899-1905). The burial ground of Holy Trinity was extended and dedicated on 12th June 1927. Further new developments took place in 1960 under the Rev. John Aubrey Davies, when an extension to the north side of Holy Trinity Church was completed. In 1960 the old vicarage was demolished and a modern one built, together with a further four houses on the old site. In 1972 Lady Cooper provided the Parish Church with an interesting memorial to her parents. This stylish cross, made of stained glass, set in resin, hangs from the open ceiling and was dedicated on 17th June 1973. Lady Cooper also opened the new church room of Holy Trinity on 26th June 1974.

Local Inns

Although the Plough pre-dates the Red Lion as a building, its existence on a tithe map of 1840 registered it as a private dwelling owned by William Halsey. The structure was re-built in 1870 and it is probable that the Plough gained a full licence shortly after this. By the end of the Nineteenth Century this Inn had been acquired by local brewers Locke and Smith, of Berkhamsted. The Red Lion was built about 1600 and the first reference to it as a beer house is 1850. In those days it was known as the Plumbers Arms, because this was the additional trade of its first licensee, Matthew Blacknell. By 1896 the Red Lion was owned by Frederick Quincy Lane of Lane Nurseries, who allowed all his workers to buy beer at a cheaper price. The present structure dates from 1924, when the property was completely re-built. Little Potten End had a beer house of its own from 1850. This was called The Fox and it stood next to the bakery.

Holy Trinity Church, Potten End, in the 1950's.

Village School, Potten End.

Village post office, circa 1919.

The Plough, circa 1919.

Early view of Potten End.

View of Potten End, 1996.

Potten End showing the Red Lion, 1996.

Frithsden

Like its near neighbour Nettleden, the community of Frithsden shares a misleading characteristic in the Twentieth Century: namely that from the few cottages remaining today, one gets little sense of how populous the hamlet once was. From the tithe map of 1840 we know that as many as 36 houses once lined the road from the Alford Arms to Frithsden Gardens. Those earlier cottages filled in many of the present gaps in the open stretch of ground between Hollybush Farm and Bede Cottage where eight dwellings once stood; one of which was a beer house. Work was plentiful on the prosperous Ashridge estate and between 1821 and 1830 a total of 85 families lived in Frithsden! Most of the early farmers at Frithsden operated on a small scale. The largest land holdings were those of John Howe at Hollybush Farm who kept some 30 acres in the Seventeenth Century, and Richard Dean who farmed 40 acres. Most of the other Frithsden holdings were scattered over the surrounding area and amounted to no more than two or three acres each. However, by the beginning of the Nineteenth Century, the Ashridge estate had acquired most of the holdings in the Frithsden valley and the farmers were all tenants.

It is worth a trip along the valley just to see the spectacularly beautiful Frithsden Beeches and adjacent row of six old cottages, originally a yeoman's house dating from the early Sixteenth Century with later additions. Near the Beeches there is also a long wall which was built to enclose the nursery gardens for Ashridge House, whose surplus produce was sent to Covent Garden. When the estate was sold in the 1920's the gardens became a prosperous family-run commercial nursery. The most notable building in Frithsden is the superb early Sixteenth Century 'Little Manor' that faces the Green. This house is much decorated with fine pargeting work, two panels of which record that the house was built in 1513 and restored in 1879. At one time the front door of this house was in Hertfordshire, whilst its back door was in Buckinghamshire and this is also true of other cottages in the valley. In the grounds of Little Manor is an old Baptist Chapel, built in 1835. It originally belonged to the next house, Frithsden Cottage, the home of the Neale family who were well known Baptists. A Nehemiah Neale farmed in Frithsden as long ago as 1669. John Bunyan is said to have ridden from Dunstable to preach at this chapel, and services were held there up until 1939. It became a school room for evacuees during World War II and its owners, the trustees of the Joanna Neale Trust, then sold it after the war.

Close by stands the Alford Arms, a Victorian public house which replaced an earlier Elizabethan Inn called the Tyrant's Arms. In 1840 it was owned and occupied by Minny and Mary Catherall and in 1851 kept by William Newman. Around 1886, when the licensee was Joseph Batchelor, this Victorian house was burnt down and subsequently re-built and renamed. The pub's new name tied it closely to the Ashridge estate, because Viscount Alford was one of the titles of the local squire, Lord Brownlow. Bede Cottage, a sizeable flint building further along the valley, was built as a village school and endowed by the Countess of Bridgewater who died in 1849. Hidden now among the trees on the south side of the main road is a beautifully built brick-lined ice hole which dates from the late 1600's. One elderly resident remembers it being filled with ice to keep the local venison for the villagers. It was also used to store lilly-of-the-valley bulbs, a flower which proliferates in the valley today.

The old country lane, known locally as Spooky Lane, starts between the Alford Arms and the old house dated 1513, and it travels over the hill to Nettleden, linking these two neighbouring communities. The most interesting feature of this old road is the derelict bridge built across it by the Duke of Bridgewater. This bridge was part of an extravagant scheme to improve his estate. The Duke altered the main carriage drive to Ashridge House in order to avoid approaching his estate through Nettleden. Where his new drive crossed Spooky Lane he ordered the construction of a deep cutting, beautifully lined with flints. This new route eliminated unnecessary encounters with farm carts travelling between the hamlets. Despite some written speculation, there is no evidence to indicate that Spooky Lane is a former Roman trackway, although local legend has it that Henry I, riding from Dunstable to Berkhamsted, was thrown from his horse on this old trackway. It is said that the King's steed was startled by the ghost of an Ashridge monk, a sinister robed and cowled figure that has given the lane its name. Another Hertfordshire tradition is that a Frithsden housewife created the famous cherry turnover. It was considered essential to use only black cherries in the turnover. These were called coroon cherries and were an important early agricultural product in this area of Hertfordshire. In the Eighteenth and Nineteenth Centuries, Frithsden was very much the centre of local cherry production and every year the village held a Cherry Fair.

Wine produced and estate bottled by P & A Latchford & Family at their vineyard in Frithsden, Hertfordshire.

Frithsden Vineyard

Established in 1971 by Peter and Ann Latchford, the Frithsden Vineyard has the distinction of being the first substantial vineyard established in Hertfordshire, since the planting of vines in Hatfield Park by the Earl of Salisbury in 1611. The tradition of English wine-making is older than many people imagine, given that the Romans grew vines in south-east England from about 300 A.D. Because substantial monasteries continued to cultivate grapes for communion wine until the Dissolution of the Monasteries in 1535, it is quite likely that the Ashridge monks themselves grew vines not too far away.

When looking for a vineyard site, the Latchfords settled on a suitable plot in Frithsden some 400ft. above sea level. Their chosen site has a south slope, which is essential for ripening. It also has a chalk soil overlaid with a flinty loam, not dissimilar to that of the famous Champagne region of France. The grape variety at Frithsden is mainly German, an offspring of Riesling called Muller-Thurgau which produces a medium white dry wine. Two and a half acres were planted in 1971 and the first harvest, in October 1973, produced 160 bottles. In 1974 the yield was 500 bottles and by 1979 the Frithsden Vineyard commenced its own bottling operation.

Frithsden, 1921.

Wine harvest at Frithsden Vineyard.

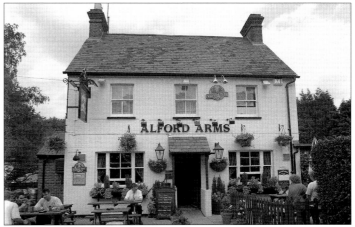

Alford Arms, 1996

Little Manor House, Frithsden, 1921.

Frithsden Beeches.

Nettleden

Church of St. Lawrence, 1921.

Nettleden, which is one of the most compact villages in Hertfordshire, lies in a pleasant valley about three quarters of a mile to the south-west of Great Gaddesden. The village's name echoes its location and simply means "valley of nettles". Until comparatively recently the village of Nettleden was included in Buckinghamshire, but was transferred to Hertfordshire in 1895. An unseen curiosity of this village is that for most of its life parts of Nettleden have lain in three different Parishes: the church side of the road in Pitstone, the northern half of the opposite side in Ivinghoe and its southern half in Great Gaddesden. Unlike its near neighbour Frithsden, which has a public house, but no church; Nettleden has a church, but no pub. At one end of Nettleden there is a house, originally two cottages, called Pipers Forge whose name commemorates a smithy which stood under a corner of its eaves, over 200 years ago.

At the other end of the village is the site of the black weatherboarded Nettleden Forge which followed it and was run by the Gash family for over two hundred years. This forge served the Ashridge estate and in its heyday employed eight men. On many of Ashridge's ironwork gates one can still see the initials "B.W.G.". "B" stood for Lord Brownlow and the "W.G." for William Gash, the Nettleden blacksmith. Between the two forge sites there are no more than a dozen houses, though it is worth remembering that the village is considerably smaller today than it was in the early Nineteenth Century. The house immediately adjoining the churchyard belongs to the Queen Anne period. Several other cottages in Nettleden, which date from the Seventeenth and Eighteenth Centuries, are modern conversions of former estate workers cottages. Out of sight of the village, tucked away in the Golden Valley, lies the beautifully restored property which was the old Nettleden Lodge of Ashridge Park. In 1933 men ploughing a field, some 400 yards to the north of the Church of St. Lawrence, broke into a Twelfth Century kiln.

This yielded up a complete jug, which can now be seen in the Medieval Gallery at the British Museum.

The first known reference to the Church of St. Lawrence at Nettleden is a document of 1285, making it part of the endowment of Ashridge Monastery. It was rebuilt in 1470, when a licence was granted to John Hunden, Bishop of Llandaff (and Prior of the Friar Preachers at Kings Langley), to consecrate altars in the church. In 1811, at the expense of the Earl of Bridgewater, the chancel and the north wall of the nave were rebuilt, possibly by James Wyatt. The building was originally a chapel of ease in the six mile long Parish of Pitstone until 1895, when diocesan changes made it a full church with its own independent Parish of Nettleden.

The tower carries three old bells, one of which, made by Thomas Harrys of London, is pre-Reformation. In 1930, during renovation work on walls in the churchyard, a stone coffin was unearthed some two feet beneath the surface. This find is believed to be connected with the Ashridge Monastery. The church also possesses an exceptionally fine pulpit. On the floor of the chancel there is a fine brass memorial, dated 1545, to Sir George Cotton who served as Vice Chamberlain to Edward VI. On the south wall there is an attractive monument to Edmund Bressy and his family, dated 1612. On the eastern side of the churchyard, there is a old yew tree and the Victorian vicar, Rev. George Spencer Cautley asked to be buried in its shade, and wrote his own verse obituary accordingly. The Rev. Cautley, who served the Church of St. Lawrence from 1857 to 1880, was a published poet and noted scholar of emblematic art. His wife Mary, the daughter of a Royal Academician, spent ten years designing and painting new stained glass windows for the whole church. The former vicarage, now called Nettleden House, was built for the Cautleys in 1856, on rising ground to the north of the church.

Nettleden Rectory in the 1880's.

Nettleden Lodge in 1928.

Nettleden villagers, circa 1920.

Pipers Forge, Nettleden, 1985.

Early view of Nettleden.

Little Gaddesden

The site of Little Gaddesden is one of the highest in Hertfordshire, some 625ft. above sea level. The village lies on the edge of the Ashridge estate, and is surrounded by glorious woodland and trees. Stretching for almost a mile, a long Green fronts some fine old houses and historic buildings which include a splendid Sixteenth Century Manor House. Little Gaddesden is one of the most interesting and distinctive villages in southern England. During the Nineteenth Century, the patronage and benevolence of the Ashridge estate was the defining characteristic in the development of Little Gaddesden. The quality and design of the village houses and gardens owe much to the wife of Earl Brownlow, Lady Marion Alford. She created, with her programme of renovation of older properties and construction of new houses for her estate workers, what some writers have called the first Garden Village of Hertfordshire.

An unusual feature of Little Gaddesden is the position of its Parish Church which stands alone in a meadow, a third of a mile away from the main community. However once found, this superb church is rewarding and its rural location, high on the scarp, offers the spectacle of commanding views north westwards across the Bedfordshire plain. There has been considerable speculation that the church's isolated position could be explained by the desertion of a previous village site during the Black Death. However, the case that villagers totally abandoned all their original dwellings in an effort to escape the Plague's contamination has not been established as the certain cause.

The Church of St. Peter and St. Paul

Early records date from 1161 when Thomas à Becket approved the granting of the rectory of Little Gaddesden to the Monastery of St. James in Northampton. It is therefore likely that an earlier Saxon or Norman church preceded the current structure. However the existing Church of St. Peter and St. Paul has a Fifteenth Century tower and nave, with part of the north arcade belonging to the same period. The exterior of the church displays gargoyles whilst the interior is richly decorated. The chancel, altar and pulpit are uniquely colourful, featuring splendid painted panelling. There are magnificent sculptures in the Bridgewater Chapel. The Bridgewater family is interred in three sections of the vault beneath the east end of the building and numerous memorials and monuments to the Egerton (Bridgewater) family adorn the church. The artistic chancel lamps are also worthy of note and the church has a fine iron-bound Fifteenth Century chest. In 1546 there were four bells in the tower and these were replaced by two new bells in 1820. Acting on the instructions of the 7th Earl of Bridgewater, James Wyatt took down the south wall of the church between 1810-12 and the south chapel of St. Peter and St. Paul was completed in 1819. The church was now closed off at its west end from the south aisle, in order to create the Bridgewater Mausoleum. Between 1813-15 Francis Bernasconi was also working on the ceiling of the mausoleum under the direction of Jeffrey Wyatt.

From 1870, working with the Rev. Charlton Lane, Lady Alford financed a new phase of support and benefaction in the life of the Church of St Peter and St Paul. She donated new pulpits and supervised the instalment of a new organ. The east wall of the church was moved further east and the gallery removed. Wyatt's arcade was now replaced by the present south arcade and the south chapel opened up to the south aisle and the church itself. The east window and the altar cross of St. Peter and St. Paul are both memorials to Lady Alford. The window was given by her son and the cross by her daughter-in-law, Adelaide. The Church of St Peter and St Paul has continued to be well cared for and in 1963 the south chapel was created out of the Bridgewater Mausoleum. A further restoration from a bequest in 1977 provided the tower with a new peal of six bells,

Early view of Little Gaddesden.

which were dedicated by the Bishop of St. Albans on 5th November 1978. In 1990/91 extensive repairs were required to the roof of the south aisle and chapel. This work cost £150,000, a sum which was successfully raised within the Parish.

Manor of Little Gaddesden

Whilst the Manor of Gatesden (Great Gaddesden) had been bequeathed by Ethelgifu to the Abbey of St. Albans 942-946, the Manor of Little Gaddesden was held by Edmar, a Thane of Edward the Confessor. The name Gatesden derives from the old English "gat/gaete" meaning goat and "den" meaning valley, so we have an early name which means "valley of the goats". Although Little Gaddesden grew to be a much more substantial community than its near neighbour Great Gaddesden, principally because it was part of the wealthy Ashridge estate, the Parish of Great Gaddesden has historically always been a significantly larger area of land.

From the time of the Norman Conquest, Little Gaddesden became one of several manors held by Robert, Count of Mortain, who was half brother to William the Conqueror. However by 1204, the manor was held by Eva de Broc who split the lands in two. She sold half to Simon de Vieleston, reserving the other half for herself including the original Manor House and estate. For Simon, she built another house of similar size. There were now two manors, Eva's remaining estate eventually became known as Lucies, whilst Simon de Vielston's lands became known as the Manor of Little Gaddesden. When Eva died unmarried, in 1221, she left her manor to her sister Juliana, wife of Geoffrey de Lucy. When Edmund, grandson of King John, became Earl of Cornwall and founded the Monastery at Ashridge in 1281, he bestowed the lands of Little Gaddesden together with the Overlordship of the Manor of Lucies on the College of Bonhommes, who then owned the estates until the Dissolution. However the Manor of Lucies remained in the hands of the Lucy family for a further six generations. Eventually the estate was conveyed to Robert Dormer whose grandson, Sir Robert Dormer, became a leading light in the court of Elizabeth I. It is likely that Sir Robert built the present Manor House because there is a stone set in its western front bearing the date 1576. In 1604 the Queen's Lord Keeper, Sir Thomas Egerton, acquired both Ashridge and Little Gaddesden. With the exception of the Halsey estate, established in 1544, Sir Thomas set about re-unifying all the historic Manors of Gaddesden which now came under ownership of the Ashridge estate. From Sir Thomas Egerton, the manor passed to the successive Earls and Dukes of Bridgewater and then through the female line to the Lords Brownlow until the break up and sale of the Ashridge estate from 1921.

The Manor House

The frontage of the Tudor Manor House faces south west and is built of local Totternhoe stone. The house consists of two projecting turrets with two main storeys, each topped by an attic and crow-stepped gables. The main entrance is in the south turret. The most note worthy part of the interior is the dining room. This room, shortened by the erection of some fine traceried Fifteenth Century panelling, was formerly part of the original Abbey of Ashridge. In keeping with the Tudor period, the room is faced with stone, decorated with stencilling. At the north west-end, there is a magnificent stone fireplace, above which are three painted panels, the centre panel still displaying the arms of Elizabeth I. This room also houses an original Tudor portrait of the Queen which is thought to show the moment of her arrest in Ashridge gardens. Upstairs is the White Room, a charming study which still has an elegant fireplace surrounded by Delft tiles and a small original Tintoretto, depicting Moses in the bulrushes.

The Manor House has survived many different phases of occupation. Given that Ashridge was, in Tudor times, a Royal residence it is likely that the Manor House could have been used as a home for the Royal Steward. During the time of the 2nd Earl, the house was home to the Maberly family who farmed 244 acres of local land in 1802. By 1810 the house had been purchased by the Ashridge estate and the last Countess of Bridgewater, who died in 1849, used the Manor House as an estate office. In 1860 the house became home to the village reading room and night school, later becoming the residence of Mrs. Cautley, the widow of the Vicar of Nettleden. On the death of Lord Brownlow in 1921, it was bought by his niece, Miss Kathleen Talbot, granddaughter of the 18th Earl of Shrewsbury and Talbot. Miss Talbot became an active and prominent member of Little Gaddesden's community.

John of Gaddesden's House.

Although this house is known as the Manor House, it is important to remember that the original Manor House site, which became the Manor House of Lucies when Eva de Broc split the estate in 1204, lay elsewhere. Historians have speculated that this first Manor House lay further north in the village and could well have been an earlier structure on the site of John of Gaddesden's House.

John of Gaddesden's House

At the corner of the main road's modern junction with Church Road is the site of an ancient cottage which is likely to have been the birthplace of John of Gaddesden (1280-1361), a leading physician in Medieval England. None of the original structure survives and the present house was built in the Fifteenth Century. This building has endured many alterations and additions over the years and only two rooms remain contemporary with its early origins. The house however still displays many Elizabethan features, with its timbers close-set in the walls and the small narrow red bricks of its chimney stacks. The fireplace in the sitting room, which was originally from Ashridge House, is decorated with roses and pomegranates and is also Elizabethan. The Solar or Medieval Hall of the house is 30ft. long by 18ft. wide. It has a fine open-timbered roof and is lit, on one side, by three oak mullioned windows. At one end of the room is a stone fireplace surrounded by Jacobean oak panelling. On a map of 1762, the plan of the house appears as a square with a courtyard in the middle. In more recent times the neglected house has served as a village reading room and even as labourers' cottages. In 1948 the property was substantially extended by Dr. Rawdon Smith who commissioned a specialist architect and employed local craftsmen on the work. These alterations and renovations to John of Gaddesden's House were conducted very carefully, using only contemporary fittings taken from the ruins of four other houses of the period. This project took four years to complete.

John of Gaddesden achieved his fame by being the first Englishman to write a textbook on medicine and also the first English physician appointed to a Royal Court. He graduated as a Bachelor of Medicine in 1307 at the age of 27. In 1314 he wrote his famous book, the Rosa Medicinae, which later became known as the Rosa Anglica or English Rose. This general medical guide had five distinct parts that dealt with fever, hygiene, diet, materia medica and drugs. This book soon established his reputation and became the standard textbook of its day. John of Gaddesden also took Holy orders and became a Master of Arts and a Bachelor of Theology. He was ordained as priest in 1320 and appointed Rector of Chipping Norton. In 1333 he became Canon of Chichester Cathedral and in 1336 Prebendary of St. Paul's, London. As court physician he served under Edward III from 1320-60. In 1339 he was also appointed Constable of the Castle of Wallingford as a reward for his war service. Many experts consider it probable that John of Gaddesden was the model for Geoffrey Chaucer's rather spiteful portrait of the "Doctor of Physick" in the Canterbury Tales.

Little Gaddesden House
This Victorian country residence was built in 1859 for Lord Brownlow and it was then used as an office for Mr. Paxton who was estate agent to the Ashridge Estate from 1854-82. Little Gaddesden House later became home to a branch of the Talbot family. Alfred Talbot was Lady Brownlow's favourite brother and, on his death in 1913, his daughter Kathleen took up residence at the Manor House. Her sister, Bridget, also lived locally, dividing her time between Little Gaddesden House and Kilpin Hall in Northallerton, Yorkshire. When Miss Bridget died, there were insufficient funds to convert the building into a charitable institution for children, as she had hoped. The property was therefore sold and later re-developed into nine separate residences by local builder E. J. Waterhouse. This work was completed in 1978.

Bede Court
These distinctive and generously proportioned almshouses were designed in 1862 by Lady Marian Alford, in memory of her late husband. When completed in 1865, they consisted of 10 pairs of rooms with gardens. They were originally called the Alford Bede Houses and were designed to provide accommodation for 10 widows of the village. Bede Court is the name of the local authority housing which was built on the site of these former historic buildings, which were demolished around 1970.

Village Green
Little Gaddesden is blessed with an unusually long village green where until a century ago the Little Gaddesden Feast was held annually; this was traditionally the first Monday following St. Peter's Day (29th June). In the first half of the Nineteenth Century this was described "as having degenerated into an annual orgy with scenes of indescribable wickedness!" The Green was sold off in the 1920's as part of the Ashridge estate, but following representations from local people, Hertfordshire County Council bought the land back from its private owner. The Green was then leased back to the Parish Council who still maintain it today. As late as the middle of the Eighteenth Century, there was no evidence of a continuous road along the Green, but by 1802 the current road existed as a lane, although at this time there seem to have been seven different paths across the Green. Standing at the end of the Green, opposite the Little Gaddesden entrance to Ashridge Drive, is the Village War Memorial which was erected in 1920/21. Built to an Italian design, its inscription carries the names of 29 men from Little Gaddesden who died in the two World Wars.

Alford and Adelaide Crosses
The Alford Cross, which is in the form of an Ionian Cross, is in memory of Lady Marian Alford. It was this lady who inspired the unique atmosphere and picturesque quality of Little Gaddesden which survives to this day. Built by public subscription, the cross stands at the Little Gaddesden entrance to the Ashridge estate and was first unveiled on Sunday 21st June 1891. Under Lady Marian's influence, the Parish Church and Village School were both improved. Most of the houses in the village were restored and beautified, whilst some older houses at Ringshall and on the Green were extended. She also ensured that piped water was brought to each dwelling in Little Gaddesden by 1858. Restored buildings were painted in the plum colour of the Brownlow family and marked with the Brownlow or Alford symbol or shield. The houses were also numbered with small blue and white tiles, similar to those in model villages in Switzerland.

The Adelaide Cross is situated at the opposite end of the Green. This cross, in memory of Lady Marian's daughter in law, stands close to the Manor House and occupies a more commanding position. It can even be seen from Ashridge House when looking up through an avenue of trees to the village green.

Home Farm
During the 1750's this was the Home Farm of the Duke of Bridgewater's estate. In 1807 the house is recorded as having a frontage of almost 50ft., with an adjoining brew house. Behind this were a malting house and various other structures. The house still bears the Brownlow shield of 1872, dating from a major restoration of the property. In the late Nineteenth Century the farm was rented out to George Underwood and his sons and at this time the main house was turned into two cottages. The property was then acquired by Cooper Macdougall and Robinson, the agricultural chemists, who used

Bede Court.

the farm for a programme of top quality stock breeding. Following their departure, it reverted to more traditional farm use, until the buildings were converted into luxury dwellings which aimed to preserve the character of the former rural homestead. The large converted dovecote is a striking feature of the farm and was designed by Jeffrey Wyatt in 1822.

Church Farm

The published work of local farmer William Ellis, who farmed at Little Gaddesden for 50 years, gives Church Farm some importance in the history of agriculture. Ellis achieved international recognition as the author of monthly guides which featured information and tips based, in part, on his experiments in cultivation at Church Farm. His key text " Chiltern and Vale Farming Explained" was published in 1733.

Village School

Little Gaddesden School first opened on the 18th May 1854 and John Worrall was appointed Schoolmaster by Lady Marion Alford. Initially the school was held in a large room at the local inn, the Bridgewater Arms, until the new schoolroom was opened on 5th June 1858. There were up to 90 children at the day school and over 130 children attended Sunday School at this time. Mr. Green was Headmaster of Little Gaddesden Church of England School for 50 years before Vicars Bell was appointed in 1929. During his time as Headmaster Mr. Bell wrote a history of Little Gaddesden, which was published in 1949. Vicars Bell left the school in 1963 and retired to Devon where, after ordination, he became Vicar of Holdsworthy; he died in 1978.

Village Hall

Little Gaddesden's early Village Hall and reading room had various sites. In 1860 its first home was a room in the Manor House and this was followed by accommodation in John of Gaddesden's house from 1894. It wasn't until 1921 that a designated Village Hall was erected on land given by Lord Brownlow. The structure provided was an old wooden army hut which had been brought from Gadebridge Park following the First World War. This served Little Gaddesden well until destroyed by fire in 1943. A new pre-fabricated Village Hall was put up near the school in 1957 on land given by the late Basil Phillips; this building was subsequently extended in 1973. In July 1948 a playing field of approximately six acres adjoining the Village Hall was bought by the Parish Council as a public recreation space. A new sports pavilion was built here between 1974-75, with funds raised by public subscription.

Robin Hood House

Formerly the Green Man and Robin Hood Inn with cellars, this house was contemporary with the Manor House and dates back to 1578. As a former public house, it has a significance relating to the 3rd Duke of Bridgewater's ownership of a string of race horses. The Duke's stable companions in this venture were the Duke of Cumberland, second son of George II, and the 4th Duke of Queensberry. Records indicate that in 1746 he was auctioning off some of his hunters from the Ashridge estate "at the sign of the Robin Hood". Robin Hood House and adjacent cottages were reconstructed by the 2nd Earl Brownlow and his wife in 1855; one of their earliest house re-constructions in the village. The house was probably used as the Ashridge estate office while Little Gaddesden House was being built. It was later leased to Fanny Halsey from 1870 until her death in 1885. During the First World War, Robin Hood House was used to house Belgian refugees.

Bridgewater Arms

The name of the Bridgewater Arms, perpetuates the memory of the various Dukes of Bridgewater who owned the Ashridge estate. On an ordnance survey map of 1878 it is referred to as the Brownlow Arms. In 1815 the Inn was kept by Nathaniel Duddlestone, a local farmer. The main part of the present building is late Eighteenth Century with Nineteenth Century additions. In 1854 the village school was held in the coffee room of the Bridgewater Arms and the children had to enter the building through the window, because they were not allowed to enter through the licensed bar. The Inn stands beside an old established track that runs from Studham to Northchurch. Until the end of the Nineteenth Century brewing took place at the Bridgewater Arms. Arthur Snelling Norris brewed here between 1870 and 1878, followed by George Allison 1882-95. There used to be two other small breweries in Little Gaddesden active during the Nineteenth Century. There was a recent short-lived revival of this brewing tradition when Bill Woods began brewing again at the Bridgewater Arms in October 1981.

ARMS OF EARL BROWNLOW.

Gerald Massey

Gerald Massey was born in May 1828. His father was a canal boatman who lived in a stone hut near Tring, and from the age of eight Gerald went to work in the silk mills. When he was 15, Gerald Massey escaped to London where he devoted his time to reading widely and became a self-taught man of letters. He was encouraged in his early literary endeavours by Charles Kingsley. By the age of 23 he had published a considerable volume of poetry which attracted the attention of Tennyson. Having established a reputation, Gerald Massey later wrote for the Daily Telegraph, before becoming involved in the Christian Socialism Movement. Partly because of his new religious pre-occupation, Gerald and his wife Rosina Jane got hopelessly in debt, but were rescued by the gift of a £100 cheque from Lord Brownlow. The owner of Ashridge also gave them a home on his estate, which was a cottage at Witchcraft Bottom. Gerald's wife, Rosina, was considered by many of the villagers to be a witch and there are several surviving tales of her supposed supernatural powers. It seems more likely however that she was a spiritualist, strongly influenced by her husband's mystical interests and researches. When his wife died Gerald became increasingly enmeshed in deeper research into the religious background of leading classical civilisations. In particular, his studies centred on Egyptian mysticism and hieroglyphics and aimed to prove that all religions derived from the same source. It is thought by many literary experts that Gerald Massey was the model for George Eliot's character of Felix Holt, in one of her major novels Middlemarch. This celebrated Victorian poet and mystic eventually died in 1907. The grave of his wife who died in 1866, can still be found in the churchyard of St. Peter and St. Paul, Little Gaddesden. Rosina Jane Massey was buried just inside the gate leading to the vestry.

John of Gaddesden's House, 1995.

Church of St. Peter and St. Paul, 1928.

Interior of the Church showing the Bridgewater Chapel (left).

The Chancel of St. Peter and St. Paul's.

Bridgewater Arms in the 1920's.

Witchcraft Bottom, 1928.

Little Gaddesden House, 1995.

Robin Hood House in the 1890's.

Village School at the turn of the century.

Adelaide Cross.

Village Green showing the Adelaide Cross.

Alford Cross.

Home Farm, 1996.

The Dovecote at Home Farm, 1996.

Manor House, 1996.

Former roadway and bridge from Ashridge to Home Farm, 1995.

The Golden Valley at Ashridge, 1995.

Ashridge

In 1275 Edmund Earl of Cornwall, who was then resident at nearby Berkhamsted Castle, ordered a house to be built in a clearing in the woods at Little Gaddesden to become a monastery for Grey Monks. Some years before Edmund himself, or more probably his father, Richard I had taken possession of a casket whilst travelling in Saxony. This devotional object was a Holy relic said to contain some of the blood of Christ. Edmund's intention was to install a group of brethren, bound by the strictest of Augustinian rules, and charge them with protecting this precious relic. Building work began on the monastery in 1276 and it was finally dedicated in 1286. The initial establishment consisted of a rector and nineteen French brethren and became known as the College of Bonhommes. The later name of Ashridge certainly derives from the ash tree, which itself has a long historical association with the establishment of boundaries and was also regarded as having sacred connotations.

Once the monastery was established, Edward I visited for an extended stay and held Parliament there in 1290. When Edward died in 1300, we are told that "his bowels were immediately buried and his heart was placed with a drop of Christ's blood in the golden tabernacle at Ashridge". The second member of the Royal family, who was a great benefactor to the monastery was the eldest son of King Edward II, the Black Prince (1330-76).

Thomas Waterhouse

allowed on the premises. Ashridge received many visitors and as it grew in prosperity the buildings of the monastery increased in number. The monastery was provided with a very handsome gateway and built around a church, which was 132ft. in length, there was a great hall (64ft. by 24ft.), an infirmary, a chapter house (33ft. by 23ft.), and cloisters (40ft. square) with passageways 11ft. wide.

Cardinal Henry Beaufort, the Bishop of Winchester who died in 1447, made substantial donations to the Ashridge monastery which allowed for improvements to the dormitory, sacristy, infirmary and cloister. A large barn was also built at the end of the Fifteenth Century to house the monks' swelling harvests. Despite all the Royal favours held since Plantagenet times, the Dissolution of the Monasteries brought an abrupt end to the College of Bonhommes in 1539. The Grey Monks, who then numbered only seventeen, were driven out by Henry VIII. The last Rector of Ashridge, Thomas Waterhouse who was known as Henry's 'gentleman priest', fared rather better. He received an income of £100 per annum with 50 loads of wood, and was later granted the Bury estate in Hemel Hempstead. Ashridge instead became a Royal residence and King Henry VIII's three children, Edward, Mary and Elizabeth, divided their time between Ashridge and Hatfield. Religious tensions were again to envelope Ashridge when Mary Tudor (1516-53) came to the throne in 1553. In 1547 the estate had been bequeathed to

Black Prince

He too was resident at Berkhamsted Castle. In his declining years, the Black Prince developed an increasing attachment to the monastery and, before his death in 1376, he endowed the altar of Ashridge with a great table of gold and silver, set with a rich selection of rubies, emeralds and pearls. For two and a half centuries the monks of Ashridge prospered, showing the 'Holy blood' to pilgrims who travelled from far and wide. The relic was so highly treasured that members of the nobility asked to be buried at Ashridge. The first resting place of the Verneys, a leading local family, was at Ashridge prior to the removal of their tombs to the Parish Church of St. John the Baptist in Aldbury. The monks continued their strict adherence to the rules of St. Augustine, wearing only ash grey tunics and cloaks, and with the exception of the Queen, no women were ever

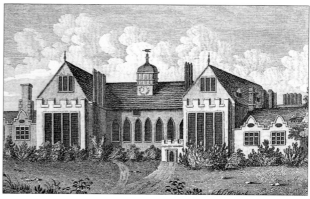

Ashridge Monastary

Princess Elizabeth in her father's will, and it was here that she was arrested in February 1554 on the orders of Queen Mary. This was for Elizabeth's alleged complicity in the revolt of Sir Thomas Wyatt against Mary's prospective marriage to Philip, King of Spain. Perhaps because of this unhappy memory, Elizabeth never returned to Ashridge after her own accession to the throne in 1558. There used to be an impressive statue of Queen Elizabeth I at Ashridge which was later presented to Harrow School in 1925. This statue remains at Harrow School to this day, on the outside wall of the famous Speechroom. A replica has been made which now stands in a niche overlooking the lawns at Ashridge.

In 1558 Queen Elizabeth granted the lease of Ashridge to Richard Combe of Hemel Hempstead, but the house remained in the possession of the Crown until the beginning of the Seventeenth Century. In 1604 Ashridge was acquired by Thomas Egerton who served first as Lord Keeper to Queen Elizabeth and then as James I's Lord Chancellor. Thomas Egerton (1540-1617), who became Baron Ellesmere and Viscount Brackley, selected Ashridge not only as a quiet retreat for his declining years, but also as a permanent family seat for his descendants. His son, who became the first Earl of Bridgewater, was rewarded as a member of one of the leading Royalist families who suffered in the Civil War, during which the mansion at Ashridge had been sacked by Cromwell's Roundheads. John Egerton, the third Earl (1646-1701), another distinguished servant of the Crown, was awarded the Order of the Bath. He built a new chapel at Ashridge and it was his son Scroop(1681-1745), who became the first Duke of Bridgewater in 1720. It was Scroop who finally cemented the family fortunes by his favourable marriages, first into the family of the Great Duke of Marlborough and also by his second marriage into the family of the Duke of Bedford.

Born in 1736 Francis Egerton became the 3rd Duke of Bridgewater at the age of only eleven, following the early death of his older brother John, from smallpox. Upon the death of his father, two years earlier, Francis was sent to Eton and therefore he did not enjoy a settled family upbringing. As an adult he grew to be rather a strange character who became obsessed with building the Bridgewater Canal from his coalmines at Worsley to Manchester. Although his ideas were destined to found an even greater family fortune, such plans initially threatened the family's prosperity. At first his scheme was regarded by many leading figures of the time as an act of madness and although his first and second Canal Acts passed through Parliament in 1759 and 1760, the ambitious project reduced the Duke to a penniless state; as his debt reached £60,000 during the canal's construction. However he was to have the last laugh, because once his expensively engineered canals were used huge savings were made as the cost of transporting coal tumbled. By 1796, when the last stretch of the Grand Junction Canal was almost complete, Francis Egerton was said to be earning in excess of £80,000 a year from the Bridgewater Canal alone. Flushed with success and great riches, the Canal Duke returned to Ashridge with ambitious plans to rebuild the crumbling Ashridge mansion, he had ignored for so long. However he died on 8th March 1803, two months after making out his will, but well before he could put his grandiose building plans into effect.

Francis Egerton had died without producing an heir, so much of the Duke's fortune was inherited by his cousin, John Egerton, the son of the Bishop of Durham, who faithfully carried out the Duke's plans for Ashridge. All the grounds were re-landscaped under the direction of Humphrey Repton, a disciple of Capability Brown, whilst the construction of the new house was the responsibility of the celebrated architect James Wyatt. This was the architect whose career had flourished when he designed the impressive Palladian villa of Gaddesden Place for the Halseys in 1768. Building work at Ashridge commenced in 1808, with the mansion's foundation stone being laid by Charlotte, Countess of Bridgewater. By 1810 the main structure of the house was complete, but further work followed. James Wyatt's Chapel was finished using fabulous Fifteenth Century glass imported from Germany, now among the treasures of the Victoria and Albert Museum. By the end of 1817 further new extensions had been added to the building which doubled its length to 1000ft. The total cost of construction for the new Ashridge was in excess of £300,000 and the new frontage created was the longest of any stately house in England. The sparkling frontage of the house was styled by the later additions of James Wyatt's nephew Jeffrey Wyatville. The modern Gothic style was not to everyone's taste, but none could ever deny the princely quality of the interior of this spectacular new house, created during the Nineteenth Century.

The interior of Ashridge had a good start in that it had been bequeathed the Canal Duke's impressive art collection, most of which was purchased from the Duc D'Orleans. Sir Matthew Digby Wyatt (1820-1877) who had worked on the restoration of Windsor Castle for George IV, re-modelled the principal rooms at Ashridge between 1857 and 1863. This work was in the Italian style and featured marble fireplaces, exquisitely painted ceilings, first class ceiling mouldings and superb panelling in Austrian walnut, some of which came from the Tuileries in Paris. The decorative ceilings were the work of

Tudor portrait showing the arrest of Princess Elizabeth at Ashridge, February 1554.

North front of Ashridge.

Staircase, Ashridge.

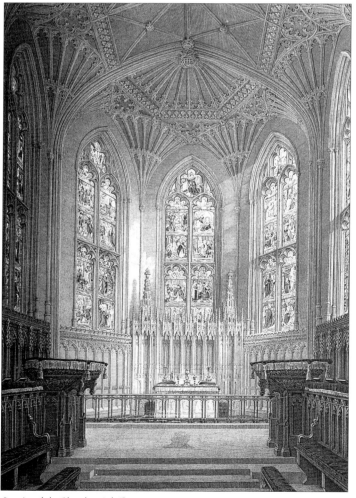

Interior of the Chapel at Ashridge.

Francis Bernasconi who was particularly skilled in scagliola work and some of the Ashridge designs were directly inspired by the Scala D'ora in the Doges Palace, Venice.

The 7th Earl, who had financed the construction of the new house, took a great interest in all aspects of life on the Ashridge estate and in the village of Little Gaddesden. He was well liked in the local community and when he died in 1823, the Duchess continued alone at Ashridge until her death in 1849. As a result of her longevity the 8th Earl, Francis Henry Egerton (1756-1829) never lived at Ashridge and following his death, the title lapsed. The next important figure in the life of Ashridge was Lady Marian Alford, daughter of the Marquess of Northampton. It was Lady Marian who supervised much of the 'Italian style' interior of Ashridge, initiated by the 7th Earl. Lady Marion Alford had married Viscount Alford (1812-1851) who succeeded to the vacant Bridgewater estate as the 1st Earl Brownlow, but he died after only two years in residence at Ashridge. Lady Marion, who died at Ashridge in 1888, remained in authority during the minority of her eldest son's (the 2nd Earl) tragically short life. John William Spencer Egerton Cust was born in 1842 and had died in 1867 at the age of 25. Her second son, Adelbert born 1844, became the 3rd Earl of Brownlow and he remained at Ashridge until his death in 1921. In 1868 Adelbert married Adelaide, the daughter of the 1st Earl of Salisbury. The time of the 3rd Earl Brownlow was very much the high society hey-day of the Ashridge estate. Ashridge could comfortably cope with weekend parties of up to 40 guests and Brownlow's shooting parties often included members of the Royal Family. Queen Mary visited Ashridge on several occasions, as did most of the nation's leading politicians, Benjamin Disraeli, William Gladstone and Stanley Baldwin. Country Life magazine described "100 acres of excellent cover

Adelbert, Third Earl Brownlow.

shooting at Ashridge, which provides six separate days of first class shooting in which a team of eight guns can easily bag 1000 pheasants a day!". The Shah of Persia paid a visit to Ashridge in 1889 and Field Marshall Lord Kitchener was taking tea at Ashridge in 1914 when he received an urgent telegram on the afternoon before war was declared on Germany.

Countess Adelaide died in 1919 and when the 3rd Earl died in 1921, the trustees were directed to sell Ashridge to meet the crippling cost of death duties. Thankfully, due to the sterling political lobbying of local luminaries such as Miss Bridget Talbot of Little Gaddesden House, and an initial anonymous donation of £20,000, a "Save Ashridge" campaign managed to prevent the break up of the estate. This eventually enabled the National Trust to acquire 3,500 acres of the Ashridge parklands. In 1928 the house and 250 acres were bought by Mr. Urban Broughton. Together with Mr. J. C. C. Davidson, M.P. for Hemel Hempstead (later Lord Davidson), Urban Broughton established a residential college. This was affiliated to the Conservative Party and known as Bonar Law College. During the Second World War, Ashridge became an emergency annexe for both University College and Charing Cross Hospitals in London. Temporary ward blocks were erected in front of the house to cater for up to 1200 injured servicemen. The wounded from Dunkirk were treated at Ashridge, as were men from the 51st Highland Division. However the majority of patients were civilians transferred from London. Between 1940 and 1946 more than 12,000 operations were performed and 3000 births were recorded at the emergency hospital.

Approximately 100 acres of the estate were leased to Ashridge Golf Club in 1932 and the newly designed course was skilfully blended into the surrounding parkland. The first President of Ashridge Golf Club was the 6th Earl of Roseberry (1932-74) and Henry Cotton, one of the greatest English golfers this century, was employed as resident professional (1937-46). After the war the house returned to its former use, but in 1959 the College at Ashridge was finally shorn of its party political affiliations. It is now an independent and prestigious Management College which enjoys an international reputation for excellence.

Ashridge Park today still comprises over 3000 acres of spectacular countryside with separate habitats of woodland, common land and down land. The National Trust estate covers over six square miles and takes in parts of Buckinghamshire and Bedfordshire, as well as Hertfordshire. Some of the woodland at Ashridge dates back over a thousand years and was once part of a vast Saxon forest situated between the ancient Manors of Berkhamsted and Gaddesden. Frithsden Beeches were an essential part of the Medieval economy providing renewable sources of wood and nuts as pannage for pigs. Two of the notable old woodlands, Frithsden Copse and Old Copse have still retained most of their native flora and fauna. Natural features of Ashridge's former glory still survive in the form of Princes Ride, a fine avenue of old oaks and chestnuts that runs from the house to the Earl of Bridgewater's Monument. The best known inhabitants of the Ashridge Park woodland are the wild fallow deer that are descendants of the deer of the original Royal park. The Ashridge parkland also offers a superb habitat for bird life and in 1965 as many as 51 breeding species were recorded.

Bridgewater Monument, 1957.

The Bridgewater Monument

On his death the Canal Duke bequeathed £13,500 for a memorial obelisk to be erected to his own design, bearing the inscription "Francis 3rd Duke of Bridgewater - Father of Inland Navigation". The Monument's somewhat remote location was dictated by Lady Bridgewater who decided its design was in poor taste and ensured that it was erected well away from the main house. The Duke, who died in March 1803, was buried in the family vault at the Parish Church of St. Peter and St. Paul at Little Gaddesden. Lord Farnborough, trustee to his will, subsequently arranged for the construction of the 100ft. Doric column, fluted in granite, which was built by Philip Newell of Pimlico. Its internal spiral stone staircase has 172 steps, leading to a viewing gallery at the top of the monument which offers an impressive panorama from 729ft. above sea level.

FRANCIS DUKE OF BRIDGEWATER.

Born 21 May 1736, Died 8 March 1803.

Ashridge Gardens

The mansion's 'pleasure gardens' were planned by Humphrey Repton in 1814 and included a circular rose garden and a monks garden. A mount garden, designed by Repton to break up the level site, was constructed using Hertfordshire puddingstone. Later additions were an Italian garden, contemporary with the interior alterations made to Ashridge House by Lady Alford 1857-63, and the more recent sunken rose garden, constructed by Malcolm Lingard in 1974-75. This new design occupies the site of an the former artificial lake that was created in the 1870's. Another major feature of the gardens, still enjoyed today, is the arboretum which is a formal avenue of wellingtonians, flanked by spectacular banks of richly coloured rhododendrons.

Other Features at Ashridge

The crypt is the only part of the old monastic building still in existence inside the main house. The term 'crypt' is misleading as it was actually the undercroft of the monastery's great hall, and James Wyatt later utilised it in his design for the new house as a wine store and beer cellar. The old Holy well of the monastery is situated directly under the south (chancel) end of James Wyatt's chapel and has a depth of 224ft. To everyone's astonishment, when it was cleaned and restored in 1970-71, the walls of the well were found to be made of over 2000 cast iron pieces. Records of 1530 indicate that the water lifting mechanism was first drawn by dogs, though the present superstructure is a Nineteenth Century donkey wheel, similar to that used at the well in the Gaddesden Parsonage at Little Gaddesden.

The ice house situated near the end of the kitchen gardens is a large cavern dug into the bank. Built entirely of Hertfordshire puddingstone, it was constructed with three layers of doors to insulate it against heat. Here in a pit 75ft. deep, ice cut from the local ponds in winter, was placed between three layers of straw, ready for use in summer days on the Ashridge estate. Beyond the quadrangle, to the west, is the Red House which is a Nineteenth Century structure that was built to provide separate accommodation for special guests and a retreat for Lord Brownlow from the main house. Stanley Baldwin always used the Red House on his frequent visits to Ashridge. It was later used as the Estate Manager's home and still features a large walk-in safe, as originally fitted.

Ashridge Lodge Houses

Old Park Lodge is a class II listed building and is said to have been formerly called King Henry VIII's Keeper's Lodge. It dates from 1619, with Eighteenth and Nineteenth Century additions and Tudor style chimneys. Thunderdell Lodge is also a class II listed building, designed either by James or Jeffrey Wyatt between 1813-19. This Lodge probably replaced an earlier building and monastic gate. Berkhamsted Lodge was built by the 7th Earl Brownlow towards the end of his life. It stands on the old road from Hemel Hempstead to Aldbury and a good example of the Brownlow coat-of-arms can still be seen in the pargeting on this old house.

Ringshall

Much of Ringshall was in the Parish of Ivinghoe and therefore belonged to the Bishop of Winchester prior to 1420, when it was given by Royal covenant to the Bonhomme Monks of Ashridge. Early dwellings of a small farming hamlet existed to the north of the Ivinghoe Ringshall road, whilst the surviving cottages built by the 7th Earl lie to the south of this. Ringshall Lodge was also part of Jeffrey Wyatt's reconstruction of Ashridge and this impressive early Nineteenth Century structure, now part of Deer Leap Garage, stood at the northern entrance of the main drive to Ashridge House. The Deer Leap Swimming Pool opened in the 1930's and was originally run from the garage by its founder, Mr. Leslie Bedford.

Rodinghead

Rodinghead was erected by the local builder Donald Lockhart in 1939, just before the outbreak of the Second World War. This was the house where General de Gaulle spent a year of his war-time exile, following France's capitulation to the Nazis. The General's family left Rodinghead in the autumn of 1942.

Ashridge, circa 1910.

Ashridge Garden (front) circa 1910.

Rose Garden at Ashridge.

Croquet at Ashridge in the 1880's.

Visit of the Shah of Persia, July 9th 1889.

Edward, Prince of Wales (centre) visits Ashridge, December 1887.

Earl Brownlow and party on the steps of Ashridge.

Ringshall Lodge, 1957.

Cottages at Ringshall, 1921.

Meet of the Hertfordshire Hunt, Ashridge, 1952.

Old Lodge Gate, at Ashridge, 1928.

Aerial view of Ashridge, 1959.

Berkhamsted

There is little mystery involved in the search for the key factor in the historic development of Berkhamsted, which today remains one of the most attractive and prosperous country towns in Hertfordshire. Whilst it is possible to overstate the importance of Berkhamsted Castle as a Royal residence, there is no denying that this ancient site played its part in the life of the Nation from the time of the Norman invasion until the end of the Plantagenet period. Furthermore the role played by the castle in the development of Berkhamsted's early prosperity and sense of importance was crucial. For nearly 400 years, the wealth and patronage emanating from members of the Royal Court living at this Medieval castle, fuelled Berkhamsted's economic growth. During this early period of English history, there were very considerable advantages to be gained by remaining in Royal favour. A Charter granted by Henry II in 1156 gave every merchant in Berkhamsted complete exemption from tolls and taxes throughout his kingdom. A further decree of Edward IV (1442-83) helped to safeguard the town's early prosperity, by declaring that no rival market was to be set up within 11 miles of Berkhamsted. Endowments, such as those established by leading courtier Geoffrey Fitz Piers, also made a valuable contribution to the local community growing up around the Royal Castle. As Earl of Essex, Fitzpiers founded two hospitals in Berkhamsted, circa 1212, and he settled local lands on the Brotherhood of St. John the Baptist.

However such a privileged position could not last indefinitely and the closure of the castle in 1495 marked the beginning of a decline in Berkhamsted's relationship with the Crown of England. In contrast, the great Tudor King, Henry VIII later bestowed Royal favours upon the rival market town of Hemel Hempstead. This neighbouring town received an important royal charter in 1539. However in 1618 James I granted Berkhamsted a further Charter of Incorporation, but its additional benefits were nominal. The civic leaders of Berkhamsted, no doubt recalling better days, began to feel aggrieved at their dwindling share of Royal revenues and privileges. Consequently the town's support for the Royal Family during the Civil Wars was at best luke warm, and it was no surprise when the Charter of Incorporation was withdrawn from Berkhamsted several years after the restoration of Charles II in 1660. This meant that the high civic status of the town, once considered sufficiently important to be returning its own Member of Parliament (1337 and 1341), was lost.

As the great agricultural industry of the nation began to blossom during the Seventeenth and Eighteenth Centuries, Hemel Hempstead with its thriving market, was well positioned to build its role as the major town in the area. This achievement was crowned by its award of Borough status by Queen Victoria in 1898, a privilege that Berkhamsted had lost some 200 years earlier. This formal recognition of Hemel Hempstead's importance gave it scope to maximise the commercial benefits of the improving transport links and early industrial developments that were already well under way. Hemel Hempstead now had the base on which to build towards its Twentieth Century destiny as the prosperous economic centre of west Hertfordshire. However it is unlikely that any Berkhamstedians would wish to swap roles with their near neighbours, given that the attractive old town of Hemel Hempstead has today become so dwarfed by the post-war development of such a large New Town. In contrast, Berkhamsted's rather gentle slide from Royal grace has perhaps more easily allowed it to maintain the attractive county town environment that better respects its historic past.

It is thought that the town's name of Berkhamsted derives from 'the place of birch trees', and was a probable reference to the dense woodland that once covered most of the Bulbourne valley. Parts of this rich woodland would first have been cleared to help support the expanding Plantagenet courts at Berkhamsted and Kings Langley. Local timber clearance was also used to provide funds for the College of Bonhommes monks at Ashridge that flourished under Royal patronage.

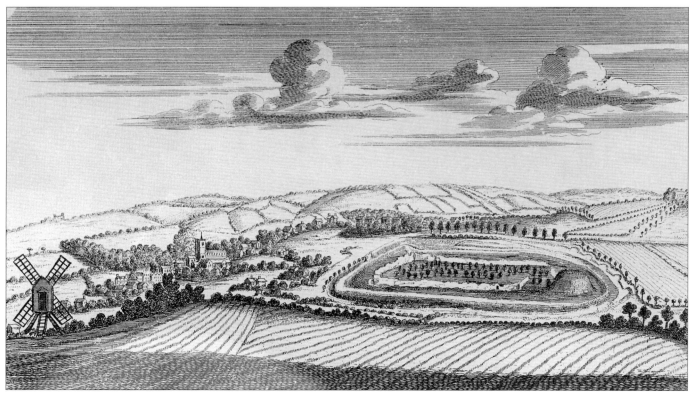

Prospect of Berkhamsted by William Stukeley, 1724.

Berkhamsted Castle

It is possible that this Norman castle was built on the site of an earlier Saxon encampment. Following the Battle of Hastings in 1066, William the Conqueror accepted the nation's surrender at Berkhamsted. He then proceeded to Westminster Abbey where he was crowned, on Christmas Day by Alfred Archbishop of York, as the newly installed King of England. The Manor of Berkhamsted was among the many grants of lands William awarded to his half-brother Robert Count of Mortain. The Count of Mortain was a military man who immediately recognised the strategic importance of Berkhamsted. The old Saxon encampment guarded the old Roman road of Akeman Street which was the main route north through the valley. Consequently he set about constructing a strongly fortified castle built on a traditional Norman plan of a defensive motte and bailey earthworks. The Count's son William, who inherited all Robert's lands and estates, later led a rebellion against King Henry I. As punishment his eyes were burned out, all his estates were confiscated by the Crown, and his father's castle was razed to the ground. Henry I then granted the Manor of Berkhamsted to his Chancellor Randolph in 1104. The Chancellor immediately started rebuilding Berkhamsted Castle and it is fragments of this structure which still remain today. The motte, on which a three storey stone tower or keep used to stand is 45ft. high. At its base it is 180ft. round with a top diameter of 60ft. The original keep would have been constructed in wood, but was replaced in the Twelfth Century by a stone building with walls 8ft. thick. The bailey of Berkhamsted Castle was oblong shaped with dimensions of 300ft. by 450ft.

A wide moat encircles the bailey area and a second large earth bank and ditch still surround the entire castle site. Around the northern quarters was a third bank of earth, acting as further protection for the keep. Apart from these impressive earthworks, the remnants of the structure are the curtain walls of the main castle (bailey) area; these are made of flint and rubble and were once 7ft. thick. The main entrance to the castle was the south gate which stood on the perimeter, close to today's railway line, but further east from the present entrance to the site. To help the community endure periods of prolonged siege, Berkhamsted Castle had two wells. One was at the sheltered northern end of the bailey in the inner ward and there was another in the keep which was designed to be the final refuge for the castle's defenders.

From 1155, Berkhamsted Castle was occupied by Thomas à Becket who diligently carried out extensive repairs and maintenance to its structure. After Thomas's death in 1170, King Henry II spent considerable time at Berkhamsted which had become his favourite residence. By 1189 the castle was owned by Prince John (later King John) brother of the much celebrated crusading monarch, King Richard I. However in the civil wars which resulted from King John reneging on pledges given in the Magna Carta, Berkhamsted Castle was attacked by Prince Louis of France. The French Prince, aided by disgruntled English Barons, finally succeeded in taking the castle on 29th December 1216, following a siege lasting 14 days. The serious damage caused by this siege was repaired during the reign of Henry III (1216-72); the work being supervised by his younger brother Richard, Earl of Cornwall. Following the death of Richard, Edmund Earl of Cornwall, duly inherited the castle where he had been born. It was Edmund who was responsible for the foundation of the important monastery at Ashridge. Because Edmund died without issue, Berkhamsted Castle then reverted to the reigning monarch, Edward I, who had established an impressive Royal Palace further to the south at Kings Langley. Nevertheless Berkhamsted Castle remained in the King's possession until Edward II granted it to his favourite and lover, the notorious Piers Gaveston.

The later reign of Edward III saw a period of much glory for the castle. The King first ordered a major survey and carried out extensive repairs before granting the building to his son Edward. His son was the Black Prince who became Berkhamsted's own favourite in history. As a young man he became a national hero who enjoyed spectacular military successes against the French, and chose many officers for his celebrated campaigns from the town. Henry of Berkhamsted was his Marshall and six Berkhamsted men fought bravely at his side in the Battle of Crecy. A defeated King John of France was actually imprisoned in Berkhamsted Castle following the Battle of Poitiers. Berkhamsted was a favourite place for the Black Prince and when he married Joan of Kent, the couple spent their honeymoon in the area. On the death of the Black Prince, the castle passed to his son who was later to become the betrayed Lancastrian, King Richard II. During this time Geoffrey Chaucer, the celebrated early English poet, acted as Clerk of Works at Berkhamsted Castle.

The last member of the Royal Family to take a serious interest in the castle was Cecily Duchess of York, who was mother to two Kings of England, Edward IV and Richard III. The infamous Richard III was slain at the Battle of Bosworth Field and Cecily's grandsons, Edward and Richard, were the two Princes who were criminally smothered in the Tower of London. Cecily had been given Berkhamsted Castle by Edward IV and lived there following the death of her husband in 1460. By the time of her own death in 1495, the House of Tudor was firmly established and the castle became deserted gradually falling into disrepair. The fact that so little of the structure remains is not due to the ravages of war, but because much of the Berkhamsted Castle's stonework was taken to build an impressive Elizabethan mansion called Berkhamsted Place. This fine old mansion used to stand high on the hill on land to the north east of Bridgewater Road. (see page 206). An architectural tragedy occurred during the 1830's when the construction of the railway caused the castle's main gate to be unceremoniously demolished. Thankfully in 1930 the surviving castle ruins were placed under the care of the Ministry of Public Building and Works, and they remain a protected historic monument today. When the Prince of Wales, the late Duke of Windsor, visited Berkhamsted Castle in 1935 it was the first time this old Royal residence had received an official visit from a Duke of Cornwall since 1616.

The Church of St. Peter

St. Peter's was not the first Parish Church in the ancient Manor of Berkhamsted. This honour belonged to the ancient Saxon Church of St. Mary's in Northchurch. As the community around the castle grew during the late Eleventh and early Twelfth Centuries, a separate Parish, originally dedicated to St. James was established for Berkhamsted. It is possible that this early Church of St. James was founded on the St. Peter's site, but much more likely that it stood somewhere on the Post Office site, which was then known as St. John's Well. This area was also home to two hospitals founded by the Brotherhood of St. John the Baptist and they are discussed in more detail on Page 206.

What is certain however is that parts of the impressive structure of the Parish Church of St. Peter date from the early Thirteenth Century. This church, built to the Italian Cross plan, has an official date of 1222, though some of the earliest work in the chancel (now the Lady Chapel) is circa 1200. The lower stages of the tower and nave would have been constructed later. Aisles were then added to the nave in 1230, St. Catherine's Chapel was built in 1320 and St. John's Chantry (now the outer south aisle) followed in 1350. One hundred years later the clerestory further enlarged the building and, when the tower was raised to its present height of 85ft. in 1545-6, the church had grown to its full dimensions. Berkhamsted's impressive Parish Church was now complete. It stretched 168ft. from east window to west door, and 90ft. across its transepts. A substantial restoration of St. Peter's was undertaken by Butterworth in 1871.

The Church of St. Peter has many interesting historical details, not least the richly decorated, Fourteenth Century tomb of a knight and his lady. This is thought to be the interment of Henry of Berkhamsted, who served as Constable to the Black Prince at Berkhamsted Castle. Another servant of the Black Prince, John Raven, is represented by a brass of a knight in armour and above this is another brass to Robert Incent, who was Secretary at Berkhamsted Castle to Cecily Duchess of York. It was Robert's son John who, as Dean Incent, founded Berkhamsted School. Other early brasses are those to Richard and Margaret Torrington (1356) which are mounted on oak panels in the nave. The church also houses memorials to residents of the castle's manorial successor, Berkhamsted Place; these are the large marble tomb of John Sayer and the charming monument to John and James Murray of Berkhamsted Place. There are also two brasses outside the vestry, on a swivel, one of which is dedicated to Thomas Waterhouse (last Rector of Ashridge Monastery). One of Berkhamsted's most famous inhabitants, the celebrated poet William Cowper 1731-1800 is also honoured in St. Peter's Church. William Cowper was born in Berkhamsted and described his childhood spent at the old rectory as "a blissful time". In 1872 the Rev. J. W. Cobb raised the necessary funds to create in the large east window of St. Peter's a beautiful and permanent memorial to the life of William Cowper. Cowper's father, the Rev. John Cowper, who served as Rector of Berkhamsted until 1772, often preached at St. Peter's and it was here that his son, destined to become a famous poet, was baptised on 13th December 1731. Southey's subsequent 'Life of Cowper', published 1833-7, confidently declared that Berkhamsted "will be better known in after ages as the birthplace of Cowper, than for its connection with so many historical personages who figured in tragedies of old". A major Twentieth Century restoration of the structure and fabric of St. Peter's was carried out between 1956-60, when the external flintwork and masonry were renewed and the church tower was given a new timber and lead roof.

William Cowper.

The Old Rectory, birthplace of William Cowper.

Dean Incent's House

Described by Nicholas Pevsner as 'the finest house in the town', the carefully restored Dean Incent's House is certainly the oldest building in the High Street. It is a picturesque half-timbered Tudor house, with some surviving Medieval traces, and was built in the later part of the Fifteenth Century. Architectural experts have indicated that they believe the original Medieval house stood at right-angles to the High Street; some of the rear part of this structure survives, but its front has been incorporated into the Tudor house that faces the main road. The minor addition of a south west wing dates from the Eighteenth Century. The interior has survived surprisingly well and many old timbers are exposed, with plaster infill, which adds to the building's authenticity. The house may well have been used first as a Medieval hall or public meeting place. We know that the house was home to Robert Incent, Secretary to Cecily Duchess of York, who was resident at Berkhamsted Castle until her death in 1496. It is also likely that the house was the birthplace of Robert's son, John Incent. This historic

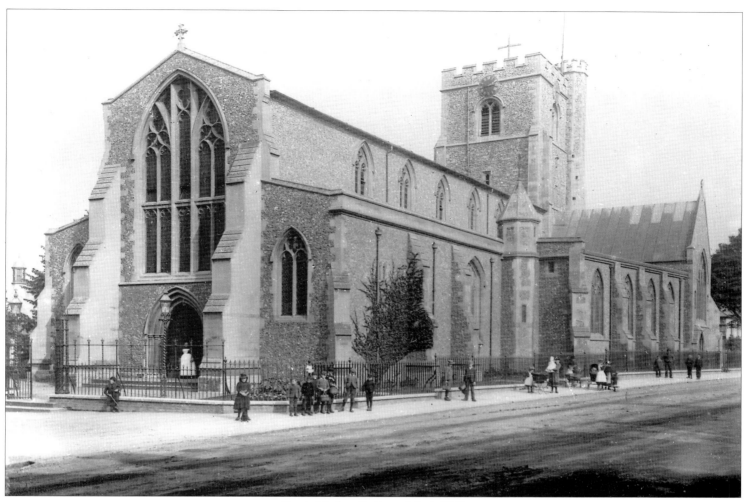

Church of St. Peter, Berkhamsted, in the 1890's.

Interior of St. Peter's Church.

figure in the life of Berkhamsted was to become President of the Brotherhood of St. John the Baptist. He was responsible for the founding of Berkhamsted School and served as Dean of St. Paul's Cathedral from 1540. In this century, the colourful arms of a Dean of St. Paul's hung outside the house which served Berkhamsted as a charming old world coffee shop from 1930-1970. More recently the house has been used as masters' accommodation for Berkhamsted School and one of those masters, David Sherratt, discovered some interesting wall paintings at Dean Incent's, which were considered to be late Tudor or early Jacobean. It is worth noting that from 1890, prior to its role as a coffee shop, the house served as both family home and studio for J. T. Newman, the noted pioneer photographer.

St. John's Well

The area of St. John's Well is now occupied by Berkhamsted's large post office. St. John's Well Lane lies down beside it, from the High Street towards the canal and railway. This however is a very early historic site. During the Eleventh and Twelfth Centuries, a small community of monks lived close by an ancient spring at St. John's Well, which had been known since Saxon times for its healing properties. It was not uncommon for Crusaders, fighting in the Holy Land, to return suffering from leprosy and the waters of St. John's Well were said to be particularly effective in the treatment of this condition. St. John's Well is also the probable site for the early church and burial ground of St. James, which preceded St. Peter's as the town's Parish Church. The main site at St. John's Well was occupied by a hospital which was founded by Geoffrey Fitzpiers, the Earl of Essex. Both the Hospital of St. John the Baptist and the Hospital of St. John the Evangelist (for lepers) at Berkhamsted, were granted by the Earl to the Brothers of St. Thomas the Martyr of Acon by 1213. King Henry II had supported these monks and Queen Isabella, widow of King John, awarded them substantial grants, which included the tithes of the mills in Berkhamsted and Hemel Hempstead. Under the umbrella of this Royal patronage, the monks' medical care at St. John's Well prospered for 300 years. When these hospitals were disbanded soon after 1520, their combined revenues were used by John Incent as part of the endowment for the foundation of Berkhamsted School. As late as Victorian times, the waters from the spring at St. John's Well were reputed to be a cure for sore eyes. Sadly, because of excessive water pumping made necessary by Twentieth Century population demands, the waters of this spring, which used to run down the slope into the River Bulbourne, ceased flowing during the 1930's. A reduced water table has however brought some benefits to the town. Early writers described how the Bulbourne often used to flood neighbouring meadows. In 1776 one account states that "Berkhamsted was an unhealthy place, stretching as it did along the south side of a swamp"! The worst of this flooding abated following the construction of the Grand Junction Canal in 1797.

Castle Street

Castle Street in Berkhamsted can lay confident claim to be one of Hertfordshire's most historic roadways. It began as an early bridle way to the newly built Norman fortress, before becoming a broad lane leading to the mighty castle of the Plantagenet Kings. Some of the great figures in national history will have ridden along this quarter mile: William the Conqueror, Thomas à Becket and the Black Prince frequently passed this way. Castle Street would have also witnessed Prince Louis' triumphant siege of 1216 and the later

humiliation of King John of France, who was imprisoned at the castle in 1356. Castle Street led directly to the main entrance and drawbridge walls of the castle and must therefore have been the route of many glittering Royal processions during Plantagenet times. By the beginning of the Thirteenth Century, Castle Street was such an important location that it was almost inevitable that the Parish Church of St. Peter would be built at its southern end. Although Castle Street had lost its status as a Royal road by the end of the Fifteenth Century, its historic character was maintained because it was now home to the churchyard of St. Peter's and also the handsome buildings of Berkhamsted School, founded in 1541 by John Incent. In earlier days Castle Street was probably lined with more houses than the High Street and, until the mid Nineteenth Century it remained the major side street in the town. Berkhamsted's first canal wharf and Railway Station were also in Castle Street and an indication of the amount of early trade and passing traffic is that there were once seven public houses scattered amongst Castle Street's shops and cottages. The most attractive cottages here dated from the late Sixteenth, early Seventeenth Century and were situated at the northern (castle) end of the street. The former Inn, the Boote dated 1604, was one of the oldest of these. Unfortunately most of these cottages were demolished in 1963 and only one now remains. The sunken appearance of this half-timbered row (see photograph) was due to the raising of the road when the canal bridge was built at the end of the Eighteenth Century. Castle Street began to lose some of its former strategic importance when Lower Kings Road became established as the main road leading to the town's second railway station, built in 1885.

Berkhamsted Place, 1856.

Berkhamsted Place

In 1580 Sir Edward Carey, Keeper of the Jewels to Queen Elizabeth I, was granted the Manor of Berkhamsted. He set about building himself a fine Elizabethan mansion at the top of the hill overlooking the derelict castle and used much of the old stonework from its ruins in the construction of his new house. It cannot have been long before Sir Edward bought the Manor of Aldenham in 1588 and decided to live there instead. Berkhamsted Place was then used by various members of his family, until it was purchased in 1612 by Henry Prince of Wales for the sum of £4,000. From Henry, the house passed to his brother King Charles I, who leased the property to his tutor and nurse, Thomas and Mary Murray. As ardent Royalists, the Murray family were not popular in a town that by now was developing parliamentarian sympathies. The great house soon bore witness to the swaying fortunes of the Civil Wars. Anne Murray (later Lady Halkett) became involved in a Royalist plot to save the young Duke of York and following the

Engraving of Berkhamstead High Street, 1857.

Old Market House and Church of St. Peter, Berkhamsted, 1852.

execution of Charles I, she fled Berkhamsted Place fearing for her life. However she was eventually rewarded 36 years later with a Royal pension by James I. Anne Murray died in 1656 and was buried at St. Andrews. Following the flight of Anne Murray, Berkhamsted Place became home to one of her opponents in this national struggle. This was Daniel Axtell, a ruthless soldier who was Berkhamsted born and who had fought his way up to become a Lieutenant Colonel of a regiment of Cromwell's foot soldiers by the age of 26. However the pendulum of fate swung again when Axtell was beheaded at Tyburn in 1660, and by 1662 Berkhamsted Place was once more in Royalist hands as home to John Sayer, chief cook to Charles II. The mansion had suffered a serious fire in 1661 and substantial reconstruction work was carried out by John Sayer; this managed to retain the original distinctive flint and stone chequerwork on its north wall. The house was built around an inner courtyard and there were large cellars under all four sides of the building. John Sayer became a wealthy man and was a leading benefactor of the town. On his death in 1681, he bequeathed the sum of £1000 in trust for the building of Almshouses in Berkhamsted. From the Sayers, Berkhamsted Place passed in 1716 to William Attwell. In 1718 he sold the property to John Roper, whose family remained in residence for nearly a century. Following this the house became home to another of the town's great benefactors, General John Finch and his wife. In the Victorian tradition the Finches helped re-build the Bourne School and generously supported the Town Hall fund. Following their period of tenure, Berkhamsted Place became the fashionable residence of Lady Sarah Spencer and Gertrude, Countess of Pembroke. Among their guests at Berkhamsted Place were the Duke of York (later George V) and the Prime Minister, Mr. Gladstone. However several years after the end of the Second World War, the house was empty and up for sale. The property then had nine bedrooms, three bathrooms and five staff bedrooms on the upper floor. Maintenance costs for such a large house were prohibitive and it was subsequently converted into flats during the 1950's. However this step was insufficient to save the Elizabethan mansion. It was allowed to fall into such a state of dereliction that its eventual demolition in 1967 was inevitable.

Sayer Almshouses

John Sayer, chief cook to Charles II, was a wealthy resident of the town who lived at Berkhamsted Place. When he died in 1681, he left the sum of £1000 in trust "for the building of an almshouse and the purchasing of lands for the relief of the poor in Berkhamsted, St. Peter". His widow subsequently supervised the construction of a single storey almshouse, consisting of 12 rooms for the habitation of six poor widows. This was provided at a cost of £269 and the widows were to be selected, alternately, by the Rectors of Berkhamsted and of Northchurch. Each widow received two shillings a week, an allowance for fuel and a further 10 shillings and sixpence at Christmas. These charming little cottages, with their latticed windows, are easy to find on the south-west side of the High Street and bear an inscription which reads: "The gift of John Sayer 1684". The tomb of John Sayer can be found in the north aisle of Berkhamsted's Parish Church of St. Peter. These days the Sayer Charity is administered by a committee of trustees.

The Court House

The Court House is one of the oldest buildings in Berkhamsted. When this Sixteenth Century structure was first built, in the shadow of Berkhamsted's Parish Church, it would have faced on to a very wide High Street. At this time the west front of St.

Peter's Church could be seen from half a mile away. The original Court House had two storeys and beneath its fine timbered roof, which is original, one can still find some of the beams that would have supported its great loft. The porch door and windows of the Court House are modern and the lower storey has been re-faced with brick and flint. The survey of 1607 tells us that the courts of the Honour and Manor of Berkhamsted, which occurred on Whit-Tuesday and the Tuesday after Michaelmas, were held at Berkhamsted Court House. By 1618, when Berkhamsted received its Charter of Incorporation from James I, the Borough Council held all its meetings at the Court House which effectively became Berkhamsted's first Town Hall between 1618-1663. It was also here that the Corporation kept its standard weights and measures. The Court House was specifically mentioned when, in 1863, Lord Brownlow's trustees paid £43,682 for the Manor and Honour of Berkhamsted. Lord Brownlow then granted the Court House to trustees at a nominal rent. From 1838 it had become part of a National School, with additional buildings that have since been demolished. The adjoining house, which later became home to the Verger of St. Peters, was built for the Headmaster of the National School. Together with Dean Incent's house, the Court House is of key significance because these two old buildings are a surviving link with Berkhamsted's Elizabethan past.

Market House

In early Tudor times the main route through Berkhamsted was only a narrow track, fringed by road-side waste which sloped down to a row of modest houses and shops in Church Lane. However around 1583, the town of Berkhamsted decided to build a Market House on this road-side waste, about 200 yards west of the Parish Church. This Sixteenth Century Market House was built on stilts and had twenty oak posts supporting a brick and timber structure. It was used chiefly for the storage of corn, pending market transactions. The town's stocks and whipping post stood in front of this new Market House. Soon the various earlier shambles and stalls gathered around it. These trading places eventually developed into buildings completely obscuring the earlier properties of Church Lane, which had formerly fronted the High Street. The lower portion of the Market House was open on all four sides, offering market vendors partial shelter from bad weather and when the High Street was widened, the public right of way actually ran through the Market House.

The tradition of a market in Berkhamsted has a long and proud history. In 1156 Henry II declared the town's merchants exempt from all taxes and when this privilege was confirmed by Edward IV; he also decreed that no other market could be established within 11 miles of the town. Berkhamsted's ancient Monday market was first inaugurated on 7th May 1217 and a later Charter from James I, dated 1619, granted the town the right to hold a second market on a Thursday.

If the Market House had survived into the Twentieth Century, its narrowing effect on this part of the High Street, would have created something of a traffic bottle-neck. The dilapidated building had already become an eyesore in the town, when it was burnt to the ground on August 23rd 1854. Berkhamsted's ancient market rights were first acquired by the Town Hall Committee after the First World War, and were subsequently transferred to the Urban District Council in 1971. Most of Berkhamsted's earliest traders and shops were situated in the High Street or Castle Street. It is worth remembering that Lower Kings Road was not built until 1885 and there were no shops there until the Twentieth Century. The Urban District

Council of Berkhamsted was formed in 1898 and later extended to Northchurch in 1935. The Berkhamsted Civic Centre was designed by the former Town Surveyor, Mr. J. R. Hadfield, and opened in 1938. Since the last war the two council estates of Durrants and Westfield have, together with the Chiltern Park development, swept across the green fields that once separated the town of Berkhamsted from the early hamlet of Northchurch.

The Town Hall

This magnificent building, which still dominates the centre of the town, was opened in 1860. Following the destruction of the town's Elizabethan Market House in 1854, it was built as a replacement. However the intention was that the building should both serve as a Town Hall for Berkhamsted and as a permanent home for the local Mechanics Institute. Over £3000 was raised towards the cost of its construction by public subscription and the Town Hall was put in the hands of a charitable trust in order to protect this endowment by the people of Berkhamsted. The design of the building was the subject of a competition won by a London based architect, Edward Buckton Lamb whose initials, decoratively carved, appear over the Town Hall entrance. The building became of particular architectural interest as Lamb's career prospered. It remains as one of the few public buildings he designed and the only one in such a decorative Gothic style. Edward Lamb was mainly involved in the planning of various churches and substantial country houses; one of his best known commissions being the re-modelling of Hughenden Manor for the Disraeli family. Apart from its decorative style, the Town Hall building is distinguished by a double staircase to the main hall and the unusual structure of its roof is the only one of its kind in Hertfordshire.

The hall initially saw the sale of corn and other produce, whilst the Institute Rooms were used for lectures and as a Library. The Town Hall was the venue for various council meetings, amateur dramatic shows, exhibitions, dinner dances and other social events. In 1895 a two storied extension was added behind the Town Hall and the large room upstairs became known as the Sessions Hall, which served as the town's Magistrates Courts until 1938. During the 1940's and 50's the building enjoyed a variety of roles serving the local community. It became a British Restaurant during wartime and later a parcels sorting office and public library. However by the 1960's the building was in serious need of repair and restoration, but because the necessary finances were not made available, the Town Hall had to be closed in 1972. Despite its status as a Grade II listed building, it was the declared intention of Dacorum District Council to demolish it in 1975. This caused a huge public outcry, with the protest joined by national conservation societies and leading old Berkhamstedians such as Graham Greene, Sir Hugh Greene and Antony Hopkins. A Rescue and Action Group was formed, from which later evolved a stalwart group of trustees. They were instrumental in first saving the building and then supporting the urgently needed process of its repair and rehabilitation. The Berkhamsted Town Hall Trust was established on 12th February 1981, under the auspices of the Charity Commission, and the ground floor of the building has since been converted into a shopping arcade which opened in December 1983. The large hall of the Town Hall, above the shopping arcade, has also now been beautifully restored.

Berkhamsted School

It was John Incent, a prominent Sixteenth Century resident of the town and Dean of St. Paul's Cathedral, who was the founder of Berkhamsted School. He was responsible for the idea of using the surplus funds from the disbanded monastic hospitals of St. John the Baptist and St. John the Evangelist to help establish a school in Berkhamsted. In 1541 Incent was given permission to open a free school which was not to exceed 144 boys on its pupil roll. This became known as 'Dean Incent's Free School and Chantry'. It soon became obvious that the old house of the Brotherhood of St. Thomas the Martyr at St. John's Well, was too small to cope. Consequently an impressive and large School House, in brick and freestone, was built in Castle Street. In fact the writer, Camden, who visited the town during the reign of James I (1603-28), commented that this fine school building was the only structure in Berkhamsted worth a second glance! The first master at the school was Mr. Reeve and John East served as its chaplain. The fortunes of Berkhamsted School fluctuated throughout the first 300 years of its life and it was not until 1841 that it was made compulsory for the masters to reside at the school. This rule was part of a new Governing Charter established by the Lord Chancellor and it was this initiative which effectively laid the foundation for the future success and prosperity of Berkhamsted School.

By 1864 Dr. Bartrum was Head of Berkhamsted School and it was during his period of tenure that the school for the first time exceeded Dean Incent's original allowance of 144 pupils. During the mid-Nineteenth Century Berkhamsted School became firmly established and, under the later headship of Dr. J. C. Fry (1887-1910), pupil numbers rose to exceed 400 boys. The magnificent school chapel, the design of which is inspired by the Venetian Church of Santa Maria dei Miracoli, was the gift of Mrs. Julia Fry in memory of her husband. Dr. Fry was succeeded as Headmaster by C. H. Greene, who oversaw the completion of his predecessor's plans. A range of new buildings now encircled the quad; a junior school block and Deans Hall had been added. In 1926 Berkhamsted's old Upper Mill was superseded by a new Music School. The old Berkhamstedian C. M. Cox served as Headmaster from 1931 until the end of the Second World War. In 1958 a further range of impressive school buildings, Newcroft in Mill Street, was officially opened by Her Majesty Queen Elizabeth, the Queen Mother. The most famous 'old boy' of the school was Graham Greene (1904-1995) who became one of the nation's most important novelists. His father, C. H. Greene, served as Headmaster of the School (1910-27) where Graham's two brothers were also educated. They too achieved their share of success, Sir Hugh Greene as a former Director General of the BBC and Dr. Raymond Greene as a leading Harley Street specialist. Berkhamsted School now has Greene's House, facing Castle Street, which was opened in 1976 to provide accommodation for day scholars. The school's tennis courts in Lower Kings Road are also named Greene's

Field in memory of a rich uncle who owned land in the town and helped establish the school's playing fields. No fewer than seventeen members of the Greene family lived in Berkhamsted during the famous novelist's time at school and he wrote in his autobiography, "If I had known it, the whole future must have lain all the time along these Berkhamsted streets". One of his later novels, 'The Human Factor' published in 1978, was partly set in Berkhamsted and filmed by Otto Premminger. However Graham Greene will be best remembered for his earlier novels, The Fallen Idol, The Third Man, Our Man in Havana , Brighton Rock and The Power and the Glory. Other famous names connected with the school are Algernon Methuen (1856-1924), the founder of the publishing firm, and millionaire Sir Jules Thorn who made his fortune in the electrical industry. Both are still remembered by significant endowments left to the school. A gift of £10,000 from Methuen's widow established entrance scholarships and leaving bursaries to Oxford, whilst a donation of £40,000 provided the funds for the construction of the Thorn Block at Berkhamsted School.

Berkhamsted School For Girls
Berkhamsted School for Girls was opened by Countess Brownlow of Ashridge on 11th May 1888. Early champions for the establishment of the town's first girls' school were John Evans (later Sir John Evans) and a local shop keeper called Henry Nash. The school began its life at 222 High Street, which had been the former home of the Bourne Charity School. However the Berkhamsted School for Girls soon began to outgrow its premises and by the time the first Headmistress Miss Disney was succeeded by Miss Beatrice Harris in 1897, there were already over 80 pupils. The school's move to the newly provided Kings Road building, which remains the heart of the institution today, was completed by September 1902. At that time girl boarders began lodging on the first floor. By 1908 the number of pupils at the girls school had risen to 200 and a new wing was opened in June 1915 by Mrs. Winston Churchill who, as Clementine Hozier, had herself been a pupil at Berkhamsted. Lady Churchill subsequently attended the opening of impressive additional buildings by Her Majesty Queen Elizabeth, the Queen Mother in 1958. Negotiations are currently underway to officially merge the Berkhamsted School for Girls with Berkhamsted Boys School.

Bourne School
Thomas Bourne (1656-1729) was one of Berkhamsted's great benefactors. He bequeathed the sum of £8000 to build and endow a charity school for up to 20 boys and 10 girls. It is worth noting that Mr. Bourne was not a resident of the town, but frequently came to Berkhamsted to visit his sister, Sarah Rolfe. In 1735 the sum of £700 was used to build the first Bourne School and adjacent teachers' accommodation. The first Master and Mistress, Edward and Elizabeth Eastmead, took up their duties in 1737. Berkhamsted's first Charity School blossomed and in 1853 public subscription was invited to provide it with a new classroom. The total cost for this addition was £391, more than half of which was provided by General John Finch of Berkhamsted Place. The Bourne coat-of-arms, together with the arms of the town and of General Finch, can still be found above the door of the old Charity School building at 222 High Street. This currently houses the Britannia Building Society. In 1875 all the pupils of the Bourne School were transferred to the National School, and the trustees established the Bourne Scholarships worth £5 per annum. These were awarded to a limited number of boys and girls attending Church of England schools. In 1949 the trustees

stopped appointing Bourne Scholars, but instead awarded a number of grants and exhibitions to children attending secondary and further education. Although the original Bourne School is no more, Thomas Bourne's endowment for the education of Berkhamsted children was commemorated in the name Thomas Bourne Middle School which opened in 1971.

Bourne School.

Ashlyns School
This historic Hospital School was founded in 1739 by Captain Thomas Coram, a caring retired sea captain. Captain Coram was mortified by the sheer numbers of orphaned babies and children being abandoned in Eighteenth Century squalor. A Royal Charter was granted to support his work and from October 17th 1739, 60 children were admitted to his temporary premises in Hatton Garden. By 1742 work had begun on the Foundling Hospital building in Lambs Conduit Fields, Bloomsbury. This Royal Charter awarded stipulated that no child could be turned away, but this proved impossible. By 1752 there were over 600 children being cared for and Parliament granted the new Foundling Hospital an income of £10,000 per annum to help it cope. Following the younger children and babies' initial admission, they were sent to foster mothers in the country to be reared until they were five years old. They were then returned to the hospital school to be educated.

The impressive hospital school founded by Thomas Coram became a well known and much respected charitable institution. In 1753 the composer Handel presented an organ to the School Chapel and, following the first performance of his 'Messiah', in Dublin, the inaugural performance of his masterpiece in London was given at Thomas Coram's Foundling Hospital. Leading artists of the day, William Hogarth, Thomas Gainsborough and Joshua Reynolds all presented paintings to the school governors. In 1926 the school's valuable London site was sold for two million pounds and the school transferred to temporary accommodation. Between 1933 and 1935, the impressive Georgian style buildings of today's Ashlyns School were erected on part of the Ashlyns Hall estate in Berkhamsted. The foundation stone of Ashlyns School was laid by the Duke of Connaught and the impressive chapel was made a central feature of the new school. By September 1935, it was ready to admit up to 400 children between the ages of 5 and 15. The school's traditional uniform survived at Ashlyn's until 1945. The boy's uniform featured brown serge suits, scarlet waistcoats with brass buttons, Eton collars and black bow ties. Subsequently in 1951, Ashlyns became a Secondary Modern school for the town of Berkhamsted. It catered for local children as well as Coram students aged eleven and upwards, and the foundling boarders had left. In 1955 Hertfordshire County Council purchased the school buildings together with 40 acres, from the Thomas Coram Foundation. A grammar stream was immediately added and under the new headmaster, Mr. J. H. Babington G.C., Ashlyns became the first bilateral school in Hertfordshire. Under its next headmaster, Mr. A. N. Johnston, Ashlyn's became Berkhamsted's senior school in a three-tier (middle) school system which was introduced in 1972.

In April 1995 the Governors of Ashlyn's School opted for grant maintained status, but the work of the Thomas Coram Foundation for Children continues, looking after deprived children. Although Handel's organ was installed in the Ashlyn's School Chapel, it was subsequently removed to a London church in 1955. However the staircase in the front hall remains the original from London, as do the columns along the main drive, which were the former light pedestals from the foundling hospital building. The name of the Hospital School's founder, Thomas Coram, is perpetuated in the Thomas Coram Middle School. This school was created in 1988 by the amalgamation of two of Berkhamsted's earlier middle schools, Thomas Bourne and Augustus Smith, on the Augustus Smith site.

Ashlyns Hall

This large hill-top estate dates back to 1314, when it was in the ownership of Richard Asselyn, and ever since then Ashlyns has been its name. During the reign of Charles II (1660-88) Ashlyns was home to Francis Wetherel who was Comptroller of Works to the King. The old Manor House was replaced by an impressive mansion towards the end of the Eighteenth Century. This house features a Welsh slate roof and its south-west gabled front has a semi-circular bow with a first floor cast iron verandah. It is now a commercially run nursing home for the elderly.

Arms of Longman Family.

In 1801 James Smith, a member of a leading Nottinghamshire banking family, bought Ashlyns Hall as his family home. Following the death of his first wife, he married Mary Isabella Pechell, who was the daughter of the owner of Berkhamsted Place. Mary bore him five children, the first of whom was Augustus Smith, born in 1804. Augustus was brought up in Berkhamsted and although he later settled at Tresco Abbey in the Scilly Isles, he remained very fond of Berkhamsted. As a young man he was deeply concerned by the appalling conditions endured by many of the labouring classes and was a great believer in the power of a good education to transform people's lives. He founded Berkhamsted's first elementary school and was one of the leading lights in the mid-Nineteenth Century revival of Berkhamsted School. Augustus Smith became M.P. for Truro in 1857, but retained a keen interest in Berkhamsted affairs. He was outraged when he learnt that Lord Brownlow of Ashridge had enclosed some 34 acres of Berkhamsted Common with iron railings. Augustus Smith will always be remembered in Berkhamsted's history for his successful and definitive rejection of this aristocratic act of enclosure. He personally financed a gang of 120 tough navvies who travelled out from London one night in March 1866 and unceremoniously tore down over two miles of these 5ft. iron railings erected by Lord Brownlow. The following morning Augustus Smith jubilantly walked across the common land of Berkhamsted which was never again enclosed. Like his fellow benefactor, Thomas Bourne, Augustus Smith is primarily remembered for his role in supporting education in Berkhamsted. His contribution was celebrated in the name of the Augustus Smith Middle School which opened in 1970.

Another notable resident of Ashlyns Hall was William Longman, who moved there from Chorleywood around 1859. He was a great lover of the countryside and also took a leading part, with Augustus Smith, in resisting Lord Brownlow's attempted enclosure. William's father, Thomas Norton Longman III (1771-1842), was the outstanding publisher of his time. The company he founded was responsible for publishing work by Wordsworth, Southey and Walter Scott. William Longman continued his father's success by buying the business of J. W. Parker in 1863 and thereby acquired the copyright to the works of John Stuart Mill. He also published Roget's Thesaurus and secured the rights to T. B. Macauley's great work the "History of England". This was the most famous publishing coup of the day. Over 3000 copies of the first two volumes were sold in the first ten days and 13,000 in less than four months. Three months after the publication of volumes 3 and 4 in December 1855, Longman paid Macauley the most famous cheque in the history of publishing. This was for the sum of £20,000, on account of the profits generated by these later volumes. Within the next 30 years over 140,000 copies of Macauley's work had been sold in Britain alone. In 1843 William Longman had married Emma Pratt Barlow, whose brother Frederick was married to the daughter of John Dickinson, the leading industrialist and paper manufacturer of Apsley. Other members of William Longman's family, notably his brother Charles Longman, lived on the Shendish estate to the north of Kings Langley, which was itself close to John Dickinson's fine country house at Abbots Hill, Nash Mills. William Longman's last great publishing feat was when he successfully negotiated the rights to the first two novels of the Barchester Chronicles by Anthony Trollope. He died in 1877, aged sixty-four.

Egerton House.

Haresfoot

The estate of Haresfoot, like its near neighbour Ashlyns Hall, has also given its name to a local school. From the Nineteenth Century, these two great houses became linked by family ties. This was when the brother of Augustus Smith, Robert Algernon Smith, married the grand daughter of John Dorrien, a wealthy banker who lived at Haresfoot. Robert changed his name to Smith Dorrien and fathered 15 children. His eleventh child, who became General Sir Horace Dorrien Smith, was born at Haresfoot in 1858. Later, Haresfoot was home to members of another leading Hertfordshire dynasty, the Blackwell family. During World War II the house was used to store art treasures for a major London gallery. Haresfoot was still standing in 1953 when Pevsner described the house as late Georgian with five bays, noted for their stucco work. One of the family pictures included a portrait of Samuel Smith, the noted goldsmith. The old house at Haresfoot was damaged by fire no less then seven times and a completely new house was built in 1962. In the churchyard at the Parish Church of St. Peter in Berkhamsted, there is a striking monument to Smith Dorrien. This takes the form of a tall stone cross in the late Gothic style, and is dated 1909.

Rossway

In 1863 Charles Stanton Hadden paid £34,000 for 577 acres of prize Berkhamsted farmland and built the family's Victorian mansion between 1865-67 for the sum of £3776. The Rossway estate prospered and by 1950 had grown to some 1300 acres, under the care of Charles' great grandson, retired Army Major Adrian Hadden-Paton. A total of 160 acres of the estate was woodland and there was a Home Farm of 180 acres, with the seven other farms let out to tenant farmers. Through the 1960's

the facade of Rossway was a frequent backdrop for the popular T.V. series of the day: episodes of The Saint, The Avengers, Father Brown, as well as Harry Worth and Jimmy Edward's comedy programmes were all filmed at Rossway. Major Hadden-Paton had the honour of being President of Berkhamsted's historic Floodlit Pageant, held at Berkhamsted Castle in 1966. The Pageant commemorated the 900th anniversary of the Norman Invasion of Britain.

Egerton House

Egerton House, with its attractive frontage, used to stand on Berkhamsted High Street, on the site of the now derelict Rex Cinema. The earliest owner of this handsome, originally Tudor house, would probably have been a member of the Egerton family. Its first role was to act as a dower house for the Ashridge estate. In 1840 Egerton House was purchased for the sum of £700 to be used by the Wesleyan Methodists. It later reverted to its role as a private house. In 1904 Arthur Llewellyn Davis, his wife Sylvia and their five sons, came to live at Egerton House. The move to this larger house came as a breath of fresh air to the family, who enjoyed the splendid garden which then had its own orchards and wisteria-clad stable. There is still a statue at the family's earlier home in Kensington Park Gardens. This commemorates the time when the author J. M. Barrie first met two of the five Llewellyn Davis boys who were to provide the inspiration for his famous tale of Peter Pan. It was specifically to entertain the Llewellyn Davis boys that Barrie's fantastic story of fairies, pirates and treasure island was created. When Peter Pan first opened at the Duke of York Theatre in 1904, all the Llewellyn Davis boys were regularly taken to rehearsals. The following Christmas, when one of the boys was too ill to attend, Barrie took some of the scenery and the entire cast to give a special command performance at Egerton House. During the Spring of 1906, tragedy struck when the boys' father Arthur, became ill with cancer. He died in 1907 and sadly his wife died only three years later. Their five boys were left in Barrie's care, a responsibility he exercised diligently until his own death in 1937. Housed in the Rex Cinema, which replaced Egerton House on the site in 1938, was a commemorative plaque which was unveiled by the actress Jane Asher on 14th February 1979. At the time Miss Asher was playing the role of Peter Pan at the Shaftesbury Theatre in London. A co-educational preparatory school was later established in Berkhamsted and this is now called Egerton-Rothesay. This school name perpetuates the memory of this fine old house that once graced the southern end of Berkhamsted's High Street.

The Hall

Situated at the southern end of the town, the Hall Park estate in Berkhamsted commemorates the name of the huge Georgian mansion that once stood about 100 yards to the east of Swing Gate Lane. After the First World War, much of the Hall's land was sold to provide a council housing estate. This magnificent old house had 17 bedrooms/dressing rooms and was ideally suited to the purpose when it became the preparatory department of Berkhamsted School. Unfortunately the building became badly affected by dry rot and was sold in 1937 and demolished.

Queen Victoria and Albert, Prince Consort, visit Berkhamsted, 1841.

Local Inns

Given that any social chronicle of Berkhamsted would be incomplete without reference to its numerous Inns and public houses, it seems invidious to pick out only a few. However the age and historic relevance of the former Swan Inn and the Kings Arms guarantee them as being worthy of special mention. The earliest known reference to the Kings Arms is 1716 and this important old coaching inn was probably built during the reign of Queen Anne, whose arms it still bears. The key historic figure at the Kings Arms was John Page who was Innkeeper here 1792-1840. He also served as local Constable and Postmaster for the area. Between 1807-14 the exiled King Louis XVIII of France, who was then resident at Hartwell House near Aylesbury, often visited the Kings Arms on his journeys to and from London. The frequency of the King's visits was on account of his affection for John Page's daughter Polly. He remained true to his English love and when he was returned to the throne in 1814, Polly the Berkhamsted barmaid, was invited to visit him at the Palace of Versailles. Another Royal honour was bestowed on the Kings Arms when, on 26th July 1841, Queen Victoria and Prince Albert stopped

at this Inn to change horses on their journey to visit the Duke of Bedford at Woburn. Throughout the Eighteenth Century the parish constables of the district would meet at the Kings Arms to submit their appeals to the justices. The Inn also served in the 1880's as the local 'Inland Revenue' office. In 1890 the Kings Arms is listed as having stabling for 40 horses, and an assembly room that could accommodate up to 400 people.

The Swan is another of Berkhamsted's notable old Inns and in common with its near neighbour, the former Crown, is actually older than the Kings Arms. Dating from the Sixteenth Century, it had a later front wall built out towards the High Street during the Eighteenth Century. The building features an old tiled roof with an oversailing double gable. The house was owned in 1607 by John Briscoe, who had inherited it from his father. In 1656 Michael Hancock was licensed to keep a wine tavern here. The surviving building is Seventeenth Century, though it is much altered and modernised. In 1792 the Swan ran its own regular coach to London and was a favourite meeting place of the local Parish Vestry until 1897. By 1806 it was owned by David Claridge, in whose family it remained up to 1923. Until 1897 there used to be a brewery behind the Inn and this was called the Swan Brewery. In the later part of the Twentieth Century, when it was run by Peter Caro, the Swan offered attractive accommodation and was a principal hotel in Berkhamsted High Street. The derelict site of the Rex Cinema (former home to the delightful Egerton House),and the abandoned historic old Inn are the saddest features of Berkhamsted's contemporary High Street. Happily the structure of the Swan is currently being renovated to turn the premises into the Swan Youth Project. This new initiative intends to offer housing for twenty homeless young people, as well as provide a bar with alcohol-free drinks.

The Crooked Billet was a small low building dating from the early Eighteenth Century, but the first known reference to an Inn is 1753. In 1792 this Inn was kept by William Chappel and between 1827-52 Robert Rance was the Inn keeper. By 1840 the Crooked Billet was owned by Isaac Winter, who also kept the George and Dragon at Northchurch. In 1964 it was replaced by a completely new building at the corner of Billet Lane. Billet Lane takes its name from the old Crooked Billet and was an important early trackway, part of the main route to Dunstable. However until the beginning of the Twentieth Century, travellers along Billet Lane had to cross a small ford over the River Bulbourne. After crossing the river, the lane climbed towards a humped back bridge over the canal, before reaching the railway bridge. As we can see from the photograph on page 219, the timber merchant Job East used to store logs near his wharf on the west side of Billet Lane.

South end of Berkhamsted High Street looking north showing the tower of St. Peter's Church, circa 1912.

Berkhamsted High Street, circa 1912.

Berkhamsted Town Hall in the early 1920's.

Berkhamsted High Street looking south, circa 1912.

Top of Castle Street, circa 1915.

Court House in the late 1970's.

Aerial view showing Dean Incent's house.

Former home of the Bourne School.

Sayers Almshouses, 1970.

Ashlyn's School showing the school chapel, 1996.

Berkhamsted School for Girls, 1912.

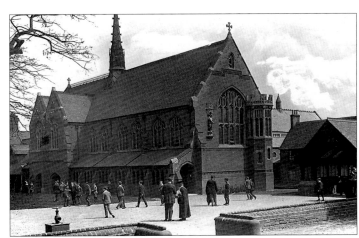

Berkhamsted Boys School, 1912.

H.M. Queen Elizabeth, the Queen Mother, visits Berkhamsted School for Girls, 1958.

Berkhamsted School with Headmaster Dr. T. C. Fry in the foreground, 1910.

Rear of Berkhamsted Place, circa 1946.

Haresfoot, circa 1908.

Ashlyn's Hall, 1960.

Rear of the Hall, circa 1910.

Egerton House, 1936.

Rear of Rossway, 1988.

Berkhamsted Common, 1905.

The Park, Berkhamsted, 1905.

Billet Lane, circa 1890.

Northchurch

Although often considered today as a suburb of the neighbouring town of Berkhamsted, Northchurch can lay strong claims to having been the earlier settlement. In fact, given the much earlier date of its church, it is probable that Northchurch was the nucleus of the much larger community that later grew up around the Norman Castle of Berkhamsted. The Parish Church of St. Mary is one of the oldest in Hertfordshire, being one of only four that still have Saxon architecture. At Northchurch a small community developed in the valley area which lay between the River Bulbourne and what was to become the Roman road of Akeman Street. The Parish Church of St. Peter dates from no earlier than 1222 and with its arrival, the village we know today as Northchurch became exactly that: the home of the North Church, i.e. the church that lay to the north of the newly established principal Parish Church of St. Peter. Historically the old River Bulbourne plays its part by uniting the parishes of Northchurch, St. Mary and Berkhamsted, St. Peter.

Apart from the main through road, the former A41 which is now the A4251, the other principal thoroughfare in the village is New Road which leads east up towards Northchurch Common and the lands of Northchurch Farm and Hill Farm. This road was an old trackway whose improvement was funded by the Earl of Bridgewater. The Ashridge estate then included all the common land which is now owned by the National Trust. During the Nineteenth Century, New Road was almost a hamlet in its own right. It included the Compasses public house, London House (which was a grocery and sweet shop), the village reading room, the church room, the policeman's cottage and the public allotments. Towards the top of New Road, near the 'S' bend, is Woodside Cottage which used to be Northchurch's former Pest House. Although the local pub the Compasses no longer exists, its name lives on in the name of the modern Compass Point housing development.

In the High Street itself, the attractive Lime Tree House was formerly a gardener's cottage. It was later home to the local Co-operative Stores and it is now a piano showroom. The main structure of the old corner shop, Bell Lane stores, has now been mainly demolished, although some Seventeenth Century chimney work still exists. Several Sixteenth Century cottages also stood on the site of today's Tudor Orchard flats. The George and Dragon Inn in the High Street was formerly known as the Swan when it was first listed in 1772. Architecturally the building shows fragments of a late Sixteenth Century house, joined by an Eighteenth Century structure with ground floor bay windows. By 1840 this Inn was owned by Isaac Winter who also owned the Crooked Billet, near Berkhamsted. At that a time braziers and blacksmith shop were attached to the George and Dragon and the village stocks stood opposite. The other principal public house in the village is the Grey Mare (Old Grey Mare), which lies further north on the other side of the High Street. This is listed as being kept by Samuel Bedford in 1806 and was later in 1840 owned by a leading Hertfordshire brewer, Samuel Salter of Rickmansworth. The original structure of the Old Grey Mare was demolished between the two World Wars and the present Inn was built to the rear of the old site. It was here, by the Springwood Estate close to the River Bulbourne, that the site of an old Roman villa was uncovered during the 1920's and re-excavated in 1973. This important archaeological find is discussed in more detail in the Early Settlement Chapter on page 14. The High Street to the north of New Road, is also home to Rosemary Cottage which was once known as Norris's

Farm. In the latter part of the Nineteenth Century, this house was the operating base for the Hertfordshire Tobacco Works run by a Mr. Page. Its structure dates from the late Sixteenth, early Seventeenth Century and is timber framed with gabled dormers. During the Eighteenth and Nineteenth Centuries the Inn yard of the George and Dragon was regularly converted into a fairground, at the time of the Statute Fair, for the hiring of farm and domestic labour. This reinforces the fact that the old village of Northchurch was essentially an agricultural community whose inhabitants were mostly farm labourers or smallholders. Many families also worked on the estates of some of the larger local houses such as Lagley, Northchurch House, Woodcock Hill and Norcott Court which are discussed later.

St. Mary's Church in the 1850's.

St. Mary's Church

The charming Parish Church of Northchurch has a cruciform plan which is typical of many Thirteenth Century churches. Most of the walls are flint though the central tower is stone-faced. The chancel and transepts are also largely Thirteenth Century, though the latter show some traces of later work. The vestries and south porch of St. Mary's were added in 1881 and, at one time, the main doorway of the church was beneath the west window. The archaeological significance of St. Mary's is that the nature and thickness of its west wall are indicative of Saxon workmanship; this wall also shows traces of a west chamber or tower once built against it. The church has some ancient windows and the chancel lancet which opens into the vestry also dates from the Thirteenth Century. St. Mary's has a finely carved Fifteenth Century Flemish chest in the chancel. In 1881 a Seventeenth Century painting of the Madonna and Child was discovered behind the chancel; this is now in the north aisle. At that time, perhaps the most interesting find of all was made in the nave; an ancient stone coffin, which probably belonged to a Crusading Knight. At St. Mary's there is a brass on the south wall to Peter the Wild Boy (1785) (see also page 221) and on the walls of the south transept are recorded the various charitable bequests made to the Parish of Northchurch. The oldest was given by Edward Young and is dated 1648, whilst the most recent is by Elizabeth Loxley of Norcott Court and is dated 1887. The stained glass window in the south transept is in memory of Peter Loxley who died in the Second World War. It depicts a local scene which includes the tower of St. Mary's and was designed by Hugh Easton, who was responsible for the Battle of Britain window in Westminster Abbey.

Marlin Chapel

The ruins of an old chapel-of-ease that survive in a field near Marlin Chapel Farm are also of Thirteenth Century origin. The Marlin (or Magdalene) Chapel is part of the old manorial site that once belonged to the small sub-manor of Maudeleynes, held by Sir Lawrence de Broc towards the end of the reign of Henry II (1133-89). There is evidence of a moated structure surrounding Marlin Chapel Farm which perhaps indicates the site of Lawrence de Broc's original Manor House. During the Eighteenth Century the old chapel building was used as a malt-house for the farm.

Baptist Chapel

In common with many other communities in the valley, especially neighbouring Tring, the non-conformist faith was well established in Northchurch. Its Baptist Chapel opened on 16th September 1840 at a total cost of £140. The Baptist community, which included neighbouring Gossoms End, Dudswell and the Cowroast, soon flourished. Expanding numbers required a new church was built and this opened on 30th May 1900. The new building, which included a school room, was constructed by J. Honour of Tring and was the gift of J. Marnham Esq., J.P. of Boxmoor. The old Baptist Chapel was disposed of in 1920 and although nothing now remains of the first building, some gravestones in the chapel's burial ground are still there.

Church House

The picturesque half-timbered Church House and cottages, dating from the Sixteenth Century and standing at the south-west corner of the churchyard, are the best known buildings in Northchurch. They are also the oldest structures fronting the main road. The principal house has an oversailing first floor and all these buildings subsequently became almshouses. Rectory Cottage is at No. 82 High Street, whilst the grounds of the old Rectory of St. Mary's were subsequently used for the housing development known as The Meads. The Rectory was demolished in 1957.

Church House.

Village School

The village school was built in the very heart of the community of Northchurch. Although the bell tower has been removed, the original building of St. Mary School still stands on the corner of New Road, close to the Church of St. Mary's. It is a good example of a Victorian village school, built in flint and brick in 1864. The land for the school site was given by Earl Brownlow of Ashridge and the building was endowed by another local land-owner, John Loxley of Norcott Court.

Peter the Wild Boy

This historic character will be forever linked to the history of Northchurch, where he was buried in a simple grave near the porch of the Parish Church of St. Mary. Born around 1713, Peter was discovered in 1725 by the Court of George I, in a field near Hanover, Germany. He was a wild, brown-skinned, semi-naked boy with no power of speech. He merely grunted

Peter the wild boy.

and was fond of resting on his knees and elbows in animal fashion. Because of his strange untamed demeanour, there was speculation that he could well have been abandoned in the dense forest lands and raised by wild animals. This curiosity delighted and amused the Royal Court who kept the 'wild boy' as a pet. Peter was brought back to England by the Princess of Wales, Caroline of Anspach (1683-1737), who later became the Queen of King George II. At the English Royal Court he was placed under the care of a tutor, Dr. Arbuthnot, but when it was found he could not be taught, even to speak, the novelty soon wore off. He was then handed over to one of the women of the Queen's Bedchamber, Mrs. Tichbourne. She periodically visited a local farmer, James Fenn of Haxters End Farm in Bourne End, and this is where Peter eventually made his home.

An annual grant of £35 was given by the Government to support Peter, who was still rather wild in his younger days. He would often vanish into the woods for days at a time, and once wandered as far as Norfolk. A labelled leather collar was specially made for him to ensure his safe return to Mr. Fenn's Farm. Peter's habits were studied by leading scientists of the day. The wild boy was very agile and preferred green twigs, acorns and bean shells to cooked meals; when given large nuts or raw onions he would beat his chest with his fists to express his pleasure. Shoes were his pet aversion; he insisted on walking everywhere bare footed, and if threatened or angry, he was quite likely to bite his tormentors. Peter was about five foot three inches tall and in his later years grew considerably tamer in his habits. This noble savage, who will always remain something of a local curiosity, died peacefully on 22nd February 1785 at the estimated age of 72. His memorial brass at the Parish Church of St. Mary, Northchurch is still well-maintained and his gravestone still stands outside the door of the church.

Edgeworth

Edgeworth stands on the other side of the main road, directly opposite the former site of Lagley House. It was built on the Sixteenth Century foundations of an earlier structure. The re-modelled house of Edgeworth dates from 1767 which can still be found carved on one of its chimneys. In 1776 the Irishman Richard Levell Edgeworth came to live in Northchurch. Richard Edgeworth had four wives and fathered 19 children. His eldest daughter, Maria Edgeworth (1767-1849) is the best remembered of his children because she grew up to become one of England's most notable women novelists. Maria Edgeworth enjoyed great fame, with the publication of her popular Irish novels, 'Castle Rackrent', 'Absentee' and 'Ormond', and her circle of friends and admirers included Sir Walter Scott and Lord Apsley. Edgeworth House was altered and enlarged in the Nineteenth Century by the addition of an east wing.

Woodcock Hill

Woodcock Hill, first mentioned in a survey of 1607, is today hidden by high boundary walls and large trees. The fine Nineteenth Century house enjoys an excellent position at the top of Durrants Lane. This old country lane was gated at both ends until 1914 and one of the old gate posts can still be seen at the top Lodge today. In 1840 the entire estate was purchased by Mr. J. Field for £2775. Later Woodcock Hill came into the ownership of Mr. F. Moore who re-built the house in 1848. Mr. Moore also built the two Lodges and extended the estate to 257 acres. This included some of the valley land where Moore Road is today and also the fields that have subsequently become the Durrants and Westfield council house estates. Mr. F. J. Moore was now a major local landowner and something of a local Squire. He served as Chairman of the Board of Governors at Berkhamsted School and in 1854 presented a set of silver for the celebration of Holy Communion to the Parish Church of St. Mary. By 1910 Woodcock Hill had become home to Mrs. McVitie, whose family were connected with the firm 'McVitie and Price', cake and biscuit manufacturers. The Lodge at the top of the lane was badly damaged by a parachute mine during the Second World War, following which Woodcock Hill was used for a while as a Nunnery for the Carmelite Sisters.

Norcott Court

Although officially listed as a Seventeenth Century house there are surviving traces that indicate the existence of an earlier Fifteenth Century structure at Norcott Court. William Edlyn is listed in 1639 as resident at Norcott Hill. For much of its history, the Loxley family were the chief residents of Norcott Court. The Loxleys were closely associated with the village of Northchurch and were great benefactors to the Parish. In 1864 John Loxley of Norcott Court provided funds for the building of the village school, and a brass dated 1887 in St. Mary's Parish Church acknowledges the public endowments given by Elizabeth Loxley. Norcott Court is now the country residence of Mr. & Mrs. Peter Rost M.P. and former family home of John Andrew Davidson, the 2nd Viscount Davidson, who between 1986-91 served as the Government Chief Whip in the House of Lords. His father, John Colin Campbell Davidson the 1st Viscount, was a leading local figure who enjoyed a prestigious political career. He held the office of Chancellor of the Duchy of Lancaster 1923-24 and again in 1931-37. He also served as M.P. for the district of Hemel Hempstead, from 1920-23 and again from 1924-37.

Northchurch House

This was a fine early Nineteenth Century, red brick, three storey house. In 1889 the house owned a substantial estate of 38 acres which included six cottages. Northchurch House was home for many years to the Barnett family and this fine residence had many attractive features. The main house offered a dairy larder, a detached boot house and bakery; with wine, beer and root cellars. During the Second World War, when Northchurch House was owned by Lady Lemon, Local Defence Volunteers met there. After the war this fine old house, like so many other substantial properties, sadly fell into neglect and disrepair and was subsequently demolished. Its grounds are now home to the Park estate.

Lagley House

The house and grounds of Lagley House were situated by Durrants Lane, on land which is now occupied by an extensive development of council-run, senior citizens' flats and bungalows. The original Lagley House stood on the main road, but Mr. W. A. Duncombe built a new mansion, behind the old house in 1832. This imposing structure featured yellow stock bricks, with a slate roof and a stone stepped porch to the front door, which was adorned by Greek Doric fluted pilasters and columns. The main entrance to the house was fronted by heavy green iron-studded wooden gates. The last resident of Lagley House was Mrs. E. Douglas who died in 1940 and who's name is commemorated in the local road name of Douglas Gardens. The house was then taken over by the army until the end of the war, when it became the home of Colonel and Mrs. Johnston. Lagley House was later acquired by the District Council and converted into flats until its demolition.

Dropshort Cottages

At the north western end of Northchurch were the former estate workmans cottage and stagecoach waiting room called Dropshort and Dropshort Cottage respectively. These Eighteenth Century houses are on the main road, opposite today's sports and recreation ground. It is said that Mr. Smart of Norcott Court would wait here in comfort for the arrival of the stagecoach. Here he employed the wife of his estate worker to help keep the waiting room clean, in readiness for his visits.

Cow Roast

This site lies to the north east of Northchurch, beyond Dudswell, and on the opposite (western side) of the valley to Norcott Hill. It was here in 1972 that substantial archaeological evidence was found of an early Romano-British settlement and this is discussed in detail in 'Early Settlement' on page 15. The earliest known reference for the old Inn at the Cow Roast is 1806, when it was called the Cow and was kept by Thomas Landon. By 1851 it was kept by Thomas Landon Junior, and had become known as the Cow Roast. The name derives from cows' rest and is explained by its location on the main droving route to London from the Midlands. Landlords at the Cow Roast would provide pens for cattle, whilst the drovers rested overnight on their long journey southwards.

Northchurch High Street, 1914.

Dropshort Cottage, 1970.

Edgeworth, 1985.

Lagley House, 1962.

Village Shop, 1971.

Church House, Northchurch, 1955.

War Memorial, Northchurch.

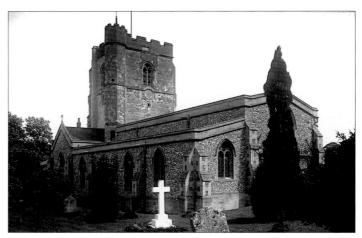

St. Mary's Church, Northchurch.

Village School, Northchurch, 1996.

Wigginton

Perched high on the crest of an escarpment, Wigginton enjoys a situation which makes it one of the highest villages in the Chilterns at 682 ft. above sea level. The village name derives from the Saxon 'wic' meaning stronghold; Wigginton was therefore a small community ('ton') belonging to a larger stronghold. Given the proximity of parts of Grims Dyke (see page 13), as well as the Romano-British encampment at Cow Roast and the presence of a major Iron Age fort at Cholesbury, this place name is not surprising. There is also evidence of early settlement at Wigginton, with some Neolithic stone axes being found in the village area.

From the time of the Norman Conquest, the manor of Wigg was part of the Honour of Berkhamsted and was held by William the Conqueror's half brother, Robert Count of Mortain. In 1219 the Lord of the Manor, Sir Geoffrey Lucy and his wife Juliana, sued the Prior of the Order of St. John of Jerusalem for the return of the Advowson of the Church of St. Bartholomew, Wigginton. This law suit unfortunately failed and the Advowson of Wigginton remained with the Knights of St. John until the village church was annexed to the Parish of Tring in 1328. Queen Elizabeth I later granted the Parsonage of Tring and Wigginton, together with the glebes, tithes and profits, to the Dean and Chapter of Christchurch, Oxford. However by the end of the Nineteenth Century the Advowson returned to Wigginton when, in 1873, Richard and Emily Valpy of Champneys, paid Christchurch College the sum of £1,800 to obtain its release. If an early Manor House existed in Wigginton, its site is unknown and it is possible that Wigginton was one of several sub-manors owned by a Lord of the Manor who lived elsewhere. The manorial seat of Geoffrey de Lucy, for example, was close by in Little Gaddesden.

The Church of St. Bartholomew

The fine Parish Church of St. Bartholomew is the only remaining evidence of Norman settlement in Wigginton and dates from the Twelfth Century. There are indications however, that it may have been built on the site of an earlier church. The design of the Norman church, containing only a small nave and chancel, produced a structure no more than 54ft. long. The piscina in the south east angle of the sanctuary is the oldest remaining feature and there are two Fourteenth Century windows in the chancel. The roof of St. Bartholomew's is mainly original and features tie beams and arched braces, with open tracery in the spandrels resting on large stone corbels carved as human heads. During the Nineteenth Century, a small Norman window was uncovered on the wall behind the pulpit. The Fifteenth Century west chamber is the only major monument at St. Bartholomew's and is known as the Weedon Chapel. The Weedons were an early Wigginton family who lived next door to the church at Penly Lodge. This house later became known as 'Farthings' and then as the 'Orchard'. In the floor of the chapel is a memorial tablet recording the burial of two members of the Weedon family in 1688. At St. Bartholomews, there is a memorial to Thomas Egerton of Champneys and his wife, dated 1764, and also a commemorative window to Emily Valpy. Members of both the Valpy and the early Sutton families, all resident at Champneys, are well recorded in this Parish Church.

In 1832 a vestry was added at St. Bartholomew's, together with a gallery able to hold 50 people. By 1853 the Rev. R. R. Anstice became the first Parson to live in the village of Wigginton, which by now had a population of over 700 and 140 children regularly attended his Sunday School. In the time of the Rev. George Gainsford (1854-8), a north aisle was added to St. Bartholomew's, the gallery removed and the Irish yews along Church Approach were planted. The church was now somewhat dilapidated and went through a further process of restoration which lasted until 1881. When this was complete, the chancel arch had been raised, the windows enlarged and an organ chamber had been built between the chancel and the vestry. Most of the roof had been renewed and the chancel floor relaid with encaustic tiles. The Advowson of St. Bartholomew's, which had been purchased from Christchurch College, Oxford, by the Valpys of Champneys, was subsequently made over to the Bishop of St. Albans in 1909.

Village Community

The first Vicarage for St. Bartholomew's had been built in 1870, and in 1896 Canon Valpy supervised the building of a church room in Chesham Road. Over the years this building became the meeting room for the social events of the village and gradually became adopted as the Village Hall. A new church room was built in 1973. In 1854 there had been two straw plait schools in the village, both held in cottages owned by Mr. Hammond of Champneys. Supported by the Rev. Gainsford, Mr. Hammond then helped to provide a village school in 1858, at a total cost of £370. This old Victorian school building was subsequently enlarged and served the village for over a century. A new modern school for Wigginton was more recently built in Cannon Field and opened in 1970. The historic old Vicarage was also replaced by a new house, erected in 1965 on part of the old school's playing field. A recent achievement by the community of Wigginton was the complete restoration of the Village Hall (the former church room) to its present attractive condition. Local people clubbed together to raise the necessary £75,000, and the newly refurbished accommodation was finally opened with a Grand Victorian Gala and Fete on Sunday 21st May 1988.

Opposite the Village Hall, is the village stores and sub post-office, currently called the 'Country Cupboard' and run by Peter Coneron. This building used to be the Pheasant Inn and was later a pub called the Travellers Rest. Of the village's five former Inns: the Fox, the Brewhouse, the Pheasant, the Greyhound and the Lamb, only the Greyhound survives. Local records indicate that Edward Eggleton was licensee of this beerhouse in 1677, although the earliest official records of a fully licensed Inn date from 1838, when it was probably kept by a Charles Soames. By 1852 a Joseph Williams was in residence at the Greyhound and he was succeeded in 1864 by Mary Williams. In previous centuries all five Inns would have been needed to slake the thirst of the village's farm labourers, because Wigginton was then an entirely agricultural community. All the men worked on the lands of the two local principal estates at Champneys and Tring Park; there was also plenty of opportunity for work as domestic staff at one of the big houses. During the Eighteenth and Nineteenth Centuries, many women and children in Wigginton supplemented the family income by their participation in the local cottage industries of lace-making and straw plaiting. From 1872 Lord Rothschild of Tring Park became the most important employer for the village and he invested heavily in the local community. He built a pumping station at New Ground and provided piped water to Wigginton. He also built several rows of cottages for his employees and will be remembered as a great benefactor to the village. Lord Rothschild gave substantial Christmas gifts to every one of his employees and ensured that they always received free medical care and attention.

Champneys

Although records of a house at Champneys go back to 1307, when a Ralph de Champneys is owner of this part of the Manor of Tring. By the Sixteenth Century this estate was known as 'Champneys and Fosters'. In 1535 the estate was owned by Richard Fitzwilliam and by 1629 it had been sold to John Baylie of Wigginton. Thomas Egerton purchased Champneys in the early Eighteenth Century and in 1781 his heirs sold the property to Major General Russell Manners who in turn sold it to Mr. John Moore in 1804. Wigginton's connection with the estate became firmly established throughout the lifetimes of father and son, William Hammond. Both men were leading supporters of the Parish Church, where the later William Hammond served as church warden in 1832. From 1839-71, the Hammonds were succeeded at Champneys by another father and son combination of Daniel Sutton. Daniel Sutton Junior's younger daughter was Emily Anne and she married Richard Valpy. It was Emily Anne Valpy who built part of the present Nineteenth Century mansion at Champneys and enlarged the estate by 200 acres. However their son, Canon Arthur Sutton Valpy, sold the Champneys estate to the Rothschilds of Tring Park in 1902. The house was purchased with the intention of providing a dower house for Lady Rothschild, but she did not occupy Champneys and promptly sold the entire estate upon the tragic death of her eldest son in 1923. However sometime prior to the

sale, Lady Rothschild had made some distinctive additions to the grand mansion. These were the turrets and red brick of the centre section which still serves as the entrance. Today these features give the entire house the authentic look of a Rothschild building.

The Champneys estate was acquired in 1925 by osteopath Mr. Stanley Lief, and during his time an 'L' shaped wing was added to the right of the entrance. Mr. Lief transferred his clinic from Orchard Leigh in Chesham to Champneys, which he then proceeded to turn into his celebrated Nature and Health Care Clinic. This soon became a mecca for the fashionably rich and famous who distrusted orthodox medicine; the Champneys massage, devised by Stanley Lief, was unique. However following his death in 1963, the clinic became less popular and by the early 1970's, Champneys had become rather run-down and outdated. However when Allan and Tanya Wheway took over the business, it was rapidly revitalised to become the world famous health resort of today. Set in some 170 acres of parkland, this delightful country mansion still provides luxurious accommodation and impressive health and leisure facilities for up to 100 clients. Champneys is currently managed by Fitness and Leisure Holdings who, amongst other activities, also maintain a London health club at Le Meriden Hotel, run the Spa at Gleneagles and operate a health clinic on the P&O cruise liner Oriana.

Church of St. Bartholomew, Wigginton.

High Street, Wigginton.

Fox Cottages, circa 1907.

Village Post Office, circa 1912.

Wigginton Bottom in the 1920's.

The Brewhouse, circa 1907.

The Greyhound, circa 1907.

Entrance to Champneys, 1996.

Frontage of Champneys, circa 1910.

Tring Park

On 18th April 1609 Thomas Egerton, Lord Chancellor to James I, was made Steward of His Majesty's Manor of Tring. By 1679 Henry Guy, Gentleman of the Bedchamber to King Charles II, was Lord of this Manor. Although never fully substantiated, local folklore persists that many of the King's romantic trysts with the legendary Nell Gwynne, took place on the Tring Park estate. In respect of this tradition, there is on the estate the avenue and an Eighteenth Century 50ft. obelisk and pavilion, named in memory of the King's lover. These structures are hidden in a wooded lane created on the hillside behind the house and have been recently purchased by the Dacorum Borough Council and leased back to the Woodland Trust in 1994. Henry Guy commissioned the building of the Tring Park mansion circa 1683, to a design by the celebrated architect Sir Christopher Wren. Although retaining the essence of Wren's design, the house was substantially altered for the Rothschild family in 1872. It can now be described as a red brick building with lavish stone dressings and slated roofs. In the French Renaissance style, the house is two storied with a basement and mansarded attics. Some of the interior remains very elaborate; a particular feature is the impressive entrance with a great staircase at the end. There is also much good plasterwork and exquisite furnishings everywhere.

In the Autumn of 1705, the house and all the manorial lands were conveyed to Sir William Gore, a former Lord Mayor of London and Under-Steward to Queen Katherine. However Sir William died soon after, on 29th January 1708, and the estate was inherited by his eldest child William Gore, husband of Mary Compton, Lord Northampton's daughter. As a leading landowner in the area William Gore did much to help the condition of the poor in Tring, and he also helped fund substantial improvements to the Parish Church of St. Peter and St. Paul. William's son, Charles Gore, inherited the manor from 1739-68 and on the death of the next owner of Tring Park, Sir Drummond Smith, the entire estate was sold in 1823 to William Kay. Mr. Kay became the leading industrialist in Tring where he established a thriving silk mill that employed many local people. However he preferred to live in Market Street, closer to his work, and he let Tring Park until his death in 1865. Tring Park estate was subsequently sold at auction, on 7th May 1872, for the sum of £230,000; this price being exclusive of the house's furniture and pictures and also the machinery and industrial equipment which had been left behind by Mr. Kay at the silk mill. At this time the estate comprised 3643 acres which produced an annual income of £6000. In addition the mansion house still had its own park of 300 acres.

The purchaser of Tring Park in 1872 was Lionel Nathan de Rothschild, a member of the international banking dynasty which had been founded in Frankfurt by the German born Jew, Meyer Amschel de Rothschild (1743-1812). By the late Nineteenth Century, the fortunes of the English branch of the family had already been established by the financial genius of Meyer's third son Nathan Rothschild (1777-1836). Nathan Rothschild had four sons of his own: Lionel, Anthony, Nathaniel and Meyer who were all made Barons of the Austrian Empire. Anthony was created an English Baronet in 1846 and settled in Aston Clinton in 1853. Nathaniel, an invalid, married a French cousin and lived in Paris, whilst Meyer established an impressive estate at Mentmore. Meyer's only child Hannah married Lord Roseberry who later became Prime Minister. Lionel lived at Gunnersbury Park and Piccadilly and wielded instead immense political and economic power as head of the Rothschild Bank in London. His own eldest son Nathaniel settled at Tring Park in 1874, whilst Lionel Rothschild's two younger sons owned estates at Halton and Wing respectively; a

cousin Ferdinand Rothschild, also lived nearby at Waddesdon.

In 1885 Nathaniel Rothschild was elevated to the English peerage as Lord Rothschild of Tring. He had also succeeded his father Lionel as head of the Rothschild Bank and, at that time, was described by leading commentators of the day as the "richest man in the whole of the British Empire". In 1897 the Rothschilds entertained the Prince of Wales at Tring Park. The huge wealth of this family exerted considerable influence on the various communities in the pleasant countryside to the north of London where they all chose to settle. There was a well established family tradition of charity work and they also took a great interest in the welfare of the small rural village which provided most of the employees on their estates. Nathaniel Rothschild was a noted authority on agriculture and served as M.P. for the Aylesbury division 1865-1885, a representation which was continued by his son Walter. On his father's death in 1915, Walter became the 2nd Lord Rothschild of Tring Park.

Walter Rothschild's enduring legacy, born of his passionate interest in natural history, is Tring Museum which was established in 1892. In 1937 the Museum became part of the British Museum and its fantastic collection, endowed by the family's wealth, is a permanent tribute to his lifelong interests and achievement. As can be seen from the photos (on page 230), Lord Rothschild enjoyed introducing some exotic animals onto his estate: kangaroos, ostriches, emus and zebra all roamed the parklands. Whilst these more spectacular animals have now all departed, one of his smallest introductions still remains. These are Hertfordshire's edible dormice, otherwise known as glis glis. Considered a gourmet delicacy by the ancient Romans, Britain now has a population of several thousand of these dormice, all descendants of the eight introduced in 1902 by Walter Rothschild. They thrived and spread in the deciduous woodland and now inhabit an area within an estimated 30 mile radius of Tring. Walter Rothschild never married and following his death in 1937, his nephew Victor, the 3rd Lord Rothschild, sold off the Tring Park mansion. However much of the parkland was initially retained in family ownership.

As a footnote it is worth stressing the wider historical influence of the Rothschild family who have left their enduring mark on the town of Tring. During the Eighteenth and Nineteenth Centuries, the Rothschilds were considered to be more significant in the shaping of international events than Kings, armies or revolutionaries and more powerful even than the Church. The family financed governments, steered international conflicts and opened up new commercial sectors, amassing vast wealth and influence in the process. Obviously such a family dynasty has a much reduced influence in the more complex world of the late Twentieth Century and the most recent figures show annual profits from the Rothschild Bank standing at no more than £16.5 million. Nevertheless the Bank's present Chairman, Sir Evelyn de Rothschild, is ranked 68th in the Sunday Times list of wealthy people, with an estimated fortune of £160 million.

In 1945 the spectacular Rothschild mansion became home to the Tring Park Educational Trust, founded by Grace Cone MBE and Olive Ripman. Set in 17 acres of secluded parkland, the school can accommodate up to 500 boarders and 50 day pupils and enjoys an enviable reputation. Tring Park specialises in offering both boys and girls, aged between 8 and 18, first class training in the performing arts, combined with serious academic studies. The President of the Arts Educational School is one of the great names in international ballet, Dame Alicia Markova.

Drawn on Stone from the Original Engravings by G.B. Tyler.

To the Honourable   Henry Guy of Tring

House, Esq.ʳ this Plate   of yᵉ Mannor House is

Humbly dedicated,   by John Oliver.

Pub.ᵈ by F.W.Hullinger,   Bps. Storfford, 1826.

Lord Rothschild, circa 1930.

Interior of Tring Museum.

Tring Museum.

View of Tring Park, 1915.

Walter Rothschild and his zebra cart.

Tring Park, circa 1919.

Tring Show in the 1920's.

View of Tring Park.

The Monument in Tring Park, 1906.

Tring

The town's name of Tring, meaning 'place of trees' could just as easily be applied to most of the other early towns and villages along the valley and gives no real clue to the significance of this particular community. From the earliest times, Tring has enjoyed a uniquely favourable strategic position which explains its successful development as a thriving country town. The settlement of Tring grew up close to the gap in the Chiltern Hills which connects London to the Midlands plain. An early community developed close to the crossing of two of the country's earliest known and most important trackways. These are the route north which became the old Roman road, Akeman Street (now the A4251 and previously the A41) and the Icknield Way (now the Dunstable Road). Whilst the old road north connected the rest of the country to the markets and port of London, the Icknield Way, which ran along the South Downs, linked the Bronze Age industrial areas of East Anglia with the country's religious and cultural centres at Avebury, Glastonbury and Stonehenge.

It is not surprising that the early community of Tring prospered, given the volume and quality of passing traffic. This made it an obvious trading place attractive to merchants and other traders. Tring's market Charter dates back to 1315. As late as 1900 Tring still maintained 3,120 acres of arable land and a further 3,310 of grass land. Given its position in the countryside, at the northern end of a river valley, it was further blessed by the rapid expansion of agriculture as the nation's principal industry during the Seventeenth and Eighteenth Centuries. Tring then became an important market town and its Agricultural Association, founded in 1840, established an annual Agricultural Show. For the next 40 years this was considered to be the finest one day show in the country and attendances of over 20,000 at the Tring Show were not unknown.

Many Tring farmers grazed sheep on the chalk slopes, whilst the beginnings of industrial manufacturing in the town sprang from lace-making, straw plaiting and canvas weaving. The early corn mills at Tring took on a new significance when Mr. William Kay, a silk throwster from Macclesfield, spent £30,000 establishing a silk mill in Brook Street. This eventually employed more than 500 local people. By the middle of the Nineteenth Century, Tring was nick-named 'Little Manchester', because of this large silk mill and several small canvas-producing factories which were flourishing. By 1891 the population of Tring had already grown to 5,426. In the Eighteenth Century the main road north had been diverted by the Gore Family, through the centre of town in order to keep it away from their mansion at Tring Park. It is ironic that Tring's motorway link, part of the A41 by-pass, now cuts a swathe through this parkland to the west of the old mansion.

The Parish Church of St. Peter and St. Paul

It is certain that an earlier Norman structure once stood on the site of Tring's handsome embattled Parish Church. Some Norman stone is built into both the east wall and the outside chancel walls. The main body of the Church of St. Peter and St. Paul was however rebuilt in the early part of the Thirteenth Century. It was subsequently enlarged during the Fourteenth Century and considerably altered again in the Fifteenth Century. The church's robust tower dates from the Fourteenth Century enlargement and has walls 5ft. thick. The tower is surmounted by a turret in one corner which has a 'Hertfordshire spike' or embryo spire at its centre. The eight bells of St. Peter and St. Paul date from between 1624-1882. The Nineteenth Century saw several improvements, with the interior of the church being thoroughly restored in 1862 and some exterior rebuilding was carried out during 1880-1882.

The most substantial memorial at the Church of St. Peter and St. Paul is the monument to Sir William Gore of Tring Park who died in 1707. At the foot of this impressive piece of masonry are more modest, but more important and rarer relics of the past. These are several small Medieval floor tiles, in yellow clay, which are believed to be connected to a further eight, now in the British Museum; there are also fragments of another two held by the Victoria and Albert Museum. The significance of these art treasures lies in the Sgraffiato technique employed in their design. The tiles are also the only known English examples of the use of this method on anything other than pottery. The scenes on these tiles portray the miraculous Childhood of Christ, as taken from the Apocryphal Infancy Gospels. Another important feature of Tring's Parish Church are its registers which date back to 1566. These contain entries which have now been proved to relate to the English born ancestors of George Washington, first President of the United States. The three grandchildren of the Rev. Lawrence Washington, who were baptised Lawrence, Elizabeth and William in Tring Church, were not the immediate forbears of George Washington, but were his Great Uncle and Aunt. The Rev. Lawrence's brother John Washington emigrated to Virginia in 1657 and George Washington was his great grandson. The Rev. Lawrence Washington was the fifth son of Lawrence Washington of Sulgrave in Northamptonshire, another mecca to American visitors in search of their early history. The Tring connection to Sulgrave was established when the Rev. Washington married Amphyllis, who was Tring born. Both she and her mother Anne, are buried in the Parish Church at Tring, as is Anne's second husband, Andrew Knowling, who was at one time church warden of St. Peter and St. Paul's. To help visitors fully understand the connection to George Washington, a family tree hangs under the church tower.

Standing a quarter of a mile to the west of the church, Tring Rectory had its own estate and was known as Parsonage House. It later became the town's Eighteenth Century workhouse, before being used to house railway workers employed in the construction of the local stretch of the London to Birmingham railway. This house was demolished circa 1860. The old Vicarage belonging to the Church of St. Peter and St. Paul used to stand on ground which is now part of Sutton Court.

Early Schools

In the early part of the Eighteenth Century, there was a parish school held daily in the old Church House by Vestry Hall. As one would expect, given Tring's agricultural character, there were also two straw plait schools established in the town, one in Akeman Street and the other in Frogmore Street. However in 1842, the old Rectory site was given by Christchurch College, Oxford, to help found a National School in the town. Built on the site where Tring's modern Library now stands, this school was an immediate success and by 1862, 550 pupils were attending the National School at Tring which was subsequently enlarged and reopened in 1866. Tring's former Library used to be housed in a room at the Victoria Hall which was built in 1886 on the site of the town's Assembly Rooms.

OLD MARKET HOUSE
TRING

Market House

Dating from the Thirteenth Century and reinforced by a later Charter of Charles II, Tring's market day has always been a Friday. Until the beginning of this century, the market was always held in the High Street, close to the early Market House which was built on timber posts with a corn loft above. This historic building stood in front of the church, but was demolished, together with some shops, in 1900 when Lord Rothschild re-built the Rose and Crown. In the process he effectively re-modelled the centre of the town. Encouraged by Lord Rothschild, a new Market House was built in the High Street by public subscription, at a cost of £2,400 and the livestock market was moved to Brook Street. Opposite this market, and closer to the old market site by the High Street, Tring's Memorial Gardens were later established to commemorate the dead of World War Two. The fallen of the Great War are remembered by a very early memorial dated 1918, which can be found on the south side of the parish churchyard. The new Market House was designed by William Huckvale as a jetted, half-timbered structure, and built on the corner of Akeman Street. In keeping with the tradition of the old Market House it replaced, the ground floor of this building was originally open to provide shelter for traders and their customers. These openings were later incorporated into the building which now serves as the Civic Centre for Tring.

Local Inns

The earliest record of the Rose and Crown is 1620 when it was kept by Thomas Robinson, but the early tavern was certainly older than this. This busy coaching Inn was one of the most important in Hertfordshire. As early as 1711, the Justices met here on highway business and from 1650-1850 it

also housed the local Excise Office. By 1852 it was the booking office for the London and North Western Railway Company and later became the Inland Revenue office. Beer was brewed on the premises until 1860 and a trading token exists dated 1668 which was issued by William Axtell, licensee of the Rose and Crown. The old Inn stood flush to the High Street and had large grounds where Fairs and Circuses were regularly held; the old Inn also had its own bowling green. It was at the Rose and Crown that William Cobbett was entertained to dinner by his supporters in 1829 and many other important figures appear in its visitors book, amongst them Edward VIII (1894-1972). The original building was largely Tudor, with the addition of an early Eighteenth Century three storey frontage. The structure of the old Inn featured a tiled roof, five dormer windows and an archway entrance to its yard. The Rose and Crown was bought by the Rothschilds of Tring, and entirely rebuilt by them at the turn of the century, partly to accommodate the regular overflow of their guests at Tring Park. The mounting block provided in the yard was for riders to the Rothschilds' hounds.

The Bell is one of Tring's oldest pubs and dates back to 1611 when licensee Henry Geary was before the Justices for drunkeness and for allowing his licence to lapse. In 1846 the Deacons of Akeman Street Chapel held their Anniversary Dinner at the Bell. The principal structure of this Inn was Seventeenth Century, but it has been heavily restored. The gateway of the Bell spans an early right-of-way and it was used by the licensees to hang meat and game, which would later be cooked and served at the Inn. The Bell stands opposite the former Tring Brewery, which was run by the Brown family until its closure circa 1900. At the southern entrance to the town, the Robin Hood is one of Tring's more notable public houses and still sits prominently on the corner of Brook Street. This Seventeenth Century Inn was first listed in 1806 when it was kept by William Topping. By 1899 the Robin Hood had been acquired by Roberts and Wilson, brewers from Ivinghoe, and at that time Jason Horwood was the licensee.

The fine old property that is now the Royal Hotel at Tring Station, was described in 1838 as a beerhouse, shed and meadow. At that time it was owned by John Brown, but kept by Thomas Coker. Samuel Brown soon took over the running of the Inn and the licence then remained in the Brown family until 1923 when it was sold to Benskins, the Watford based brewery. John Brown had built the house under contract for the London to Birmingham Railway Company, who then granted him the freehold for £232 10s 6d. When the railway opened in 1837, Tring Station was rather isolated in the countryside. The railway station clearly required the support of an Inn offering rest and refreshment, and the Royal Hotel was born of this need. However in its early years it was named after the Lords of the Manor of nearby Pendley and called the Harcourt Arms. By 1851 this Inn had officially become the Royal Hotel. The property had extensive stables which were used by the Rothschilds' Hunt and subsequently, owing to the patronage of Lord Londsdale in particular, the hotel was enlarged and a fine ballroom was added. During the latter part of the Nineteenth Century, the Royal Hotel was the venue for many fine dinner parties and in 1881 it hosted a special dinner given to celebrate the marriage of Leopold Rothschild.

Mills

Tring flour mill is situated on the Wendover arm of the canal in an area known by the ancient name of Gamnel. It is not to be confused with an old water mill built by John Grace at New Mill, which was bought in 1799 by the Grand Junction Canal Company. The stream which powered this mill was then used to feed the canal, leaving the mill idle. The old mill head had been used by the early Baptist community at New Mill. When the mill was demolished by the Canal Company, the Church people were given some compensation to provide a new baptistry within their chapel. The first mill at Gamnel was a windmill and is shown on a map of 1822 when its miller was William Grover. From about 1842 there was a working partnership here between the Mead and the Grover families. In 1892 Edward Mead also owned the mills at Hemel Hempstead and Piccotts End. In 1875 another member of the family, Thomas Mead, had built a new mill close to the old windmill, powered instead by a beam engine. This was a fine tower mill with at least five storeys. The windmill was demolished in 1910 and in 1911 William Mead erected a large silo which was capable of holding 2000 quarters of grain. Three years after the death of William Mead in 1941, Heygates an established firm of millers and merchants, acquired the business and became the largest private flour millers in the country. They funded a programme of modernisation and Tring flour mill is the only surviving mill in the valley, representing a trade which dates back to Saxon times.

What became known as Tring Dockyard was a boat building yard initially owned by the milling firm William Mead & Co. It was later acquired by the boat building company of Bushell Brothers in 1912 (see page 40). In 1824 a silk mill was established in Tring by William Kay of Macclesfield. He built his 'silk throwing' mill in Brook Street and in order to provide a head of water sufficient to drive the mill wheel engines, he diverted the Miswell and Dundale Springs in culverts to the mill pond. His factory was a great success and Mr. Kay employed over 500 permanent workers, who were supplemented by a small army of girl apprentices, the majority of whom were hired from the local workhouse. When the Rothschilds purchased the Tring Park estate from Mr. Kay, they subsequently leased the silk mill to Messrs. Evans of Wood Street, London. Although employees at the mill totalled 600 in 1836, numbers had fallen to 400 by 1879. Cheap foreign imports eventually put paid to Tring's only major manufacturing industry and when hard times hit the mill, Lord Rothschild initially took over the business to help cushion the economic effects for all the employees in Tring.

Grace's Mill and mill house, at 15 Akeman Street, date back to the Sixteenth Century and were built by a Mr. John Harding. The Grace family had been farming and milling at Tring Ford since the beginning of the Sixteenth Century. The activities of this fine old Tring family flourished and by the end of the Eighteenth Century, Carter Grace (1796-1863) had become an important corn merchant and maltster, but no longer had any milling interest. Carter Grace's son, Thomas (1826-1904), took over at the mill in 1863 as a maltster, but also ran a business as a corn and seed merchant. One of the next generation, Frank Grace (1872-1945), gave up the declining malt trade and returned to milling, operating a steam powered mill. He continued as a corn and seed merchant and farmed at Parsonage Farm, whilst his sons, Tom and Bob Grace, worked Little Tring and Miswell farms. Though power for the mill was later supplied by a Crossley gas engine, the mill ceased working on 1st November 1975. The buildings, listed in 1953 as being of historical and architectural interest, have now been carefully converted into mews style homes. The restored gas engine from Grace's mill is now in the Pitstone Farm Museum.

Goldfield Mill, on the northern borders of the town, is a good example of a medium sized, four storey, mid Nineteenth Century mill. Built by Mr. Grover around 1840, its sails were removed in about 1906 and it was last operated by steam during the 1920's. In 1900 the mill had four double shuttered patent sails and flytackle for winding. From 1883 it was operated by James Wright, who held the contract for the crushing and grinding of oats from Lord Rothschild's farms. This provided him with good business until Lord Rothschild built his own mill at Hastoe. James Wright left Goldfield in 1908 and took over the running of Pitstone Mill. Goldfield Mill ceased operating during the 1920's, but had already achieved the accolade of being the last windmill to be working in this part of Hertfordshire. Today only the tower still stands.

Tring Chapels

Non-conformist faith which is so marked in most communities in the valley reached its peak in the town of Tring. In the Nineteenth Century, the famous satirical magazine 'Punch' once described Tring as "Baptist Chapelled". This is hardly surprising considering that in the 1880's there were no less than five Baptist Chapels serving a community of over 500 adult members, and 800 children. At that time Baptist believers represented nearly 40% of the towns' population of 3,500. As early as 1662, fifty two local people (some Baptist, some Quaker) were prosecuted for offences relating to non-conformity. However by 1694 Baptists in Tring felt secure enough to purchase their first public meeting place which was a cottage at New Mill. By 1705 this early community had flourished and there were as many as 62 Baptist families in the town. A second group of Baptists, then built their own chapel in Frogmore End. This initially accommodated up to 200 people, but by 1818 a further enlargement was necessary to cope with a congregation of 600. In 1799 another place of worship, known as the Tabernacle, was opened in a barn in Levatts Yard, Akeman Street. This building was also enlarged in 1820 and a Sunday School added. In 1808 another splinter group, combining some of the congregations from New Mill and Frogmore End, built a new Meeting House in Akeman Street and by 1832, a brand new chapel was erected by them to seat up to 85 people. Finally a fifth Baptist Church was opened in Western Road. Tring also has a Methodist chapel which was established in Langdon Street.

Tring Museum

Walter Rothschild's boyhood interest in natural history and collecting butterflies continued into his adult life. The family's wealth enabled him to indulge his passionate hobby and his work became firmly established on a scientific basis. He travelled widely to secure specimens and also employed a network of agents and collectors throughout the world. As his collection grew, it became necessary to house it in protective conditions, so the first Tring Museum, together with an adjoining caretaker's lodge, was built in 1889. This original building was a 21st birthday present for Walter, from his father Lord Rothschild. As the collection increased, the buildings were enlarged and the museum was first opened to the general public on August 12th 1892. When Walter Rothschild died in 1937, he bequeathed the museum and entire collection to the trustees of the British Museum and it subsequently became part of the British Museum (Natural History). The British

Museum had inherited an amazing collection, which included over 2000 mounted mammals, 355 pairs of horns and antlers, 227 marsupials, 2,400 mounted birds, 680 reptiles, 144 tortoises, 914 fishes and a representative collection of invertebrates. The collection also featured over two million butterflies and moths, and an entomological collection of over three million insects and 50,000 birds eggs. Also at Tring Museum, is a unique collection of dogs and the present display features over 60 breeds. It is thought that Walter Rothschild must have spent over £500,000 assembling this collection and many of the specimens on display are outstanding examples of the taxidermist's art. In 1972 new building work included an extensive modernisation of the public galleries. This improved both storage conditions and study facilities, whilst still retaining the original arrangement and character of Walter Rothschild's great museum.

Louisa Cottages

These almshouses for the town of Tring were built by Lady Rothschild on the corner of Akeman Street, opposite the museum. They were designed by William Huckvale, the architect also employed to plan the construction of the museum for Walter Rothschild. Numbers 1-5 of the cottages were built in 1893, followed by numbers 6-8 in 1901. These attractive houses have a timber-framed front, with a red brick rear wall and tall pilastered chimneys. They also feature gabled rectangular bays with leaded-light mullioned casement windows and are among the most photographed buildings in the town.

Louisa Cottages in the 1950's.

High Street, Tring, showing Market House (left), circa 1904.

High Street, Tring, showing the Bell (right), circa 1914.

High Street, Tring, looking south.

High Street, Tring, looking north.

Western Road, circa 1910.

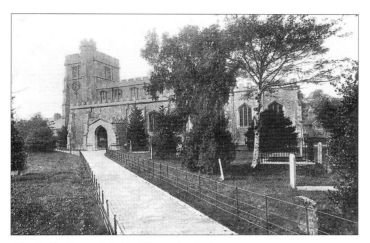

Church of St. Peter and St. Paul, Tring, circa 1910.

Tring Vicarage, circa 1906.

Church Lane, Tring.

Rose and Crown, Tring, circa 1919.

Tring Market.

Interior of Grace's Mill.

Grace's Mill, 1962.

View of Tring War Memorial, 1926.

Goldfield Mill, circa 1904.

Home Farm, 1909.

Tring Reservoir.

New Mill, Tring, circa 1912.

Bushell's Boat Yard, circa 1920.

Pendley

At the time of the Domesday Book, Pendley was a manor in its own right, with lands which lay between the neighbouring Manors of Aldbury and Tring. It was one of the many manors given to Robert Count of Mortain, following the Norman Invasion. It may surprise many people to know that, prior to 1440, Pendley was not merely an early manorial estate, but a peopled settlement comprising eight larger tenements and a further eight crofts. This early small village was said to offer "work for more than 13 ploughs, some handicraft men, tailors, shoemakers, cardmakers and divers others". However the social life of this early settlement was brought to an abrupt end in 1440 by Sir Robert Whittingham, who systematically demolished the village and laid all the ground to pasture. Having cleared his land, this despotic new Lord of Pendley promptly built a Manor House at the west end of his estate, although the old village had been situated in the south-east corner. His only son, Sir Robert the second, died only twelve years after this clearance in 1452 and his fortune was inherited by the third Robert Whittingham who was Keeper of the Wardrobe to Margaret of Anjou. This Robert Whittingham played a full part in the historical struggles of the time and consequently spent little or no time at Pendley. He fought at Guines and Dieppe (1458-60) and was knighted by the Prince of Wales, following the Battle of St. Albans in 1461. However when Edward IV was proclaimed King in March 1461, a price of £100 was put on his head. He was accused of treason and, with his lands confiscated, he fled to join Queen Margaret in Scotland. He was eventually captured and sent to the Tower of London in 1468. Two years later Henry VI was restored to the throne, but Whittingham did not enjoy his return to favour for long as he died at the Battle of Tewkesbury in May 1471.

Robert Whittingham's daughter, Mary, married John, the son of the Yorkist Sir Ralph Verney. Out of respect for the Verney family's loyalty and her father's stalwart record, the couple were allowed to inherit the Whittingham estates. Four generations of Verneys are listed as living at Pendley during the next hundred years, whilst other members of the family resided at their principal and current country estate of Middle Clayton in Buckinghamshire. A raised tomb bearing the effigies of Sir Robert and Lady Whittingham was first erected in the chapel of the Monastery of Bonhommes at Ashridge. Following the Dissolution of the Monasteries, Edward Verney removed the tomb to the Parish Church of St. John the Baptist, Aldbury, in 1575. Sir John and Lady Verney's son, Ralph Verney, became Lord Mayor of London and also made Pendley his home. His own sons, Ralph and John, and his grandson Edmund, all lived at Pendley and a likeness of Edmund as a child can be seen on the fine brass of his parents, which is in the Leeds Chapel of Aldbury Church. It is likely that Sir Edmund substantially rebuilt the old Manor House at Pendley to produce the distinctive 'U' shaped group of buildings around a main courtyard. Sir Edmund Verney will always be remembered as the loyal standard bearer to King Charles II who met his end at the Battle of Edgehill, aged 52. When his body was found on the battlefield it is said his hand was still firmly clasped around the Royal Standard, although his arm had been severed from his body. Following the death of Sir Edmund, Pendley was sold to Richard Anderson, whose family lived on the estate for a further four generations. The Andersons were a worthy family, but a good deal less colourful than the Verneys, their predecessors at Pendley. The Andersons however were also staunch Royalists; Sir Henry Anderson was committed to the

Tower for taking up arms against Parliament, but was later pardoned in 1647. A bewigged bust of a later Sir Richard Anderson of Pendley, can still be found in the Parish Church of Aldbury. Sir Richard's daughter and heir, Elizabeth, married the dandy Simon Harcourt who was Squire of Pendley from 1703 until his death in 1724. The estate was subsequently inherited by Colonel Charles Anderson, the Marquis d'Harcourt of Normandy. However the Marquis was greatly displeased when the construction of the Grand Junction Canal spoiled the river fishing on his estate and withdrew rather sulkily to his family's principal property in France. The Pendley Manor House was then left empty and fell into disrepair. The old Manor House, whose ownership reverted to the Crown, is said to have burnt down in 1835 and was never rebuilt.

The contemporary Pendley Manor was built 165 yards west of the old house, with the modern Pendley Farm some 80 yards to the north. Much of the old land and derelict site of Pendley was bought by James Grout, a Dutchman, who had been a tenant at Tring Park in 1872. When the Rothschild family purchased Tring Park, James Grout's son James, who had taken his wife's maiden name of Williams, decided to rebuild Pendley Manor. In deference to the age of the estate, the architect was instructed to design the building to look like an old Tudor manor house that had subsequently been enlarged. The Rev. James Grout Williams died before his newly-planned house was finished and it was his son J. G. Williams who supervised the completion of a building programme which took nearly five years. The result was a symmetrical $2\frac{1}{2}$ storey Jacobean style house, whose irregular east front features three gables. Mr. J. G. Williams then lived at Pendley until his death in 1922, but was survived there for a further 22 years by his wife. When Mrs. J. G. Williams died in 1944, part of Pendley was being used as a local base for the Womens' Land Army. The heir to Pendley was Colonel V. D. S. Williams, father of Dorian Williams (1914-85), the former well known television commentator on show jumping. It was Dorian Williams' idea to use Pendley as an Education Centre and he was assisted in his plans by Mr. J. L. Newson, Director of Education for Hertfordshire. Both men were keen to experiment with adult education programmes following the war. Together they created a thriving Adult Education Centre, which also offered overnight accommodation for its students. It was officially opened on 31st October 1945.

Much more recently in October 1989, Pendley Manor opened under new management as an extensively refurbished luxury hotel. In May 1991 another wing provided an additional 47 bedrooms, to add to the 24 luxury bedroom suites remaining in the old Manor House. Set in an impressive 35 acres of wooded parkland, Pendley Manor now offers impressive hotel and conference facilities with meeting/presentation rooms that can cope with an audience of up to 200 delegates. Despite this redevelopment, the estate's educational tradition established by Dorian Williams, lives on in the shape of Pendley Arts Centre, which is located in the old stable block. Another tradition is the on-going success of its world famous Shakespeare Festival which is held each summer in Pendley's outdoor Glade Theatre. The 46th season in 1995 featured productions of 'Much Ado About Nothing' and 'Richard II'. Part of the old farm estate is now home to the Pendley Racing Stables, which are used by leading racehorse trainer, Peter Harris.

Pendley Manor in the 1950's.

Aldbury

Aldbury is situated one mile from the border of Buckinghamshire and three miles east of the market town of Tring. The old Norman spelling of 'Aldeberie' reflects the unspoilt nature of this picture book English village, thought by many to be the prettiest in Hertfordshire. Like Tring, Aldbury was too near to both the Icknield Way and the old Roman road of Akeman Street not to be concealing some evidence of early settlement. The discovery of Roman coins gave the local lane Moneybury Hill its name. Also in 1943 schoolchildren found evidence of a sizeable Belgic burial site, close to the village in the form of a cremation cemetery dating from the 1st Century A.D. At the heart of the village is a tear-shaped pond which, prior to the Twentieth Century, would have been considerably deeper than it is today. Lined with layers of puddled clay, like a dew pond, it was regularly filled with rain that ran off the surrounding hills. The pond was an essential resource for this small community, providing water for the horses and cattle, as well as a home for the village ducks and geese. Two old roads cross at the south east corner of the village pond. The road from Ivinghoe forms the main highway through the village and continues on past the Valiant Trooper to Berkhamsted. This is now called Stocks Road (north of the pond) and Trooper Road (south of the pond). The road crossing this old street comes in from Tring, along Pendley Lane (today's Station Road) and leads up Toms Hill to the Common. The remains of Aldbury's old stocks and whipping post are preserved on the village green, but they are thought to be replacements for earlier fittings. Standing to one side on the Green is a fine old elm tree which was planted in 1897 to commemorate the Diamond Jubilee of Queen Victoria. Here there is also a seat which was given by the Hon. Mrs. Blezard, who was then living at Stocks House. Although the surroundings of the Green have altered considerably over time, one can still appreciate the large Sixteenth Century timbered yeoman's house with the Parish Church of St. John the Baptist beyond. Together with the surviving cottages and the two old public houses, they complete a picture of an archetypal English village. Not surprisingly, Aldbury has always been a popular choice for television and film producers. An entire television series called 'Shillingbury Tales", was set in Aldbury and filmed there during the 1980's.

'Aldeberie' was one of the many local manors awarded to the Count of Mortain following the Norman Invasion of England. At that time it was assessed as comprising approximately 1200 acres with 500 sheep. By 1203 William de Bocland was holding the manor which, in 1309, was sold by Sir Richard de Rokeslegh to Walter de Aylesbury, whose family held it for the next hundred years. The ancient ecclesiastical Parish of Aldbury consisted of the Manor of Aldbury and part of Pendley Manor. The remainder of the Manor of Pendley was situated in the Parish of Tring and was held as a sub manor of that town. The Manor of Aldbury had become rather fragmented by the beginning of the Sixteenth Century until John Hyde started to buy it back. Historically Aldbury's most notable Lord of the Manor was the last Hyde at the Manor House, Sir Thomas Hyde. He died in 1665, aged 71, having founded a local charity which is still administered and bears his name. Thomas Hyde's only child, his daughter Bridget, subsequently married Peregrine Osborne, the 2nd Duke of Leeds. By 1736 the 4th Duke of Leeds had sold the Manor of Aldbury to the 1st Duke of Bridgewater who by then had built up a very large estate around the former monastic site of Ashridge.

Church of St. John the Baptist

About 1213 Aldbury's Parish Church (then called St. James's) was given to Missenden Abbey who held it until the Reformation. In 1335 the Lord of the Manor Philip de Ailesbury, founded a chantry with its own chaplain which existed until 1548. This chantry chapel may have occupied the site of the Pendley Chapel in the Parish Church. Aldbury Church, dedicated to St. John the Baptist, stands a little to the west of the village centre and dates from the Thirteenth Century. The existing nave arcades and aisle walls are Fourteenth Century and the tower was built in the Fifteenth Century. Much of the building however was altered when the church was extensively restored in 1866. During this restoration most of the windows, which were originally square-topped, were replaced by the present fittings. Prior to the

A brass of Sir Ralph Verney.

Restoration of 1866, the services at Aldbury were read from a magnificent 'three decker' pulpit in the middle of the church. The rector preached from the top deck, from the middle deck he read the service and in the lowest deck sat the clerk who led the 'Amens' and the singing. In 1905 the tower of St. John's underwent extensive repairs.

At the east end of the south aisle of the church is the Harcourt Chapel, also known as the Verney or Whittingham Chapel. The beautiful stone screen which encloses the chapel was brought from the monastery at Ashridge, following the Dissolution. It was accompanied by the magnificent tomb of Sir Robert and

Lady Whittingham. Sir Robert, who lived at Pendley Manor, was slain in 1471 at the Battle of Tewkesbury, while fighting in the Lancastrian cause. In the Leeds Chapel, at the end of the north aisle, there is the splendid marble altar tomb which contains the fine brass portraits of Sir Ralph Verney and his wife, together with their twelve children. This chapel was the Mortuary Chapel of the Hyde family. It is believed that the second Duke of Leeds and his wife are buried somewhere in the church, but it is unclear where. Their family acquired the Manor of Aldbury when Thomas Hyde's daughter married Viscount Dunblane, who was later to become the 1st Duke of Leeds. A monument to Sir Thomas Hyde and his son, who died in 1580, can be seen in the church. Near a window in the north wall of the chapel there are also two monuments to the Duncombes, another leading local family. William Duncombe

A brass of Lady Elizabeth Verney.

acquired Stocks in 1503 and this house remained in the possession of the family until the Nineteenth Century. Some beautifully decorated Medieval tiles can still be found in the Church of St. John the Baptist. Most of these are located in the tower floor, by the font, and also in the nave of the Pendley Chapel. The soft colours and floral geometric designs are characteristic of the early Chiltern tileries which were centred on Penn in Buckinghamshire. Some experts have speculated that at least some of the Chiltern tiles at Aldbury were brought from the monastery at Ashridge in 1575, when Sir Edmund Verney supervised the moving of the Whittingham tomb and screen.

Manor House

Aldbury's old Manor House, the family seat of the Hyde family, is no longer standing. However we know that the old manorial site was in the field behind the Parish Church. In 1545 John Hyde, a wealthy official of the King's Exchequer, built the property on his newly acquired estate and some elements of this site can be identified from surviving structures still visible in the field, behind the church. The last known Lord of the Manor at the old Manor House, was Sir Thomas Hyde who abandoned the village some years before his death. By the time the agent for the Duke of Leeds assessed the state of the manor in 1688, it was in a derelict condition and was pulled down in 1691. However it was decided to restore the old manorial farmhouse, brew house and barn. What today is often called Aldbury's Manor House is nothing of the kind. This is a large timbered Sixteenth Century house which stands to one side of the village pond and is best described as a former yeoman's house, which was acquired by John Duncombe in 1722. In 1802 this fine old house still stood in more than an acre of ground.

Local Inns

One attractive Aldbury Inn stands at the centre of the village close to the stocks and the pond. The Greyhound is a purpose built Georgian structure and the first record of a licence being held is dated 1760, when George Brooks was the innkeeper. For nearly a hundred years from 1763, the Inn was owned and kept by the Elliott family, although for some of that period it was run by one Lovi Elliott, using the surname of her second husband, East. After this the Greyhound continued to be privately owned and leased to a variety of brewers, until it was finally purchased by Benskins in the late 1920's. Aldbury's other public house dates from a similar period to the Greyhound. From 1771-1851 the Valiant Trooper was owned by Thomas Ing and his heirs, the Parrot family. In 1858 it was bought at auction by Joseph Simmons who let it to the Berkhamsted brewers, Locke and Smith. Sometimes known simply as the Trooper, this pub like its village rival, the Greyhound was by 1923 under the control of the Watford brewers Benskins.

Aldbury Murders

A notorious crime was committed on the evening of December 12th 1891, in the normally tranquil village of Aldbury. The shooting rights at Stocks had been let to Mr. Joseph Williams of Pendley. However during the evening unlicensed shots were heard in Aldbury Nowers, the local woods. Headkeeper James Double and second keeper William Puddiphat took turns, with help from the estate night-watchman Joseph Crawley, to search the woods in an attempt to catch the suspected poachers. Neither Puddiphat or Crawley returned from their patrolling and when James Double went the following morning to look for them he found them shot dead. The bodies were taken to the Greyhound Inn. Three men from Wigginton, Walter Smith, Frederick Egleton, and Charles Rayner were subsequently charged.. Egleton and Rayner were convicted of murder and Smith was dealt with on the lesser charge of manslaughter. The incident is recounted in Mary Humphry Ward's novel 'Marcella' which paints an authentic picture of village life in Aldbury.

Brightwood

As a young boy Henry Robert Craufurd had lived with his aunt, Mrs. Bright at Stocks in Aldbury. He married a local girl, Alice Jane, who was the daughter of the Rev. R. M. Wood, the

Rector of Aldbury. In 1883 he bought some land at the foot of Toms Hill and here he built a charming house called Brightwood, on a site surrounded by rich woodland. Brightwood was inherited by his son, subsequently Sir James Craufurd (1886-1970), who became a favourite resident in the village community. Local children were always welcomed to Brightwood for a party at Christmas and in the summer there were regular village festivities with Morris dancing on the Brightwood lawns. During the Second World War, Sir James's wife, Ruth, Lady Craufurd, served as a W.V.S. Group Organiser for six villages in the Berkhamsted Rural District. She was also the Billeting Officer and regularly welcomed evacuees to Brightwood where she fed and housed them until she could find them suitable billets.

The Wellhouse

The distinctive building of Aldbury's wellhouse is sometimes known locally as the bakehouse, because part of the building was later used to house ovens. This building, with its verandah extension covering the well, was originally built on the instructions of Lord Brownlow of Ashridge who owned the adjacent cottages during the second half of the Nineteenth Century. In 1972 the wellhouse was designated a Grade II listed building and described as still having a pumping wheel, a tiled roof with three panels over the verandah and a very tall brick chimney. This old well has a long history and dates from the chantry which was founded in 1335. The chantry farm buildings used to stand closer to the well, but many years after their demolition, the tithe map of 1838 shows that the present row of cottages was erected further back. During the Nineteenth Century, this well served these newer cottages, although many other households had their own fresh water wells. The chantry well was still supplying drinking water as recently as 1910 and, when it was prepared for use as a supply in case of emergency during the Second World War, tests showed that the water rising from it had remained pure.

The Village

The joy of Aldbury is that, despite the fact that not all the old buildings have survived, Twentieth Century developments have been unable to spoil the picture in this charming country village. The remaining buildings at its centre still manage to portray the authentic atmosphere of Aldbury's past as a thriving agricultural community, which successfully established itself in the surrounding fertile countryside. With the exception of various local squires in the large houses, Aldbury was a community of working people who were either local craftsmen, tenant farmers, agricultural labourers or estate workers. Throughout much of the Nineteen Century, the traditional cottage industries of lace making and straw plaiting helped to augment the modest incomes of most village households. Many local people worked on the lands which belonged to the Ashridge estate. From the beginning of the Nineteenth Century, the working population of Aldbury were fortunate that successive Lords of the Manor at Ashridge took such a benevolent interest in the village. The positive effects for Aldbury of having such a huge source of wealth nearby were considerable. By 1811, and after only eight years of the 7th Earl's interest and benefaction, there was a house for everyone, with 123 families then listed as living in 123 houses in Aldbury. The needs of such a large estate meant that there was plenty of employment available and, by 1841, Aldbury's population had soared to 790. This was already a 73% increase on the beginning of the century. Endowed by

the Brownlows at Ashridge, Aldbury's Church of England School opened in 1856 and soon flourished, being expanded and rebuilt in 1878.

If a tour is started at the north (Ivinghoe) end of the village one can soon find a typical example of Nineteenth Century improvement in housing stock in a row of cottages which are now called Barrack Row (formerly known as Slated Row). By 1830 these eight cottages had been built, well back from the road, and were all given expensive slated roofs, hence their name. Opposite Barrack Row are the old almshouses, two thatched and one tiled, which were once known collectively as the Town House. There was accommodation for another four almspersons in a house on the edge of the churchyard, but this was pulled down around 1866. On the same side of the road as the almshouses, there was a blacksmith's shop and an orchard. Further along is the tiny Baptist Chapel, which was erected by the publican at the Trooper Inn, Ann Hall, in 1840. There is a strong history of non-conformity in Aldbury. This was encouraged by leading local families such as the Emertons and also the Edlyns of Norcott Hill, near Northchurch. Near the chapel stands the old village Inn, the Greyhound. Opposite this public house is a group of buildings which first became known as Town Farm when they were sold to the Duncombe family at Stocks in 1757. This name was presumably given in order to distinguish them from their own Home Farm on the Stocks estate. The cottage which stands next to Town Farm was once a village beerhouse.

Approaching the pond, on the east side there is the former site of an old row of cottages known as Turnip Top Row, demolished between 1861-71. On the opposite side still stands the fine timbered Sixteenth Century yeoman's house which was in the ownership of John Duncombe by 1722. Beyond the church is the Nineteenth Century church farmhouse which was built circa 1830. It is a good example of a Georgian style building and was originally 50ft. square. On the road leading up Toms Hill to the Common, the Rectory was rebuilt between 1805-06 by local rector Rev. David Jenks 2nd. It replaced what must have been an impressive thatched 'L' shaped structure. This was a four bay dwelling set in half an acre which included two barns, a stable, a wheat house, a wood barn and brew house for malt storage. When the new house was finished it was one of the largest in the village and at this time the church's glebe land extended to about 40 acres.

The southern end of the pond was dominated by the baker's shop during the Nineteenth Century. This is now the village stores and post office. It is thought probable that John Grover's home in Toms Hill Road was the subject of one of Peter de Wint's notable paintings. This was formerly hung in the Royal Academy, and is now displayed at the Usher Gallery in Lincoln. On the east side of what is now Trooper Road was the site of Cooley's forge which was built in 1835. It survived until the 1960's, when it was demolished and incorporated into the Garage site. At the bottom of Trooper Road stands the other village Inn, the Valiant Trooper, once known as the Royal Oak. Opposite this is a sizeable timber framed house and thatched barn, which was home to Martha Culverhouse. From here she ran a small farm of ten acres at the turn of the Nineteenth Century. Outside the village, to the south east, lay the old maltings. The highest spot on the west side of the parish lies off Windmill Hill and was the site of an early village windmill long since demolished.

Aldbury in the landscape.

View of Aldbury from the church tower.

Church of St. John the Baptist, 1957.

Wooden Sundial at Aldbury Church, 1955.

Sixteenth Century Yeoman's House, 1958.

View of Aldbury from the crossroads, 1915.

Village Stocks, circa 1957.

Pond at Aldbury, 1996.

Stocks

The name of this country house and estate probably dates from 1503 when William Duncombe acquired the property from a Richard Stokkis. For over 250 years Stocks continued as the family home of a branch of the Duncombe family who themselves can be traced back to 1488, when a Ralf Duncombe lived in Ivinghoe with his four sons. John Duncombe (1691-1746) added to what was then a relatively small estate from the dowry of his wife Elizabeth Lowndes, who died in childbirth in 1712. Both John Duncombe's sons by his first wife died of smallpox. He then had another three children by his second wife, the daughter of Nehemiah Arnold. John Duncombe's son, Arnold, inherited the house from his father and later decided to build an entirely new house, 300 yards to the west. This new house was finished in 1773 and part of the old family house became the main farmhouse for the estate. Stocks was now an impressive white Georgian house with a fine situation and excellent views. Arnold unfortunately did not enjoy his new residence for long as he died in March 1774. Arnold Duncombe never married and, when his eldest sister Martha died in the same year, his other sister Clara and her husband, William Hayton of Ivinghoe, inherited the estate. Although the new house was originally smaller than it is today, it was still a fine gentleman's residence which rivalled any other house in the area. Architecturally the structure still features stuccoed brick work with additional mouldings and steep hipped roofs with parapets. The estate of Stocks which had begun with only 33 acres in the Sixteenth Century, had now grown into a home farmstead of 225 acres with a further 330 acres of tenanted land.

In 1811 the Hayton family were succeeded at Stocks by the society beauty Harriet, Lady Gordon, who was the wife of James Gordon of Knockespoch and the daughter of the brewer, Samuel Whitbread. The great artist Joshua Reynolds visited her at Stocks to paint her portrait, for which she posed in a splendid gown of dark red velvet. On the death of Harriet Gordon in 1832, Stocks was inherited by her son, James Adam Gordon, who was said to be "cultured, artistic and with ideas ahead of his time". James Gordon was very wealthy, having inherited four sugar plantations in Antigua from his father. He owned 26 cottages, three farms and some 847 acres of land in 1846. During his tenure Stocks became something of an artistic community, the census of 1841 recording that the household included Samuel Lover, the Irish painter and poet and William Thorn, a Scottish weaver and poet. Lover was a well known portrait painter, but he also wrote ballads and novels, collaborating with Charles Dickens in founding 'Bentley's Magazine'. James Gordon himself was a leading romantic artist and minor poet of his day. He lived happily at Stocks with his wife Emma Katherine Wolley, daughter of the Admiral Sir James Wolley who had served with Nelson. It is said that James Gordon fell in love with her at first sight in a country churchyard when he was 32 and she was only 17. They were married in a romantic torch-light ceremony at St. Albans Abbey. However when he died in 1854 his widow re-married, becoming the wife of Richard Bright M.P. As Emma Bright, she enlivened the country house of Stocks which became a highly fashionable venue with many fine dinner parties, musical soirees and artistic gatherings attended by leading figures of the day. Emma Bright lived at Stocks until 1898, but following her second husband's death, the next owner of the house was Sir Edward Grey who subsequently sold Stocks in 1892 to Mr. & Mrs. Humphry Ward who did much to maintain the tradition of artistic and literary interests. Humphry Ward was a leading critic who wrote for 'The Times', whilst Mary Humphry Ward enjoyed great success as a popular novelist. Born in Tasmania in 1851, Mary was the granddaughter of Dr. Thomas Arnold, Headmaster of Rugby School and the niece of Matthew Arnold, the poet. Her literary lineage however was more extensive than this: she was also sister-in-law to T. H. Huxley and therefore aunt to Julian and Aldous Huxley, who often visited her at Stocks. Later she also became mother-in-law to the historian G. M. Trevelyan. "Robert Elsmere", her first great success, was published in 1888. It sold over 70,000 copies in Britain, during its first year of publication, and later sold over half a million copies in America. This made it one of the outstanding literary successes of the Nineteenth Century. Two of her later novels, 'Marcella' and 'Bessie Cottrell' both feature Aldbury as a country setting. Tolstoy described Mrs. Ward as the "greatest living novelist" and in 1908, at the height of her success, she visited the United States where she was entertained by Theodore Roosevelt.

Whilst she was away on her travels there was much renovation work carried out on the decaying fabric of the old house. It eventually required the demolition of over three-quarters of its structure, but the final result gave us the handsome building of today. Mrs. Ward and her husband were great entertainers and during this time the celebrated American novelist Edith Wharton stayed at the house. Bernard Shaw stayed at Stocks in the Spring of 1896 and other celebrated guests at the house during this period included Henry James, the Asquiths, the Darwins, the Wedgwoods and the Rothschilds. In later life Mary Humphry Ward also became a social worker and magistrate; she joined Beatrice Webb in founding the Anti Suffrage League. She worked tirelessly on behalf of the poor of London's East End and a lasting tribute to her work was the founding of the Passmore Edwards Settlement. Later renamed Mary Ward House, this opened in Tavistock Square, Bloomsbury in 1897.

After his wife's death in 1920, Mr. Humphry Ward sold Stocks and after a quick succession of owners and occupants, the house eventually became the Brondesbury School. This was a boarding school for girls, under headmistress Miss Forbes-Dunlop. Brondesbury had originally been founded in 1932 at Warrington Crescent in Maida Vale by Miss Margaret Clarke. The school had its own riding stables at Stocks and hunted with the Vale of Aylesbury Hunt, which met there each March. A cottage and chapel was added by the school and various classrooms filled the old house. However the main structure was not altered. In 1972 Stocks was sold by the school to Victor Lowndes for £115,000. He was then a chief executive of the International Playboy Organisation founded by Hugh Hefner and this made Mr. Lowndes one of the highest paid business executives in Britain. Victor Lowndes incorporated his house into the Playboy Organisation, adding a discotheque, jacuzzi and gambling rooms; he even converted the old school chapel building into a training room for the former Playboy hostesses, who were called 'Bunnies'.

By 1981 the Playboy Organisation was having trouble renewing its gaming licence in London; there were accusations of malpractice and Victor Lowndes was dismissed by Hugh Hefner. However Mr. Lowndes decided to try and maintain a business at Stocks by turning it into a residential country club for members who already belonged to his town club in the Kings Road, Chelsea. The attractions he offered at Stocks were 17 bedrooms with saunas, swimming and riding. Following the death of Victor Lowndes, Stocks Country Club continues under new management, offering a golf course and much improved sporting facilities.

Stocks, 1996.

Western aspect of Stocks, 1996.

Chronology

8000 BC	The last Ice Age begins to retreat from the Chilterns.
6000 BC	Mesolithic hunters roam southern England.
3000 BC	First Neolithic settlements in the Gade Valley.
2000 BC	Bronze Age burial mounds built at Chipperfield.
150 BC	The Belgic tribe of Catuvellauni now rule most of south east England.
54 BC	Julius Caesar invades Britain.
60 AD	Roman roads and farming estates established locally.
450 AD	Saxon tribes begin to colonise both the Gade and Bulbourne Valleys.
705 AD	Hamele (Hemel Hempstead) granted to Bishop of London.
793 AD	Abbey of St Albans founded by King Offa.
942 AD	Manor of Little Gaddesden is held by Edmar.
1045	'Langlei is given forever to the monks of St Albans'.
1066	William the Conqueror accepts the nation's surrender at Berkhamsted.
1104	The Norman structure of Berkhamsted Castle is overhauled by Chancellor Randolph.
1154	Nicholas Breakspear, born in Bedmond, becomes Pope Adrian IV.
1156	Henry II grants total tax exemptions to all of Berkhamsted's merchants.
1160	Nunnery of St Margarets is founded at Great Gaddesden by the Bishop of Winchester.
1213	Two Hospitals are endowed at St John's Well in Berkhamsted by Geoffrey Fitzpiers.
1216	Berkhamsted Castle is besieged by Prince Louis of France.
1276	Royal Palace built at Kings Langley by Edward I and Queen Eleanor of Castile.
1286	Monastery at Ashridge is dedicated.
1309	Walter de Aylesbury now holds the Manor of Aldbury.
1312	Church of the Dominican Friary at Kings Langley is dedicated.
1314	Publication of Rosa Anglica written by John of Gaddesden.
1337	Berkhamsted returns its own member of Parliament.
1349	Black Death devastates the local population.
1356	King John II of France imprisoned at Berkhamsted Castle.
1381	Peasants Revolt produces unrest around the 1402 Edmund the first Duke of York is buried at the Dominican Friary, Kings Langley.
1431	Disastrous fire wrecks Royal Palace at Kings Langley.
1440	Sir Robert Whittingham orders the clearance of Pendley village.
1495	Closure of Berkhamsted Castle.
1539	Dissolution of the Monastery at Ashridge.
1539	Royal Charter awarded to Hemel Hempstead by Henry VIII.
1541	Dean Incent founds Berkhamsted School.
1544	Gaddesden granted to William Halsey by Henry VIII.
1554	Princess Elizabeth arrested at Ashridge for plotting against her sister Queen Mary.
1575	Tomb of Sir Robert Whittingham is moved to Aldbury.
1580	Berkhamsted Place constructed for Sir Edmund Carey.
1595	Richard Coombe builds the Bury in Hemel Hempstead.
1604	Sir Thomas Egerton is granted the manors of Ashridge and Little Gaddesden.
1616	Prince Charles is Lord of the Langleybury estates.
1618	King James I grants Berkhamsted a Charter of Incorporation.
1648	English Civil Wars begin.
1665	Death of Sir Thomas Hyde, Lord of the Manor at Aldbury.
1674	Cassiobury House redesigned by Hugh May.
1679	Henry Guy resident at Tring Park.
1700	Thomas Lomax rebuilds Westbrook Hay.
1705	Golden Parsonage built at Great Gaddesden.
1711	Langleybury is constructed for Sir Robert Raymond, Lord Chief Justice of England.
1731	Poet William Cowper is born at Berkhamsted.
1736	Francis Egerton becomes the 3rd Duke of Bridgewater.
1750	Langley House is built in Abbots Langley by Sir John Cope Freeman.
1756	The Grove, near Watford, is rebuilt by Thomas Villiers.
1762	Sparrows Herne Turnpike Trust established.
1768	Gaddesden Place designed by James Wyatt.
1773	Stocks House built at Aldbury by Arnold Duncombe.
1780	Tooveys Flour Mill in business at Kings Langley.
1793	Construction work begins on Grand Junction Canal.
1798	Ironworker Joseph Cranstone starts his business at Hemel Hempstead.
1801	Ashlyns Hall bought by James Smith.
1803	The Fourdrinier Brothers making paper at Frogmore Mill.
1809	John Dickinson acquires Apsley Mill.
1809	Boxmoor Trust created by an Act of Parliament.
1811	Astley Paston Cooper purchases the Gadebridge Estate.
1817	A new Mansion is created at Ashridge.
1824	William Kay opens his Silk Mill at Tring.
1836	Abbots Hill House is built by John Dickinson.
1837	The local stretch of London to Birmingham Railway is complete.

1840	Lane's Nurseries are established at Potten End.
1841	Timber Merchant Job East is trading at Berkhamsted.
1843	William Cooper, the veterinary chemist, arrives in Berkhamsted.
1847	Baron Rokeby creates the Hazelwood Estate near Abbots Langley.
1850	Robert Blackwell inherits the Manor House at Chipperfield.
1854	Shendish House is built for Charles Longman.
1867	Benskins Brewery established in Watford.
1868	Foundation stone is laid for Leavesden Hospital.
1872	Tring Park estate purchased by Nathaniel Rothschild.
1873	Pendley Manor built by J.G. Williams.
1875	Thomas Mead builds new Flour Mill at Tring.
1877	West Herts Infirmary opens.
1881	The Ryder Memorial is erected at Bovingdon.
1883	Brightwood is built at Aldbury by Henry Craufurd.
1887	Two local tramway projects are proposed.
1889	Tring Museum is constructed.
1891	Alford Cross is unveiled in Little Gaddesden.
1898	Borough of Hemel Hempstead created by Charter awarded by Queen Victoria.
1901	Kent Brushes build a new factory at Apsley.
1905	Original Gaddesden Place is destroyed by fire.
1909	First local bus services provided by LNWR.
1913	Wander's Ovaltine Factory established at Kings Langley.
1914	First World War begins and a large military camp is built in Gadebridge Park.
1916	Three German Zeppelins raid the local area.
1918	Sun Engraving are now the leading local printers based in Watford.
1918	Influenza epidemic sweeps through the local population.
1919	Peace Day celebrations.
1923	Champneys Estate becomes a Nature and Health Care Clinic.
1924	Sale of the Ashridge Estate.
1927	Cassiobury House is demolished.
1927	Major and Lady Motion are resident at Serge Hill, Bedmond.
1929	Grand Junction becomes part of the Grand Union Canal system.
1935	Ashlyns School built in Berkhamsted.
1936	Odhams create the largest photo-gravure works in the world at Watford.
1938	New railway station opened at Apsley.
1939	Second World War begins.
1940	Food Rationing is introduced.
1940	Leavesden Aerodrome built for wartime aircraft production.
1940	London Blitz brings first flood of evacuees to the area.
1941	Worst local bombing incident kills nine people in Belswains Lane, Apsley.
1941	Full-scale Invasion practice is held in the countryside around Tring and Berkhamsted.
1942	Bovingdon Airfield becomes a base for US Air Force.
1944	D Day Invasion.
1945	Victory in Europe is proclaimed.
1948	Construction work begins on Hemel Hempstead New Town.
1952	Queen Elizabeth II visits Adeyfield.
1953	Important medieval wall paintings discovered at Piccotts End.
1959	MI Motorway opens.
1962	Construction work begins on the Civic Centre at Hemel Hempstead.
1963	Major Roman Villa discovered in Gadebridge Park.
1966	Electrification of local railway services into London.
1966	Leavesden Aerodrome becomes home to the Small Engine Division of Rolls Royce.
1966	Local stretch of the main A41 road subject to substantial overhaul.
1968	Grand Union Canal re-classified as a cruiseway.
1971	Kodak build their office skyscraper in Hemel Hempstead.
1972	Stocks purchased by Victor Lowdnes of the Playboy Organisation.
1973	Tring Bypass is opened.
1977	Work draws to a close on Hemel Hempstead New Town.
1986	Gade Valley Viaduct of the M25 Orbital Motorway is complete.
1988	Bovingdon Prison opens.
1988	BP Oil UK build new office headquarters near Hemel Hempstead.
1989	DRG at Apsley is taken over by Biber Holdings A.G..
1991	Important Neolithic finds made during the A41 Bypass construction work.
1992	Dickinson's Apsley Mill factory is demolished.
1993	A41 Bypass is finished.
1996	Principal buildings of Leavesden Hospital are demolished.

Bibliography

BALL,A.W. Street and place names in Watford.
ISBN: 0903408023 Pub. 1973
BALL,A.W. Watford: A Pictorial Record 1922-72
ISBN: 0903408007 Pub. 1972
BASS,M.& FOWLER,J. Tring in old picture postcards Vol.2
ISBN: 9028856390 Pub 1993
BAYNE,R. Moor Park
Pub. 1977
BELL,V. Little Gaddesden
Pub. 1949
BENSON, Captain L. Remarkable Trials and Notorious Characters
Pub. 1850
BIRTCHNELL,P.C. Short history of Berkhamsted
ISBN: 1871372003 Pub. 1972
BIRTCHNELL,P.C. Bygone Berkhamsted
ISBN: 0900804149 Pub. 1975
BOURNE,T.C. London and Birmingham Railway
Pub. 1839
BRANCH-JOHNSON,W. Hertfordshire Inns: Vol 2 - West Herts
Pub. 1963
BRANCH-JOHNSON,W. Industrial Archaeology of Hertfordshire
Pub. 1970 ISBN: 0715247756
BRANIGAN,K. Archaeology of the Chilterns
Pub. 1994 ISBN: 0951634518
BRITISH RAILWAYS BOARD. The Grove Story
Pub. 1948 ISBN: 0950932000
BRYANT,V.J.M. History of Potten End
Pub. 1986
CANNON,J.& H. Nicky Line
ISBN: 0860230503 Pub. 1977
CHIPPERFIELD PARISH COUNCIL. Village Appraisal
Pub.1994 ISBN: 0952337606
COCKMAN,F.G. Railways of Hertfordshire
2nd ed. Pub 1983 ISBN: 0901354112
COULT,D. A Prospect of Ashridge
ISBN: 0850333601 Pub. 1980
CULL,E. Wigginton
ISBN: 0952041715 Pub. 1993
CUSSANS,T.E. History of Hertfordshire
Orig.Pub. 1870/1. Reprinted in 3 vols 1972
ISBN: 085409883X
D.H.T. Agriculture in Dacorum
Exhibition Catalogue Pub 1990
D.H.T. Dacorum Canal
Exhibition Handbook Pub 1980
D.H.T. Dacorum at War
Exhibition Handbook Pub 1995
D.H.T. Education in Dacorum
Exhibition Catalogue Pub. 1992
D.H.T. Highways and Byways of Dacorum
Exhibition Handbook Pub. 1985
D.H.T. Railways of Dacorum
Exhibition Catalogue Pub 1983
D.H.T. Roman Dacorum
Exhibition Catalogue Pub 1993
DAVIS,E. Hemel Hempstead in Camera
ISBN: 0860233405
DAVIS,E. Hemel Hempstead
Pub. 1995 ISBN: 075240167X
DIPLOCK,M. History of Leavesden Hospital
Pub. 1991
DONY,J.G. Flora of Hertfordshire
Pub. 1967
EDWARDS,D.F. Hemel Hempstead in old postcards
Pub. 1994 ISBN: 9028857974
EDWARDS,D.F. Watford: a pictorial history
Pub: 1992 ISBN: 0850338344
EVANS,J. Endless Web:Dickinson and Co. Ltd.
Pub. 1954
FAULKNER,A.H. Grand Junction Canal
ISBN: 0951792318
FAULKNER,A.H. Grand Union Canal in Hertfordshire
Pub. 1987 ISBN: 0901354643
FIELD,J. Place names of Dacorum District
ISBN: 0903978083 Pub. 1977
GARDNER,H.W. A Survey of Agriculture in Hertfordshire
Pub. 1967
GOVER,J.E.B. Place names of Hertfordshire
Pub. 1938 ISBN: 0521049083
HANDS,R.& J. Book of Boxmoor
ISBN: 0860234193 Pub. 1989
HANDS,R.& J. Boxmoor in Camera
ISBN: 0860233863 Pub. 1993
HASTIE,S. Abbots Langley: An Outline History
Pub. 1986
HASTIE,S. Abbots Langley:A Hertfordshire Village
ISBN: 0952092905 Pub. 1993
HASTIE,S. Kings Langley: A Hertfordshire Village
ISBN: 095076471X Pub. 1991
HAY,D.& J. Tring and district in old picture postcards
ISBN: 9028822739 Pub. 1983
HEDDLE,L.W. The Chilterns
ISBN: 085033943X Pub. 1994
HERTFORDSHIRE ARCHAEOLOGY
All Vols, 1969-
HERTFORDSHIRE COUNTRYSIDE.
All Vols, 1949-
HERTFORDSHIRE LIBRARY SERVICE. Brief History of the Grand Union Canal in Hertfordshire
Pub. 1993
HERTFORDSHIRE PAST.
All Vols, 1976-
HOLGATE,R.(Ed.) Chiltern Archaeology: Recent Work
ISBN: 187199522 Pub. 1995
HOSIER,B. Hedgehog's Northchurch
ISBN: 0952288206 Pub. 1994
JOLIFFE,G.&JONES,G. Hertfordshire Inns and Public Houses
ISBN:0901354791 Pub. 1995
JONES,A. Hertfordshire
Pub. 1988 ISBN: 0852639333
JONES,K.R. Companion around Watford
Pub. 1971
KITCHENSIDE,G. The West Coast Route To Scotland
Pub. 1976 ISBN: 0715372106
KNIGHT,J. Watford
Pub. 1995 ISBN: 0752403559
LIDDLE,H.G. Notes on old Chipperfield
Pub. 1948
LONGMAN,G. A corner of England's garden 1600-1850
Pub. 1977
MARGARY,I.D. Roman Roads in Britain
3rd ed. Pub. 1973 ISBN: 0212970011
MUNBY,L.M. Hertfordshire Landscape
ISBN: 0340044594 Pub. 1977
MUNBY,L.E. (Ed.) History of Kings Langley
Pub. 1963
NUNN,J.B. Book of Watford
Pub. 1987 ISBN: 0951177710
PENDLETON,J. Our Railways
Pub. 1894
PENROSE,R.J. Hertfordshire Valley (Arc in the Park)
Pub. 1993 ISBN: 0952257904
PEVSNER,N. Hertfordshire (Buildings of Hertfordshire)
2nd ed. Pub. 1977 ISBN: 0140710078
POOLE,H. A fair and large house, Cassiobury Park 1546-1927
ISBN: 0907958036 Pub. 1985
RICHARDS,S. History of Tring
ISBN: 0950413003 Pub. 1974
ROBINSON,G. Book of Hemel Hempstead and Berkhamsted
ISBN: 0860230112 Pub. 1975
ROBINSON,G. Hertfordshire
ISBN: 0860230309 Pub. 1978
ROLT,L.T.C. Inland Waterways of Britain
Pub. 1950 ISBN: 0043860060
ROOK,T. History of Hertfordshire
ISBN: 0850335809 Pub. 1984
RUTHERFORD DAVIS,K. Deserted medieval villages in Hertfordshire
Pub 1982 ISBN: 0901354236
ST PAULS LANGLEYBURY. The First Hundred Years (1864-1964)
Pub. 1964
SALISBURY,E.M. Miss Salisbury's notes on Bourne End
Pub. 1985
SAUNDERS,W.R. History of Watford
Pub. 1931
SENAR,H. Little Gaddesden and Ashridge
ISBN: 0850334608 Pub. 1983
SHELDRICK,G. Hart Reguardant - Hertfordshire County Council (1889-1989)
Pub. 1989 ISBN: 0901354503
SHIPMAN,C. & JACKSON,R.
Dacorum within living memory
Pub. 1988 ISBN: 095117737
SHIRLEY, D.(Ed.) Hertfordshire:a guide to the countryside
ISBN: 0905858069 Pub. 1978
SMITH,A.C. WIndmills in Hertfordshire
ISBN: 094875401X Pub. 1986
STOKES,P. From Gypsy to Gem (with diversions) 1926-86
Pub. 1987 ISBN: 095117102X
STURGESS,M.& R. Hertfordshire Vol1. (South & East)
ISBN: 187070830X
THICKNESSE,S.G. Abbots Langley
Pub. 1946
VICTORIA COUNTY HISTORY: Hertfordshire (4 Vols)
Orig.Pub. 1902-25. Reprint 1971
WARD,P. & LACEY,R. Apsley and Nash Mills in Camera
ISBN: 0860233529 Pub. 1989
WARE,M.E. Canals and Waterways
Pub. 1987 ISBN: 0852638787
WATFORD BOROUGH COUNCIL. Watford: A Pictorial Record
Pub. 1951
WATFORD MUSEUM. Here for the beer Pub. 1984 ISBN: 0907958028
WATFORD WEA. Aspects of Nineteenth Century Watford
Pub. 1987
WHITMORE,R. Hertfordshire Headlines
ISBN: 0950392957 Pub. 1987
WILKINSON,R.S. Church and Parish of Abbots Langley
Pub. 1957
YAXLEY,S.(Ed.) History of Hemel Hempstead
ISBN: 0950274305 Pub. 1973

Index